# Global Convulsions

SUNY Series, The Social Context of Education
Edited by Christine E. Sleeter

# GLOBAL CONVULSIONS

Race, Ethnicity, and Nationalism
at the End of the Twentieth Century

Edited by
Winston A. Van Horne

STATE UNIVERSITY OF NEW YORK PRESS

Published by
State University of New York Press, Albany

Printed in the United States of America

For information, address State University of New York Press,
State University Plaza, Albany, N.Y., 12246

Production by Cathleen Collins
Marketing by Theresa Abad Swierzowski

**Library of Congress Cataloging in Publication Data**

Global convulsions : race, ethnicity, and nationalism at the end of
    the twentieth century / edited by Winston A. Van Horne.
        p.   cm. — (SUNY series, the social context of education)
    Includes bibliographical references and index.
    ISBN 0-7914-3235-1 (hc : alk. paper.) — ISBN 0-7914-3236-X (pbk. :
alk. paper)
    1. Race relations.   2. Racism.   3. Ethnicity.   4. Nationalism.
    I. Van Horne, Winston A.   II. Series: SUNY series, social context of
    education.
    HT1521.G54   1997
    305.8—dc20                                                96-15321
                                                                  CIP

10 9 8 7 6 5 4 3 2 1

Cheeks drowned in tears translucent,
Hands awash in crimson red,
Legs drenched by rich new blood,
Feet shrouded by death's dark vapors.

Last night did I behold
Hot violent death,
Cold violent death,
Strike through vapors sickly sweet.

Crouch bent he stalked,
Mighty swift to strike,
Upright quick he fled,
Outstretched still they lay.

Who was he? What was he?
Criminal? Revolutionary? Both?
Why struck he?
To cleanse a wretched soul.

No! No! No!
Never! Never! Never!
Shout of anguish, cry of sorrow,
Never shall violence cleanse a wretched soul.

Winston A. Van Horne

# Contents

# List of Figures

# List of Tables

# Foreword

This volume presents the culmination of over three years of on-going efforts—planning, organization, and implementation—by the sponsors of the conference on "Race, Ethnicity, and Nationalism at the End of the Twentieth Century," and includes the edited academic manuscripts of sixteen of the internationally recognized scholars who participated in that conference. It addresses a complex and multifaceted theme which has come to dominate the international relations of the post-Cold War era. Not one of the problems discussed at the Fall 1993 conference has been "resolved" (although some progress, however tenuous, has been made in relation to the Middle East peace process, peace in Northern Ireland, and the stabilization of Canada), and all of the issues addressed remain as relevant to national, regional, and international conflict and peace as they were when the conference was first conceived in 1990.

It is not an overstatement to say that the conference brought together at the University of Wisconsin–Milwaukee (hereinafter UWM) an assemblage of impressive international stature and included some of the most respected scholars of these issues in the world. The presentations were of the highest quality originally, and as now edited, they have benefited additionally from the comments that were made at the time of their initial presentation. The conference also provided a unique opportunity to address problems concerning race, ethnicity, and nationalism in both their domestic and international dimensions. The collaboration of the University of Wisconsin System's Institute on Race and Ethnicity with UWM's Institute of World Affairs drew upon the resources of both Institutes to promote this national/international perspective.

The issues of race, ethnicity, and nationalism are crucially significant for their impact on international peace and stability not only in and of themselves, but also because of the compounding effects produced by their interactions with one another. This conceptual and pragmatic linkage was alluded to repeatedly by conference speakers, but was particularly stressed by Martin Bernal in his discussion of "Race in

History," by Brian Porter in his analysis of "Concepts of Nationalism in History," and by Martin Marty in his presentation on "Cultural Foundations of Ethnonationalism: The Role of Religion." The case studies dealing with the Middle East and with the former Yugoslavia were especially illustrative of this multiple linkage and the multiplying effect it has had on the beliefs, emotions, and actions of individuals and nations alike.

Equally significant, however, has been the impact of racial and religious strife, as well as ethnonational conflicts, on the integrity of the sovereign state, particularly multiethnic or multinational states or those divided by racial or religious sectarianism. The actual break-up of the Soviet Union and of Yugoslavia attests to the pervasiveness and virulence of the emotions attached to these concepts, and the case studies concerning Canada, Nigeria, and Ireland, as well as Israel and the Palestinians, clearly illustrate the range of problems created when state borders fail to coincide (as they seldom do) with the national, ethnic, racial, or religious groups which comprise those states. The plight of stateless nations is illustrated ever so eloquently by George Harris in his discussion of the Kurds, and by Galia Golan and Muhammad Hallaj in their observations pertaining to Palestinian statehood.

Many have been the costs that attend ethnonationalism and cultural nationalism. Still, ethnonationalism need not undercut the integrity of the state, and cultural nationalism is by no means synonymous with cultural chauvinism. These observations find good support in David Buck's presentation on attempts to "contain" ethnonationalism in China, and Kosaku Yoshino's discussion of cultural nationalism and "internationalization" in an ethnically homogenous Japan.

In the opinion of all concerned—organizers, presenters, and attendees—the conference on "Race, Ethnicity, and Nationalism at the End of the Twentieth Century" presented an array of thorough and perspicacious scholarly analyses of vital national and international issues. And so it is with much satisfaction that we invite you to read this book.

Carol Edler Baumann, Director
UWM Institute of World Affairs

# Acknowledgments

In the fall of 1993, the University of Wisconsin System Institute on Race and Ethnicity, of which I was then director, the University of Wisconsin–Milwaukee Institute of World Affairs, and the University of Wisconsin–Milwaukee jointly sponsored an international conference on race, ethnicity, and nationalism at the end of the twentieth century. The conference was very well received by the hundreds who attended, and its value now persists through the chapters of this book. Given the amount of work and time that have gone into making this volume possible, it is fitting and proper that thanks should be said to a number of persons.

It is well to begin by recognizing the contributors of the volume's chapters, for they substantially rewrote the manuscripts which they initially presented at the conference, and so to them goes whatever credit accrues to the book. Many made the success of the conference what it was, most especially Thomas Tonnesen, the associate director of the Institute on Race and Ethnicity, Judy Treskow, Thelma Conway, and Sandra Fuller—the staff of the Institute on Race and Ethnicity. Director Carol Edler Baumann and members of her staff at the Institute of World Affairs—Gareth Shellman, Frances Luebke, and Jane Austen—were invaluable to the remarkable success that the conference enjoyed. The support of President Katharine C. Lyall and then Senior Vice-President Stephen R. Portch of the University of Wisconsin System, as well as Chancellor John H. Schroeder, Provost Kenneth Watters, Dean George Keulks, and Associate Dean Robert Jones of UWM made possible resources without which the conference could not have been held. A word of thanks should also be extended to Kenneth Buelow, Nicholas Schultz, Neil McIntosh, and Vicky Everson of the Graduate School.

I should now like to say a most generous thank you to Christine E. Sleeter for believing that this volume would make an important contribution to her series, and for the richness of her ideas and support. I also would like to thank my editor, Priscilla C. Ross, at SUNY Press for her belief in distinction, and the skill and care with which she guided this book. And to Cathleen Collins, the production editor, many thanks for a book well done.

For listening endlessly to my musings about this manuscript, I say to my colleagues—Osei-Mensah Aborampah, Bartholomew Armah, Patrick Bellegarde-Smith, Lennell Dade, Joyce Kirk, Doreatha Mbalia and Ahmed Mbalia—in the Department of Africology, thanks ever so much for your patience and insights. A word of thanks goes to Kimberly Sampson, the department's student help, for the cheerfulness with which she undertook the tasks that were assigned to her. I extend an expansive thank you to Teresa Shannon, program assistant in the Department of Africology. With a sound grounding in philosophy, a keen eye for lucidity of presentation as well as conceptual flaws, superb technical skills (which are ever so evident in the figures, tables, notes, and index of this book), she kept me sharp as the manuscript was organized for the publisher. Finally, to Mary Ann, my intellectual companion and wife for more than a quarter century, and Maxwell my son, to you go the largest chunk of the credit for my intellectual and personal growth across the years—thank you beyond measure.

# About the Editor and Contributors

**Winston A. Van Horne** is professor and chair of the Department of Africology at the University of Wisconsin-Milwaukee. For seven years he was the director of the University of Wisconsin System Institute on Race and Ethnicity, and for eight years the chair of the University of Wisconsin System American Ethnic Studies Coordinating Committee, which preceded the formation of the Institute. He edited eight books in the Institute's *Ethnicity and Public Policy* series. His articles have appeared in a number of journals, including *Philosophy and Phenomenological Research*, *The Journal of Religious Thought*, and the *Journal of Caribbean Studies*. He is currently working on transforming his lectures of twenty years on urban violence, both domestically and globally, into a book.

**Claude Ake** was the director of the Center for Advanced Social Science, Port Harcourt, Nigeria. He served as president of the Council for the Development of Economic and Social Research in Africa (CODESRIA)—the umbrella social science organization in Africa—as well as president of the Nigerian Political Science Association. He also was a Woodrow Wilson Scholar, a Research Fellow at the Brookings Institution, a member of the Social Science Research Council of the United States, and a consultant to the World Bank, UNESCO, UNDP, as well as the UN Economic Commission on Africa. Among his numerous publications are: *A Theory of Political Integration* (Dorsey Press, 1967), *Revolutionary Pressures in Africa* (Zed Press, 1978), *A Political Economy of Africa* (Longman, 1981), *Political Economy of Nigeria* (Longman, 1985), and *Democracy and Development in Africa* (Brookings Institution, 1996). Editor's note: Claude Ake, a distinguished international scholar, a man of unusual insight and uncommon courage, and a great humanitarian, suffered an untimely death in November of 1996.

**Mark R. Beissinger** is professor of political science and director of the Center for Russia, East Europe, and Central Asia of the University of Wisconsin-Madison. In

xvii

addition to publishing numerous articles and book chapters, he is the author of *Scientific Management, Socialist Discipline, and Soviet Power* (Harvard University Press, 1988), and a contributing coeditor of *The Nationalities Factor in Soviet Politics and Society* (Westview Press, 1990).

**Martin Bernal** is a professor of government and an adjunct professor of Near Eastern Studies at Cornell University. His chief publications are the critically acclaimed *Black Athena: The Afroasiatic Roots of Classical Civilization*, vols. 1 & 2 (Rutgers University Press, 1987 and 1991) and the *Cadmean Letters* (Eisenbrauns, 1990). His works have been widely reviewed, won high praise, and engendered intense controversy. Two films have been made about the academic and political controversies that his work has stimulated.

**David D. Buck** is a professor of history at the University of Wisconsin-Milwaukee and a former editor of the *Journal of Asian Studies* (1990–95). He specializes in Modern China, and has lived and conducted research in Shandong and Jilin provinces, as well as in Taiwan. His books and articles cover a wide range of topics including urban development, rural-based popular uprisings, educational modernization and bureaucratic administration in Modern China. He is currently working on a book dealing with China's role in the world tea trade during the nineteenth century.

**Marianne Elliott** is the Andrew Geddes and John Rankin Professor of Modern History at the University of Liverpool. She is the author of various works on Irish and French history, which have been awarded a number of prizes, including the AHA Leo Gershoy prize, the Irish Independent/Irish Life biography prize, and the American Conference of Irish Studies J.R. Donnely, Snr., prize. Her works notably include, *Partners in Revolution, the United Irishmen and France* (Yale University Press, 1982) and *Wolfe Tone, Prophet of Irish Independence* (Yale University Press, 1989). Her contribution to this volume derives from her work as a member of the Opsahl international commission on Northern Ireland, which reported its findings in *A Citizens' Inquiry: The Opsahl Report on Northern Ireland* (1993). She is currently writing *A History of the Catholics of Ulster*.

**Galia Golan** is the Jay and Loni Darwin Professor of Russian and East European Studies at the Hebrew University of Jerusalem. A former chair of the Department of Political Science, her research focuses primarily on Soviet foreign policy. She is a frequent commentator on Middle East politics and the Arab-Israeli conflict, and is the author of eight books including, *The Soviet Union and the Palestine Liberation Organization: An Uneasy Alliance; Soviet Policies in the Middle East From World War Two to Gorbachev*; and, most recently, *Moscow and the Middle East: New Thinking on Regional Conflict*.

**Muhammad Hallaj** is the director of the Center for Policy Analysis on Palestine in Washington, D.C. He has served as director of the Council for Higher Education in the West Bank and Gaza, as the director of the Institute of Arab Studies in Boston, and as a visiting scholar at Harvard University's Center for International Affairs. He has taught at Jacksonville University in Florida, the University of Jordan, and Birzeit University in Palestine. He served for two years as a member of the Palestinian delegation to the Arab-Israeli peace talks, and is a member of the Board of Commissioners of the Palestinian Independent Commission for Citizens' Rights in Jerusalem, as well as the Palestine National Council (PNC). He has authored eight books on Palestinian affairs and the Arab-Israeli conflict, and published extensively in Arabic and English in a variety of journals and magazines.

**George S. Harris** retired at the end of 1995 after sixteen years as the director of the Office of Research and Analysis: Near East and South Asia, U.S. Department of State in Washington, D.C. He was awarded the Presidential rank of Distinguished Executive in 1992 for his contributions to the understanding of that region. He has served as Professorial Lecturer in Middle East studies at the School of Advanced International Studies of The Johns Hopkins University, 1968–81, and intermittently at the George Washington University Faculty of Political Science. He is the author of several books on Turkey, has written numerous articles on the Kurds, and edited several volumes on the Middle East including *Law, Personalities, and Politics of the Middle East.*

**Marc V. Levine** is an associate professor of history and the director of the Center for Economic Development at the University of Wisconsin-Milwaukee. He has written numerous scholarly articles on language and nationalism in Quebec, and on economic trends in Montreal, including "Au-delà des lois linguistiques: la politique gouvernementale et le caractère linguistique de Montréal dans les années 1990," in *Contextes de la politique linguistique québécoise* (Quebec: 1993). He authored *The Reconquest of Montreal: Language Policy and Social Change in a Bilingual City*, a revised and expanded French-language edition of which was published in the fall of 1996 by VLB Editeur of Montreal. He has served as a consultant to Quebec's Conseil de la langue française, and is currently Professeur invité at l'Institut national de la recherche scientifique-Urbanisation in Montreal.

**Martin E. Marty** is the Fairfax M. Cone Distinguished Service Professor at the University of Chicago, where he has taught since 1963 in three faculties. A specialist in American religion, he directed a six-year, five-volume study comparing varieties of militant fundamentalisms around the world, which has been published by the University of Chicago Press. His three-volume *Modern American Religion* was also published by the University of Chicago Press. The third volume, *Under God, Indivisible*, covering 1941–60, appeared in 1996.

**Brian E. Porter** is Honorary Lecturer in International Relations at the University of Kent at Canterbury and a Fellow of the Royal Historical Society. He has lectured in France, the Sudan, China, Russia, and for twenty years at the University of Wales.

Among his publications are *Britain and the Rise of Communist China* (1967), and *The Aberystwyth Papers: International Politics 1919–1969* (1972). He also has contributed to a number of theoretical and historical works, including "Nationalist Ideals and Ethnic Realities" in *Community, Diversity, and a New World Order: Essays in Honor of Inis L. Claude, Jr.* (1994). In 1991 he and Gabriele Wight published the late Martin Wight's celebrated lectures, *International Theory: The Three Traditions*, which took over five years to reconstruct and edit from notes.

**Robin Alison Remington** is a professor of political science at the University of Missouri-Columbia. Since 1970–71 she has been doing fieldwork in the former Yugoslavia, first as an exchange scholar from MIT at the Institute for International Politics and Economics in Belgrade, then funded by the American Council of Learned Societies, the University of Missouri-Columbia Graduate Research Council, and the Fulbright Faculty Research Abroad Fellowships. She has published numerous articles and chapters on the collapse of the former Yugoslavia into civil war and subsequent Yugoslav wars of secession. Her latest essay, "The Yugoslav Army: Trauma and Transition," appers in Constantine P. Danopoulos and Daniel Zirker, eds., *Civil-Military Relations in Soviet and Yugoslav Successor States* (Westview Press, 1996). Her works have been published in Greece, India, Spain, and in the former Yugoslavia in both Belgrade and Zagreb.

**Alfred Erich Senn** is a professor of history at the University of Wisconsin-Madison, and a Foreign Member of the Lithuanian Academy of Sciences. He has written a number of works on Russian and Lithuanian history. In 1992, a Lithuanian translation of his doctoral dissertation *The Emergence of Modern Lithuania* (1959) was published. He was in Lithuania in 1988, where he participated in the process of the rebirth of Lithuanian national consciousness and recorded his experiences in the book, *Lithuania Awakening* (University of California Press, 1990). His most recent book, *Gorbachev's Failure in Lithuania* (St. Martin's Press, 1995), examines Lithuania's role in the collapse of the Soviet Union.

**Linda Vigilant** is a research associate in anthropology at The Pennsylvania State University. Her research includes human genetic diversity and evolution, in particular, using molecular genetic data to reconstruct the origins of modern humans. Most recently, she has been analyzing mitochondrial DNA variation in African populations. Her articles have appeared in a variety of publications, notably, *Science* and *Systematic Biology*, as well as the proceedings of the National Academy of Science of the United States of America.

**Kosaku Yoshino** is an associate professor of sociology at the University of Tokyo. He specializes in the study of nationalism and cultural identities in Asia. He is the author of *Cultural Nationalism in Contemporary Japan: A Sociological Enquiry* (Routledge, 1992, 1995), and is currently working on a study of "the cross-culture industry."

# Introduction

WINSTON A. VAN HORNE

The tug of the familiar and the pull of the unfamiliar have fired the imagination and fashioned the conduct of wo'man over untold generations. In the familiar there is reassurance; in the unfamiliar there is uneasiness. In their familiarity and unfamiliarity, race, ethnicity, and nationality both reassure and unsettle. "We" don't mix with "them," for "they" stick with "their kind" and we stick with "our kind." "They" are different from "us," and "we" are not like "them." "We" go "our" way, and "they" go "their" way. The antinomies here are largely a function of what B. F. Skinner calls "contingencies of reinforcement"[1] which shape the personalities and mold the characters of individuals. Stern have been the societal fault lines occasioned by contingencies of reinforcement regarding nationality, ethnicity, and race. Concerning race specifically, the following example, though anecdotal, is most instructive.

I recall vividly my Dad, George Wilton Van Horne, now deceased, telling me more than forty years ago, that a friend of the owner (FF) of the thirty-two hundred acre estate where he worked as an overseer told him that one evening just before dinner at the local country club FF remarked aloud: "How good it is to look around and don't [sic] see a black face." Ironically, all of the faces that served dinner were black (in the American usage of the term); all the faces of those who were served were white; and, excluding the family of FF, the faces of all of those who lived and worked on FF's estate were black. I know that the anecdote just presented has no standing as legal testimony, yet it is ever so poignant. Assuming that FF's friend did not lie to my Dad, who, in turn, did not mislead his son, one cannot but be struck by the full force of we/us versus they/them. We employ them, and they work for us. In a very real sense, for FF that evening, and who knows how many other evenings and mornings, black faces were simply invisible. They were seen but not beheld; observed

1

but not discerned; apprehended but not comprehended. Or as Ralph Ellison, the great twentieth-century American novelist, puts it:

> I am an invisible man. No, I am not a spook like those who haunted Edgar Allan Poe; nor am I one of your Hollywood-movie ectoplasms. I am a man of substance, of flesh and bone, fiber and liquids—and I might even be said to possess a mind. I am invisible, understand, simply because people refuse to see me. . . . When they approach me they see only my surroundings, themselves, or figments of their imagination—indeed, everything and anything except me.
>
> Nor is my invisibility exactly a matter of a biochemical accident to my epidermis. That invisibility to which I refer occurs because of a peculiar disposition of the eyes of those with whom I come in contact. A matter of the construction of their inner eyes, those eyes with which they look through their physical eyes upon reality.[2]

And so, though they serve us dinner, speak the same language as we do, attend the same church as ourselves, and generally vote for the same political party as we do (all of which, incidentally, were true in relation to these who lived and worked on FF's estate), they nonetheless are not like us. In the case of FF, as well as the numberless ones that it represents, what set "them" apart from "us"?—race.

# I

Race and its cognate racism are among the most malodorous and disgusting concepts with wide currency at the end of the twentieth century, just as was true of them at the end of the fifteenth, sixteenth, seventeenth, eighteenth and nineteenth centuries, especially in the West. But race did not have its origin in the fifteenth century. As Martin Bernal points out, a concept of race, in the sense of varieties of colors of wo'man, did obtain in the ancient world prior to 500 BCE. Yet it did not ground feelings of superiority and inferiority. It expressed an aesthetic—one in which, for example, "[t]he beautiful and erotic lover in the *Song of Songs* is called in both the Hebrew and Greek texts as 'black *and* beautiful'."

Sentiments concerning race in the ancient world do change starting around 500 BCE, according to Bernal, so that by the time of the *New Testament* "the description of the heroine . . . in the Latin Vulgate translation of the *Song of Songs* is changed to 'black *but* beautiful'." Black and beautiful gave way to black but beautiful as black, unlike heretofore, became "the color and complexion of evil and white that of purity and goodness," says Bernal. Racial prejudice, in the sense of preference based on somatic or physical norms, was now observable. Still, malodorous racism, grounded in putative racial superiority and racial inferiority, had not yet fully reared its monstrous head.

By the seventeenth century, however, armed with Christianity, capitalism and muskets, Europeans in ships that bore such names as *John the Baptist, Gift of God, Jesus, Brotherhood, and Liberty*[3] set sail and pillaged with utter rapacity the indigenous peoples of the Americas and West Africa, among others. As the greed, fraud, and profit that Karl Marx diagnosed as intrinsic attributes of capitalism conjoined with the proselytizing religiosity of Christianity, many peoples were trampled upon and reduced either to slaves or colonial subjects. Indeed, if Bernal is to be believed, modern racism, not simply racial prejudice as it was known in the ancient world, "has its origins in the European need to justify their inhuman behavior in the genocide, colonialism, and slavery inflicted upon peoples of other continents by dehumanizing them and turning their victims into devils or animals." And although Brian Porter does not address directly the origin of modern racism in the way that Bernal does, he too notes that "a strong racial . . . prejudice . . . exists at a deep level in many European societies." But racism never has been, nor is it now, the exclusive province of Europeans and their societies, even though over the past five centuries they have constructed the most elaborate and tortured explanations of, and justifications for, racist behaviors. What grounds racism, the sheer racial arrogance that continues to overspread the planet? The false belief that race is a biological phenomenon; that "we" are more aesthetically attractive and intellectually endowed than "they" are; that "we" are "their" betters; and that "us" and "them" are never equals, either by nature or by society when it is properly constituted. Given the persistent noxiousness of racism, and the deep fault lines that are drawn racially all over the planet, it is well to pause for a moment on the phenomenon of race.

In her chapter that leads off this book, Linda Vigilant reinforces what already is known concerning race as a putative biological phenomenon. She writes: "There is a great longing for uniqueness [us/them, we/they] lurking in the members of the human species. People seem to want to believe in uniqueness, if not superiority. . . . However, evidence of intrinsic, biological superiority is sorely lacking. . . . In fact, the entire concept of race as applied to the human species is not scientifically justifiable. The sorting of individuals into discrete categories ignores the genetic similarity of all humans and is biologically, and socially, inappropriate. . . . [Accordingly, r]ace is by definition a biological entity yet it has no true justification in biology." Regarding a supposed biological foundation for race, Vigilant thus tells the world at the end of the twentieth century precisely what the United Nations Educational, Scientific, and Cultural Organization (hereinafter UNESCO) had told it at mid-century through its statements on race of 1950 and 1951. The "Statement of 1950" reads in part:

1. Scientists have reached general agreement in recognizing that mankind is one: that all men belong to the same species, *Homo sapiens*. It is further generally agreed among scientists that all men are probably derived from the same common stock; and that such differences as exist

between different groups of mankind are due to the operation of evolutionary factors or differentiation such as isolation, the drift and random fixation of the material particles which control heredity (the genes), changes in the structure of these particles, hybridization, and natural selection. In these ways groups have arisen of varying stability and degree of differentiation which have been classified in different ways for different purposes.

2. From the biological standpoint, the species *Homo sapiens* is made up of a number of populations, each one of which differs from the others in the frequency of one or more genes. Such genes, responsible for the hereditary differences between men, are always few when compared to the whole genetic constitution of man and to the vast number of genes common to all human beings regardless of the population to which they belong. This means that the likeness among men are far greater than their differences.

3. A race, from the biological standpoint, may therefore be defined as one of the group of populations constituting the species *Homo sapiens*. These populations are capable of interbreeding with one another but, by virtue of the isolating barriers which in the past kept them more or less separated, exhibit certain physical differences as a result of somewhat different biological histories. These represent variations, as it were, on a common theme.

4. In short, the term "race" designates a group or population characterized by some concentrations, relative as to frequency and distribution, of hereditary particles (genes) or physical characters, which appear, fluctuate, and then often disappear in the course of time by reason of geographic and/or cultural isolation. The varying manifestations of these traits in different populations are perceived in different ways by each group. What is *perceived* is largely *preconceived*, so that each group *arbitrarily* tends to misinterpret the variability which occurs as a *fundamental difference* which separates that group from all others.

5. These are the scientific facts. Unfortunately, however, when most people use the term "race" they do not do so in the sense above defined. To most people, a race is any group of people whom they choose to describe as a race. . . .[4] [How powerfully is the last sentence instantiated when Justice Antonin Scalia, in concurring with the Supreme Court's decision in *Adarand Constructors, Inc.*, v. *Federico Peña, et al.*, wrote: "Individuals who have been wronged by unlawful racial discrimination should be made whole, but under our Constitution there can be no such thing as either a creditor or a debtor race. . . . To pursue the concept of racial entitlement even for the most benign of purposes is to reinforce and preserve for future mischief the way of thinking that produced race

slavery, race privilege and race hatred. *In the eyes of government, we are just one race here. It is American*"[5]—the American race.]

The "Statement of 1951" reads in part:

1. Scientists are generally agreed that all men living today belong to a single species, *Homo sapiens*, and are derived from a common stock, even though there is some dispute [which continues into the 1990s] to when and how different human groups diverged from this common stock. . . .

4. Broadly speaking, individuals belonging to different major groups of mankind are distinguishable by virtue of their physical characters, but individual members, or small groups, belonging to different races within the same major group are usually not so distinguishable. Even the major groups grade into each other, and the physical traits by which they and the races within them are characterized overlap considerably. With respect to most, if not all, measurable characters, the differences among individuals belonging to the same race are greater than the differences that occur between the observed averages for two or more races within the same major group. [It is well to note here that Vigilant makes this very same point.]

5. . . . It often happens that a national group may appear to be characterized by particular psychological attributes. The superficial view would be that this is due to race. Scientifically, however, we realize that any common psychological attribute is more likely to be due to a common historical and social background, and that such attributes may obscure the fact that, within different populations consisting of many human types, one will find approximately the same range of temperament and intelligence.

6. The scientific material available to us at present does not justify the conclusion that inherited genetic differences are a major factor in producing the differences between the cultures and cultural achievements of different peoples or groups. It does indicate, on the contrary, that a major factor in explaining such differences is the cultural experience which each group has undergone.

7. There is no evidence for the existence of so-called "pure" races. . . . In regard to race mixture, the evidence points to the fact that human hybridization has been going on for an indefinite but considerable period of time.[6]

The UNESCO statements of 1950 and 1951 pertaining to race have been cited at some length for two basic reasons. First, I wanted to make crucial portions of their substance available to the readers of this volume, who, for whatever reason, may be unable to get their hands on the UNESCO documents. Second, and critically important, I wanted to call out from a source bearing the imprimatur of the international community that the rubbish which is abroad over much of the planet in the 1990s concerning racial superiority and racial inferiority anchored biologically was debunked nearly half a century ago, and nothing of scientific repute—that is, open to critical, rigorous testing and intersubjective corroboration—has since undercut the debunking that was done. Indeed, just the obverse is true.

In the most comprehensive study of human genetic patterns ever published in a single volume, L. Luca Cavalli-Sforza, Paolo Menozzi, and Alberto Piazza in *The History and Geography of Human Genes* observe the following:

> The classification into races has proved to be a futile exercise for reasons already clear to Darwin. Human races are still extremely unstable entities in the hands of modern taxonomists, who define from 3 to 60 or more races. . . . To some extent, this latitude depends on the *personal preference* of the taxonomists, who may choose to be "lumpers" or "splitters." . . . Statistically, genetic variation within clusters is large compared with that between clusters. . . . All populations or population clusters overlap when single genes are considered, and in almost all populations, all alleles are present but in different frequencies. No single gene is therefore sufficient for classifying human populations into systematic categories. . . .
>
> From a scientific point of view, the concept of race has failed to obtain any consensus; none is likely, given the gradual variation in existence. . . . By means of painstaking multivariate analysis, we can identify "clusters" of populations and order them in a hierarchy that we believe represents the history of fissions in the expansion to the whole world of anatomically modern humans. At no level can clusters be identified with races, since every level of clustering would determine a different partition and there is *no biological reason* to prefer a particular one. The successive levels of clustering follow each other in a regular sequence, and there is no discontinuity that might tempt us to consider a certain level as a reasonable, though arbitrary, threshold for race distinction. . . .
>
> [Accordingly, t]here is no scientific basis to the belief of genetically determined "superiority" of one population over another. None of the genes that we consider has any accepted connection with behavioral traits, the genetic determination of which is extremely difficult to study and presently based on soft evidence. The claims of a genetic basis for a general superiority of one population over another are not supported by any of our findings.[7]

What one learns here from Cavalli-Sforza, Menozzi, and Piazza is what one had learned already from L. C. Dunn, who, writing for the UNESCO volume *Race and Science* cited earlier, observes:

The judgment of biology . . . is clear and unequivocal. The modern view of race, founded upon the known facts and theories of heredity, leaves the old views of fixed and absolute biological differences among the races of man, and the hierarchy of superior and inferior races founded upon this old view, without scientific justification. Biologists now agree that all men everywhere belong to a single species, *Homo sapiens*. As is the case with other species, all men share their essential hereditary characters in common, having received them from common ancestors. . . . [And so, t]he persistence of race prejudice where it exists is a cultural acquisition which . . . finds no justification in biology.[8]

When the UNESCO statements of 1950 and 1951 are conjoined with the observations of Vigilant, Dunn, and Cavalli-Sforza and colleagues, a clear, distinct and incontrovertible pattern emerges concerning race as a biological phenomenon. Race is not a biological phenomenon; it is a social phenomenon transmuted by culture into a biological one. It names a classificatory preference that finds no sound empirical mooring in biology. If racial classifications are largely a function of the "personal preference" of taxonomists, as Cavalli-Sforza and colleagues, believe, or any group of people whom one "choose[s] to describe as a race," as the UNESCO "Statement of 1950," calls out, there is indeed "no biological reality to the concept of race."[9] This truth was announced to the readers of *The Milwaukee Journal* on the evening of February 20, 1995, in a bold headline that read: **Race has no scientific basis in biology, researchers say**. I was both pleased and distressed by the headline. Pleased because a major newspaper made known to its readers a truth that had been well established for nearly half a century; distressed because I asked myself how many times was it necessary to rediscover fire or to reinvent the wheel. The paper cited, among others, C. Loring Brace, an anthropologist at the University of Michigan, Ann Arbor, who observed that "[r]ace is a result of the human tendency to categorize, but it has no biological basis."[10]

So there it is: Unless the world were to learn otherwise from the Human Genome Project and the Human Genome Diversity Project that are now underway, in the context of the best objective knowledge[11] that has been extant since the mid-twentieth century, race is not a biological phenomenon—neither is ethnicity nor nationality for that matter. There is no superior race biologically; there is no inferior race biologically. This being so, it would be well were the twentieth century to be remembered as the one in which the biological stake was driven irretrievably through the deformed heart of race, and its malformed but tenacious multicolored body burned, scattered, and forgotten. But alas, this is not likely to be, for all around the world an assumed biology animates the commonplace understanding of race. Put differently, in the commonplace of everyday life concerning race, biological myths all too often overwhelm biological facts, and a sort of mythological biology, if one may so speak, comes to supersede empirical biology.

Interesting, here, is the fact that there are those who claim to believe that race is not grounded in biology yet behave in their daily lives as if it were. In this, the empirical reality of what Charles Stevenson called out as a logical possibility nearly two generations ago comes into play, namely, a clash of belief and attitude. Stevenson wrote: "It is logically possible, at least, that two men should continue to disagree in attitude even though they had all their beliefs in common, and even though neither had made any logical or inductive error, or omitted any relevant evidence. Differences in temperament, or in early training, or in social status, might make the men retain different attitudes even though both were possessed of the complete scientific truth."[12] What Stevenson said concerning two individuals is true also for a single individual. One always has to proceed with the utmost caution when one uses the term "personal knowledge."[13] Still, I do know, of my own personal knowledge, of individuals who have claimed forcefully that they did not believe that race really had a sound biological anchor, yet continually behaved as if it did. In short, "a commonly accepted body of scientific beliefs [does not necessarily] cause us to have a commonly accepted set of attitudes."[14] Dunn thus hits the mark when he writes:

> We know now why certain views about race uniformity and purity and the fixity of racial differences were[/are] wrong; and why social and political views of race inequality were[/are] wrong. Since the former were often used as a justification for the latter, we should as reasonable beings like to believe that, if we get rid of our biological misconceptions, we should thereby cure the social and political ills of injustice and exploitation which appeared to be based upon wrong biology. Eventually we may expect this to happen, but we should not forget that the way in which human beings as individuals and as groups have acted with regard to race differences has more often stemmed from *feelings and from prejudice* than from knowledge.[15]

Racial prejudice, racial hatred, and boorish racism persist in spite of scientific knowledge about the biology of race. They persist because of their social value and social utility. They persist because they are perceived to reinforce the safety, security, and comfort of the familiar in the face of the anxiety, insecurity and discomfort of the unfamiliar. Gordon Allport tells us that "what is familiar tends to *become* a value."[16] Racism bounds that which is familiar, sets it apart from what is unfamiliar, and is a value—albeit an ignoble one. In this regard, Sidney Willhelm touched a raw nerve a generation ago when he wrote that in the United States "racism . . . must now be taken for a dominant, autonomous social value."[17] Mythic biological superiority and mythic biological inferiority undergird racism as a value. How well was Abraham Lincoln cognizant of this value when he made plain that he had "no purpose to introduce political and social equality between the white and the black races," and was "in favor of the race to which [he belonged] having the superior position;" for "[t]here is a physical difference between the two which . . . will probably *forever* forbid their living together upon the footing of perfect equality."[18] In the United States, and elsewhere around the world at the end of the twentieth century, one observes starkly the effects of racism as a social value as those who have been the beneficiaries of what I term *racial inheritance* struggle to maintain what Lincoln understood to be "the superior position."

In the nineteenth century, Arthur de Gobineau and Charles Carroll, among others, constructed frameworks based on the supposed biological superiority of whites and inferiority of nonwhites to justify the social advantages that accrued from white racial inheritance. At the end of the twentieth century, Richard Herrnstein and Charles Murray have imitated de Gobineau and Carroll, though they have been less conspicuous in calling attention to their biological assumptions. What all of these men seek is the continued transgenerational, racial inheritance of the superior position—whether the superior position takes the form of control of major institutions in, say, the United States, or northern hegemony in the North-South divide vis-à-vis the global political economy of which Claude Ake makes mention. But "[s]uperiority is a political and socioeconomic concept, tied to events of recent political, military, and economic history and to cultural traditions of countries or groups. This superiority is rapidly transient, as history shows, whereas the average genotype does not change rapidly."[19] The critical term here is "cultural traditions."

The superior positions that wo'men strive for, and seek to maintain, come their way not by dint of their racial superiority biologically, but in virtue of the cultural traditions which support and sustain the biological machinery they obtained at birth. It is thus well to turn to culture to illuminate race, ethnicity and nationalism, which, at the end of the twentieth century, constitute the most explosive societal fault lines on the planet.

## II

Concerning *"The Fate of the Earth,"* a subheading in his chapter entitled "The Biological Consequences of Nuclear War" in *The Cold and the Dark: The World after Nuclear War*, Paul Ehrlich writes:

> Plausible war scenarios can be constructed that would result in the dominant atmospheric effects of darkness and cold spreading over virtually the entire planet. Under those circumstances, human survival would be largely restricted to islands and coastal areas of the Southern Hemisphere, and the human population might be reduced to prehistoric levels. . . . [T]here probably would be survivors scattered throughout the Southern Hemisphere and, perhaps, even in a few places in the Northern Hemisphere. . . .
>
> But one has to ask about the long-term persistence of these small groups of people, or of isolated individuals. Human beings are social

animals. They are *very dependent* upon the social structures that they have built. . . . The survivors [of a large-scale nuclear war] will be back in a kind of hunter and gatherer stage. But hunters and gathers in the past always had an enormous *cultural knowledge* of their environments; they knew how to live off the land. But after a nuclear holocaust, people without that kind of cultural background will suddenly be trying to live in an environment that has never been experienced by people anywhere. . . . If the groups are small, there is a possibility of inbreeding. And, of course, social and economic systems will be utterly shattered. The psychological state of the survivors is difficult to imagine.

[In this context,] the possibility that the scattered survivors simply would not be able to rebuild their populations, that they would, over a period of decades or even centuries, fade away [cannot be excluded, nor can] the possibility of a full-scale nuclear war entraining the extinction of *Homo sapiens* [be excluded].[20]

The grim picture painted by Ehrlich calls out most starkly the cultural imperative in relation to the biological survival of *Homo sapiens sapiens*. Cultural extinction and biological extinction are but two sides of a single coin. Culture affords individuals and groups the wherewithal to adapt to their environments. Such adaptation fosters the biological survival of individuals and groups, and of culture itself. As Skinner notes, "[a] person is not only exposed to the contingencies that constitute a culture, he helps to maintain them, and to the extent that the contingencies induce him to do so the culture is self-perpetuating."[21]

The self-perpetuation of a culture presumes that its members and it, itself, survive. "[A] culture," says Skinner, "which *for any reason* induces its members to work for its survival, or for the survival of some of its practices, is more likely to survive. Survival is the only value according to which a culture is eventually to be judged, and any practice that furthers survival has survival value by definition."[22] Moreover, in relation to survival, "[e]ach culture has its own set of goods, and what is good in one culture may not be good in another. To recognize this is to take the position of 'cultural relativism.' What is good for the Trobriand Islander is good for the Trobriand Islander, and that is that."[23] The cultural relativism of which Skinner speaks is most healthy, for its recognizes the authenticity, integrity, and intrinsic value of diverse cultures in terms of the survival of their own members. This tolerance of cultural diversity—a sound term that, regrettably, has been sullied at the end of the twentieth century by much that is pejorative—is the very antithesis of the "missionary zeal [that seeks to convert] all cultures to a single set of ethical, governmental, religious, or economic values."[24]

Vodun, Christianity, Judaism, and Islam, for example, all serve their believers equally well, just as Danbala Wedo[25] serves with equal facility the ones who believe in him as does Jesus Christ those who worship him. It was rank cultural chauvinism and imperialism that, in part, impelled European Christians to spread out around the world to impose their version of religion upon presumably less fortunate races. And it was acute cultural myopia that moved the French of the Enlightenment to believe that French-based Enlightenment rationality was the foundation for a world culture. In this regard, Brian Porter writes that "[t]he French were to be the core nation of a universal republic. And the criterion for membership of that republic was to be one's philosophy of life rather than one's ethnic origins or racial background. Such a basis for a reorganization of world society might have worked had not the French, in Martin Wight's words, been 'sublimely incapable of distinguishing between the universal Rights of Man and French culture.' Napoleon's armies entered the surrounding countries of Europe as liberators, but to those being liberated it came increasingly to look like political and cultural imperialism on the grandest scale."

Grand cultural designs and schemes, then, are all too often repressive and oppressive, as one culture either is unmindful of, or simply elects to ignore, the empirical fact that what is good in one culture may not be good in another. "[W]hat makes so-called universal religions so pernicious," says Patrick Bellegarde-Smith in his penetrating discussion of Vodun, is that "[t]hey rob the world of its richness and imply cultural and racial hierarchies by establishing bad and good religions. Alienation follows the erosion of one's spiritual and cultural heritage."[26] No religion that serves the good of a culture is a bad religion. This is a cardinal truth of cultural relativism. Still, cultural relativism does not mean that all cultures do not share much, indeed very much, in common. "Vodun is the national religion of Haiti,"[27] according to Bellegarde-Smith, and if Christianity is not the national religion of the United States it comes pretty close to being so. Here Christianity is juxtaposed to Vodun to call out what is of singular importance, that is, both are religions, and both serve the good of their respective cultures.

Cultural relativism notwithstanding, all cultures share in common at least seven attributes. These are: species life, species being, language, religion, literature-art-science-technology, institutions, and transgenerational memory.

Species life is a unique organic property which only nature itself produces and reproduces, and without which there is no culture. In this sense, species life is prior to culture, but without culture, as Ehrlich makes plain, species life may survive for a while but it is unlikely to persist. Species being entails the ontological and cosmological percepts and precepts around which species life is organized. Species being ascribes value and worth to species life. The value and worth that it ascribes to any life are contingent on the place of that life in the order that it creates. The more the species life of individuals or groups is valued in the order of species being, the greater is the likelihood that the ones who lead those lives will adapt well to the contingencies of their environment. The sorts of interaction that obtain between species being and species life thus structure the possibilities for wo'men to grow, develop, adapt, create, and reproduce themselves in their work and their progeny.

Over historical time, competing, conflicting, contradictory, and asymmetrical conceptions and constructions of species being have occasioned profound variations in the valuation of species life and its products. The value and worth of the species life of the West African and his descent, both in Africa and in the Diaspora, over the past five hundred years have been nominal in European constructions of species being. This opened wide the path to slavery, colonialism, and Jim Crowism in both its de jure and de facto forms. If Africans were "slavish by nature," they could indeed be "bought and sold, and treated as . . . ordinary article[s] of merchandise and traffic, whenever a profit could be made by it."[28] Bernal is most powerful here, as he discusses racism's degradation of the species being not only of Africans, but also of others who were to suffer the anguish of European cultural arrogance.

The deformation of the species being of individuals and groups affords justification for all sorts of conduct that distort, distract and corrode their species life. Thus, for example, in spite of its empirical falsity, were policymakers in the United States to agree with William Schockley—twice a Nobel laureate in physics, and now deceased—that "the major cause of the American Negro's intellectual and social deficits is hereditary and racially genetic in origin, and thus not remedial to a major degree by practical improvements in [the] environment,"[29] all sorts of what Skinner calls "aversive consequences"[30] could come to bedevil the species life of African-Americans.

As one gazes back over the twentieth century from the vantage point of the 1990s, one cannot but be struck by the expansiveness of cultural aggression in the deformation of the species being of "them" by "us." One of its most nefarious and rapacious manifestations, "ethnic cleansing," has reemerged with a vengeance in the 1990s. Marianne Elliott observes that in Northern Ireland "[t]he IRA's border attacks were seen as 'ethnic cleansing'" by the Protestants. Robin Remington makes mention of Dr. Ante Pavelic's "SS [which] set out on a campaign of 'ethnic cleansing'" when the Nazis controlled Yugoslavia, as well as the "rising body counts, untold numbers of wounded, and the 2–3 million refugees created by war and deliberate policies of ethnic cleansing" that accompanied the disintegration of Yugoslavia in the 1990s. Furthermore, in Rwanda, in three short months between April and July of 1994, the United Nations estimated that half-a-million to one million persons were killed and roughly three and a half million made refugees, in a country of approximately eight million people. Most of those who were killed were Tutsis, at the hands of Hutus. (The Tutsis won the civil war.) This is without a doubt one of the greatest holocausts of the twentieth century, yet it has passed as merely one manifestation of what I heard a former U.S. ambassador call "nasty bits of disorder." A million lives lost to human hands in three months was but a nasty bit of disorder. Thus the inevitable questions arise: Is racial cleansing to be next?—in spite of what has been said pertaining to the biology of race. Given the longanimity of the world community in relation to the evil of "ethnic cleansing," would like forbearance obtain were racial cleansing to occur? I am not sanguine concerning the answer to either of these questions.

One of the means through which the deformation of species being occurs is the use of language. Language may be used to exalt or to diminish. In the texture of their language is the species being of a people woven. It is a well-known adage but worth repeating: Language is a people's mirror. They see themselves in it; they see others through it. Images of a people are conveyed to the world through the language by which they are made known. These images cover quite a spectrum. They may be sharp or blurred, simple or complex, coarse or refined, solicitous or provocative, accurate or distorted, and so on. What is critical is that they impress themselves upon the mind and leave impressions that incline, guide, and/or occasion conduct. How well does the African intellectual and spiritual father of the Catholic Church, Saint Augustine of Hippo, whom Bernal mentions in relation to the African mind in European religion, understand this when he writes:

> After the state or city comes the world, the third circle of human society—
> the first being the house, and the second the city. And the world, as it is
> larger, so it is fuller of dangers, as the greater sea is the more dangerous.
> And here, in the first place, man is *separated* from man by the *difference
> of languages*. For if two men, each ignorant of the other's language, meet,
> and are not compelled to pass, but, on the contrary, to remain in company,
> dumb animals, though of different species, would more easily hold
> intercourse than they, human beings though they be. For their common
> nature is no help to friendliness when they are prevented by diversity of
> language from conveying their sentiments to one another; so that a man
> would more readily hold intercourse with his dog than with a foreigner.
> But the imperial city has endeavored to impose on subject nations not
> only her yoke, *but her language, as a bond of peace*, so that interpreters,
> far from being scarce, are numberless.[31]

Why did the imperial city strive to impose on subject nations not only her yoke but also her language? To make her dictates readily comprehensible. But even more important, so that the many would discern, understand, and internalize the customs, traditions, norms, mores, and ethos that animated Roman civilization. Rome sought to lighten the weight of her yoke through the spread and acceptance of her language. Through her language and her laws, she endeavored to make those whom she had conquered participants in her culture—to bind, as it were, their spirits with her language and their bodies with her laws. European colonial overlords imitated Rome in imposing their languages on those whom they colonized and enslaved. But they never learned well the art of the imperial city in making "them" truly as part of "us."

Looking around the world, one observes society after society where language, rather than being "a bond of peace," is actually a wedge of discord. Language is especially a wedge of ethnic and national discord as it separates individuals and groups, many of whom, if one might borrow from Saint Augustine, would rather hold intercourse with their dogs than with "them," whoever them might be. As one reads the chapters in this volume by Elliott, Muhammad Hallaj, George Harris, Mark Beissinger, Alfred Senn, Marc Levine, Kosaku Yoshino, and David Buck, one observes language both as a bond of peace and a wedge of discord.

Hallaj makes known that once the PLO accepted "the legitimacy of [a] Jewish presence in Palestine . . . [and] adopted the democratic-secular state idea, PLO schools began to teach Hebrew to Palestinian children to prepare them for the eventuality of coexistence with a Jewish community in Palestine." What was the purpose of this? It was not merely that Palestinian children would know the vocabulary and grammar of Hebrew, important though this was. It was, rather, that Palestinian children and Jewish children of today, who would be the adults of tomorrow and the ancestors of the day after, would come to share a common language. "A common language is not intrinsically one official or unofficial natural language, but the capacity and ability of large numbers of persons to make common sense of a given phenomenon or range of phenomena and share like sentiments pertaining to it. This is so regardless of whether one, two or more natural languages are used in the emergence of such common sense and [shared] sentiments."[32] In having its youngsters learn Hebrew, just as many Jewish youngsters learn Arabic, the PLO realized that if a bond of peace were to obtain between Palestinians and Jews instead of merely tolerable order, it was essential that a common language bridge the Jewish community and the Palestinian community. The bridge of a common language would not necessarily conflate the two communities, but it would most assuredly make less likely the many irritations, vexations, torments, vulgarities, brutalities, and horrors that separated them. Policies and conduct that foster the development and spread of a common language among peoples thus have much to commend them.

The PLO sought the evolution of a common language in a land where more than one natural language is a commonplace. In Northern Ireland, English, a natural language, serves as a linguistic bridge between the Catholic and Protestant communities, yet by and large no common language obtains between them. How compellingly is this point instantiated by Elliott, who observes: "The kind of mutual incomprehension of the other community's core values that has been outlined [in Elliott's chapter] owes not a little to the way in which they are expressed. 'The talks failed for lack of language,' wrote Professor Edna Longley of the breakdown of interparty talks on the future of Northern Ireland in November 1992." The talks failed not for the lack of a mutually understood natural language but for the absence of a shared common language. A common language may be conflated into many natural languages, yet one natural language may not bear a common language for all of those who make use of it in a given society.

This very point resonates in Yoshino, who notes that

[t]he *nihonjinron* and their popularized cross-cultural manuals offer abundant examples to suggest that Japanese patterns of behavior and use of

language are so peculiar that one has be born a Japanese to be able to grasp the intricacy of the Japanese language and the delicacy of the Japanese mode of thinking. For example, one writer observes that, though he knows of some Europeans whose Japanese is accurate and quite fluent, and though some Korean residents in Japan have won literary awards for their prose or fiction in Japanese, he knows of no foreigner who can compose good *waka* (or thirty-one syllable Japanese poetry). This sort of remark may be taken as suggesting that the Japanese language "belongs exclusively" to the Japanese, in the sense that it can truly be appreciated only by the Japanese.

This assessment of Japanese as a natural language precludes those who are not born Japanese from participating in a common language through its use. In this sense, though a Korean resident of Japan acquires Japanese in his childhood, or a European lives his whole life in Japan speaking flawless Japanese, neither is ever a full participant in the common language of the society, and thus is never wholly familiar to the Japanese. In this regard, Porter points out that Japan is "the notable exception of . . . the modern industrial state," insofar as it has not "sought to distance itself from its ethnicity." The conflation of natural language and common language in Japanese as "the exclusive property of the Japanese people," to use Yoshino's terms, oftentimes serves to drive a wedge between the Japanese and those who may well speak the natural language but are perceived to lack a sound understanding of its common language. Accordingly, a bond of peace among the Japanese themselves becomes a potential wedge of discord between the Japanese and their resident aliens, as well as foreigners.[33]

The value of a common language was not lost to the men of the Kremlin who ruled the former Soviet Empire, and Russian was used as an instrument for constructing it. But just as the spread of Latin did not bring peace to the Roman empire, the spread of Russian did not bring peace to the former Soviet Union. Rome succeeded more than perhaps any other empire in making "them" a part of "us"; still, for most her language, like her arms, was a weapon of order, an instrument to promote the tranquility of the empire. As was true of Rome, the former Soviet Union did succeed in imposing upon those who fell within its imperial bounds a measure of tranquility and order, but failed to occasion true peace. This it could not impose.

It could impose its language, and this it did. It could impose its laws, and this it also did. It could wield its arms, and this too it did. But it could not impose its peace, that well-ordered concord that binds wo'man to wo'man both near and far, opening wide the gates to shared symbols, myths, values, beliefs, and attitudes concerning the organization of political society, as well as the bounds of right, fitting, and proper conduct. The language it strived to impose was in reality no bond of peace but a wedge of discord, which was to be of no little import in its undoing. This point emerges most forcefully in the chapters by Beissinger and Senn. Moreover, one cannot but be intrigued by the fact that problems attending language that so harassed the former Soviet Union continue to bedevil the new states that emerged from it.

Senn observes that

> [i]n the 1980s Soviet nationalities' policy focused on the concept of *sliianie* (merging), an effort to do away with the differences between nationalities by the general acceptance of the Russian language. Soviet educators advocated "bilingualism," providing children with better instruction in Russian than in their mother tongues. Teachers of Russian, moreover, received higher pay than did teachers of the local language. . . . Those who specialized in the use of language reacted first to bilingualism. . . . Within the cultural elites of the various nationalities many saw in bilingualism the decline and even destruction of their basic vehicles of communication.

Thus did reaction against Russian—as the language of intruders and an occupation regime in the Baltics and elsewhere in the former Soviet Union—drive a wedge between those who saw themselves as being forced to make use of an alien tongue for the sake of their well-being, and ones who perceived the language to be essential to peace, order and tranquility. A measure of order and tranquility did obtain, but not peace in the sense that I have used the term. Russian was "their" language not "ours"; it wedged "them" against "us" both symbolically and substantively; and so it largely failed to forge a sense of oneness out of "we" and "they" that would bond the peace of all. How exquisitely does Senn capture this idea when he makes known that "[i]n 1988, the head of the Lithuanian Writer's Union told [him] of his concern that the Soviet requirement that dissertations be written in Russian would undermine the development of critical thought in the Lithuanian language." Thus "[i]n one republic after another, the local writers' union took the lead in demanding stronger efforts to preserve the national language and culture." With lightning speed did the Soviet Union collapse in 1991. Though its arms were still strong, and its laws made less repressive and oppressive under *glasnost* (openness) and *perestroika* (restructuring), it could not withstand the assault of those who saw in its language no bond of peace, and for whom there was no common language. With no common language, the Republic fell apart.

There is a truth most old but still very salutary here. The Soviet Union disintegrated, and though language was not the efficient cause, it most assuredly was a significant contributory factor. The people did not share a common language as a bond of peace. Without such a common language, natural languages became wedges of discord—the most prominent, of course, being Russian. Today, a markedly similar state of affairs obtains in many of the new states of the former Soviet Union. In Lithuania, for example, Senn points out that "Poles have . . . demanded that Polish be recognized as an official language in Vilnius and certain other cities of the republic"; and in the Donbass region of Ukraine, Beissinger mentions the miners "who called for the resignation of the Kravchuk government because of excessive taxes and price rises, [and] advocated as well special autonomous status for the Donets region . . ., largely as a means of protecting economic interests and language rights." What is being called out here is that insofar as many natural languages are spoken by the people of a given state and/or society; insofar as most of them speak fluently one or at most two natural languages; and insofar as there is no common language that binds them together, absent the strong hand of an imperium, language becomes a centrifugal force that impels toward the emergence of ever smaller units of social organization. How well is this observation borne out by what is being witnessed in the former Soviet Empire in the 1990s. Beissinger and Senn are most helpful here.

The centrifugal potentiality of language in relation to the cohesion of society and the integrity of the state, and the effort of states to counter it, resonate in the chapters by Harris, Levine, and Buck. Mindful of the relation between language and ethnonational identity; aware of the sorts of transgenerational sentiments that are transported through language; sensitive to the costs of inflexible heavy handedness in the suppression of a language; and conscious of the effect that large minority populations can have on the stability of the state, Turkey has played the language of its Kurdish minority like an accordion. Beyond the restrictions already in place, in the 1980s "[l]aws were passed further restricting the use of Kurdish in any of its varieties," says Harris. But "language is the surest touchstone of Kurdishness," according to Harris, and so as violence by the Kurds mounted at the outset of the 1990s, "steps were taken [by the regime in Ankara] to acknowledge Kurdish identity and to ease restrictions on the use of the Kurdish language in publications." In matters of language policy vis-à-vis social cohesion and the integrity of the state, draconian heavy-handedness as well as supine flaccidity are formulae for the full centrifugal potentiality of language to be unleashed. The true integration of those who speak different natural languages into a common language of political society is the surest means for a regime to escape the unforgiving trap of either of these extremes.

Although to date it has sort of "muddled through," to use Levine's term, Canada thus far has avoided the regime extremes of Turkey or the state and societal fragmentation of the former Soviet Union. Why has muddling through been possible? I suggest the existence of a common language that draws Canadians together in spite of centrifugal forces, language being the most prominent, that would tear them apart. Levine observes that "by the early 1970s linguistic trends in Montreal seemed to threaten the *cultural survival* of Francophones, . . . [and] by the mid-1970s . . . the most burning policy question in Quebec [was] the issue of language policy." The outcome of these was the 1976 election of the Parti quebeçois, and "[f]or the first time in an advanced Western democracy an ethnonationalist separatist party was elected to control a subnational government." Canada seemed on the verge of splitting apart. Yet it did not. Despite Bill 101 and Bill 178 pertaining to language policy (see Levine), Quebec's desire to be recognized as a "distinct society," and persistent dissatisfaction among Quebec Francophones over Canada's constitutional misadventures, most especially the Meech Lake Accord, Canada has nonetheless held together thus far, and the integrity of the Canadian state has been preserved.

There is something at work here that transcends the wedge of English and French as natural languages. It is a common language drawn around shared economic interests, political limits, and a liberal democratic tradition. People can only muddle through where there is a willingness to do so. Such willingness emanates from a sense that things will work out, if not optimally, at least in a manner that does as little harm and promotes as much good as is possible within extant constraints. A common language makes this possible. For it does not compel universal agreement, it simply inclines the wills of individuals to will within the limits of mutually acceptable bounds, and induces them to act accordingly. And a common language is precisely what the new Communist government in China aimed for in 1949 when, to cite Buck, it "banned derogatory terminology about minorities in published pronouncements, improved minority peoples' schools and education in their respective languages, and tolerated the practice of many minority customs and life styles that differed from the Han majority."

Given my longstanding fascination with comparisons between the United States and Rome, and my current interest in the United States of 1991 (the year of America's unchallenged supremacy in the world) through 2011 set against Rome of 390 (the year in which the Emperor Theodosius boldly proclaimed Christian times throughout the empire) through 410 CE—the year in which Alaric the Visigoth caused so much psychological pain to the imperial city with so little actual physical damage— I cannot leave the discussion on language without asking: Of what significance is all that has been said for the United States?

The accretion of natural language enclaves in the United States at the end of the twentieth century is not a good thing. Its potential harm both to the state and the society is of great moment. The United States has always been fortunate in having a common language that could sustain it in spite of its many divisions, trials and tribulations. Frederick Douglass summoned it after the *Dred Scott* decision when he said: "The Constitution, as well as the Declaration of Independence, and the sentiments of the founders of the Republic, give us a platform broad enough, and strong enough, to support the most comprehensive plans for the freedom and elevation of all the people of this country, without regard to color, class, or clime."[34] And Abraham Lincoln invoked it on the evening of June 16, 1858, in the Hall of the House of Representatives in the Illinois State House as he began his campaign for the U.S. Senate, when he declared: "'A house divided against itself cannot stand.' I believe this government cannot endure, permanently half *slave* and half *free*. I do not expect the Union to be *dissolved*—I do not expect the house to fall but I *do* expect it will cease to be divided. It will become *all* one thing, or *all* the other."[35] Lincoln engaged the same common language in defense of liberty in the Republic as Frederick Douglass did. But Stephen Douglas tapped deep into another common language, as he mocked Lincoln in their first debate, concerning the matter of a divided house. Said he: "Mr. Lincoln . . . says that this government cannot endure permanently in the same condition in which it was made by its framers—divided into free and slave states. . . . Why can it not exist divided into free and slave states? Washington, Jefferson, Franklin, Madison, Hamilton, Jay, and the great men of that day, made this government divided into free states and slave states, and left each state perfectly free to do as it pleased on the subject of slavery. . . . Why can it not exist on the same principle on which our fathers made it?"[36] Here we have it: two common languages struggling for the soul of one Republic.

The common language to which Lincoln and Frederick Douglass appealed emerged triumphant for seven generations—using twenty years for a generation. But at the end of the twentieth century, the language of Stephen Douglas has had a new rebirth, and one can only ponder what it portents for the future of the Republic. On the front cover of *U.S. News & World Report* of July 10, 1995, was a likeness of the Statue of Liberty with the caption: "Divided We Stand: America's New Cultural Landscape." In a story entitled "The New America," the magazine observed that

> America has always been a divided nation. *E pluribus unum* may be a national motto and the melting pot a national metaphor, but the reality has been patriots and Tories, free whites and black slaves, Philadelphia bankers and Tennessee woodsmen, Northern abolitionists and Southern slave owners, free silver and hard currency, natives and immigrants, Wall Street and Main Street, Republicans and Democrats, hawks and doves, liberals and conservatives. [Christians and non-Christians could have been added.]
>
> Today America is divided in new and different ways. The South, once solidly Democratic, is fast becoming Republican. . . . African Americans and Hispanics are divided about affirmative action and welfare reform. There is a gulf between women who work outside the home and women who stay at home with their children. . . . "Are we a nation?" are the first words of Michael Lind's *The Next American Nation*. "Social classes speak to themselves in a dialect of their own, inaccessible to outsiders," wrote Christopher Lasch in *The Revolt of the Elites*. Republican analyst William Kristol warns of "the Balkanization of America."
>
> We can see these new divisions every day—living in geographical and cultural enclaves; sitting in walled back yards, not open front porches; listening to our own music and watching our own cable-television channels.[37]

*U.S. News & World Report* is correct in saying that "America has always been a divided nation." But the triumph of the common language shared by Frederick Douglass and Lincoln provided the substratum for a sufficiency of shared purpose which, in spite of grave lacerations upon the body politic, has sustained the Republic over these past seven generations. But at the end of the twentieth century one increasingly observes enclave America replacing access America. Enclaves are not new social phenomena in the United States. They have always existed. What is new is the doubt that expands ever the more concerning the bridging of these enclaves by a common language. This becomes especially troublesome when differences in natural languages serve to reinforce the enclaves. It has been estimated that in Los Angeles alone more than one hundred and fifty different languages are spoken—a virtual Tower of Babel. To the extent that these languages serve to buttress enclaves, where individuals live in the United States but are at best only marginally steeped in its common language, they open seams in the tapestry of the Republic.

Abraham Lincoln and Stephen Douglas represent two radically different concepts of America. One is grounded in the belief that a house divided against itself cannot stand. The other is anchored in the conviction that it can. Lincoln carried the day—even though he did not win the senate seat that he sought—yet one cannot but wonder at the end of the twentieth century whether Douglas is on the verge of emerging victorious after all. It is this writer's conviction that should Douglas come to supersede Lincoln, Alaric will assuredly visit the American republic sooner rather than later. There is no need for an official natural language in the United States, and a constitutional amendment to make English *the* national language is likely to have the obverse effect of its intended purpose. What is needed are expanded contingencies of reinforcement for the common language that knits together the diverse groupings of the society in a bond of peace.

Just as language may divide or unite the members of a society, so too does religion. In the language of a people is their concept of the divine made known. And in a divine Godhead, whether within wo'man or without her/him, do all religions rest. Both Lincoln and Douglas appeal to the Christian God. "[A]s God has made us separate," says Lincoln, "we can leave one another alone and do one another much good thereby. . . . [L]et us discard all this quibbling about . . . this race and that race and the other race being inferior, and therefore must be placed in an inferior position. . . . Let us discard all these things, and unite as one people throughout the land, until we shall once more stand up declaring that all men are created equal."[38] With equal conviction, Douglas declares: "I do not believe that the Almighty ever intended the negro to be the equal of the white man. . . . He belongs to an inferior race, and must always occupy an inferior position."[39] Here, then, are two radically different concepts of race in American society, both anchored in the same Christian God. The crucial point is that the very same divine Godhead can sustain fundamentally different conceptions of man and the organization of political society. Proslavery and antislavery forces solicited with equal confidence the favor of the same Christian God. Interestingly, on June 20, 1995, one hundred and fifty years after it was formed, "the Southern Baptist Convention, America's largest Protestant denomination and one founded in large part in defense of slavery, voted overwhelmingly in the annual meeting . . . to 'repent of racism of which we have been guilty' and to apologize to and ask forgiveness from 'all African-Americans'."[40]

Of much interest here is the fact that ex-slaves in the United States largely retained the religion of their former masters. Though Christian slaveholders debased, despoiled, depreciated, and demeaned the Gods of the Africans, and strived to depose ancestral Gods with the Christian God, they did not attempt to extinguish the longing of the Africans for the divine. To the contrary, they sought to tap into the Africans' religion, which "was nature-worship, with [a] profound belief in invisible surrounding influences, good and bad, and . . . [their] worship . . . [was] through incantation and sacrifice."[41] Thus were slaveholders, for example, able to evoke a sense of sacrifice steeped deep into the psyches of Africans through their intercourse with the divine. And despite a substitution of the Christian God for African Gods, which did separate Africans from *their* archetypes of the divine, their connectedness with the divine was nonetheless preserved.

How strikingly does this contrast with communist overlords of the former Soviet Union who sought to extinguish the role of the divine in structuring the contours of their peoples lives. Unlike American Christian slaveholders who recognized the value of religion in sustaining organized, legal, and constitutional racial oppression, communist overlords failed to make use of this value of religion. Marxism-Leninism had much to do with this. Ironically, communists sought to set religion aside, yet they could not escape it; for peoples are not readily severed in their spirits from the Gods in whom they trust. The regime in Beijing may well have come to terms with the societal significance of this truth, and found it prudent since 1978, as noted by Buck, to permit "minority peoples in China . . . to revive religious practices previously suppressed." It is thus well that leaders should recognize that peoples have need of their Gods, for in them is life sustaining hope.

In *Our Oriental Heritage*, Will Durant writes: "[B]eneath and above everything in Egypt was religion. . . . We cannot understand the Egyptian—or man—until we study his gods."[42] Why does Durant stress the relation between wo'man and religion? The divine is the ultimate wellspring of hope. Hope, that balm of life. Where hope abounds a people strive; where hope evanesces a people atrophy. Hope imbues individuals with the feeling that they have some measure of control over their destinies. It stimulates in them a consciousness of their abilities, potentialities, capacities and capabilities. Hope fosters in one a sense that one can master impediments in one's path, transcend given limitations, open up possibilities that have been closed heretofore, and create satisfactory, perhaps even good, options where none appear to be present. It gives one a sense of confidence to believe that one can make things happen, and affords reasonable grounds for this belief. Believing that one can make things happen, one is impelled to make the sorts of sacrifices which are necessary to bring them to pass, especially if they either are needed greatly or desired strongly. Hope thus kindles desires and ignites expectations, which, when satisfied, reinforce it.

If the radiance of hope quickens the spirit and encourages, the gloom of hopelessness deadens the soul and discourages. Even as hope lifts one up, hopelessness drags one down. Just as hope makes lighter one's difficulties, problems, troubles, vexations, cares and worries, hopelessness makes heavier whatsoever that weighs upon the heart. Hopelessness magnifies inadequacies and undercuts resolve. Corroding optimism, hopelessness diminishes effort.

This is of the utmost importance, for where effort is lacking that which could have been accomplished is usually left unrealized. Wherever a state of hopelessness obtains, individuals tend to believe that much is beyond their reach that actually may be within their grasp. Believing that they have little control over the present, virtually none over the future, and that it is useless to contend against what is beyond their control, they often resign themselves to what is, settling for less than they either can or ought to secure.

By constricting sharply images of the possible and conceptions of the probable, hopelessness undermines the willingness of individuals to make sacrifices in the present for gains in the future. Hopelessness thus fosters and reinforces present-oriented behaviors, as individuals and groups discern rigid limits to their life chances. If wo'man is by nature a creature that works, strives and creates, hopelessness wars against human nature. For it undermines the striving purpose of wo'man's very being, and so induces individuals to acquiesce to limits which they may well have the potentiality, capacity, and capability of pushing beyond. By suffocating creativity, as well as dulling insight and foresight, hopelessness diminishes individuals, and corrodes their self-respect, self-esteem and dignity.

In hopelessness does despair inhere, with offshoots of resignation and desperation. Despair tends to distort vision and skew perception. Those who despair are prone to all sorts of errors in their reading of the social universe in which their lives are played out. Upon these errors is the flaccidity of resignation oftentimes evinced or the unbridled fury of desperation unleashed. And even where those who despair do read their social universe accurately, they may well sense either that they can do nothing to alter their lot or they must rage against it. Despair thus destroys, either by corrosive inertia or by violent explosions.

It is in the context of hope and hopelessness that the divine becomes a nexus of human survival. Gods animate the human spirit, and bring hope out of hopelessness, joy out of despair. John Blassingame tells of a slave, William Webb, who said: "'As soon as I felt in my heart, that God was the Divine Being that I must call on in all my troubles, I heard a voice speak to me, and from that time I lost all fear of men on this earth.'"[43] A loss of fear is a commonplace among those who feel themselves connected with the divine, and it may be put to uses that are noble or ignoble. Fiendishly was it manifested in the demolition of the No. 5 bus in Tel Aviv on October 19, 1994, with the slaughter of twenty-two persons and the wounding of forty-six. The suicide bomber, Saleh Abdel Rahim al-Souwi, left a videotape in which he made known that "[i]t is good to die as a martyr for Allah."[44] Diabolically was it instantiated in the shooting spree of Dr. Baruch Goldstein on the morning of February 25, 1994, at the Cave of the Patriarchs, which left forty Muslim worshipers dead and another one hundred and fifty wounded. Goldstein himself was beaten to death by some of those who escaped his fusillade. According to *The New York Times*, one supporter of Goldstein said that "'[h]e loved Jews. He was a righteous man.'" Another one remarked: "'This act, which sanctified God's name, shows Arabs that we will not remain silent and watch them spill Jewish blood with impunity.'"[45]

But how much do these abominable deeds pale against the historic radiance of hope that enveloped the handshake between Israeli Prime Minister Yitzhak Rabin and PLO Chairman Yasir Arafat on the South Lawn of the U.S. White House on September 13, 1993.[46] Each time I look at it in my clip file of "historically famous handshakes," I see the hope of bridging two religious traditions by a common language and am moved deeply by the fearlessness and courage that it represents. For that handshake symbolized openly and publicly two recognitions: for the Israelis, a recognition of the Palestinians as a people, and by extension their right to self-determination; for the Palestinians, a recognition of the legitimacy of the state of Israel, and its right to exist. The divine, then, may be used to rend in despair or to build in hope—a weapon of oppression or a tool of liberation. It is to build in hope that Golan and Hallaj writes, and in this they stand out beautifully as bold exemplars of what might be in a land and among two peoples who subscribe to fundamentally different concepts of the divine.

The divine implies that which is pure, sacred, holy, worthy of worship and all praise, and from which issues precepts that give meaning and purpose to the lives of those whose conduct they guide. The divine unites a people in a shared purpose, and impels them to strive to give it objective form and substance. By objective signs, symbols, and works are individuals and groups bound together in relation to a given concept of the divine. This a point of critical importance; for those who are bound together are expected to behave in certain ways.

Thus, are Christians and Muslims, for example, called upon to proselytize their religion, in conformity with their respective precepts of the divine, in order to redeem and save those who are supposedly lost. And who are the lost? Those who do not serve the one true God. But *the* one true God of Christians is not identical with *the* one true God of Muslims, and each true God admonishes followers to behave in clearly defined ways. Herein, then, lay the germs of intolerance emanating from different concepts of the divine, especially in relation to proselytizing religions. In this regard, Bernal submits that "[s]ome scholars today argue that there has always been a particular Christian affinity for tolerance. [However, t]his is clearly untenable. Believers in revealed religions find it hard to tolerate what for them is error and sin. The Western liberal tradition of religious tolerance did not arise from Christianity. Its origins are firmly linked to upper class skeptics and deists of the seventeenth and eighteenth centuries." Bernal goes on to say that "[t]here is no doubt that in its early heyday from 650 to 1100 CE Islam was far more religiously tolerant than Christianity," though he does observe tragic examples of intolerance in contemporary Islam. What is crucial, in Bernal's view, is that "[t]he correlation with tolerance appears to be with having confidence in the success of one's faith. Thus,

Muslims on the defensive today, can behave almost as badly as Christians did when Islam tore the heart out of Christendom in the seventh century. . . . [Yet,] success and confidence are only necessary and not sufficient conditions for religious . . . toleration." What else is necessary, if not sufficient?

A concept of the divine that is amenable to the coexistence of more than one true God, and ascribes to none the status of "the Elect of God," or "God's Chosen People." Such an open-textured concept is inconsistent with mythic constructions that frame the divine particularistically, that is, there is but one true God. With much force is this point illustrated in the following passage:

> Joshua gathered all the tribes of Israel to Sheehem . . . and they presented themselves before God. And Joshua said unto all the people, . . . choose you this day whom ye will serve; whether the gods which your fathers served that *were* on the other side of the flood, or the gods of the Amorites, in whose land ye dwell: but as for me and my house, we will serve the Lord.
>
> And the people answered and said, God forbid that we should forsake the Lord, to serve other gods. For the Lord our God, he *it is* that brought us up and our fathers out of the land of Egypt, from the house of bondage, and which did those great signs in our sight, and preserved us in all the way wherein we went, and among all the people through whom we passed. And the Lord [drove] out from before us all the people, even the Amorites which dwelt in the land: *therefore* will we also serve the Lord; for he is our God.
>
> And Joshua said unto the people, Ye cannot serve the Lord; for he *is* a holy God; he *is* a jealous God; he will not forgive your transgressions nor your sins. If ye forsake the Lord, and serve strange gods, then he will turn and do you hurt, and consume you, after that he hath done you good. And the people said unto Joshua, [n]ay; but we will serve the Lord. And Joshua said unto the people, [n]ow therefore put away . . . the strange gods which *are* among you, and incline your heart unto the Lord God of Israel. And the people said unto Joshua, The Lord our God will we serve, and his voice will we obey.[47]

A chosen people shall serve their God and none other; for none other has the same standing. Ones who are among the elect shall serve their God and none other; for none other is of equal estate. For Chosen Jews, Yahweh and Allah are not substitutable; for Elect Christians, Jesus Christ and Danbala Wedo are not interchangeable.[48] Hard mythic boundaries circumscribe these manifestations of the divine, and shape fundamentally the behaviors of those who fall within them. Thus did Oliver Cromwell and John Milton "amongst many others, . . . see the English as being chosen of God" (see Porter), at the very time that Englishmen were setting out to make colonial subjects and slaves of peoples around the world. And, as Galia

Golan points out, "the ideologically motivated right wing" in Israel after the 1967 Arab-Israeli War denied that the Palestinians had any claim to Palestine, since they were not a people, and in any case all the land of Palestine had been "given by God to his Chosen People."

The mythic boundaries of the divine fold believers together, as well as differentiate them from others. They separate our God from their god; and, in the words of Martin Marty, "solidify tribalist groups and impulses; they do legitimate exclusion of the 'other,' . . . stress . . . 'difference,' [and] exaggerat[e] . . . the flaws of non-members and the virtues of adherents." Given significantly different images of the world, expectations framed within these boundaries tend to erect high walls of separation between "us" and "them," "ours" and "theirs." Retribution, sometimes very severe, often attends those who breach those expectations. The murder of Anwar el-Sadat after he concluded a peace treaty between Egypt and Israel is but one distressing, yet all too familiar case in point. Also, in Northern Ireland, Elliott notes that mixed-religion couples are generally not looked upon with favor. "There is more hostility to mixed marriages among Protestants than Catholics, even liberal-minded Protestants thinking it 'something that's morally wrong.'" Elliott also observes that "there has always been an inferiority/superiority dichotomy in Catholic thinking, the belief that they hold the moral high ground. . . . At its more extreme, this inferiority/superiority syndrome induces self-righteousness and moral elitism. Republicans are particularly skilled at exploiting Catholic's shared memory of disadvantage, and any effort to break away from it risks the accusation of selling out," with its potential costs.

As mythic boundaries are folded around the divine, contending claimants to the divine divide themselves up into all sorts of groupings. In these groupings are what Porter calls the *ethnie* born. All religious groupings are not instantiations of the *ethnie*, but wherever the *ethnie* obtain so too do mythic boundaries of the divine. Religion is separable from ethnicity, but ethnicity is inseparable from religion. "Myth," says Porter, "not only plays an essential part in group identity, but is continuously created to preserve and enhance that identity." When a myth of religion is combined with an attachment to language, the life-giving fluid of ethnicity issues forth—to be renewed generationally and transgenerationally by kin and quasi-kin relationships.

For many people, religion is simply a way of expressing the belief that wo'man is not the ultimate source of moral authority, and that it is right, fitting, and proper that individuals should lead good and decent lives. No church is needed. Religion, here, is "ecumenical, rational, reconciliatory, semi-indifferent and tolerant," to use Marty's terms. For many persons, language is purely instrumental. It is simply a means by which society is organized, and individuals and groups transmit bits of information. But for the *ethnie* religion and language entail much more, so very much more. It is, as it were, that language and religion inhere in their very being, and as such delimit the contours of their lives. In this context, Marty's concept of "'retribalist' religions" is potent; for it directs attention to the sorts of forces which are at play around the world that have inflamed religious and linguistic passions in both the *ethnie* and nations.

An ethnic group may or may not be a nation. Interestingly, one concept of a nation is that of "an aggregation of persons of the same ethnic family, often speaking the same language or cognate languages."[49] Yet all ethnic groups are not nations, and all nations are not ethnic groups. (Despite the troublesome, perhaps even dangerous, social and political fraying that is occurring in the United States, it still makes empirical sense to speak of the Republic as one multiethnic nation.) "In nationalist doctrine," says Elie Kedourie, "language, race, culture, and sometimes even religion, constitute different aspects of the same primordial entity, the nation."[50] But it is the *ethnie* not nation that is primordial, according to Porter. "What makes them special," says Porter, "is a distinct cultural character usually expressed in language, origins in the remote past, a long-settled homeland, and a sense of kinship." A nation, on the other hand, is an aggregation of persons who feel themselves attached to what Porter calls "a national idea," and whose behaviors are animated by it. A national idea pertains to what a nation is about—for example, life, liberty and the pursuit of happiness in the case of the Americans of 1776, and liberty, property, security, and resistance to oppression in regard to the French of 1789. In the American Revolution of 1776 and the French Revolution of 1789, those who perceived themselves to constitute a nation were almost solely of European stock. It is a measure of the elasticity of the concept of nation that both the American nation and the French nation of the 1990s are far more heterogeneous than they were at the time of their respective revolutions. Nations can be drawn very broadly or most narrowly. The Nazis, for example, drew the German nation exceedingly narrow. Contrariwise, the American nation is drawn most broadly at the end of the twentieth century. Porter is thus truly profound when he observes that "[t]he world of nations is primarily and essentially a world of the mind."

It is the narrow drawing of "nation" conflated with the "*ethnie*" that spawns ethnonationalism. Here the *ethnie* perceive themselves to be nations, and, concomitantly, demand national rights, often including the right of self-determination. The rise of ethnonationalism within a nation-state or a state nation (Porter elucidates both terms) invariably puts the integrity of the state at risk. Indeed, the seeking of their own state either by nationalists when two or more national ideas collide, or by ethnonationalists when a state is deemed to be essential to their well-being, undercuts the integrity of the extant state of which they are a part.

## III

At the very outset of his chapter Beissinger cites John Stuart Mill, who adduced that the well-being of political society necessitates "that there be in the constitution of the state *something* which is settled, something permanent, and not to be called in question." The *something* constitutes the "fundamental principles" upon which the integrity of the state and the good order of the society rest. At the end of the twentieth century, in country after country, and society after society, the questioning of fundamental principles have become a commonplace, and much of what was thought to be settled has been pried wide open for rancorous disputation. Into oblivion have many states disappeared, which, but a short decade ago, few thought would not persist for generations. In their place have come new and mostly smaller ones, which in many ways are like rudderless boats upon a vast ocean, as national and ethnonational groupings have had their claims to self-determination recognized.

In the last half of the twentieth century, self-determination has been a battle cry, the sovereign state the prize. The revolt against Western European colonialism issued forth an array of new states in Africa and Asia in the 1950s and 1960s. And out of the revolt against the former Soviet Empire has come many new sovereign states. "Ironically," says Beissinger, "the revolt against communism was supposed to be a revolution against the state, not a struggle for it." But this is precisely what has happened. And so, in Beissinger's words, "[t]he breakup of the former Soviet Union was more than simply the end of a regime. It was the beginning of an era. When future historians determine the global significance of the chain of events that stretched from 1988 through 1991 in the former USSR, they will be as likely to focus on the death of communism as on the phenomenal growth in nationalist mobilization that accompanied communism's demise and the persisting consequences which that mobilization has had for the rest of the world." It is in this context that Beissinger introduces the concept of "state-seeking attitudes and behaviors."

State-seeking attitudes and behaviors encompass

> not only the desire on the part of a group for the creation of its own independent state, . . . [but also] other types of demands as well: for the creation of autonomous state formations within another state; for merging the territory of a group to that of another state; for upgrading the sovereignty and authority of existing territorial units with the purpose of group empowerment; or for changing the rules of the state to gain group control over access to state resources (for instance, changing the official language or altering group representation in positions of power). The common denominator here is the desire on the part of an ethnic or territorially based group to gain more direct control over or access to a state where such control or access had been denied previously.

I have cited Beissinger at length, and in his own words, because his concept of state-seeking behaviors and attitudes helps one to clarify and explain congeries of behaviors that mark national and ethnonational groupings in relation to the state.

Multinational and multiethnic states, if they are to persist, require institutions that engender the loyalties of "we," "us," and "our," as well as "they," "them," and "their." In these states, the surest means by which to obviate state-seeking attitudes and behaviors is to make the ones who would hold these attitudes and engage in these behaviors reject them of their own volition. A colleague of mine—now retired, and who never received the recognition he deserved for his work on what he termed the "submerged nations" of Eastern Europe and the Soviet Union—was fond of saying that institutional illegitimacy would one day destroy the Soviet Empire. The submerged nations, said he, would rise up and claim what was legitimately theirs. Neither he nor I expected to live to see that day, but we both have.

State-seeking attitudes that obtain in a given state may be masked by conformity insofar as it is deemed to be unwise objectively to engage in state-seeking behaviors, and this can readily give a false reading concerning institutional legitimacy. Such was the case regarding the Baltic republics of the former Soviet Union, as one readily discerns in Senn's chapter. So effective can this masking be that, as Senn notes pointedly, "common wisdom among Soviet experts in the United States discounted the national question as a factor in Soviet affairs. In 1984 an official of the American Central Intelligence Agency (CIA) flatly predicted that national minorities in the Soviet Union would play no significant role 'in this century.'" These national minorities were the very ones whom my colleague termed submerged nations, and how very wrong was the official. Masked conformity can be so effective that even as prescient an observer of societies and states around the world as Samuel P. Huntington, in discussing the United States, Great Britain, and the Soviet Union, would say, in his now classic *Political Order in Changing Societies* (1968) that "[e]ach country is a political community with an overwhelming consensus among the people on the legitimacy of the political system. In each country the citizens and their leaders share a vision of the public interest of the society and of the traditions and principles upon which the political community is based. . . . These governments command the loyalties of their citizens."[51] Senn, on the other hand, makes plain that once "central control faltered," the Soviet regime soon realized that it did not command the loyalties of much of its citizenry, and of the Baltic republics in particular. The Baltic republics saw themselves as being under occupation, and not as legitimate parts of the Soviet Union; and so, when the opportunity afforded itself, they revolted against the Soviet state in order to secure states of their own. Could this also happen in China?

Buck is helpful here. He writes:

> Among China's many minorities there is reason to be concerned that certain groups—particularly the Tibetans, the Moslem peoples of central Asia, and possibly the Mongols or Koreans—may try to break the existing political order to establish their own states or associate with preexisting nation-states. . . . In the case of Tibet, for example, where the Han Chinese find control necessary, but little to praise in either past or present Tibetan culture, it is easy to imagine the breaking away of the region as a parallel

to Mongolia's independence in the 1920s. If Tibet can go its own way, why would not large sections of Inner Mongolia become part of an enlarged Mongolian republic, or the Korean minority in Northeast China be joined in some way to the burgeoning state of South Korea with all its wealth and dynamism? Clearly these most populous minority groups, with strong linguistic, cultural, and religious identities who occupy an identifiable territory, have all the standard markers of ethnonationalism. If political leadership emerges, and the increasingly familiar politics of ethnonationalistic fragmentation appear, they could break away.

It is doubtful whether the extant structure of institutional legitimacy is sufficiently strong to prevent such an occurrence. At this juncture, it is well to pause and ask: Why is the legitimacy of institutions of such importance?

Institutions are patterns of behavior organized around rules through which they are replicated generationally and transgenerationally. There is a reciprocity between "rules" and "patterns of behavior"; each can and do affect the structure of the other. Well-established patterns of behavior can be highly resistant to changes in the rules governing them, and rule changes can alter significantly a given pattern of behavior. The persistence of a given institution, then, is largely a function of the symmetry between a set of rules and the pattern of behavior it organizes.

The capacity of individuals and groups to cope with the contradictions, ambiguities, and vagaries of social life is in large measure contingent on the strength of their institutions. Legitimacy increases the strength of an institution. The legitimacy of an institution presumes that the rules and patterns of behavior that cohere to form it are sound, fitting and proper. As the strength of their institutions increases so too does the capacity of individuals and groups to adapt, survive, grow and develop. The obverse also is true—even though given individuals and groups may engage in particular activities of note. Such activities are not, however, readily transmitted transgenerationally. Thus, for example, there were among the free black population in the United States at the time of Martin Delany, individuals who were quite successful as entrepreneurs. However, the failure to develop institutions whereby their success could have been replicated transgenerationally makes a paragraph penned by Delany roughly seven generations ago as poignant in the 1990s as it was in the 1850s. He wrote:

> White men are producers—we are consumers. They build houses, and we rent them. They raise produce, and we consume it. They manufacture clothes and wares, and we garnish ourselves with them. They build coaches, vessels, cars, hotels, saloons, and other vehicles and places of accommodation, and we deliberately wait until they have got them in readiness, then walk in, and contend with as much assurance for a 'right,' as though the whole thing was bought by, paid for, and belonged to us. By their literary attainments, they are the contributions to, authors and teachers

of, literature, science, religion, law, medicine, and all other useful attainments that the world now makes use of. We have no reference to ancient times—we speak of modern things.[52]

Institutions connect individuals and groups not only to modern things but also to ancient times. It is precisely the failure of Soviet institutions to connect Lithuanians, Estonians, and Latvians, for example, to ancient times that undercut their legitimacy, and kept state-seeking attitudes smoldering until the time was propitious for them to be manifested as state-seeking behaviors. One observes this very same state of affairs today in relation to Russia and the Chechens. And as Beissinger points out, "Chechnya's declaration of independence . . . has unleashed other processes of state-seeking throughout the northern Caucasus, weakening further Russia's control over this volatile region." Yet, on the other hand, China's economic success has muted state-seeking attitudes and behaviors, at least among some of its large minorities. Buck notes that "for some large minorities in China, the results of recent economic growth, combined with the promise of the future, will serve as a major break on the genesis of new ethnonational states. In markets and streets in China's largest cities, central Asian minorities prosper through trade and commerce. If they lost their ability to travel and do business in China through national separation, they would lose access to the source of their prosperity." Economic prosperity, then, can be an antidote to state-seeking attitudes and behaviors, but it is no substitute for legitimate institutions. For once the bloom of economic prosperity fades, as it always does, an array of societal fissures invariably open wherever institutions do not command the loyalties of those whom they serve.

The institutions of a people bridge not only generations but also subjective reality and objective reality. When there is little or no incongruity between how individuals discern an institution in "their *inner* eyes, those eyes with which they look through their physical eyes upon reality," to borrow again from Ralph Ellison, and what they actually behold with their physical eyes, it is invariably strong. Subjective expectations and objective actualizations conflate in institutional legitimacy. Here institutions are often able to shut out, crowd out, or diminish the full impact of aversive consequences for the ones who suffer them in a given environment. Contrariwise, where the images of the inner eyes and the physical eyes conflict sharply over extended periods of time, institutions are put at risk as time-honored beliefs, conventions, and indeed the fundamental principles of which Mill spoke, are called into question.

As fundamental principles are called into question, and national and ethnonational groupings come increasingly to perceive an array of institutions that sustain the extant state as static, ossified and bankrupt, the impetus for new institutional formations tend to become ever the stronger. This does not necessarily mean that the extant state itself is always immediately at risk, even though it may eventually crumble in consequence of a push for new institutional formations. This point emerges forcefully in Remington's discussion of Slovenia and Croatia vis-à-vis the Yugoslav state. Though both were troubled deeply by the tattered institutional framework left in place by Josip Tito, and each had declared itself to be a sovereign republic, as the Yugoslav state began to unravel both "came to the defense of the federation, and allows one," says Remington," to assume that as late as March 1991 all parties still engaged in a choreography of struggle over a shared Yugoslavia." If Remington is correct, as late as March 1991 the state-seeking behaviors of the Slovenes and the Croats did not necessarily entail and independent Slovenia and Croatia, even though both were soon to declare their independence thereafter.

The power of Beissinger's concept of state-seeking attitudes and behaviors is readily evinced here. Had the sorts of institutional constructions and reconstructions occurred that would have increased the legitimacy of the Yugoslav state, especially for, say, the Slovenes who deemed it unduly burdensome and resented "the flow of Slovene foreign currency to the federal government in the form of subsidies to their southern neighbors," according to Remington, state-seeking behaviors in the republics may well have stopped short of independence, as has been true thus far for Quebec. The construction of new institutions, as well as the reconstruction of old ones, by changing the rules of the state so the republics and autonomous provinces could develop a sense of enduring loyalty to the Yugoslav state that transcended the national identities with which they were largely coterminous, may well have choreographed Yugoslavia to a different outcome than the one that now obtains.

Yet insofar as the "republics and autonomous provinces were largely synonymous with national identities," as Remington points out, and insofar as the national and ethnonational cleavages that divided the country were such that only the forceful hand of an imperium could keep them in check, perhaps no amount of institutional tinkering could have saved the Yugoslav state. Increased autonomy for the republics and the autonomous provinces would only have widened the emotive distance that already existed between them and the state, and decreased autonomy would surely have exacerbated existing tensions. And so, given the national and ethnonational composition of the republics, the die for independence may well have been cast once the international environment became hospitable to such an outcome. For unlike Canada, a context that was amenable to muddling through just did not exist. Thus did state-seeking attitudes and behaviors destroy Yugoslavia.

The success of state-seekers, especially where this involves an independent state recognized by the international community, is contingent on the logic of the domestic situation, as well as the receptivity of the international community. This emerges with striking clarity in the chapters by Beissinger, Senn, Remington, and Harris. There are twenty million Kurds, who, in spite of deep divisions among, as Harris calls out, desire to see an independent Kurdistan. Harris' chapter makes plain that state-seeking among the Kurds covers Beissinger's spectrum. But even more critical than this is the fact that the three states—Iraq, Iran, and Turkey—out of which the bulk of an independent Kurdistan would have to be carved object vehemently to the creation of any such state, and the international community evinces no disposition to contravene that objection. Thus are the Kurds forced to employ other paths of state-seeking short of securing a fully independent state.

On the other hand, 1.7 million Slovenes, and 3.675 million Lithuanians each have their own independent state. This is largely a function of the state of affairs that existed at the time of the disintegration of Yugoslavia and the Soviet Union. In the case of the former Soviet Union, Beissinger notes that

> other than Stalin's self-serving decisions about which peoples' deserved their own republics and which would have units subordinated to union republics, there is no justification for why peoples with union republics deserve independence and those without do not. Kazakhstan and Kyrgyz-stan, for instance, were not originally assigned union republican status when the USSR was created, but were instead autonomous republics within the Russian Federation. Had they not been separated by Stalin into union republics in 1936, it is doubtful that they would be independent states today.

An accident of history, state-seeking behaviors, and the hospitableness of the inter-national community all conflated to produce independent states which might not have come into being otherwise. As for the Lithuanians, the "family of nations" stood ready to receive them, given what was perceived to be the illegality of their absorption into the Soviet Union. And Slovenia, like Croatia, with strong backing from a newly reunited Germany, rode the tide of unravelling communism to full independence.

Whether state-seeking attitudes and behaviors end in full independence, some variant thereof, or in misadventure, they point ever so compellingly to the allure of the state. Still, state-seeking and state-acquisition are one thing, state-building and state-maintenance are another. Many of those who seek a state soon find out that securing it, difficult though this might have been, is easier than building and main-taining it. For the sorts of behaviors that might have been both justifiable and effec-tive in gaining independence often cease to be so once the state has been won. This is demonstrated forcefully and convincingly in Ake's chapter. I find this chapter to be particularly distressing personally, for I have long believed that Nigeria has the potential to be to Africa and the world what Germany is to Europe and the planet in terms of prestige, influence and power.

Ake points out "that the colonial state in Nigeria inevitably relied heavily on force to subjugate the indigenous peoples and to carry out its mission. That made it threatening, and induced some of its subjects to regard it as a hostile force. Many of them were driven to traditional solidarity groups"—some drawn along ethnic or national lines, and others structured in the form of clubs or associations—which "became centers of resistance, means of self-affirmation against the colonizers' aggressive de-culturing of the indigenous people, as well as networks for survival."

Since "[c]olonial rule was cheap rule," utterly lacking a social welfare system, traditional solidarity groups, particularly in the cities, were crucial to the survival of individuals. Intense loyalties developed around them, and "[t]hey became vehicles of political participation as well as group solidarity against the impositions of an arbitrary and coercive state." Where traditional solidarity groups coalesced persons of the same ethnicity in forming "functional safety net[s] in the face of a predatory state and a total absence of a social welfare system, they effectively displaced the state as the primary focus of political loyalty." To this day, the Nigerian state has not overcome this displacement of loyalty.

Ake makes plain that the nationalist movement that struggled against colonialism "initially evolved as a network of ethnic associations and mass organizations." And insofar as ethnicity and region were usually linked, regionalized ethnicity provided the foundation for those who evinced state-seeking attitudes and behaviors. Once the state was won, full independence having been achieved and recognized, state-seekers now had before them the task of becoming state-builders. But by and large they proved to be wanting. They were unable to transcend and supplant regionalized political ethnicity with a nationalized common language.

The state, rather than being an instrument for the common good, became a thing to be owned. Possessory title to the state in behalf of regional and ethnic interests became a norm. Replicating their colonial predecessors, those who have controlled the state have failed to build institutions that were recognized as legitimate and could engender the loyalties of most of the populace. Coupled with the absence of a social welfare system, and the continued reliance of large numbers of persons on variations of the old traditional solidarity groups for their sustenance, "[t]he Nigerian state, already displaced by ethnic and national groups and local communities, is becoming irrelevant except as a nuisance," says Ake. This is true whether civilians or the military have controlled the state. "However tempting it may be," observes Ake, "it is not very useful to dichotomize between military rule and civilian rule in the Nigerian context; it is far more useful to regard them as moments of the same political dynamics. . . . [For both,] the Nigerian state is perceived as an exploitable resource, a contested terrain where all struggle to appropriate and privatize some or all of its enormous powers and resources. . . . [Moreover,] by all indications, many Nigerians think it is quite proper to appropriate and privatize the resources of the state." Thus does Ake conclude that "[t]he official Nigerian state— for all of its apparatuses, its enormous power, and all of the resources that it controls—is only nominally a state. It is no *res publica*. Its citizens do not constitute a 'public.' They share no strong sense of corporate identity, and do not see the state as a collective enterprise of overriding importance deserving commitment. . . . [And so,] the state-building project must now be pronounced a failure, inasmuch as the state has lost the bid to be the repository of the primary loyalty of Nigerians to ethnic and national groups as well as local communities." If Ake's assessment is correct, of what significance is it both for the Nigerian state and others?

First, absent the guiding hand of an imperium, Nigeria could very well go the way of Yugoslavia (or China the way of the former Soviet Union), for the centrifugal forces at work pull in that direction. More and more states, which now number thirty, have been created in recognition of the social and ethnic plurality of the society, and a commitment to the federal character of the national state. But insofar as these states serve to reinforce local loyalties counterpoised to the national state—"a hostile, predatory force with enormous power" (see Ake)—they simply reinforce the fragmentation of the society. Likewise did the Baltic republics perceive the Soviet state, and, most perturbing, so too do increasing numbers perceive the American state.

Second, national institutions that fail to legitimize the state undercut its integrity. Herein lay a profound difference between the United States and Nigeria, or the former Soviet Union, Yugoslavia, China, and even Canada for that matter. The undeniable fraying that is occurring notwithstanding, there is still a strong emotive attachment to the critical national institutions of the American state. This gives the United States room to maneuver in the face of escalating racial and ethnic cleavages that Nigeria does not have, and neither the former Soviet Union nor Yugoslavia ever had.

Third, perceptions of the state as irrelevant, except as a nuisance, are of the utmost gravity in relation to the integrity of the state. That which is irrelevant is extraneous, and may be gotten rid of; whatever is a nuisance is an irritant, and may be expunged. The more the state is perceived as irrelevant except as a nuisance the greater is the likelihood that its integrity will be undermined by those who feel set upon by it. An extraneous and irritant state is to be shunned; thus are loyalties eroded.

Fourth, a widespread perception that the state is a drain on society's resources and beneficial only to those who are positioned to make use of it erodes the legitimacy of the state. But, in Ake's view, this is precisely what obtains in Nigeria, and troublingly, one observes the same sort of perception becoming increasingly common in the United States. Perceiving diminishing or no benefits from the state, individuals and groups become increasingly reluctant to pay for its cost, and strive to find ways to circumvent their obligations. Under the rules of the state, they may have an obligation to pay, but in the context of their perception of the state they may not feel obliged to do so.[53] When individuals have an obligation to do something but do not feel obliged to do it, the obligation is usually fulfilled only grudgingly, if at all. A state may multiply endlessly the rules whereby individuals and groups incur obligations to it, but if they do not feel obliged to fulfill those obligations disaster awaits the state. This is exactly what befell the former Soviet Union; could very well befall Nigeria; and even the United States could fall victim to it.

Finally, and to my mind most important in relation to the United States, the expansion of local autonomy with a corollary diminution of central authority, especially when this is accompanied by relentless attacks on waste, fraud, abuse, and unwarranted privilege at the center, has the effect of illegitimizing the institutions of the state and thereby corroding the state itself. Federal systems that lack strong, vibrant, and highly adaptable institutions are constantly at risk of *dis*integration. And even a federal system such as the United States, with institutions that by and large serve it well, is set at risk when presumably settled questions concerning the legal and legitimate sources of federal authority are reopened, eliciting fearsome quarrels and vexations. Perhaps the most compelling lesson of this volume for the United States, then, is that the trauma (Nigeria and Canada) and demise (Yugoslavia and the Soviet Union) of federal systems point to two corollary dangers: an excessive concentration of power, authority, and resources at the center, so that it is too intertwined with the daily lives of the citizenry; and a copious devolution of power, authority and resources from the center, such that it becomes too removed from the everyday lives of the populace. An old Aristotelian maxim comes into play here. It is well that states should strive ceaselessly to strike a sound balance between extremes of too much and too little.

The timeless wisdom of Aristotle's admonition is all too often unheeded by politicians who seek to advance given agenda. Levine underscores this in pointing to critical costs of the conservative agenda of former Canadian Prime Minister Brian Mulroney. He writes:

> Mulroney Conservatives' attack on the Canadian state after 1984 . . . unwittingly helped unleash centrifugal tendencies in the country. Put simply, cutbacks in social programs and, in particular, slashes in transfer payments to provinces helped lessen the importance of the central government in the daily lives of Quebecers (and other Canadians) and refocused citizens' attention on provincial governments as their primary states. "Fiscal decentralization" during the Mulroney years resulted in important expenditure shifts that de-emphasized the centrality of the federal government in Canadian life. . . .
>
> Furthermore, the anti-state rhetoric of the Mulroney government depreciated the value of the central government, an approach to political economy that could only enhance nationalists' argument that Ottawa offered little of importance to Quebecers. Each time the Mulroney government reduced the scope of national institutions—the CBC [Canadian Broadcasting Corporation] or Via Rail, for example—it eliminated some of the glue binding together Canada's regions. The Quebec nationalist rhetoric that "Canada doesn't work anymore," received ample support in the devaluing of the Canadian state that occurred during the Mulroney years. Thus, by attacking the state as well as "unloading" social programs on the provinces, Mulroney unwittingly undercut his government's ability to bridge Canada's regional/linguistic cleavages.

The relevance and portentousness of Levine's observations for the United States are so compelling that no elucidation nor elaboration are needed here. True, the United States does not now suffer the sort of linguistic cleavage that continually lurks just beneath the surface as a threat to the integrity of the Canadian state. This could well change in the years ahead. But it is my hope that the common language of Abraham Lincoln and Frederick Douglass, as well as the strength and adaptability of its institutions, will continue to sustain the United States.

Institutions tap old memories and create new ones. The memories they tap and the ones they create help to bridge generations one to another. But not all memories that link generations are institutional ones. Many are simply handed down by word or other sufficient sign generation after generation. These are the transgenerational memories that relay deeds and misdeeds, hopes and fears, enmities and friendships, successes and failures, as well as pleasures and pains of a collective. They shape the legends, customs, norms, and traditions by which a people live. They mold attitudes and reinforce beliefs. They justify conduct. Transgenerational memory is thus a form of individual and generational immortality, for in it and through it both individuals and generations live on to do good or ill.

The strength of a generation, an ethnic group, or a nation is not the material abundance that each produces but its capacity to reproduce progeny whose ability to survive, grow, and develop is greater than its own. Transgenerational memory kindles hope, induces sacrifice—to the end of the good and well-being not just of this or that individual but of the collective of which s/he is a part—and fosters the survival of a culture. In the context of the survival of cultures, transgenerational memories can draw unyielding lines of demarcation between peoples or open paths of crosscultural intercourse. Where transgenerational memories draw stern lines of demarcation—as they do, for example, between the Catholics and Protestants in Northern Ireland, or Israelis and the Palestinians in the Middle East—and there are few, if any, institutions to intersect those lines, conflicts are not readily resolved. Indeed, they may continue for generations, as is true both in Northern Ireland and the Middle East.

Sound institutions ameliorate the effects of bad transgenerational memories. Such has been the case in the United States. But defective institutions, or an absence of institutions, only compound the effects of bad transgenerational memories. The chapters by Golan, Hallaj, Elliott and Remington are ever so instructive here. When Hallaj, for example, writes that "Palestinian-Israeli peace must be understood as a process of reaching compromises to end a struggle between enemies who have compelling reasons to be enemies, not as a process of reconciling estranged lovers," he captures with much exactitude the power of transgenerational memories in the conflict between the two peoples. Their memories of one another are as enemies, not as lovers. This shapes profoundly the way they perceive each other, and the extent to which they are willing to trust one another. In the absence of shared and sound institutions to ameliorate distrust and suspicions flamed by bad transgenerational memories, the Israelis and Palestinians have had to employ truly extraordinary ingenuity to bridge the differences that have brought them to the point in the peace process called out by Hallaj and Golan.

Recognizing the effects of the high emotive charge that attend bad transgenerational memories, both Golan and Hallaj have strived to expand the scope of what is technical and legal and contract the domain of that which is symbolic and sentimental, as they think aloud about matters germane to the peace process in their respective chapters. And so, concerning the really thorny matter of the future of Jerusalem, Hallaj writes: "Even the question of Jerusalem, widely advertised as the Gordian knot and the obstacle over which all efforts to make Israeli-Palestinian peace are likely to flounder, is not insoluble . . . [once t]he problem of how to make the transition from belligerency to peace becomes essentially a technical one which, freed of its emotional burdens, becomes more manageable." Likewise, Golan observes: "With regard to Jerusalem, sentiment and symbolism are often stronger than legalities and technicalities, but it may well be through the latter that a solution emerges." What one discerns here in both Golan and Hallaj is a formula whereby emotions charged by transgenerational memories may be assuaged, thereby opening a path to outcomes once thought to be unattainable. The same basic formula is applicable to countless like situations around the world.

Such is the emotive power of transgenerational memories that where they do not furnish a desired remembrance, it is oftentimes manufactured and inserted in them by those who wish to make use of it. Elliott taps this element of transgenerational memory in calling attention to the desire of Protestants to secure an "origin legend" as a counterpoint to that of the Catholics. She notes that "[t]o grow up as a Catholic in Northern Ireland—particularly in working class areas—is to grow up convinced that you occupy the high moral ground, as a descendant of the true Gael, your ancestors were deprived of their land and persecuted for their religion." These are potent memories, especially the memory concerning descent. To counter this particular memory, Elliott points out that "[t]here is already a search underway among some Protestants for an equivalent origin legend to that of the Gaels for the Catholics. The argument is that Ulster has always been a distinct nation; that Protestants are not Johnny-come-latelys, but descendants of the ancient Celtic people of Ulster, the Ulaid, the people of the Ulster Cycle and the heroic tales of Cuchullain—the central theme of which is the struggle of the Ulster people against the rest of Ireland." This origin legend provides an alternative "for those arguing for an independent Ulster against the territorial claims over the province made by the Republic's Constitution. In other words, it is the Protestants who are the natives, not those of Gaelic stock," says Elliott, who goes on to observe that "[i]t is interesting that this origin legend should extract similar romantic views from the past for incorporation into a future state as the Gaelic revival did for the future Irish state, notably, a rejection of materialism and an idealization of life on the land."

Reason is no match for romance. Transgenerational memories are grounded more in romance than reason. They tend to be the way that those who recollect and make use of them would like them to be. If some memories have little or no foundation in empirical fact it matters not so long as their bearers believe they do. Thus do Ulster Protestants harbor fears of "'popery,'" since "'Catholics are taking their lead from Rome and Rome is out to get rid of Protestants,'" and Catholics nurse apprehensions about Protestants' desire for "'ascendancy'" over them, says Elliott. "Originally defined in the eighteenth century to describe exclusive Protestant rule of Ireland, [ascendancy] is a word embedded in the Catholic psyche. It acquired a new resonance after the creation of the Northern Ireland state in 1921, and the embers of resentment are easily ignited. It is such memories which unites SDLP and Sinn Fein supporters (though they agree on little else) against anything savoring of restored majoritarian Unionist rule," Elliott points out. In this is to be found a grave pitfall of transgenerational memory. It may continue to sustain an enmity and induce adversaries to continue a fight, missing good opportunities for its cessation. How very true is the adage: "The combatants continued the fight, though there was no longer a reason to fight."

Bad transgenerational memories may be as important to the survival of a people and their culture as are good ones. Both fortify the will to persist. In good memories are a people's thought, intelligence, values, pleasant encounters, gains, and hopes recorded; in bad memories are their disappointments, fears, tribulations, and losses recollected. Together, these steel them against the vicissitudes of their environment. Grave defeat at a given point in time is often viewed as but a temporary setback where a people are animated by strong transgenerational memories, which stretch ever the more their horizon of time. How well is this captured in the passages that opens Golan's chapter when Neguib Azoury, a Christian Arab, said in 1905 that "[i]t is the fate of the Arab and Jewish national movements to fight until one or the other prevails," which was affirmed in 1936 by Arthur Ruppin, a Zionist leader, who stated that "[i]t is our destiny to be in a state of continual warfare with the Arabs and there is no alternative but that lives should be lost." The triumph over transgenerational memories that gave rise to these sentiments makes the symbolic value of the handshake between Yasir Arafat and Yitzhak Rabin all the more profound historically.

Still, bad transgenerational memories do carry the germs of vengeance, retribution and distrust. This is instantiated ever so plainly and painfully in Remington's observation that "Serbian memories of what happened to the Serbian minority in the last independent Croatia combined with Croatian fears of Milosevic's hegemonic ambitions to destroy the fabric of Yugoslav national/ethnic coexistence." Bad transgenerational memories played no little role in the fragmentation of Yugoslavia, especially as the obviating effects of economic prosperity and strong, unifying leadership, in the person of President Josip Tito, gave way to economic distress and leadership woes.

As one reads the chapters of parts II and III of this volume, one discerns clearly the undertow of transgenerational memories in the state-seeking attitudes and behaviors of those who have strived either for greater autonomy within an existing state or to win their own independent states. They strive for the sake of the right and freedom to realize their capacities, capabilities and potentialities through their work. By their works are peoples made known to the generations and the ages. The literature, art, science, and technology of a people lay bare their sense of space and time, measure and proportion, value and worth, purpose and achievement, the ephemeral and the enduring. In their literature and art a people express their sense of the good, the beautiful, and the ugly; in their science and technology they display their capacity to order and manipulate nature. In their science, technology, literature, and art a people, as it were, make their nature—that is, character, personality, individuality, ego, and so forth—known to the world.

It is interesting to observe here that in Northern Ireland, for example, according to Elliott "Protestants think they are culturally more inclined to the useful scientific subjects, whilst Catholics prefer 'soft' subjects like history and the arts." The cultural divide between Catholics and Protestants is thus also drawn by art and literature on the one side, and science and technology on the other. In all of my studies, I never have come across anything convincing pertaining to the putative superiority of cultures and societies in which science and technology were emphasized in comparison with those in which art and literature were stressed. Insofar as science and technology contribute to material abundance, this assuredly is no ultimate measure of either strength or superiority. To loop back to a point made much earlier in this presentation, if survival is indeed *the* ultimate measure of a culture, whatsoever fosters its survival is of value for that culture. In this context, it serves no useful purpose to talk in terms of cultural superiority and cultural inferiority based on science and technology, or any other criteria for that matter.

At the end of the twentieth century, insidious and pernicious fabrications concerning intellectual deficits and cultural lags are abroad. One observes the very same state of affairs at the end of the nineteenth century, especially regarding race. The dominance of Europeans at the end of the nineteenth century, and Europeans and Asians writ large at the end of the twentieth century, in science and technology has been construed by some to mean that "others" are less gifted, and, by extension, their cultures less well-developed. This sentiment at the nineteenth century's end, wrought havoc to untold numbers of racial, ethnic, and national groupings in the twentieth century at the hands of those who thought they were superior. This pattern could well be replicated in the twenty-first century, unless the putatively less gifted take the sorts of action which demonstrate empirically that they possess the wherewithal to fight and succeed in any arena. Otherwise, the prospect of indeed becoming what Samuel F. Yette, a generation ago, called "obsolete people"[54] looms ever the larger.

## IV

As a son of the twentieth century, were I asked what has been my inheritance, I should say: the taint of genocidal wars; hard barriers of race, ethnicity, and nationalism; and pitiful destitution amidst heretofore unknown abundance. Mine is not a unique inheritance, for the century has spread out to all that which I have inherited.

In this it has made some filled with hopelessness and despair, others hopeful concerning their lots, and still others just fed up with what they observe around them.

In her chapter, Golan makes use of the concept of "fed-up-ness," which I find to be most intriguing. She observes that "the most salient effect of the [Palestinian] intifada was its stimulation of a certain realism among Israelis, and what might be called 'fed-up-ness.' It was not, for the general public, a matter of now understanding or perhaps even sympathizing with the Palestinians; nor was it a recognition of their rights. It was, instead, a sense that matters could not continue as they were. [Where fed-up-ness obtains, muddling through is not an option.] Something had to be done." Fed-up-ness, says Golan, "is . . . akin to the feeling of simply having had enough."

Something must be done to overcome the absence of a common language. Our God and their God cannot continue to separate "us" from "them." Something must be done to overcome the effects of bad transgenerational memories. Weak institutions cannot continue to stifle growth and development. Something must be done concerning attainments in science and technology, given their bearing on material abundance. The deformation of species being cannot continue to destroy species life. I speak here not of the Israelis and Palestinians, but of the untold numbers in the many societies of the planet who feel that they have had enough of racial, ethnic, and national putrefaction, and things cannot continue the way they are. But how, and by whom, shall they be changed?

This question is beyond the scope of the introduction, and is not really discussed in the volume, yet I do feel constrained to offer an observation. In 1995 there were one hundred and eighty-five countries represented in the General Assembly of the United Nations. Most of these bear a striking family resemblance to the now thirty states of Nigeria that Ake mentions—they are not developed politically, and they are not economically viable. Drawn substantially along racial, ethnonational, and national lines, many of these countries are akin to racial and ethnic enclaves in the United States. And just as the United States will not endure the erosion of its institutions and common language by enclaves, the information superhighway notwithstanding, in like manner, many of the now independent states of the world will not persist without a common language and well-developed institutions.

A great task of the moment, then, is the building of institutions and a common language that abate the hardening of racial, ethnic, and national lines of demarcation globally. Fed-up-ness could be a vital stimulus to this. For insofar as it impels people to act, what was heretofore presumed to be intractable may well become tractable. Thus fed-up-ness—animated by realism, purpose, resolve, and results—has within it the seeds of compromise and reconciliation. Out of these could emerge the formation or re-creation of larger states out of a number small ones that now exist, as more and more people come to feel that cleavages drawn racially, ethnically, and nationally only serve to limit their life chances on the planet.

There is assuredly no one-to-one correspondence between the size of a state and the well-being of its people. Still, the travails of many a small state around the globe afford one reasons to believe that they might well have been better off had they been incorporated into some larger unit. Hence do I believe that the stage has now been set for the reconstruction of larger entities, with substantial amounts of formal power, that hold forth the possibility of transcending narrow racial, ethnic, and national boundaries with purposes that call out that *Homo sapiens sapiens* is but one species, though divided by the vagaries of geography and culture.

There will not be one hundred and eighty-five countries in the United Nations, assuming that it persists, in the year 2020. There may be more before then, but by that year there will be far fewer. Many small states shall have disappeared, either absorbed by new imperia or integrated into larger entities whereby shared purposes and common interests can be advanced. Thus shall patterns pertaining to race, ethnicity, and nationalism in the twenty-first century be determined.

## Notes

1. B. F. Skinner, *Beyond Freedom and Dignity* (New York: Alfred A. Knopf, 1971) p. 37.

2. Ralph Ellison, *Invisible Man* (New York: Vintage Books, 1972), p. 3.

3. Vincent Harding, *There is a River* (New York: Vintage Books, 1983), p. 3.

4. UNESCO, *Race and Science* (New York: Columbia University Press, 1969), pp. 496–97. Author's italics.

5. See "Excerpts From the Decision on Justifying Affirmative Action Programs," *The New York Times*, June 13, 1995, p. A8. Author's italics.

6. Ibid., pp. 502–5.

7. L. Luca Cavalli-Sforza, Paolo Menozzi, and Alberto Piazza, *The History and Geography of Human Genes* (Princeton, NJ: Princeton University Press, 1994), pp. 19-20. Author's italics.

8. L.C. Dunn, "Race and Biology," in UNESCO, op. cit. note 4, pp. 263, 298.

9. *The Milwaukee Journal*, February 20, 1995, p. A1.

10. Ibid.

11. By objective knowledge, I mean hypotheses that have been subjected to rigorous, critical scrutiny involving intersubjective testing and corroboration. See Karl Popper's *Objective Knowledge: An Evolutionary Approach* (Oxford: The Clarendon Press, 1974); and also Popper's *Conjectures and Refutations: The Growth of Scientific Knowledge* (New York: Harper & Row Publishers, 1968).

12. Charles L. Stevenson, *Facts and Values: Studies in Ethical Analysis* (New Haven and London: Yale University Press, 1964), p. 7.

13. See Michael Polanyi, *Personal Knowledge: Towards a Post-Critical Philosophy* (New York and Evanston: Harper & Row Publishers, 1964). Polanyi writes:

We shall find Personal Knowledge manifested in the appreciation of probability and of order in the exact sciences, and see it at work even more extensively in the way the descriptive sciences rely on skills and connoisseurship. At all these points the act of knowing includes an appraisal; and this personal coefficient, which shapes all factual knowledge, bridges in doing so the disjunction between subjectivity and objectivity. It implies the claim that man can transcend his own subjectivity by striving passionately to fulfill his personal obligations to universal standards. (p. 17)

14. Stevenson, op. cit. note 12, p. 7.

15. Dunn, op. cit. note 8, p. 269. Author's italics.

16. Gordon W. Allport, *The Nature of Prejudice* (Garden City, NY: Doubleday & Company, Inc., 1958), p. 28.

17. Sidney M. Willhelm, *Who Needs the Negro?* (Garden City, NY: Doubleday & Company, Inc., 1971), p. 2.

18. "Ottawa: Lincoln's Reply," in Paul M. Angle, ed., *The Complete Lincoln-Douglas Debates of 1858* (Chicago and London: The University of Chicago Press, 1991), p. 117. Author's italic.

19. Cavalli-Sforza, op. cit. note 7, p. 20.

20. Paul R. Ehrlich, "The Biological Consequences of Nuclear War," in Paul R. Ehrlich, Carl Sagan, Donald Kennedy, and Walter Orr Roberts, *The Cold and the Dark: The World After Nuclear War* (New York and London: W. W. Norton & Company, 1984), pp. 58–59. Author's italics.

21. Skinner, op. cit. note 1, p. 128.

22. Ibid., p. 136.

23. Ibid., p. 128.

24. Ibid.

25. For an intriguing and insightful discussion of Vodun in Haitian culture and society, see Patrick Bellegarde-Smith, *Haiti: The Breached Citadel* (Boulder, CO: Westview Press, 1990); concerning Vodun cosmology in particular, see pp. 9–22.

26. Ibid., p. 22.

27. Ibid., p. 9.

28. See the infamous *Dred Scott* v. *Sandford*, 60 U.S. (19 How.) 393 (1857) in *Civil Rights: Leading Cases*, Derrick Bell, Jr., ed. (Boston and Toronto: Little Brown and Company, 1980), p. 6.

29. *Time*, October 6, 1986, p. 67. This is a sentiment shared by many in the society including, perhaps, Herrnstein and Murray.

30. Skinner, op. cit. note 1, p. 35.

31. St. Augustine, *The City of God* 19.7. Translated by M. Dods in Whitney J. Oates, ed., *Basic Writings of Saint Augustine* (New York: Random House Publishers, 1948), vol. 2. Author's italics.

32. Winston A. Van Horne, "Epilogue," in Winston A. Van Horne, ed., *Ethnicity and Language* (Milwaukee: University of Wisconsin System Institute on Race and Ethnicity, 1987), p. 214.

33. One cannot but wonder about the extent to which the sarin gas attack on the Tokyo subway system on March 20, 1995—during the Monday morning rush hour, and in which ten people died and about 5,500 were injured, *The New York Times*, March 24, 1995, p. A4—calls into question the expansiveness of the common language that is generally presumed to be shared by the Japanese. Since then, Shoko Asahara, the leader of the Aum Shinrikyo religious sect which has been charged with responsibility for the attack, has been arrested and, as of this writing in July of 1995, is awaiting trial.

34. Frederick Douglass, "Speech on the Dred Scott Decision," in Howard Brotz, ed., *Negro Social and Political Thought, 1850-1920* (New York and London: Basic Books, Inc., 1966), p. 253.

35. "Lincoln at Springfield, June 16, 1858," in Angle, op. cit. note 18, p. 2. The italics are Lincoln's.

36. "Ottawa: Douglas' Opening Speech," in Angle, op. cit. note 18, pp. 109–10.

37. "The New America," *U.S. News & World Report*, July 10, 1995, p. 18.

38. "Lincoln at Chicago, July 10, 1858," in Angle, op. cit. note 18, pp. 39, 42. One has here a foundation for the doctrine of "separate but equal," which was constitutionalized by the Supreme Court in *Plessy v. Ferguson* (1896).

39. "Ottawa: Douglas' Opening Speech," in Angle, op. cit. note 18, p. 112. In the Galesburg debate of October 7, 1858, Douglas attacked Lincoln for the apparent inconsistency between his belief that all men were created equal and his stand that he was in favor of white men having the superior position in society. Lincoln responded by pointing out that he was mindful of "the necessities that [sprang] from the actual presence of black people" in the society, but were legislation being drawn for "new countries" what he said concerning all men being created equal would stand. See "Galesburg: Douglas' Opening Speech," and "Galesburg: Lincoln's Reply," Angle, op. cit. note 18, pp. 291–94, 299–300.

40. "Baptist Group Votes to Repent Stand on Slaves," *The New York Times*, June 21, 1995, p. A1. "Further, the resolution said, 'We lament and repudiate historic acts of evil such as slavery from which we continue to reap a bitter harvest, and we recognize that racism which yet plagues our culture today is inextricably tied to the past.

"It asked for 'forgiveness from our African-American brothers and sisters, acknowledging that our own healing is at stake'" (p. A13). Here one observes a frank, lucid, and unequivocal recognition of a relation between Christian slavery and racism in the United States. In many important respects, American Christian slavery was more stringent than Roman pagan slavery.

41. W. E. B. DuBois, *The Souls of Black Folk* (New York: The New American Library, Inc., 1982), pp. 215–16.

42. Will Durant, *Our Oriental Heritage* (New York: Simon & Schuster, 1954), p. 197.

43. John W. Blassingame, *The Slave Community* (New York and Oxford: Oxford University Press, 1979), p. 147.

44. "'Living Martyr' Leaves Taped Statement," *The New York Times*, October 21, 1994, p. A3. *The New York Times* of October 20, 1994, reported that:

> The red-and-white No. 5 bus was rocked so hard that it seemed to leave the ground, witnesses said. The blast ripped away a metal panel that flew at least 20 feet into the air, catching overhead electrical wires as it fell and dangled there all morning. In one third-story apartment overlooking Dizengoff at Esther Hamalka Street, blown-out balcony windows flew across three rooms, scattering across the floor of a bedroom at the back. . . . Pieces of human flesh landed on terraces and in trees. Firemen trimmed branches to make sure no body parts were left there. Rescue workers, including Orthodox officials from burial societies, sifted through the wreckage for arms, legs, hands—anything they could find—putting them in clear plastic bags so they might be identified later. Some police officers were so overwhelmed that they wept. (pp. A1, A7)

45. "A Seething Hate, a Gun, and 40 Muslims Died," *The New York Times*, February 28, 1994, pp. A1, A6. The story reads in part:

> The doctor, who was well-known to soldiers and settlers, arrived at the Cave of the Patriarchs at about 5:30 [a.m.], entering through a side entrance and passing by soldiers, who did not challenge him. He moved swiftly toward the door of the mosque, where hundreds of Arabs were saying their Friday morning prayers in observance of Ramadan, the Muslim holy month of penance.
>
> Muhammed Abu Saleh, a guard at the mosque door, said that Dr. Goldstein had demanded to enter, saying he was the duty officer, and that when Mr. Abu Saleh objected, the doctor knocked him down with the but of his rifle. . . .
>
> Dr. Goldstein slipped a clip into his assault rifle, put on what witnesses described as protective ear cups to deaden the noise and opened fire on the Muslims kneeling in tight rows, heads bowed to the ground. . . .
>
> The doctor fired 111 rounds from three and a half clips, army investigators said. . . . As the dead and wounded lay on their blood-soaked prayer rugs, [some] survivors stampeded for exits . . . [even as others] rushed to help the wounded. (pp. A1, A6)

46. See *The New York Times*, September 14, 1993. The across-the-page headline read: "RABIN AND ARAFAT SEAL THEIR ACCORD AS CLINTON APPLAUDS 'BRAVE GAMBLE'."

47. Joshua 24:1–2, 15–24, *The King James Bible*.

48. What I have always found to be most intriguing is not that some people are called "God's Chosen People," or "the Elect of God." They simply chose themselves or elected themselves by their particular construction of the divine. It is, rather, how they actually got other people to believe that they were chosen or elected, and to behave towards them as if they were—especially where there was no *quid pro quo* in the context of earthly gains. As for heavenly gains, surely those could be made without treading in the footsteps of ones who claim either to be chosen or elected.

49. *The Random House Dictionary of the English Language: Second Edition Unabridged* (New York: Random House, 1987), p. 1279.

50. Elie Kedourie, *Nationalism* (New York: Frederick A. Praeger, Publisher, 1962), p. 73.

51. Samuel P. Huntington, *Political Order in Changing Societies* (New Haven and London: Yale University Press, 1968), p. 1.

52. Martin R. Delany, "The Condition, Elevation, Emigration, and Destiny of the Colored People of the United States," in Brotz, op. cit. note 34, pp. 53–54.

53. For the critical distinction between to *have an obligation* and *to feel obliged*, see H. L. A. Hart, *The Concept of Law* (Oxford: Clarendon Press, 1961), pp. 79–88.

54. Samuel F. Yette, *The Choice: The Issue of Black Survival In America* (New York: Berkley Medallion Books, 1972), p. 14.

# Part I

## Race, Ethnicity, and Nationalism: Concepts and Images

# 1

# Race and Biology

LINDA VIGILANT

> You, created only a little lower than
> The angels, have crouched too long in
> The bruising darkness. . . .
> Do not be wedded forever
> To fear, yoked eternally
> To brutishness.
> —Maya Angelou

The simplest definition of race that I could construct would be a group of people containing physical similarities generally sufficient to distinguish them from other groups. Unfortunately, this definition is vague, subjective, circular and ultimately useless. In fact, the entire concept of race as applied to the human species is not scientifically justifiable. The sorting of individuals into discrete categories ignores the genetic similarity of all humans and is biologically, and socially, inappropriate.[1]

A problem with a race concept as applied to the human species is that there are no meaningful barriers to the interbreeding of individuals of different races. A species is defined biologically as the total members of a group of populations that share a common gene pool and actually or potentially interbreed with one another under natural conditions.[2] The term subspecies is not a synonym for race. In humans there are no geographic barriers for the formation of subspecies, and physical and genetic variation fails to consistently distinguish one population from another.[3] Races are not subspecies and are therefore not meaningful biological terms.[4] Unfortunately, a need for organizing information often precipitates the use of racial categorization.[5]

I do not include here pictures of people from different places that demonstrate the wide range of human appearance (phenotype). I believe that to do so would perpetuate the erroneous idea that there are biologically significant differences between peoples. The phenotypic variation so apparent to us is not very significant overall, and our awareness of it clearly comes from societal custom rather than biological assessment. People within our own racial division may be clearly distinguished, while ones of other groups "all look alike."[6] But our awareness of race generally does not extend to other species, many of which, like chimpanzees, may also be said to contain races.[7]

### I can't define it, but I know it when I see it

Scientists, and others, have wrestled with theories on race formation for generations. Nonscientific ideas with wide currency include the idea that races have independent, pure origins in the past. Some interpretations of the Bible have a black race descending from one of Noah's sons.[8] Another confused idea imagines human history as a climb from brutish animality to enlightened reason, with some races farther along than others.[9] Always under appreciated, however, is the extent to which biological theories of race are misled by the environment and social class of the individual.

Ancient racial prejudices found their first scientific home in the works of Carolus Linnaeus.[10] In 1758 he not only classified humanity by color, but also listed personality traits.[11] Along with classificatory schemes arrived the concept of the "great chain of being," upon which all organisms could be arrayed in order of their proximity to heaven. Caucasoids occupied the topmost human rung. The distance between the rungs was emphasized by the newly emergent theory of polygenism, or separate origin of the races. Thus, scientific racism was firmly established by the mid-eighteenth century.[12]

The racial myth that lead directly to the genocide of World War II had its origin in the mid-1800s in the writings of Arthur de Gobineau and others. He promoted a myth in which everything of value in human history could be attributed to the white race and particularly its imaginary Aryan branch. This Aryan population was granted both superior physical and mental capabilities, and was naturally suited to lead the world. Hitler modified these ideas already in existence to create a justification for his own tyrannies.[13]

The notion of ideal types for human races has long held sway in the general mind. The classification proposed by the German physician J. F. Blumenbach in 1795 still has a place in the mind of the public.[14] He divided humanity into Caucasian, Mongolian, Ethiopian, American and Malay races. This scheme leaves many out—Polynesians, Australian Aborigines, etc.,—but more detailed schemes ultimately collapse because of the impossibility of dividing a polytypic, interbreeding mass of humanity into neat compartments. Classificatory schemes err in expecting all characteristics to be shared by all members of the same group, and in mixing unrelated characteristics.[15] Tracing the frequency of a trait over space reveals to one the geographic cline. One physical trait may appear in a distribution supporting a particular classification scheme, only to be contradicted by other traits.[16]

## The Biology of Race

The total genetic variation found in humans is markedly less than in other, older species. In fact, the genetic distance between human and chimpanzee is much less than that between sibling species of rodents or of Drosophila (fruit flies).[17] It is the partitioning of the total human genetic variation that is of interest in discussions of race.

Over twenty years ago, Richard C. Lewontin demonstrated that the greatest amount of genetic variability is found within, and not between, races.[18] Diversity calculations ask for the probability of finding differences in two individuals within a particular grouping. For example, it asks about the relative chances of finding two differences in two individuals from the same race as opposed to two individuals of different races. When calculations of this type are performed, it is found that about 85 percent of human genetic diversity is found within races.[19] And so, only a small amount of genetic diversity actually distinguishes races.

More extensive studies of nuclear DNA polymorphisms by Masatoshi Nei and others confirm and extend these findings.[20] The total of the gene differences between Europeans, Asians and Africans is less than the differences found between individuals of the same race, but the small inter-race differences do provide information about the time of divergence of the races. It has been estimated that these three major human races were in existence about 50,000 to 100,000 years ago. Thus, racial differentiation in humans is a relatively recent occurrence.[21]

The basis of the racial characteristics observed in humans is the variable genetic response to variable environments.[22] These biological changes may be adaptive, and enhance the survivability of a gene pool, or random, and persist merely by chance. Adaptive traits may include skin color and B-globin genotype, while blood group characters previously thought to be distributed randomly may have some adaptive value as well.[23] Racial characteristics in humans have a pattern of continuous variation, rather than appearing in a few alternate forms. For example, skin color varies widely, and continuously, around the world. Continuous variation is the result of multigenic control of traits.[24] A large number of genes determine skin color, so a wide range of results is possible.[25]

With many exceptions, lightest skin color is found at northern latitudes with an progressive increase in pigmentation along a southward cline.[26] There are some notable exceptions, however. For example, some of the darkest African populations live in equatorial rain forest, where the intensity of the sun is less than in the open savanna. Similarly, people of the intensely irradiated Kalahari do not possess very dark skins.[27] Migrations in the past are likely to explain some of the anomalies.[28] But, generally there is a correlation between skin color and distance from the equator. Since exposure to UV light also varies with distance from the equator, it has been hypothesized that skin color varies as an adaptive response to UV exposure.[29]

It is variation in quantities of the pigment melanin that produces variation in skin color.[30] Melanin protects skin from deleterious effects of UV light exposure, including sunburn and skin cancer.[31] The vast amount of time spent by early hominids in Africa hunting and gathering under intense sunlight would have exerted an important selective force against light skin.[32] Given the benefits of darker skin pigmentation, it is a reasonable question to ask why all humans do not possess large amount of photo-protective melanin. One explanation is the necessity for efficient vitamin-D production in the sun-starved regions distant from the equator.[33]

The principal source of vitamin D synthesis in the skin upon exposure to UV light. Vitamin D promotes calcium absorption from food and controls bone calcification. A deficiency of vitamin D can lead to rickets, a condition that produces malformations of the skeleton.[34]

Although appealing, there is no good evidence for the hypothesis that the need for efficient vitamin D production in northern climes leads to the development of lighter skin. In his presentation on skin pigmentation, Ashley Robins methodically shreds the claims for the necessity of lighter skin for vitamin-D production.[35] Rickets is principally a disease of the industrial age, and it would have been unlikely to affect early humans that spent most of their time outdoors. Also, even cold winters provide sunlight and the reflection of UV light off the snow. Vitamin D can be stored in fatty tissues for many months as well.

A newer, more substantiated explanation for the evolution of light skin color in northern latitudes proposes that lighter skin is less susceptible to injury by cold.[36] According to Army data, the incidence of frostbite is higher in darker- rather than lighter-skinned troops. Frostbite would have had a very deleterious effect upon early humans moving northward out of Africa, and an advantage conferred by lighter skin color could have had a significant selective effect. One difficulty for this hypothesis is the poorer cold tolerance of Caucasians as compared to relatively darker Inuit and Amerindians.[37] Clearly, the evolution of varied skin color has been a complicated process with many selective pressures and a wide range of genetic responses.

Hemoglobin is the carrier of oxygen in human red blood cells. The hemoglobin molecule is composed of four polypeptide chains: two alpha chains and two beta chains. The beta globin chain contains 146 amino acids. Variants in beta globin chain compositions exist in humans, and affect the functioning of the hemoglobin.[38]

One of the most common mutations is a substitution of the amino acid valine for glutamic acid in position six of the beta globin.[39] This change alters the binding properties of the molecule and is manifested as sickle cell anemia. Individuals with sickle cell anemia have a portion of red blood cells that is dysfunctional. Inheritance of the sickle cell trait from both parents is extremely disadvantageous to the individual, who will then suffer from the disease. However, possession of one gene for the sickle cell trait, that is, to be heterozygous for the trait, may confer an advantage in certain parts of the world.[40] Areas of the world where the trait is common include parts of west and central Africa, southern India, and around the Mediterranean, where the frequency of the Hemoglobin S allele can range as high as 25 percent.[41] The frequency of this allele is high because of the resistance to malaria experienced by heterozygotes.

This dramatic case of single gene interaction with an environmentally selective force resulting in advantage to heterozygotes and great disadvantage to homozygotes is unusual. Possibly, this is a relatively new response, arising in the last few thousands of years, as agricultural and herding patterns changed and exposed more populations to malaria.[42]

For many physical traits, humans have a genetic range of responses, and the potential realized depends upon the environment experienced. One of the most physically demanding of living environments is at high altitudes. Nonetheless, people have occupied areas above three thousand meters, such as the Andes, for centuries.[43] Humans have a range of adaptive responses to hypoxia, or low oxygen levels in the body. Physiological features characteristic of high Andes populations, such as barrel chest or comparatively better resistance to cold, are doubtless traits selected for from generations of mountain dwellers.[44] However, physiological responses to hypoxia, such as increased red blood cell count, can be elicited even in adults from low altitudes moving to the mountains, just as these traits diminish in mountain dwellers who leave for the lowlands.[45]

**Misuses of the Biology of Race**

The failure to recognize the tremendous impact of environment upon the complex genetic background of human variation has led in the past, and probably present, to poor science. Biological determinism is the argument that intrinsic qualities of human groups produce the social and economic differences manifested between different races, classes and sexes.[46] Deterministic studies can be difficult to counter, as they are couched in putative scientific objectivity, and are firmly in line with the prevailing political winds of the day.

Racial prejudice has existed at least since Plato.[47] For centuries, the idea of a natural hierarchy of human races and classes has held sway. Thomas Jefferson, Benjamin Franklin, and Abraham Lincoln did not hesitate to express a belief in the biological inequality of races.[48] Biological studies add a depressing note of inevitability and immutability to it all, by purporting to demonstrate that races deemed inferior were of less intelligence and ability.

Before the advent of evolutionary theory, two lines of thinking explained the racial ranking of humans.[49] In one view, monogenism, all humans share a single origin in Adam and Eve. Current social patterns could be explained as the result of the races degenerating to different extents, most likely under the influence of different climates. Polygenism, instead, argues that the races have separate origins, and in fact, represent distinct species. The interfertility of races presented a difficulty for this argument. Polygenism was an idea of American origin, and particularly popular in a nation practicing slavery and forcibly removing the native inhabitants. Louis Agassiz, a Harvard naturalist, was a stout defender of polygenism with a horror of racial intermixture.[50] Yet he amassed no data, unlike the anatomist Samuel George Morton.

Morton amassed over one thousand skulls of different races for the purpose of constructing a hierarchy of races based upon physical characteristics of the brain.[51] He measured the volume of the cranial cavity of each skull in order to infer the size of the brain it once contained. The results neatly ranked people as follows: Caucasian, Mongolian, Malay, (native) American, and Ethiopian. Stephen Jay Gould has shown that Morton, probably unconsciously, biased his measurements and calculations in order to arrive at these socially acceptable results.[52]

It is not true in the matter of brains that bigger is necessarily better; in fact, brain size varies with body size and sex.[53] But in Morton's time it was assumed that brain size must have something to do with intellectual ability. The second half of the nineteenth century saw the development of craniometry, the meticulous measurement of the skull and the brain.[54]

This field was grounded in the belief that the truth about human origins and racial variation would emerge from methodical unbiased measurement.[55] Its master exponent, Paul Broca, sought to ascertain the intellectual value of the human races through measurement.[56] At the time there was little doubt of a link between brain size and intelligence. Broca criticized those who, in his view, allowed egalitarian views to influence their science, while being influenced himself by prior, socially acceptable, conclusions.[57]

Gould has outlined in detail the convoluted path between Broca's exemplary method of data collection and the selective, unconscious manipulation of the data to yield the expected results.[58] His fundamental error was the assumption that human races could indeed be ranked by intellectual ability. With this as the starting point, it merely remained to find, and measure, characters that followed the expected distribution. Inevitably, some of the characters did not vary in the expected pattern. Broca used a variety of ingenious arguments to explain each seemingly anomalous result.

One of the most obvious, and vexing, measurements was that of brain size. People of Asian origin tended to have brains of surprisingly heavy mass, even surpassing Europeans.[59] This disappointing result was minimized by instead stressing the importance of a finding of small average brain size in West Africans. The argument of large body size correlating with large brain size was used to dismiss a finding of larger brain size in Germans than in French, but not used to explain the socially acceptable male-female difference in brain mass.[60]

The size of the brain was not the only feature deemed important. The anterior regions of the cortex were believed to be the site of higher mental functions, while the posterior of the brain was assigned mundane roles in physical function.[61] Hence races possessing a bias towards anterior size or positioning must be superior. Many convoluted arguments were employed to reconcile the results of measurement with expectations.

Broca sought to rank the men of different races, and measure the brains of deceased great men. Some races may have been deemed inferior, but *all* women were clearly subhuman. Broca's support for the natural inferiority of women was based upon both the smaller brains of women and a purported increase in the male-female difference through evolutionary time.[62] A difference in body size was dismissed out of hand as an explanation for the smaller brains in women. The finding of a more similar brain size in a few male and female prehistoric skulls was interpreted as evidence that the struggle for existence had edified and civilized men, while passive women had stagnated.[63] The difference between men and women, and most important the inferiority of women, was taken as a fact so indisputable that no analysis of data need even be done.

The concept of recapitulation provided a theoretical underpinning for the attempts to rank human races. Extremely popular in the late nineteenth century, this idea proposes that in its development an individual passes through all its ancestral adult forms.[64] Thus, a child of a superior race would be expected to resemble an adult of an inferior race. In comparison with a white male child, everyone was inferior—nonwhite adults, all women, southern Europeans, Jews, members of lower classes, and so on. Anatomical data were collected selectively to support these rankings.[65] The idea was also popular as a justification for imperialism.[66]

After almost seventy years, the idea of recapitulation lost favor and was supplanted in the late 1920s by its complete opposite, the concept of neoteny.[67] Neotenic features are those possessed by the juveniles of ancestors, but adults of their descendants. Thus the most advanced race would be that with the most childlike features. The data required to support this theory were exactly the opposite of those used to promote recapitulation, and supporting data were promptly culled.[68]

In the late nineteenth century, physician Cesare Lombroso described the physiology of the born criminal and founded the discipline of criminal anthropology.[69] He claimed, based upon anthropometric data, that criminals are evolutionary throwbacks. Lombroso also saw a kinship between criminals and inferior, savage races.[70]

Despite criticisms, Lombroso's ideas were widely influential, in both science and in law. Belief in innate criminality shifted attention away from the context of the crime and the life history of the individual. Factors such as education, social standing, or deprivation need not be considered.

Arguments based upon craniometry are now a relic of the past. But deterministic thinking does not fade away so easily. The modern substitute for craniometry, intelligence testing, purports to quantify the innate ability of the brain.[71]

Alfred Binet, the parent of intelligence testing, had tried craniometry and been disappointed.[72] The tests he developed in the early years of the twentieth century were devised to identify children in need of additional help in the classroom. Binet realized that a single number was not enough to describe something as complex as intelligence.[73] Nonetheless, within twenty years the pervasive misuse of IQ testing influenced the passage of the Immigration Act of 1924, which severely limited the number of persons entering the United States from particular countries.[74]

The Stanford-Binet test developed in 1916 rewarded conformity and penalized originality. Correct answers required knowledge of society's conventions.[75] These characteristics were present in the IQ tests given to 1.75 million World War I recruits.[76] The army tests viewed intelligence as a single, heritable quality unaffected by environment. An individual's allotment of intelligence was thought to destine him to a particular level of society.

The mass testing of army recruits had significant effects upon social policy in the United States.[77] One shocking finding was of an astoundingly low mental age of 13 for the average white male. This finding was seized upon by eugenists eager to curtail the pollution of the native gene pool by blacks, immigrants from eastern and southern Europe, and the prolific breeding of the dimwitted. Eastern and southern Europeans were judged to be duller than northern Europeans, while blacks scored at the bottom of all. Some used the results to support segregation and the denial of educational opportunities to blacks. However, the largest impact of the army test results was in immigration policy.

The Immigration Act of 1924 not only limited immigration, but it specifically targeted countries judged to contain genetically inferior people.[78] In the years preceding World War II, the number of immigrants from southern and eastern Europe was severely limited, with tragic results for some. Ironically, by 1930 the developer of the army tests recognized that both the tests and conclusions drawn from them were without validity.[79]

**Crime and Heredity**

It is unlikely that criminal tendencies are genetically determined. The social explosiveness of the topic is marked by the inability to even hold a conference to discuss the ethical implications of investigating a link between heredity and crime.[80] The conference in question was entitled "Genetic Factors in Crime: Findings, Uses and Implications," and was to have occurred in October of 1992 at the University of Maryland. The meeting was to be funded by the National Institutes of Health (NIH), which suspended, and one year later cancelled, the funding after adverse publicity.[81]

Experts involved with the conference have observed that rather than seek to link crime and genes, there would have been discussion of the ethics of any such studies.[82] In addition, it is commonly accepted that any genetic traits linked to crime would be dwarfed in importance by environmental conditions promoting criminal behavior. Instead of protecting some groups in society from racist investigations of the genetics of criminality, those who objected to the conference may have done them a disservice. Results from the conference reaffirming the overwhelming social and psychological causation of crime, could well have been valuable in relation to the articulation, design, and implementation of policies that targeted a given range of socially corrosive inequalities.

**I Wanna Be Me**

There is a great longing for uniqueness lurking in the members of the human species. People seem to want to believe in the uniqueness, if not superiority, of their family, neighborhood, racial group, religious group, country and, of course, species. However, evidence of intrinsic, biological superiority is sorely lacking.

The last common ancestor of chimpanzees and humans likely lived no more than five million years ago.[83] The recency of human origin, a fact still only grudgingly accepted by some members of the scientific community, is almost completely unappreciated by nonscientists. Similarly, findings over the last half-century concerning the close interrelatedness of all human racial groups are still not appearing in every college biology classroom.[84]

The reception accorded my own research has impressed upon me the strength of people's (erroneous) convictions regarding race, and the origin of the human species. Studies of human mitochondrial DNA, a special part of our genome, have emphasized the recency of modern human origin and placed our point of origin in Africa.[85] This work has attracted much attention in the popular press, and I would like to describe it here briefly.

**Human MtDNA**

I am a geneticist by training, investigating molecular variation in the human species. The molecule in use is mitochondrial DNA (mtDNA), a small genome separate from our chromosomes. Mitochondria are the organelles responsible for energy synthesis for cells, and contain their own DNA. MtDNA has been useful for evolutionary studies in part due to its rapid rate of evolution and unusual mode of inheritance.[86]

MtDNA evolves at a rate of about 2–4 percent per million years, or 5-10 times more quickly than single-copy nuclear DNA.[87] This enables us to obtain data about events in human history that, in terms of evolutionary time, are very recent.

MtDNA has an unusual mode of inheritance. It is transmitted strictly maternally (figure 1.1), without a contribution from the male parent as is the case for the rest of our genes.[88] This is useful for evolutionary studies, for we can look at variation in people today and trace a maternal family tree of the past. When a large number of individuals of different worldwide origin are studied, inferences about human evolution may be made.

A phylogenetic tree relating the mtDNAs found in contemporary individuals (figure 1.2) has several notable features.[89] First, individuals are not all grouped according to geographic origin, due to the retention of genetic changes occurring far in the past. Second, there is a tendency to find mtDNAs from Africa at the root of the tree. The simplest explanation for the distribution of individuals seen is an African

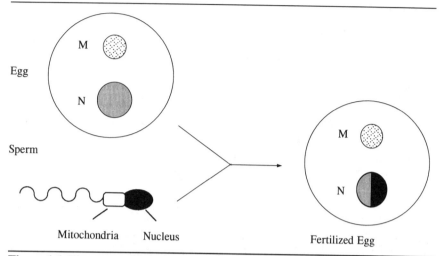

**Figure 1.1.** The maternal inheritance of mitochondrial DNA. The illustration depicts how the nuclear DNA of the fertilized egg is provided equally by both parents while the mtDNA is of maternal derivation.

origin for mtDNA, with subsequent migration out of Africa. The individual at the deepest branchpoint of the tree is the most recent common mitochondrial ancestor of us all, and is inevitably called "Eve" in the popular press.

The term "Eve" is quite unfortunate for it gives to its possessor a rather undeserved air of uniqueness. There is actually no reason to believe that the most recent mtDNA ancestor was in any way special, merely lucky in that her mtDNA lineage persisted through random chance over the generations. She was not the only female in existence at the time, and indeed our other genes doubtless trace back to many individuals, male and female, of other generations.

Many, judging by the sometimes anonymous and often emotional correspondence received, are uneasy with the implications of the mtDNA work. The best known human fossils are millions of years old, and may or may not be ancestors of any of us. The mitochondrial ancestor is linked to all of us be a distance of only 1,000 generations. All of our racial characteristics have developed in a relatively short space of time.

### Conclusion

Race is by definition a biological entity, yet it has no true justification in biology. The need to organize information makes the use of racial terms too often unavoidable. The author of a recent monograph on human pigmentation had to regretfully make use of

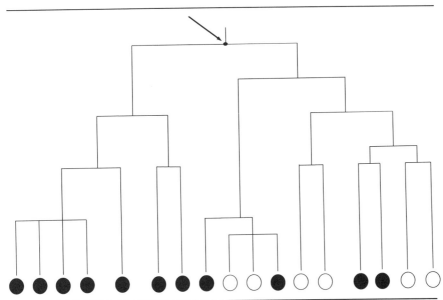

**Figure 1.2.** A hypothetical tree presenting relationships among mtDNAs found in contemporary humans. Filled circles indicate mtDNA types of African origin, while empty circles represent non-African types. The arrow points to the most recent common ancestor of all types depicted.

the racial terms Caucasoid, Mongoloid, Negroid, and so on, while admitting to the lack of biological validity to such classificatory schemes.[90]

Society at this time still pays a great deal of attention to classification, whether by race, or under the guise of ethnic group. The category of ethnic groups invokes culture and moves yet further from any purported biological justification.[91] The most recent U.S. census, in 1990, became tangled in questions of racial background and ethnic self-designation.[92]

The U.S. census contained four basic categories: white, black, American Indian/ Alaskan Native, and Asian/Pacific Islander. Ten million people checked the "other" category. Many of these people were determined to be Hispanic, which has been an ethnic category (since 1970) not a race (as before 1930). The movements of ethnic groups in and out of racial groups, overall, resembles a tale from Lewis Carroll.

I am unsure whether racial categories will continue to fractionate, under the pressures of ethnic group pride and affirmative action opportunities, or amalgamate into groups. Some respondents with parents of different races describe themselves as "mixed," a conclusion perhaps at once both less precise and more accurate in describing most of the residents of this and other countries.[93]

## Notes

1. Douglas J. Futuyma, *Evolutionary Biology* (Sunderland, MA: Sinauer Associates, 1986), p. 109; Paul R. Spickard, "The Illogic of American Racial Categories," in Marla P. Root, ed., *Racially Mixed People in America* (Newbury Park: Sage Publications, 1991), p. 18.

2. Futuyma, op. cit. note 1, p. 111; Ernst Mayer, *Systematics and the Origin of the Species* (New York: Columbia University Press, 1942), p. 111.

3. Alice Littlefield, Leonard Lieberman, and Larry T. Reynolds, "Redefining Race: The Potential Demise of a Concept in Physical Anthropology," *Current Anthropology* 23 (1982): 641–55.

4. Edward O. Wilson and W. L. Brown, "The Subspecies Concept and its Taxonomic Application," *Systematic Zoology* 22 (1953): 97–111.

5. Ashley H. Robins, *Biological Perspectives on Human Pigmentation* (Cambridge: Cambridge University Press, 1991), p. xi.

6. Richard C. Lewontin, *Human Diversity* (San Francisco: W.H. Freeman, 1982), p. 7.

7. Jared Diamond, *The Third Chimpanzee* (New York: Harper Collins, 1992), p. 8.

8. Robins, op. cit. note 5, p. 166.

9. James C. King, *The Biology of Race* (Berkeley: University of California Press, 1981), p. 111.

10. Spickard, op. cit. note 1, p. 13.

11. Robins, op. cit. note 5, p. 171.

12. Ibid., p. 172.

13. Ibid.

14. King, op. cit. note 9, p. 111.

15. Stephen Molnar, *Human Variation* (Englewood Cliffs: Prentice Hall, 1992), p. 20.

16. Ibid., p. 208.

17. Futuyma, op. cit. note 1, p. 510.

18. Richard C. Lewontin, "The Apportionment of Human Diversity," *Evolutionary Biology* 6 (1972): 381–98.

19. Lewontin, op. cit. note 6, p. 120.

20. Masatoshi Nei and Arun Roychoudhury, "Gene Differences Between Caucasian, Negro, and Japanese Populations," *Science* 177 (1972): 434–36.

21. Futuyma, op. cit. note 1, p. 522.

22. Molnar, op. cit. note 15, p. 3; Lewontin, op. cit. note 7, p. 65.

23. Molnar, ibid., p. 223.

24. Futuyma, op. cit. note 1, p. 44.

25. Robins, op. cit. note 5, p. 22.

26. Ibid., p. 187.

27. King, op. cit. note 9, p. 140.

28. Ibid., p. 141.

29. Robins, op. cit. note 5, p. 189.

30. Ibid., p. 3.

31. Ibid., p. 59.

32. Ibid., p. 189.

33. Ibid., p. 200.

34. Ibid., pp. 197–200.

35. Ibid., pp. 202–8.

36. Ibid., p. 209.

37. Ibid., p. 210.

38. Lewontin, op. cit. note 6, p. 30.

39. Molnar, op. cit. note 15, p. 106.

40. Ibid., p. 105.

41. Ibid., p. 108; Lewontin, op. cit. note 6, p. 29.

42. Molnar, ibid., p. 239.

43. Ibid., p. 215.

44. Ibid., pp. 220–23.

45. Lewontin, op. cit. note 6, p. 16.

46. Stephen Jay Gould, *The Mismeasure of Man* (New York: W. W. Norton, 1981), p. 20.

47. Ibid., p. 19.

48. Ibid., p. 35.

49. Ibid., p. 39.

50. Ibid., p. 43.

51. Ibid., p. 50.

52. Ibid., p. 54.

53. Ibid., pp. 61–62.

54. Ibid., p. 74.

55. Molnar, op. cit. note 15, p. 16.

56. Ibid., p. 14; Gould, op. cit. note 46, p. 85.

57. Gould, ibid., p. 84.

58. Ibid., pp. 85–105.

59. Ibid., p. 87.

60. Ibid., p. 104.

61. Ibid., p. 97.

62. Ibid., p. 103.

63. Ibid., p. 104.

64. Ibid., p. 114.

65. Ibid., p. 116.

66. Ibid., p. 118.

67. Ibid., p. 119.

68. Ibid., p. 120.

69. Ibid., p. 123.

70. Ibid., p. 125.

71. Lewontin, op. cit. note 6, p. 92; John Maddox, "How to Publish the Unpalatable," *Nature* 358 (1992): 187.

72. Gould, op. cit. note 46, p. 149.

73. Ibid., p. 151.

74. Ibid., p. 157.

75. Lewontin, op. cit. note 6, p. 93.

76. Gould, op. cit. note 46, p. 194.

77. Ibid., pp. 196–99.

78. Ibid., p. 232.

79. Ibid., p. 233.

80. Daniel Coleman, "New Storm Brews on Whether Crime has Roots in Genes," *The New York Times*, September 15, 1992, p. C1.

81. Christopher Anderson, "NIH Under Fire, Freezes Grant for Conference on Genetics and Crime," *Science* 358 (1992): 357.

82. Coleman, op. cit. note 80.

83. Satoshi Horai, Yoko Satta, Kenji Hayasaka, Rumi Kondo, Tadashi Inoue, Takafumi Ishida, Seiji Hayashi, and Naoyuki Takahata, "Man's Place in Hominoidea Revealed by Mitochondrial DNA Genealogy," *Journal of Molecular Evolution* 35 (1992): 32-43.

84. Leonard Lieberman, Raymond E. Hampton, Alice Littlefield, and Glen Hallead, "Race in Biology and Anthropology: A Study of College Texts and Professors," *Journal of Research in Science Teaching* 29 (1992): 301–21.

85. Rebecca L. Cann, Mark Stoneking, and Allan C. Wilson, "Mitochondrial DNA and Human Evolution," *Nature* 325 (1987): 31-36; Linda Vigilant, Mark Stoneking, Henry Harpending, Kristen Hawkes, and Allan C. Wilson, "African Populations and the Evolution of Human Mitochondrial DNA," *Science* 253 (1991): 1503–7.

86. Allan C. Wilson, Rebecca L. Cann, Steven M. Carr, Matthew George, Ulf B. Gyllensten, Kathleen M. Helm-Bychowski, Russel G. Higuchi, Steven R. Palumbi, Ellen M. Prager, Richard D. Sage, and Mark Stoneking, "Mitochondrial DNA and Two Perspectives on Evolutionary Genetics," *Biological Journal of the Linnaen Society* 26 (1985): 375–400.

87. Ibid.

88. Ibid.

89. Cann et al., op. cit. note 85; Vigilant et al., op. cit. note 85.

90. Robins, op. cit. note 5, p. xii.

91. Lieberman et al., op. cit. note 84.

92. Felicity Barringer, "Ethnic Pride Confounds the Census," *The New York Times*, April 25, 1993, p. A3.

93. Ibid.; Spickard, op. cit. note 1, p. 22.

# 2

# The Bell Curve
## A Cross-Century Tradition Concerning Race and Intellect

WINSTON A. VAN HORNE

Tradition is a wellspring of human life. From it issues forth sentiments, beliefs, customs, mores, and norms that are handed down by speech, writing or other sufficient signs from generation to generation. Long-established ways of thinking and/or acting ground tradition, which shapes the contours of conscious and unconscious, as well as rational and irrational behavior. It also is shaped by these behaviors. In tradition inhere the best and the worst of the thought and conduct of *Homo sapiens sapiens*. Through it, guideposts of acceptability and the pathways of permissibility are made known, whereby individuals are inclined to behave in ways that make them better or worse, when judged against standards of human decency.

A tradition that has drawn determinate contours of life in the United States, with searing social effect, is racism. The conscious and unconscious, rational and irrational impulses that radiate from this tradition are a commonplace in the everyday life of the society. They find expression in articulate, conceptual discourse no less than in inarticulate, discursive diatribe. Richard J. Herrnstein's and Charles Murray's *The Bell Curve* is masked behind articulate, conceptual discourse, though steeped in an all too familiar racialist tradition. Before discussing The Bell Curve directly, it is well to arc back to the mid-sixteenth century when Englishmen first made contact with Africans, in order to provide an historical context for the racialist tradition that envelops the book, in particular, and American society in general.

I*

In his now classic work *The White Man's Burden*, Winthrop D. Jordan observes that "Englishmen found the peoples of Africa very different from themselves. 'Negroes' looked different to Englishmen; their religion was un-Christian; their manner of living was anything but English; they all seemed to be a particularly libidinous sort of people."[1] It is proper to note here that in their initial contact with Africans, Englishmen observed that Africans were not without religion; it was just that the form and substance of the Africans' religion differed from Christianity with which Englishmen were *familiar*.

I should like to stress the term familiar. At the very outset of their interactions with Africans, Englishmen imputed to the unfamiliar countenance and behaviors of Africans all sorts of wretchedness out of their own myopia, ignorance, arrogance, lack of understanding, and cultural chauvinism. Many an European has mindlessly imitated the English in this regard.

Still, it was color that most engaged Englishmen in relation to Africans. Jordan notes that "[f]or Englishmen, the most arresting characteristic of the newly discovered African was his color. Travelers rarely failed to comment upon it; indeed when describing Africans they frequently began with complexion and then moved on to dress (or, as they saw, lack of it) and manners."[2] What was it about the African's complexion that so arrested Englishmen? Its blackness. Jordan writes that "Englishmen actually described Negroes as *black*."[3] Given the powerful impact that the black color of Africans had upon Englishmen, it is fitting and proper to ask: What were the cultural cognates of the term black into which Englishmen were socialized? Again, Jordan is helpful. He observes: "No other color except white conveyed so much emotional meaning. As described by the *Oxford English Dictionary*, the meaning of *black* before the sixteenth century included, 'Deeply stained with dirt; soiled, dirty, foul. . . . Having dark or deadly purposes, malignant; pertaining to death, deadly; baneful, disastrous, sinister. . . . Foul, iniquitous, atrocious, horrible, wicked. . . . Indicating disgrace, censure, liability to punishment, etc.' Black was an emotionally partisan color, the handmaid and symbol of baseness and evil, a sign of danger and repulsion."[4]

Jordan continues, "[e]mbedded in the concept of blackness was its direct opposite—whiteness. No other colors so clearly implied opposition. . . . White and black connoted purity and filthiness, virginity and sin, virtue and baseness, beauty and ugliness, beneficence and evil, God and the devil. Whiteness, moreover, carried a special significance for Elizabethan Englishmen: it was, particularly when complemented by red, the color of perfect human beauty, especially *female* beauty. . . . By contrast, the Negro was ugly, by reason of his [black] color and also his 'horrid Curles' and 'disfigured' lips and nose."[5]

I have cited Jordan at some length because his observations afford critical insights into the rise of a racialist tradition in colonial America/the United States. Given its British origins, the dominance of the English in colonial America, and the powerful emotive charge attached to color in the psyches of Englishmen, it was empirically inescapable that color would come to permeate the culture of American society. Insofar as the English conflated color and race in relation to themselves and

Africans, Chief Justice Roger Taney simply expressed with stark forthrightness sentiments pertaining to racial superiority and inferiority, carried transgenerationally in the culture, when he wrote in the infamous *Dred Scott* decision that neither the Declaration of Independence nor the Constitution embraced the African in the United States—regardless of whether s/he was enslaved or free. Moreover, said Taney, blacks "had for more than a century before been regarded as beings of an inferior order, and altogether unfit to associate with the white race, either in social or political relations; and so far inferior, that they had no rights which the white man was bound to respect. . . . This opinion was at that time fixed and universal in the civilized portion of the white race. It was regarded as an *axiom in morals as well as in politics*, which no one thought of disputing, or supposed to be open to dispute.[6]

There are those who have quarrelled with Taney's observation concerning the axiomatic assumption of moral and political inferiority in relation to black people. Still, no less an intractable foe of slavery than Harriet Beecher Stowe, of *Uncle Tom's Cabin* fame, believed that though slavery was morally wrong, a hard boundary of demarcation along the color-line would continually separate blacks and whites, with blacks being the social inferiors of whites. And Abraham Lincoln, in the first of seven truly historic debates with Stephen Douglas between August 21 and October 15, 1858 (one of the seminal events of the decade prior to the Civil War) observed: "I will say here . . . [that] I have no purpose to introduce political and social equality between the white and black races. There is a *physical difference* between the two, which in my judgment will probably *forever* forbid their living together upon the footing of perfect equality, and . . . I, as well as Judge Douglas, am in favor of the race to which I belong, having the superior position. . . . I agree with Judge Douglas [that blacks are] not my equal in many respects—certainly not in color, perhaps not in moral or intellectual endowment."[7]

In the third debate Lincoln reinforced the aforementioned points by observing: "[T]here is a physical difference between the white and black races which I believe will for ever forbid the two races living together on terms of social and political equality. And inasmuch as they cannot so live, while they do remain together there must be the position of superior and inferior, and I as much as any other [white] man am in favor of having the superior position assigned to the white race."[8] And meeting with a group of black men at the White House after he had become president, Lincoln said: "You and we are different races. We have between us a broader difference than exists between almost any other two races. Whether it is right or wrong I need not discuss, but this physical difference is a great disadvantage to us both. . . . [O]n this broad continent, not a single man of your race is made the equal of a single man of ours. . . . I cannot alter it if I would. . . . It is a fact. . . . *It is better for us both, therefore, to be separated.*"[9] What is the empirical fact that Lincoln perceives himself unable to alter?—the social, political, moral, and intellectual inferiority of blacks, which emanate from a physical difference grounded in color.

Lincoln's stance concerning white superiority, and his sentiment pertaining to the moral and intellectual inferiority of blacks, merely echoes Thomas Jefferson's belief that "[i]n general, [blacks] appear to participate more in sensation than reflection. . . . Comparing them by their faculties of memory, reason, and imagination, it appears to me [,says Jefferson,] that in memory they are equal to whites; in reason much inferior, as I think one could scarcely be found capable of tracing and comprehending the investigations of Euclid; and that in imagination they are dull, tasteless, and anomalous."[10]

The moral vulgarity of Jefferson saying that a black person could scarcely be found who could trace and comprehend the investigations of Euclid, when he knew full well the stringency of state-imposed sanctions against black people receiving even the barest trace of an education, is so stark that no comment is needed here. What is critical to call out is the presumption of white aesthetic, moral, and intellectual superiority vis-à-vis blacks, and all others for that matter, that coursed the culture and society of colonial America/the United States through the Civil War was to persist after the Reconstruction of the Union. The nineteenth century was to close with the revalidation of the archetype of white superiority in the Supreme Court's *Plessy* v. *Ferguson* decision of 1896, which constitutionalized Jim Crow in the United States through the cunning—one might even say fraudulent—doctrine of "separate but equal." Indeed, Justice Henry Billings Brown, who wrote the decision, was to observe that "[i]f one race be inferior to the other socially, the Constitution of the United States cannot put them upon the same plane."[11] And where inferiority does obtain, such could not pertain to "the white race, [which] . . . would not acquiesce [to] a badge of [racial] inferiority."[12]

The twentieth century was to open with the cocoon of racial inferiority drawn tightly over blacks, and close with the unrelenting struggle of black people to break free from it. But the full and complete shedding of the cocoon of racial inferiority has proven to be a task of truly monumental proportions, for it chips away the very foundations of white racial and cultural hegemony. In the twentieth century, *the beneficiaries of racial inheritance*—carried in the tradition of archetypal white superiority, which Jefferson, Lincoln, Taney, and Brown symbolized ever so potently— have fought just as hard, through a range of direct and indirect measures, to assure the persistence of racial advantage. It is in this context that *The Bell Curve* must be evaluated.

## II

*The Bell Curve*, anchored securely in the tradition that has been just called out, rooms most comfortably with Arthur de Gobineau's *The Inequality of the Races* (1854) and Charles Carroll's *"The Negro a Beast"; or, "in the Image of God"* (1900). De Gobineau has the dubious distinction of being the father of modern racialist theories, and Carroll was one of Jim Crow's clarion voices. What, then, are the fundamental, unifying themes of the volumes just mentioned regarding black people?

Like Jefferson and Lincoln before them, de Gobineau, Carroll, Herrnstein and Murray posit an *intelligence gap* between blacks and whites. Regarding this putative gap, de Gobineau writes: "Do all men possess in an equal degree an unlimited power of intellectual development? . . . If it is admitted that the European cannot hope to civilize the negro, and manages to transmit to the mulatto only very few of his own characteristics; if the children of a mulatto and a white woman cannot really understand anything better than a hybrid culture, a little nearer than their father's to the ideas of the white race,—in that case, I am right in saying that the different races are unequal in intelligence."[13] Carroll observes: "The negro possesses the erect posture, a well-developed hand and foot, articulate speech, and is withall, a tool-making, tool-handling animal. These characteristics pre-eminently fit him for the position of servant, while the low order of his mentality disqualifies him for a higher sphere [of life]. . . . The gulf is far too wide and deep, which separates between the mental indolence and incapacity of the negro, which accomplishes nothing, and the flashing intellect, the restless energy, and the indomitable courage of the white, which enables him to discover, conquer, and develop continents."[14] Herrnstein and Murray ask: "*Do Blacks Score Differently from Whites on Standardized Tests of Cognitive Ability?* If the samples are chosen to be representative of the American population, the answer has been yes for every known test of cognitive ability that meets basic psychometric standards of reliability and validity. . . . *How large Is the Black-White Difference?* The usual answer to this question is one standard deviation. In discussing IQ tests, for example, the black mean is commonly given as 85, the white mean as 100, and the standard deviation as 15."[15]

Resonating through the passages just cited is the intellectual inferiority or cognitive deficit of blacks. Given the conceptual and empirical significance of cognitive ability in relation to what may loosely be called the progress of wo'mankind, one perforce must ask: From whence comes the supposed transgenerational cognitive deficit of black people? Again one turns to the quadrumvirate of de Gobineau, Carroll, Herrnstein and Murray.

De Gobineau observes: "The animal character, that appears in the shape of the pelvis, is stamped on the negro from birth, and foreshadows his destiny. His intellect will always move within a very narrow circle. He is not however a mere brute, for behind his low receding brow, in the middle of his skull, we can see signs of a powerful energy, however crude its objects. If his mental faculties are dull or even non-existent, he often has an intensity of desire, and so of will, which may be called terrible. Many of his senses, especially taste and smell, are developed to an extent unknown to the other two races . . . the yellow and the white."[16] Carroll notes that "diminutive brain weights, carrying with them a corresponding diminution of intelligence"[17] are a defining attribute of blacks. Referring to a study done by Sanford B. Hunt on the brain weights of white soldiers and black soldiers at the time of the Civil War, which found the weights to be 1424 grammes and 1331 grammes respectively, Carroll calls out the diminished intelligence of blacks. He goes on to observe that this and all other "scientific investigation of the subject proves the Negro to be an ape; and simply stands at the head of the ape family, as the lion stands at the head of the cat family. . . . And we feel assured that a careful consideration of this subject must lead any rational mind to decide that the White, with his exalted physical and mental characters, and the Negro, with his ape-like physical and mental characters, are not the same progeny of one primitive pair." He continues: "This being true, it follows that, if the White was created 'in the image of God,' then the Negro was made after some other model. And a glance at the Negro indicates the model; his very appearance suggests the ape."[18]

Concerning the intelligence gap or cognitive deficit of blacks in relation to whites, Herrnstein and Murray note that it cannot be wholly explained by social and environmental considerations. They observe that "whites are characteristically stronger than blacks on subtests involving spatial-perceptual ability, blacks are characteristically stronger than whites in subtests such as arithmetic and immediate memory, both of which involve retention and retrieval of information."[19] (Jefferson's remarks concerning memory, reason, and imagination should resonate loudly here.) This difference, along with a host of others pertaining to cognitive ability, is "not the result of biased tests in the ordinary sense of the term. [It] may well include some (as yet unknown) genetic component, but nothing suggests that [it is] *entirely* genetic."[20] The term *entirely* is critical here. It plays the customary role of a hedge word. The cognitive deficit of blacks may not be entirely genetic but it is at least *partially* so. This is the only sound conceptual inference that can be drawn from the language of Herrnstein and Murray—assuming that they do not play Alice in Wonderland with the use of words.

And so, God and nature afford the racist answers adduced by de Gobineau, Carroll, Murray and Herrnstein to a question that unites them all: From whence comes the transgenerational cognitive deficit of black people? De Gobineau rejects the view "that between some human races and the larger apes there is only a slight difference of degree, and none of kind [a belief shared by Carroll, as] an insult to humanity, [though it is his conviction] that human races are unequal."[21] Herrnstein and Murray share de Gobineau's sentiment pertaining to the inequality of the races—they prefer to speak of ethnic groups—at least in relation to putative differences in cognitive ability. They do not dirty themselves with Carroll's diatribe concerning whites being God-like, and blacks being ape-like. Yet, intriguingly, insofar as intelligence and cognitive ability ground the fields of work for which one is equipped, and the spheres of life properly open to one, Murray and Herrnstein come mighty close to Carroll.

It is Carroll's belief that "scientific research demonstrates that [the white] man, whom God designed, equipped, and clothed with authority to subdue the earth, never descended to savagery. On the other hand, the Negro, when uncontrolled by the White, becomes 'a mere wanderer in the woods,' and like any other animal, subsists upon the spontaneous products of the earth, and the proceeds of the chase. This indicates that the natural relation between the White and the Negro is that of master and servant. . . . [The] mass of scriptural and scientific evidence clearly indicates that the pure-blooded White is the creature whom God designed should perform the mental labor necessary to subdue the earth; and that the Negro is the creature whom God designed to perform the manual labor."[22] For Carroll, as is true also for de Gobineau, blacks lack the intellect to fill a variety of societal roles. Cognitive deficit delimits their life chances, and their proper place in society. One finds in Herrnstein and Murray a remarkable similarity.

They ask: "Inasmuch as cognitive ability is related to job performance and as minority workers[, especially blacks,] are entering professions with lower ability distributions than whites, is there evidence of lower average performance for minority workers than for whites?"[23] Calling attention to affirmative action, for example, they observe that "the same degree may not have the same meaning for blacks, Latinos, and whites in terms of cognitive ability. . . . In the NLSY [National Longitudinal Survey of Youth], the black-white differences for every educational level, from high school diploma to Ph.D., are large, with the smallest being a difference of 1.2 standard deviations."[24] Given these differences in cognitive ability, and given the correspondence between cognitive ability and job performance, "[p]art of the reason . . . that employers hire blacks and whites of differing cognitive ability [may be] because of pressures brought on them by government policies regarding representation of minority groups. Without such pressures and in a race-blind labor market, blacks and whites should be equal in those traits that best predict performance on the job."[25] Absent governmental pressures to hire minorities, if a disproportion were to obtain between blacks and whites in job categories that are cognitively demanding, such disproportion would be fair, and attempts at "'correcting' it—making it proportional—may [well] produce unfairness along with equal representation."[26]

Like de Gobineau and Carroll before them, Murray and Herrnstein perceive the majority of blacks to fit most neatly into societal roles that do not make weighty cognitive demands. Indeed, one observes in their text that of the approximately thirty million blacks in the society as of 1990, only 100,000, or 0.33 of 1 percent, fall into "Class I of [their] five cognitive classes [Very bright, Bright, Normal, Dull, Very dull], with IQs of 125 or higher."[27] In a very real sense, at the end of the twentieth century, IQ plays for Herrnstein and Murray the very same pseudo-scientific role that the since long-discredited brain weight did for Carroll at the close of the nineteenth century, namely, providing an anchor for a presumed intelligence gap between blacks and whites. And so, the sort of racial stratification grounded in the putative inequality of the races that one observes in de Gobineau and Carroll, also can be found in Herrnstein and Murray, who decry antidiscrimination laws that sunder what they deem to be the proper relation between cognitive ability and societal role.

The societal costs of cognitive deficit are profound, the quadrumvirate believe. De Gobineau informs us that "[m]ankind is . . . divided into *unlike* and *unequal* parts, or rather into a series of categories, arranged, one above the other, according to differences of intellect. . . . [Moreover], all civilizations derive from the white race, [and] none can exist without its help, . . . [given the] immense superiority of the white peoples in the whole field of intellect, . . . and a society is great and brilliant only [in] so far as it preserves the blood of the noble group that created it, provided that this group itself belongs to the most illustrious [white] branch of our species."[28] It is de Gobineau's belief that civilizations have been degraded by the loss of white dominance through what he calls "the mixture of blood."[29] (We know today that, strictly speaking, blood does not mix.) He notes that "[t]he small have been raised [through the mixture of blood]. Unfortunately, the great have been lowered by the same process; and this is an evil that nothing can balance or repair. . . . [W]hen . . . mediocre men are once created at the expense of the greater, they combine with other mediocrities, and from such unions, which grow ever more and more degraded, is born a confusion which, like that of Babel, ends in utter impotence, and leads societies down to the abyss of nothingness whence no power on earth can rescue them."[30]

Sharing de Gobineau's sentiments, Carroll writes:

> [m]ixed-bloods are "an unnatural production," and being altogether "out of the common order of nature," they are simply monstrosities, no odds what their social, political, or religious standing may be. Even the atheist, who denies the existence of God and the inspiration of the scriptures, will insist that an amalgamation between Whites and Negroes is "a violation of natural law". . . . [Accordingly], so long as we [whites] allow the negro and his amalgamated progeny imposed upon us as "lower races of men," with who we may associate on terms of social, political, and religious equality, just so long will we labor under the curses of God, just so long will these degraded creatures have political domination over us, just so long will the youth and the manhood of the land be debauched by amalgamation, just so long will the chastity of our wives and the virginity of our daughters be subjected to their brutal assaults.[31]

De Gobineau's and Carroll's sentiments find expression in Herrnstein and Murray's theme of dysgenics. They write: "Mounting evidence indicates that demographic trends are exerting downward pressures on the distribution of cognitive ability in the United States and that the pressures are strong enough to have social consequences. . . . In trying to foresee changes in American life, what matters is *how* the distribution of intelligence is changing, more than *why*."[32] In response to their own question, "Can we find evidence that dysgenesis is actually happening?" (after citing a range of data) they observe: "[T]he case is strong that something worth worrying about is happening to the cognitive capital of the country. . . . The social phenomena that have been so worrisome for the past few decades may in some degree already reflect an ongoing dysgenic effect. It is worth worrying about, and trying to do something about."[33] In this regard, they note, for example, that there is a "kernel of evidence that must . . . be acknowledged . . . [namely,] that Latino and black immigrants are, at least in the short run, putting some downward pressure on the distribution of intelligence."[34]

The dysgenics of Herrnstein and Murray is nothing but a late twentieth century version of de Gobineau's racial degradation from the mixing of blood, and Carroll's "unnatural production" of blacks and whites. They all perceive blacks to be not only an intellectual drag on white society but also corrosive of its civility and civilization. This is especially troublesome, insofar as they all perceive individuals with lower levels of cognitive ability to reproduce quicker and in greater numbers than those with higher levels of cognitive ability. If, as Herrnstein and Murray opine, "[a] smarter population is more likely to be, and more capable of being made into, a civil citizenry;"[35] if blacks were to have the cognitive deficits that have been ascribed to them; and if a highly civil society is most conducive to the persistence of civil order, as well as civilization itself; it follows that a more cognitively gifted—less black— society ought to be a goal of sound public policy in the United States. Thus, for example, public policy should be designed to discourage cognitively deficient blacks from procreating as quickly, and in the numbers, that they do. The objective necessity for this sort of public policy has been shrouded by "[t]he ideology of equality,"[36] which now guides the behavior of policymakers in the United States, Herrnstein and Murray believe.

Like de Gobineau and Carroll before them, Herrnstein and Murray believe in inequality as an organizing social principle. De Gobineau says explicitly: "I believe . . . that human races are unequal."[37] Carroll states unequivocally: "[I]t was man's social equality with the negro which brought sin into the world; and it is man's social equality with the negro and the evils which inevitably grows out of it that keeps sin in the world."[38] Herrnstein and Murray are not as blunt as either de Gobineau or Carroll.

With more racial circumspection, but with the same rancid effect, they posit: "Cognitive partitioning [of the society, which has been ongoing] will continue. It cannot be stopped, because the forces [especially the natural ones, to wit, genetic differences] driving it cannot be stopped."[39] There is an iron determinism here. The continued cognitive partitioning of the society is inevitable, for "[i]nequality of endowments, including intelligence, is a reality. [Moreover, t]rying to pretend that inequality does not really exist has led to disaster. Trying to eradicate inequality with artificially manufactured outcomes has led to disaster. *It is time for America once again to try living with inequality, as life is lived.*"[40]

Given the intelligence gap between blacks and whites that Murray and Herrnstein claim to exist; given what they deem to be the inevitable partitioning of the society along the cognitive-line; and given the correspondence between the *cognitive-line* and the *color-line*, differential cognitive ability becomes a justification for the racial stratification of the society. Put differently, on grounds of purported racial differences in cognitive ability, the call that America should once again try to live with inequality is nothing but a not too subtle admonition to keep black people in their place.

What Herrnstein and Murray either may be ignorant of, or conveniently elected to ignore, is the historical fact that of the approximately eighteen generations of black people in colonial America/the United States since the 1630s—a twenty-year floor is used for generation—each and every one, barring the generation born since the Civil Rights Act of 1968, passed its life under state-imposed inequalities, under-girded by an extremely color-conscious culture. For black people, then, there is absolutely nothing to be desired, or is desirable, about America trying once again to live with inequality.

But there is an equally compelling point to be made here. Herrnstein and Murray are at war with the very foundations of the American republic. Though Taney was correct in observing that neither the framers of the Declaration of Independence nor the Constitution envisaged a state of equality between blacks and whites, it is nonetheless the case that the United States committed itself to principles of equality, and *not* inequality. The Republic did live with inequality, but always within the framework of principles of equality. There was, then, a persistent contradiction between the egalitarian principles of the Republic and its inegalitarian practices, especially in relation to black people. Since the mid-1960s, the United States has strived hard to conform egalitarian principles with egalitarian behaviors.

In admonishing America to try living with inequality again, Herrnstein and Murray would have the Republic undercut its efforts to harmonize its principles and its practices. Indeed, one may well say that they would organize it around principles of inequality, which would be transformative of its original conception. In this regard, Herrnstein and Murray are radicals at war with the ideals of the United States. Their racial agenda are commensurate with the practices of the society in a bygone era, but incommensurate with its ideals.

Herrnstein and Murray claim that it is fitting and proper that individuals should be able to lead lives of dignity. However, it is not the business of the government to formulate and implement policies designed to give people dignity, rather, it is to make the leading of lives with dignity "accessible to all."[41] Such accessibility, though, will ever be delimited by differences in cognitive ability, for example, that which obtains between blacks and whites. Here, then, is the hard edge of the racial politics of Herrnstein and Murray. Presumed natural differences in cognitive ability ground the racial partitioning of American society, and legitimizes the under-representation of black people in all spheres of social life that are cognitively demanding. Since such underrepresentation is supposedly fair and just, it is assumed to be right and proper that the weight of crucial governmental institutions be brought to bear in the defense of inequality. And so, the pseudoscience of Herrnstein and Murray, like that of de Gobineau and Carroll before them, undergirds a politics of perpetual-black-social marginalization.

## III

In conclusion, it is well to make the following points. First, *The Bell Curve* is simply a late-twentieth-century version of the well-worn theme of the racial inferiority of black people. Second, unmasked of its academic regalia, *The Bell Curve* bears a striking family resemblance to the discursive diatribe of *The Inequality of the Races* and *"The Negro a Beast;" or "In the Image of God."* Third, Herrnstein and Murray room comfortably in the racialist tradition of Jefferson, Taney, Lincoln, and Brown.

Finally, and most important, *The Bell Curve* is a gauntlet thrown down before black people at the end of the twentieth century. It is an attack manifesto. The challenge to black people in general, and to black politics in particular—with the assistance of those whose sense of proportion is not skewed, distorted and distracted—is to continue, resolutely and with unflinching courage, the articulation and implementation of measures designed to make ever the more commensurate the egalitarian principles and practices of the Republic.

## Notes

* Portions of this section will appear in a forthcoming issue of the *Journal of Black Studies*.

1. Winthrop D. Jordan, *The White Man's Burden* (New York: Oxford University Press, 1974), p. 4.

2. Ibid.

3. Ibid.

4. Ibid., p. 6.

5. Ibid.

6. *Dred Scott v. Sandford*, 60 U.S. (19 How.) 393 (1857), in Derrick A. Bell, *Civil Rights: Leading Cases* (Boston and Toronto: Little, Brown and Company, 1980), p. 6. Author's italics.

7. See "Ottawa: Lincoln's Reply," in Paul M. Angle, ed., *The Complete Lincoln-Douglas Debates of 1858* (Chicago & London: The University of Chicago Press, 1991), p. 117. Author's italics.

8. See "Charleston: Lincoln's Opening Speech," ibid., p. 235.

9. See "Address on Colonization to a Committee of Colored Men, Washington, D.C.," in *Abraham Lincoln: Speeches and Writings 1859–1865* (New York: The Library of America, 1989), pp. 353–54. Author's italics.

10. Thomas Jefferson, *Notes on the State of Virginia*, William Pede, ed. (Chapel Hill: The University of North Carolina Press, 1954), p. 139.

11. *Plessy v. Ferguson*, 163 U.S. 537 (1896), in Bell, op. cit. note 6, p. 71.

12. Ibid.

13. Count Arthur de Gobineau, *The Inequality of the Races* (Los Angeles: The Noontide Press, 1966), pp. 155, 179.

14. Charles Carroll, *"The Negro a Beast;" or, "In the Image of God"* (St. Louis, MO: American Book and Bible House, 1900), p. 99.

15. Richard J. Herrnstein and Charles Murray, *The Bell Curve: Intelligence and Class Structure in American Life* (New York: The Free Press, 1994), p. 276.

16. De Gobineau, op. cit. note 13, p. 205.

17. Carroll, op. cit. note 14, p. 109.

18. Ibid., pp. 87, 90.

19. Herrnstein and Murray, op. cit. note 15, p. 302.

20. Ibid., p. 312. Author's italic.

21. De Gobineau, op. cit. note 13, p. 73.

22. Carroll, op. cit. note 14, pp. 101–2.

23. Herrnstein and Murray, op. cit. note 15, p. 492.

24. Ibid., p. 502.

25. Ibid., pp. 488–89.

26. Ibid., p. 501.

27. Ibid., p. 278.

28. De Gobineau, op. cit. note 13, pp. 181, 210, 207, 210. Author's italics.

29. Ibid., p. 209.

30. Ibid., pp. 209–10.

31. Carroll, op. cit. note 14, pp. 116, 291.

32. Herrnstein and Murray, op. cit. note 15, p. 342.

33. Ibid., pp. 345, 364–65.

34. Ibid., pp. 360–61.

35. Ibid., p. 266.

36. Ibid., p. 533.

37. De Gobineau, op. cit. note 13, p. 73.

38. Carroll, op. cit. note 14, p. 219.

39. Herrnstein and Murray, op. cit. note 15, p. 551.

40. Ibid. Author's italics.

41. Ibid.

# 3

# Race in History

MARTIN BERNAL

At the outset, I should like to make it clear that following nearly all physical anthropologists, I do not believe that "race" is a useful biological concept. In the first place, the genetic make up of all humans is quite exceptionally similar. There are fewer genetic differences among us than there are, for instance, within the far smaller population of gorillas. Second, human populations do not vary sharply or neatly but with gradations. These are sometimes steep but more often they are gradual and inconsistent. Nevertheless, race, based arbitrarily and very loosely on physical appearance, is enormously important today as a social construct. As I hope to make clear, this has not always been the case, but we live in an age and society in which race has become obsessional and has pervaded every nook and cranny of our social life and culture.

When considering the title, "Race in History," I have found it useful to distinguish between "race" in history and "race" in historiography. By historiography, I mean the thinking about and writing of history. The historical and historiographical aspects are, of course, intertwined. Writing about places and periods in which the concept of race has been important is bound to influence one's historical writings about them. From the other side, racist and ethnic histories have themselves been major factors in the emergence of racism and ethnocentrism as social or political forces. Still, I believe that the distinction between the history and the historiography of race is worth making, if only because attitudes that we should now recognize as racially prejudiced or ethnocentric have existed for more than two thousand years, and full blown racism has existed since the seventeenth century; while systematic racist historiography only emerged some 180 years ago in the early nineteenth century.

I shall begin with the concept of race in history but before I do so, I should like to try to distinguish ethnicity from racism. The word *ethnicity* is commonly used to denote the consciousness of solidarity beyond real or fictitious kinship, based on shared symbols or images (a particular territory, history, religion, flag, currency, law, etc.), but above all, it can come from a shared language. In a wonderful book entitled *Imagined Communities*, my colleague at Cornell, Benedict Anderson, maintains that this kind of nationalism is a positive force inspired by love and is completely unlike the evil racism.[1]

I cannot accept this sharp distinction. There is no doubt that nationalism has many attractive features. It can inspire great and moving heroism as well as magnificent artistic achievements. Above all it can provide purpose and dignity to lives that are often desolate in every other respect. However, I do not believe that people can celebrate their own nationality without in some way deprecating those who do not "belong" to it. As we can see only too well today, nationalism—sometimes combined with racism, but often without the slightest indication of physical difference—is leading to the committing of frightful atrocities.

One of the shared images or symbols of ethnocentricity is frequently the ideal national physical type, which can easily lead to racism. Yet, nationalism, unlike racism, has the possibility of open-endedness. That is to say, in certain societies, if someone lives in a territory, knows its culture, and speaks its language fluently he— or more likely she—can be accepted as one of the community regardless of physical appearance. This appears to have been the case in ancient Egypt, among the Iroquois, other North American nations, and—with limitations—in the Arab world. Until recently, it was largely true even in France. This lack of overlap between ethnicity and physiology has usually been the result of the "national" culture being shared by peoples of varied physical appearance. In theory this should provide some hope for the United States. Unfortunately, though, racist nationalism is not so flexible. Someone who differs substantially from the Northern European physical ideal type is not, and can never be, fully accepted in German, British, or North American societies as they are presently constituted.

In many cultures, people who vary greatly from the somatic or physical norm are treated differently, some are especially respected, but more often they are treated with corrosive scorn. Despite the biological imprecision, this can usefully be called racial prejudice. But "racism" of the sort that is experienced today is a modern phenomenon, until quite recently restricted to peoples of European descent. It clearly has its origins in the European need to justify their inhuman behavior in the genocide, colonialism, and slavery inflicted upon peoples of other continents by dehumanizing them and turning their victims into devils or animals.

As most populations vary a great deal in height and body build, the two features that are picked out most frequently to define a race are facial features and skin, hair and eye color. According to the social psychologist Kenneth Gergen, and Carl Degler, an historian, the contrast between black (evil) and white (good) is a human universal, because all peoples prefer day to night, milk to dirt, and so forth. They go even further to claim as universal the application of this abstract color scheme to what the author, E. M. Forster, described as the "pinko-grey" skin color of Northern Europeans and the shades of brown of other peoples.[2]

The structural anthropologist Edmund Leach pointed out that although color codes and opposition between colors are important in all societies, they do not necessarily have the values white equals good, black equals bad. For instance, in East Asia and many other cultures, including Europe before the late Middle Ages, white or paleness—the color of corpses—symbolizes death, and the darkness, gained from exposure to the sun, virility.[3]

St. Clair Drake, the great anthropologist and historian, attacked the ideas associated with Gergen and Degler both on these grounds and by using historical counter-examples. He showed that there have been major societies in which there has been no social or religious hierarchy associated with color or physiognomy.[4] The most significant of these was ancient Egypt. We have considerable knowledge of this society, beginning with the unification of the country by the First Dynasty around 3,400 BCE, and there is no trace of any racial preference, let alone prejudice in it for the next 2,900 years.

The population of Ancient Egypt was extremely mixed. Nubia and Upper Egypt where Pharaonic civilization was formed, had a basic population very similar to that of the modern Nubians, that is to say East African with Central African admixture. Lower Egypt had a basic population of North African "Caucasoids." However, after the fifth millennium BCE this was differentiated from that of north-west Africa or the Maghreb, because while the latter was separated from the rest of Africa by the growing Sahara, the Nile continued to link Lower Egypt to the rest of the continent. The mixture of populations between Upper and Lower Egypt accelerated with the establishment of a single Egyptian state.

After unification, the population of the Lower Nile Valley became extremely heterogeneous. This was not only because Southerners moved down the Nile and Northerners moved up, but also because of immigration into Egypt from Nubia and even more from southwest Asia. The latter process intensified after the fall of Pharaonic civilization and the rise of Islam in Arabia; thus the Egyptian population of today is almost certainly lighter and more "Caucasoid" than it was 2,000 years ago.[5] Nonetheless, the old pattern survives to the present in that the further up the Nile one travels, the darker and more "Negroid" the population becomes.

Ancient Egypt was extremely ethnocentric. For Egyptians of that time, speaking Egyptian and worshipping the Gods of Egypt were of critical importance. What is more, Egyptian artists tried to convey "Egyptianness" by representing a more or less homogenized population of red-brown men and yellow-white women. They played down the huge variety of physical types actually present, as indicated by mummies and other physical remains. The artists did this so that Egyptians should not be confused with southwest Asians, who were stereotyped as pale, and Nubians, who were generally portrayed as black with broad noses and tight curly hair.

As elsewhere, there was a strong symbolic color code in Egypt. Red was the color of the desert and death, while black was that of fertility, life, and rebirth. Egypt itself was known as Kemet, the Black Country. There is no doubt that at least in part, this referred to the black soil of the Nile Valley. On the other hand, written with the determinative or symbol for people, the word Kemet also meant "Egyptians" literally "black people." Nonetheless, there is no sign of preference for black skin and or Negro appearance. There is absolutely no indication that any hierarchical social value was placed on skin color or facial features. Egyptian Pharaohs and slaves alike could be black, brown, or olive with Negro, East African, or Mediterranean features.

This also seems to have been the case in early southwest Asia, which I shall examine from the regional culture which we know best, that of Israel. It is clear that there were people of African appearance in Ancient Israel. The name Pinchas comes from the Egyptian P3 Nhs "The Nubian" and Sim(e)on may well come from Sm3w "Upper Egyptian."[6] This does not necessarily mean that the individuals so named were themselves black; but the names do indicate *both*, that there had been people of this type in Israel *and* that they differed from the southwest Asian norm.

In the Old Testament, the predominant color of sin is scarlet—the color of blood and sex—a tradition preserved today in the color of the devil. And there is no doubt that black had unfortunate associations in ancient Israel. It was used to portray psychological as well as natural gloom. But black also had positive connotations. It could represent night as a relief from the heat of the day and the color of the clouds that brought the precious rain. The beautiful and erotic lover in the *Song of Songs* is called in both the Hebrew and Greek texts as "black *and* beautiful."[7] White also had both negative and positive connotations. It was sometimes the color of purity; but it was also the color of leprosy. In the labelling of people, the ambivalence was made still more acute by the uncertainties involved in transposing the abstract color to human complexions.

Ancient Greece too had conflicting color codes. There was certainly no pre-judice against men who had dark brown or black skin. Memnon, "the most beautiful," noble and brave Ethiopian prince who marched to Troy's rescue and died there heroically was known by the earliest Greek poets whose works survive, Hesiod and Homer, who lived in the tenth or ninth centuries BCE.[8] There is some confusion as to whether Memnon was an Asian "Ethiopian" or an African one.[9] But "Aithiops" meant "black," and there is no doubt about his pigmentation.

Memnon was not the only Ethiopian to play a prominent and positive role in the Homeric epics. In the first book of the *Iliad*, Zeus goes with the other Gods to feast with "the blameless Ethiopians."[10] The *Odyssey* opens with Poseidon visiting them.[11] Thus, for Homer and presumably other Greeks of his time, the Ethiopians were seen as a particularly virtuous people with especially close associations with the Gods. Homer also saw Africans in Greece. For example, Odysseus' herald Eurybates, who accompanied him on important missions, was described as having "black skin and woolly hair."[12]

There was a lord called *Aigyptios* on Odysseus' island, Ithaca. This name and others suggesting African origins also have been found in Bronze Age texts from

Greece before 1200 BCE. As in Israel, such evidence indicates both that Egyptians and other Africans were present in Greece, and that they were unusual there. There was also an ambiguity about Greek color codes. There is no doubt that at least as far back as Homer, blackness was associated with night and death, as well as with the terrors that these inspire. Yet, black also had positive aspects in early Greece. It was seen as the color of bravery and manliness, while white was that of effeminacy and lily-livered cowardice.

Asian and European attitudes towards Africans and skin color appear to have begun to change around 500 BCE. The favorable impression of Egyptians and Ethiopians did not disappear immediately. Herodotus, the earliest Greek historian whose work is extant, wrote in the fifth century BCE that the Ethiopians (by which he meant the Nubians of the Upper Nile) were "said to be the tallest and best-looking people in the world."[13] By this time though, a prejudice against both darkness of skin and "negroid" physiognomy was growing around the Mediterranean world and a clear association of blackness with evil began to be established in Greece.[14] A similar shift took place in the Hebrew tradition. By the time of the New Testament, black had become the color and complexion of evil and white that of purity and goodness.[15] The shift is symbolized by the fact that in the Latin Vulgate translation of the *Song of Songs* the description of the heroine is changed to "black *but* beautiful." It was also around this time that the long and sickening tradition began in which people with dark skins were patronized by others or excused themselves with the argument that their souls were white.

The biblical story of Noah's punishment of his son Ham, by a curse on Ham's son Canaan, had originally been used to justify the Israelites' extermination and enslavement of the Canaanites. In both Jewish and Christian biblical interpretations, written in the new atmosphere around the beginning of the Common Era, the curse was transferred to Ham himself, the African, and was believed to have taken the form of "ugly" blackness and perpetual slavery.[16]

What had caused this change of attitude? The standard explanation is that it was the first encounter between Mediterranean peoples and black Africans. This does not work, because of the evidence of substantial contact between the two groups during the Bronze Age and the period up to 500 BCE. There are two other explanations for diminution of the positive connotations of blackness and the exaggeration of the negative ones around this time. The first, which only applies to Greeks, is that when they began to dominate darker peoples in southwest Asia and Egypt during these centuries they found complexion a useful marker for themselves and justification of their rule. The second explanation is influence from Persia.

During the second millennium BCE Indo-European speaking invaders, calling themselves "Arya" or Aryans, invaded the older civilizations of Elam (in what is now Iran) and the Indus Valley from the north. The "Aryans" were generally lighter in color than the natives, who seem to have resembled the South Indians of today. During these struggles, a cult of lightness, associated with the sun and the sky grew up. The Hindu *Vedas* or scriptures contain violent images of the destruction of natives described as "darker" and were clear-cut in their preference for the invaders own lighter skins, though black has continued to be valued in some respects in Indian culture.[17] Although the linkage between caste and skin color is now loose, the Sanskrit word for "caste" Varṇa means "color" and in the Hindu symbolic color scheme the higher castes are associated with lighter colors.[18]

In Iran, these struggles between the lighter invaders and the more civilized natives were integrated into the Zoroastrian religion. This, like its later branch Manichaeism, sees the whole universe as a finely balanced and perpetual conflict between the forces of good and evil seen as those of light and darkness, which can be transposed to skin color.

In the sixth century BCE, Persia erupted into the Mediterranean, conquering the Levant and Egypt, as well as many of the Greek city states. In Egypt, the emphasis on the value and moral superiority of lightness was useful both to the Persian conquerors and to Greeks, who played an increasingly important role there even before the conquest by Alexander the Great and the establishment of the Macedonian or Greek Ptolemaic Dynasty there around 300 BCE. This preference for the invaders and paler Lower Egyptians introduced a new sense of "race" to Egypt. Resistance to the Persians and later to the Greeks involved a cultural "return" among Egyptians to African blackness—to the art of the great southern dynasties in Upper Egypt, and to an image of a dark Nubia as a source and refuge for true Egyptian culture.[19]

These new "racial" attitudes also spread into Greece itself. I must insist, though, that the prejudice against people of evident African descent which grew up at this time, was qualitatively different from the "caste racism" found in the modern world.

The presence of many Africans in classical antiquity is indicated by the large numbers of blacks represented in Greek and Roman art.[20] We know that some were slaves, although most slaves of the period were of Mediterranean or northern European origin. Some Africans were important free craftsmen. For instance, the best known and most admired potter in fifth century Athens, had the Egyptian name of Amasis and was portrayed by a rival as a black African.[21] Blacks also were admired and feared as warriors. The bulk of Hannibal's Carthaginian army, that crossed the Alps and invaded Italy, was African and some were "Negroid." The coin struck to pay the troops and symbolizing his army, had a Negro head on one side and an elephant on the other.[22]

This leads us to consider Greek and Roman relations with Africa beyond Egypt. The name "Africa" probably comes from the Afar people, who lived and live at the southern end of the Red Sea. In Roman times, however, "Africa" was used as a euphemism for the hated Carthage, for the territory we now call Tunisia. Some of these northern "Africans" played significant parts in Roman history. The early Roman playwright Terence (190–159 BCE), who played a central role in the formation of Latin drama from imperial times to the Middle Ages, was surnamed Afer and was born in North Africa. The Severans, the Roman imperial dynasty, who ruled the empire from 193 to 235 CE, were originally Punic or Phoenician in culture and came from the coast of what is now Libya. A number of the most important Christian church fathers came from northwest Africa, the most important of whom was St. Augustine of Hippo (354–430 CE), the chief founder of the theology and philosophy of the Roman Catholic Church.

For the Romans and Greeks, there were three types of blacks. First, there were those who lived within the empire, who were generally, though not always in the lower classes. Then there were the admired civilized and philosophical "Ethiopians," who were usually located in the Nubian state of Meroë near the modern Khartoum. The name "Ethiopia" maintained this high status into the modern period. There was also a third type of black, the fierce nomadic "Ethiopians" of the desert from Egypt to the Atlantic, who resisted Roman attacks and raided cities within the empire. From these and from black forces in the Roman legions, Africans had a reputation for soldierly qualities. In Christian times, the patron saint of soldiers became St. Maurice, a soldier from Upper Egypt of the third century CE, who was always portrayed as a "negro."[23]

Ptolemy, the mathematician and astronomer of the second century CE, was also an Upper Egyptian, and known to Arab writers as a black.[24] Thus, despite the widespread fear and suspicion of blacks among Western Europeans of the Middle Ages, the dominant figures or authorities in their theology, warfare and science, namely, St. Augustine, St. Maurice, and Ptolemy were Africans, and the last two were generally held to be blacks.

Some scholars today argue that there has always been a particular Christian affinity for tolerance.[25] This is clearly untenable. Believers in revealed religions find it hard to tolerate what for them is error and sin. The Western liberal tradition of religious tolerance did not arise from Christianity. Its origins are firmly linked to upper-class skeptics and deists of the seventeenth and eighteenth centuries, who saw tolerance and the separation of church and state as a way to avoid religious upheavals and preserve social order.

There is no doubt that in its early heyday from 650 to 1100 CE, Islam was far more religiously tolerant than Christianity. This was partly the result of historical chance, Islamic armies conquered Christian countries, not vice versa. Thus, while Christian communities have always existed under Islamic rule, no Muslims were tolerated in European Christian countries until the late nineteenth century. The contrast can be seen in the tolerance and sensitivity towards other religious communities shown when the Caliph Omar and the Kurdish ruler Saladin took Jerusalem in 638 and 1187 CE respectively, as opposed to the massacres of Muslims and Jews that followed the Crusaders' conquest of the city in 1099 CE.

This is not to say that Islam is inherently more tolerant on religious issues than Christianity. One can readily observe tragic counter examples today in the Sudanese treatment of the non-Islamic South, the Muslim Indonesian massacres of Christian Timorese, and the *fatwa* against Salman Rushdie. The correlation with tolerance appears to be with having confidence in the success of one's faith. Thus, Muslims on the defensive today, can behave almost as badly as Christians did when Islam tore the heart out of Christendom in the seventh century. I insist, however, that success and confidence are only necessary and not sufficient conditions for religious or other toleration.

By contrast, there is no doubt that, Islamic attitudes on race have been better than those of Christianity. The basic reason for this is the insistence that all men are equal in the face of Allah, and that the critical divisions among people are not those of physical appearance, but ones of gender and religion, men/women, Muslim/non-Muslim, Peoples of the Book/nonbelievers.

Still, in spite of the Prophet's special relationship with Ethiopia, Islam was affected by the earlier developments of color prejudice in South West Asia, to which attention has been directed already. What is more, stereotypes of and prejudices against Africans were intensified by the increase of slavery in Mesopotamia from Africa under the Muslim caliphs. But slavery was not restricted to Africans, there were also white slaves from the Caucasus and Europe, though they were less discriminated against than the blacks.[26]

In the Christian world, there persists a tension between the official view of black as the color of evil and the folk belief found earlier in Egypt, of black as the color of life and fertility. This tension is illustrated by the conflicts between peasants in most Catholic countries with a passionate attachment to Black Madonnas and the church authorities who constantly want to destroy or whiten them.[27]

Blacks were to become associated with the hated Muslims, and the images of St. Maurice and the Christian Nubians, who aided the Crusaders, would be overshadowed by those of the Berber and black Almoravids from Senegal, who massively defeated Spanish Christian kings and Crusaders in the twelfth century. In modern Greek and Russian, the words for "negro" are Arapes and Arap, and the association between black and Muslim can still be seen in England today, where the pubs named "The Turk's Head" have as their sign the head of a stereotypical West African.

## Modern Racism

Racism of the modern type only began in the fifteenth century, when Portuguese ships started to outflank Islamic power by sailing round the coast of West Africa and immediately began kidnapping anybody they could find and taking them back to Portugal to sell as slaves. Their justification for this was that those who were taken were prisoners of a just war, and any war fought by Christians against non-Christians qualified as a just war. Quite soon however, a new justification grew up, that of racism. Africans were claimed to be "slavish by nature." The new concept was powerfully reinforced by developments in America.

By the end of the fifteenth century, Europeans were in Central and North America, where within a century—aided by disease—they succeeded in obliterating

90 percent of the population. To begin with, they attempted to enslave native Americans, but this was quickly found to be far less profitable than importing Africans. This is commonly explained in racial terms, that Africans were physiologically suited to hot climates and psychologically suited to slavery, where the primitive Americans could only resist or die. There is no doubt that during periods of intense genocide some native American societies simply gave up. But many African slaves also committed suicide.

There is a much simpler nonbiological explanation for the successful exploitation of African slaves in America. If slaves could run home they would, and the cost of preventing this could easily become prohibitive. Thus, chattel slavery was usually only economically possible on an extensive scale where the slave owners controlled the sea passage. In this case, slaves had only four unpleasant choices: (1) run to hostile natives whose language(s) they did not understand; (2) rebel knowing it to be futile; (3) commit suicide; and (4) acquiesce. On islands where there had been genocide, the first option was not available, and it is remarkable how frequently slavery has flourished on islands.

The connection between ancient and early capitalist slavery were the continuing slave plantations on Cyprus. In the fifteenth century, Spanish and Portuguese massacred the populations of the Canaries and Madeira and imported slaves. This can be seen as a rehearsal for slavery in the West Indies. Black slaves were brought there from the beginning, but it was not until the end of the seventeenth century that the enslavement of whites stopped and slavery *as an institution* became identified with Africans.

In the Middle Ages, Christians had seen Islam as both the location and the source of pure evil. This type of *projection* of the ugly and fearful aspects of one's own character and society onto others was now systematically applied by Europeans, calling themselves white, in relation to Africans, whom they labelled as "black." Whites saw blacks as the epitome of evil. Hence, modern racism is particularly vicious because it maintains absolute lines of caste and insists that the worst white is better than the best nonwhite.

It is precisely in the period of the establishment of race-based slavery, in the 1660s, that scholars tried to provide academic rationality for these beliefs and to establish racial schemes dividing humankind into European, African, American, and Asiatic races.[28] It was widely believed that the differences were so extreme that there must have been "polygenesis" or many separate creations. Though extremely attractive to those who wanted to justify slavery, such speculation was handicapped by both Christianity and nature. The new racists tried to enlist religious backing for their ideological requirements. There was an emphasis among Christians in the seventeenth century for the Talmudic interpretation of the story in Genesis mentioned earlier, in which it was Ham, the ancestor of the Africans, and not Ham's son Canaan, who had been cursed by his father Noah and that the curse had consisted of blackness, ugliness, and the fate of perpetual slavery. Yet there was no getting around the biblical insistence that all people were the children of Adam. Thus, suggestions that there had been multiple creations were clearly heretical. Even so, the passionate desire for a categorical distinction between peoples who were of European descent and those who were not led many scholars and others to be drawn to the idea of polygenesis.

Another strategy to dehumanize Africans and other non-Europeans was the scheme of a "great chain of being." According to different versions of this, one could begin with God and His angels going down through white men, to white women, Asiatics, Africans, apes, and so on. This hierarchy blurred the category of "man" which philosophers like John Locke, who was personally involved with American slavery, found extremely inconvenient.[29] The "great chain of being" too was unacceptable to orthodox Christians, because of the categorical distinction between men created in the image of God and with a soul, and all other creatures.

The *natural* difficulty the racists had to face, was that the new taxonomy of animals into species was defined by what could or could not produce fertile offspring. As all humans were only too capable of this, the much less well defined subclassification of "race" had to be employed. This problem came out clearly in the last quarter of the eighteenth century in the work of the German professor, J. F. Blumenbach, who attempted a "scientific" study of human races along the lines set out by the Swedish scholar Carolus Linnaeus in the 1750s for the classification of natural history. Blumenbach did not believe in human progress or polygenesis. He maintained, with complete religious orthodoxy, that there had been a single creation of a perfect man. Blumenbach's explanation for what he perceived as important racial differences followed the Eurocentric pattern set out earlier in the eighteenth century by the French naturalist Comte Georges de Buffon. De Buffon had argued that the *normal* type of species found in Europe had degenerated in other continents because of their unfortunate climatic conditions. Species had become too big, too small, too weak, too strong, too brightly colored too drab, and so forth.

Blumenbach was the first to publicize the term "Caucasian." According to him, the white or Caucasian race was the first and most beautiful and talented race, from which all others had degenerated to become Chinese, Negroes, and so on. He justified the curious name "Caucasian" on "scientific" and "racial" grounds, since he believed the Georgians to be the finest "White Race." However, there was much more to it than that. First, there was the religious belief that people emerged from the Ark, which the Bible tells us landed on Mount Ararat in the Caucasus. There was also a Romantic tendency to see human and European origins, not in river valleys like those of the Nile and Euphrates, but in high and imposing mountains.[30]

There is a wonderful irony in Blumenbach's own life, in that after he had completed what became the academic bible of racism, he fell in love with a black midwife he saw in Switzerland. He then wrote a little book of the biographies of blacks who had succeeded in European society. The most notable of these was the life story of the Ethiopian Abram Hannibal, who became the leading military engineer of Peter the Great of Russia. After Blumenbach's book was completed, Abram Hannibal was immortalized in a biography by his great grandson, the Russian poet Aleksandr Pushkin. Blumenbach's change of heart did not lessen racist reliance on his earlier larger work to provide academic backing for their ideological position.[31]

Although Blumenbach and his retrogressive scheme of decline from the original Caucasian remained central to racist thinking in the nineteenth century, the concept of race was also taken up by progressives. This division overlaps the racial aspects of the conflict between the Enlightenment and Romanticism. The men of the Enlightenment valued stability and permanence. For them, the classification of natural species and human races was part of the project of establishing timeless conceptual order. This fitted well with their general racism, but their racism conflicted with their overall view that reason was accessible to men of all cultures. (I use the word "men" deliberately because they tended to be extremely sexist.)

The Romantics opposed the Enlightenment and insisted that reason was inadequate. They believed that what really mattered was feeling. Thus, the conflict between racism and the enlightened belief that "all mankind are brothers plighted" did not exist for consistent Romantics. They saw nations and races as communities bound together by emotions and feelings, which by definition could not be shared with others.

Where the Enlightened were concerned with space, Romantics were obsessed by time. The passage of time could be seen as a decline or as progress, and both views appear in Romantic racism. Thus, in the nineteenth century there were what one could call optimistic and pessimistic racists. As an example of the "optimistic racists," I raise Robert Knox.

Knox was an anatomist at the University of Edinburgh in the 1820s. He became notorious as the patron of the grave robbers and body snatchers Burke and Hare. When Knox complained that the bodies they delivered were too old and withered, Burke and Hare turned to murder to provide him with fresh ones. Both eventually were caught and hanged. Knox, as a gentleman, was merely obliged by the bad publicity to resign his academic chair. He then went on to become a distinguished writer on race. Taking the exterminations of the American and Australian populations to be natural and desirable, he believed that what he saw as the superior white race should complete the job in Africa and Asia. Indeed, he even congratulated his contemporaries for living in an age when it was possible to collect so many fascinating human specimens.[32]

An outstanding example of a pessimistic racist is Knox's younger contemporary, Comte Josephe-Arthur de Gobineau. De Gobineau saw Caucasian man as having originated somewhere in the cold parts of Asia. He then saw three branches, the Hamites, the Semites, and the Indo-Germans having divided very early. According to his idiosyncratic history, the Hamites went south to Palestine and North Africa where they were corrupted by the blacks. De Gobineau claimed religious orthodoxy, but his scheme required that Africans were descendants of a different creation. Sometime later, the Semites followed their brothers, where they too were made impure both by the blacks and the now thoroughly corrupted Hamites. Only the Germanic peoples had stayed in the cold north and had thus preserved their purity. Now they too were in danger of mixture and corruption from the Semites.

For de Gobineau, there was the unbearable paradox that superior races lost to inferior ones in any competition.[33] As with Knox, de Gobineau's racial imagery had clear connotations of gender. The Caucasians and Germans were male and the lesser races somehow female. However, where Knox saw virility—at least when armed with guns—as invincible, de Gobineau believed that the soft seductive black forces could sap the manhood of the poor, pure white males.

The congruence or overlap between the social constructions of race and gender remain centrally important today. It is still widely believed that Europeans and men think more rationally, work harder, and fight more fiercely than Africans and women. The qualities of human warmth, social supportiveness, intuition, artistic creativity, and, above all, a close relationship to, if not control by, their emotions and biology are attributed to Africans and women. This is not only an image seen by men and Europeans; it is often accepted by women and blacks themselves. It may be that there is some biological basis for women's caring. But I am convinced that the fundamental similarities in the attributes come from power and the lack of it. The qualities of blacks and women are those helpful for living a satisfactory life in a position of relative or absolute powerlessness. Moves towards sexual and racial equality reveal that qualities of both types are far more evenly distributed throughout humanity than has been conventionally supposed.

To return to Knox and de Gobineau. These two white men also illustrate another major pair of strands in nineteenth century racism, namely, anatomy and language. Steven Jay Gould has shown brilliantly, in his *The Mismeasure of Man*, how early-nineteenth-century anatomists and physiologists spent an inordinate amount of time and effort trying to provide scientific evidence to back the huge inequalities they knew to exist between races. Gould demonstrates their total debacle.[34] The story would be comic were it not for the powerful social forces motivating them, and the uses that racists made even of their failures.

De Gobineau relied heavily on linguistics, the other prop of racism. His three groups came, of course, from Noah's sons. However, by the 1840s these had become linked to language families. Hamitic was the name used for what we now call the Afroasiatic language family, including: the Cushitic languages of East Africa, Hausa, and other languages in Chad and Northern Nigeria, the Berber language of northwest Africa, and Ancient Egyptian. Semitic is the family including Hebrew, Arabic, Babylonian, South Arabian, and Ethiopian languages. Today this is considered to be a single branch of the Afroasiatic family. The other language family with which de Gobineau was concerned was the recently discovered Indo-European. This includes the languages of northern India, Iran, and nearly all of Europe. De Gobineau accepted the conventional view of the time that the purest Indo-Europeans were first, the speakers the ancient Indian language of Sanskrit, who, sadly, had become corrupted by the dark natives of the subcontinent. Second were the pure Germanic speakers. But de Gobineau, like most of his contemporaries, slipped all too easily from language to physiology, and speakers of the "pure" Indo-European were often seen as the Aryan race.

## Anti-Semitism

Blumenbach had classified Jews, Arabs, and other speakers of Semitic languages as "Caucasians." Moreover, a number of mid-nineteenth-century thinkers, denying the massive evidence of African, East Asian, and American civilization, saw the Semites and the Aryans as the joint creators of all human culture. The Semites had contributed monotheistic religion and a noble simple poetry, while the Aryans had given the world politics, the arts, science, philosophy, and heroism. All the time, though, there was the feeling that this was granting too much to the Semites; thus great efforts were made to build up alleged Persian and Greek influences on Judaism and Christianity.

Religious hatred of and intolerance towards Jews is almost as old as Christianity. In general, however, the converted Jew was accepted as a Christian. Still, in fourteenth- and fifteenth-century Spain the mass conversion of large numbers of Jews, many of whom were rich, talented and influential, led to a violent hostility by those of Christian ancestry against the so-called "New Christians." They were suspected—sometimes rightly—of carrying on Jewish rites in secret; but beyond that, there grew up the notion of Jewish "blood" which was seen to be polluting Spain.[35]

This idea remained a minor strand in European thought until the intellectual triumph of racism that came with the dominance of Romanticism in the nineteenth century. By 1870, the idea of a Semitic race was generally accepted. This was seen to include not merely the distinctively dressed Orthodox Jews of, or from, Eastern Europe, but also the assimilated Jews *and* those who had converted to Christianity or had become completely secularized. Believers in European purity saw the latter as particularly evil and threatening precisely because they were invisible. Thus, by the 1890s, racial anti-Semitism had become a major cultural and political force not merely in Eastern and Central Europe, but also in Western Europe and America.

Fears of assimilated and converted Jews were intensified by the fact that some of them were extremely successful in business, particularly banking, and as intellectuals. In fact, their position *in but not of* nineteenth- and twentieth-century Europe gave them a marginality that allowed them a radical stance, and provided fruitful insights not so easily available to other Europeans. Two obvious examples of this are Sigmund Freud and Albert Einstein. Politically, by far the most important is Karl Marx. There is no doubt that the paroxysm of anti-Semitism in the 1920s and 1930s came from a horrified reaction to the Russian Revolution of October 1917. Its leaders claimed to have been inspired by Marx and many of them, including Leon Trotsky, were Jewish. And so, most rightwingers saw communism as a Jewish conspiracy against the European order that had been widely believed to exist since the 1880s.

There was another source of anti-Semitism that became particularly attractive in Germany during the hyperinflation of the 1920s, and throughout Europe and America in the Depression of the 1930s. This was the belief that a Jewish conspiracy controlled the financial world, and that it had caused these economic catastrophes to destroy the "pure" Europeans whom they so hated. Thus, the "National Socialist" ideology of the Nazis could be against both Jewish capitalists, who were supposedly responsible for their unemployment and hunger, as well as Jew-Communists who were putatively trying to subvert the Aryan order.

It was in this atmosphere that the ultimate absurdity of racism was achieved, the intellectual construction of a "race" that was physiologically and phenotypically indistinguishable from the surrounding population. This construction was able to strip some Europeans of their Europeanness. Previously, Jews had been victims of massacres and pogroms, but something qualitatively different now took place. In the Holocaust, Jews were treated in a way that Europeans had previously reserved for non-Europeans: the Spanish and English genocides in the Americas, the British genocide in Australia, the German genocide of the Herero in Namibia, and the Belgian genocide in the Congo.

Since the end of the Second World War, while anti-Semitism is far from dead, there has been a general reclassification of Jews as Europeans, which has been accelerated by the role and style of Israel as a bastion of European civilization in the so-called Third World.

## Historiography

I should now like to focus attention on the role of racism in historiography. In the 1760s a new movement began among some German historians to leave the listings of kings and battles to look at social history, and the stories or biographies of nations or races—their birth, rise, and decline. This approach, which was the result of Romantic concerns with the community, or *Volk*, was intensified and altered by contemporary historical events.

In the 1780s, just before the first French Revolution, some French aristocrats, finding their extreme privileges difficult to defend in the rational atmosphere of the Enlightenment, were driven to the extraordinary expedient of trying to justify them on grounds of the right of conquest. They maintained that they were the descendants of the Germanic Franks, who had conquered the territory now called France some 1,300 hundred years earlier. The tactic proved disastrous for the French aristocrats, especially when it was combined with their flight to Germany. The revolutionaries were able to rally the population by calling themselves the true patriots who wanted to drive out the German invaders. Ethnicity also became central to the wars fought in Russia, Germany, and Spain against the occupying Napoleonic armies. In each case, resistance based its popular appeal on Romantic nationalism. Thus, both the revolution and the reactionary wars against it, which traumatized those who lived through them, were seen by many as national or racial conflicts, and this had an impact on all historiography.

In early nineteenth-century Germany and England, the historical myth concocted by the French aristocrats took on new life, and a new Germanic ideology grew up. According to this, the Germans, through their tribes, the Anglo-Saxons in Britain, the Franks in France, the Visigoths in Spain, and the Lombards in Italy, were the true aristocrats of all Europe. They were seen as responsible for all the military and cultural achievements of Europe. The view that social classes originated from races was taken up by the man who is still generally considered to be the founder of modern "critical" historiography of the ancient world, the German historian Barthold Niebuhr. Niebuhr argued, for instance, that the Roman patricians had come from farther north in Germany than the plebeians.

In the new world of systematic racism, such ideas were quickly taken up by other historians such as Jules Michelet in France, and Niebuhr's translator into English, Thomas Arnold, the famous Dr. Arnold of Rugby in *Tom Brown's School-days*.[36] For them and their pupils, race and ethnicity became the exciting new principles of historiography that previous historians had missed. They saw racial competition and conflict as the motor of historical progress. This notion had a crucial impact on both of the major theoretical developments of the nineteenth century. Charles Darwin extended racial conflict to what he saw as the struggle between species in natural history, and Karl Marx removed the alleged racial origin of social classes to posit class conflict itself as the engine of human history.

The idea that history should consist of the "biographies" of superior races flourished throughout the nineteenth century. It has survived even longer among the wider public, instantiated in the immense popularity of Winston Churchill's *A History of the English-Speaking Peoples*.

The wider concern with ethnicity and alleged purity of race, especially that of Europeans, was still present in modern historiography in the denial of extra-European influences on Europe or its development. Historians have consistently underplayed the importance of such outside inventions as Arabic numerals, optics, perspective, the compass, gun powder, paper, printing, sugar, pasta, the potato, and maize. Their foreign origins are conceded singly. Moreover, their cumulative impact, not merely on the European material progress, but also on the crucial concept of progress itself, tends to be neglected or denied altogether.

A particularly crude form of history glorifying Europe, and by implication the "white" race, was promoted under the Reagan and Bush administrations of the 1980s and early 1990s. European history was seen as a succession of glorious moments: Periclean Athens, Renaissance Florence, the seventeenth-century scientific revolution, the French Enlightenment, the German Philosophers, Victorian England, and twentieth-century America. Each of these was seen as having been built upon the others; they were assumed to be purely European phenomena. This splendid sequence was perceived as a sacred shrine of "Western Civilization" to be worshipped, treasured, and defended at any cost.

Moderates have been pushing for a more critical approach and an appreciation of non-European civilizations. Even they, however, tend to balk at the idea that European civilization has always been heavily dependent on other cultures, both materially and intellectually. Interestingly, this is particularly true of the glorious "moments." Ancient Greek language, religion, art, politics, philosophy, and science were all massively influenced by Egypt and Semitic-speaking southwest Asia.[37] The Florentine Renaissance and humanism were heavily indebted to the Ancient Egyptian Hermetic tradition.[38] The scientific revolution depended substantially on Islamic mathematics and astronomy. Hermetic influences, development and application were only possible in a Europe made wealthy by the exploitation of America and other continents.[39] The leaders of the French Enlightenment constantly looked to China for inspiration.[40] The later "moments" took place in European societies in which exploration, conquest, and exploitation of other continents were central to their political, economical, and cultural life.[41]

It is impossible to have a full historical understanding of any culture without taking external influences into account. Yet this is what most historians of Europe have been doing for the past two hundred years. In general, historians should realize that mixture is a far more effective stimulus to innovation than isolation and purity. If one recognizes an equal potential in all human beings, it is not only socially immoral, but also historically mistaken, to treat Europeans as the sole actors on the historical stage, and to privilege Europeans and peoples of European descent above those of the rest of the world.

**Notes**

    1. Benedict Anderson, *Imagined Communities: Reflections on the Origins and Spread of Nationalism* (New York: Verso, 1987).

    2. Kenneth Gergen, "The Significance of Skin Color in Human Relations," *Daedalus* 96.2 (1967): 390–407; Carl Degler, *Neither Black nor White: Slavery and Race Relations in Brazil and the United States* (New York: Macmillan, 1971), p. 211.

    3. Edmund Leach, *Culture and Communication: The Logic by which Symbols are Connected* (Cambridge: Cambridge University Press, 1976), pp. 57–74.

    4. St. Clair Drake, *Black Folk Here and There*. 2 vols. (Los Angeles: Center for Afro-American Studies, 1987–90), Vol. 1, pp. 146–332.

    5. Shomarka Keita, "Studies of Ancient Crania From Northern Africa," *American Journal of Physical Anthropology* 83 (1990): 35–48; "Further Studies of

Crania from Ancient Northern Africa: An Analysis of Crania from First Dynasty Tombs, Using Multiple Discriminant Functions," *American Journal of Physical Anthropology* 87 (1992): 445–54; and "Black Athena: 'Race,' Bernal and Snowden," *Arethusa* 26.3 (Fall 1993): 295–318.

6. For other names, see Frank Snowden, *Blacks in Antiquity* (Cambridge, MA: Harvard University Press, 1970), pp. 16–18.

7. Drake, op. cit. note 4, p. 307.

8. For this dating see Martin Bernal, *Black Athena: The Afroasiatic Roots of Classical Civilization.* Vol. 1: *The Fabrication of Ancient Greece 1785–1985* (New Brunswick: Rutgers University Press, 1987), pp. 86–88.

9. Snowden, op. cit. note 6, pp.151–52 and Bernal, *Black Athena: The Afroasiatic Roots of Classical Civilization.* Vol. II, *The Archaeological and Documentary Evidence* (New Brunswick: Rutgers University Press, 1991), pp. 258–60.

10. Bernal, op. cit. note 8, pp. 423–24.

11. Ibid., pp. 22–24.

12. Iliad, 2.184, 9.170 and Odyssey 19.245; Snowden, op. cit. note 6, p. 102 and Drake, op. cit. note 4, pp. 318–19 accept the plausible argument that Eurybates was black. The latter also shows the contortions made by some white scholars to avoid this unpalatable conclusion.

13. Herodotus 3. 20.

14. Drake, op. cit. note 4, pp. 31–34.

15. Ibid., vol. 2, pp. 4–5.

16. Ibid., pp. 15–23.

17. Ibid., p. 309.

18. Benedict Anderson, "Race and Descent as Social Categories in India," *Daedalus* 96.2 (1967): 444–63.

19. Drake, op. cit. note 4, vol. 1, pp. 259–65.

20. Snowden, op. cit. note 6.

21. Ibid., pp. 16–17.

22. Ibid., pp. 70–71.

23. Drake, op. cit. note 4, vol. 1, pp. 214–20.

24. Martin Bernal, "Animadversions on the Origins of Western Science," *Isis* 83.4 (December 1992): 596–607, 606.

25. Charles Taylor, *Multiculturalism and The Politics of Recognition* (Princeton: Princeton University Press, 1992), p. 62.

26. See, Bernard Lewis, *Race and Color in Islam* (New York: Harper, 1970).

27. Ean Begg, *The Cult of the Black Virgin* (London: Arkana, 1985); and Lucia Chiavola Birnbaum, *Black Madonnas: Feminism, Religion & Politics in Italy* (Boston: Northeastern University Press, 1993).

28. L. Poliakov, *The Aryan Myth: A History of Racist and Nationalist Ideas in Europe* (London: Chatto and Windus, 1974), p. 143.

29. Bernal, op. cit. note 8, pp. 202–4.

30. Ibid., pp. 219–21.

31. H. W. Debrunner, *Presence and Prestige: Africans in Europe: A History of Africans in Europe before 1918* (Basel: Basler Afrika Bibliographie, 1979), pp. 140–45.

32. Robert Knox, *The Races of Man: A Philosophical Inquiry into the Influence of Race Over the Destinies of Nations* (London, 1862).

33. Bernal, op. cit. note 8, pp. 240–45, 338–64.

34. Stephen Jay Gould, *The Mismeasure of Man* (New York: W. W. Norton, 1981).

35. See Ronald Sanders, *Lost Tribes and Promised Lands: The Origins of American Racism* (Boston and New York: Little Brown and Company, 1978), pp. 17–29, 65–91.

36. For Michelet, see Edmund Wilson, *To the Finland Station* (New York, 1940); Bernal, op. cit. note 8, pp. 297–308, 317–20.

37. See David Pingree, "Hellenophilia Versus the History of Science," *Isis* 83.4 (1992): 554–63; and Bernal, op. cit. notes 8, 9, 24; idem, "Phoenician Politics and Egyptian Justice in Ancient Greece," pp. 241–61, in Kurt Raaflaub ed., *Anfänge politischer Denkens in der Antike: Die nah-östlichen Kulturen und die Griechen* (Munich: Historisches Kolleg, 1993). See also Walter Burkert, *The Orientalizing Revolution: The Near Eastern Influence on Early Greek Culture in the Early Archaic Age* (Cambridge, MA: Harvard University Press, 1992).

38. See Eric Iversen, *The Myth of Egypt and its Hieroglyphs in European Tradition* (Copenhagen: Gad, 1961); "God and Egyptian and Hermetic Doctrine," *Opuscula Graecolatina*, Copenhagen: Supplemental Musei Tusculani, 27 (1984); and Frances Yates, *Giordano Bruno and the Hermetic Tradition* (London: Routledge and Kegan Paul, 1971).

39. See Yates, op. cit. note 38, and N. M. Swerdlow and O. Neugebauer, *Mathematical Astronomy in Copernicus's De Revolutionibus*, 2 pts. (New York and Berlin: Springer, 1984). See also J. M. Blaut, *1492: The Debate on Colonialism, Eurocentrism and History* (Trenton: Africa World Press, 1992).

40. See S. Etiemble, *L'Europe chinoise.* vol. 1: *De l'empire romain à Leibniz* (Paris: Gallimard, 1988); and vol. 2: *De la sinophilie à la sinophobie* (Paris: Gallimard, 1989); and G. Blue, "The Chinese Presence in Europe," *Comparative Criticism* 12 (1990): 283–98.

41. See Edward Said, *Culture and Imperialism* (New York: Alfred A. Knopf, 1993).

# 4

# Concepts of Nationalism in History

## BRIAN E. PORTER

Nationalism is both a conscious movement or doctrine and part of the instinctive group behavior of mankind. In the first sense it is comparatively new, in the second very old. People were behaving like nationalists long before nationalism was ever heard of, let alone investigated and analyzed. It is nationalism in the behavioral sense that is the subject of this chapter. The "concepts" then are our own, and the "history" as much of the recorded past as may prove helpful as source or illustration. In a study of this scope, however, some limitation is inevitable. An historical sociologist will find evidences of strong, even fierce, loyalty to the nation, national idea, or ethnic group, in many parts of the world, and from ancient times, but for our purpose, and as a help to understanding what this loyalty is, and involves, we shall trace its development chiefly through the history of Europe since the early Middle Ages.

### Origins

The basis of Roman society was citizenship. This, with its rights and obligations, was the link between the individual and the state. But when a Roman looked at, say, the Germans, he saw no equivalent. North of the Alps there was no state, only a number of tribes characterized by common language, religion and customs. Germans were Germans not by legal status, as Paul of Tarsus was a "Roman," but by being born German: they were a *natio*. Throughout the Dark and Middle Ages, "nation" continued to have this inherently ethnic meaning. It involved awareness of certain cultural affinities, and a degree of xenophobia towards those of alien cultural or racial background (as between, for example, the Anglo-Saxons and the Celtic British). None of this implied political obligation. For many centuries this remained the highly personalized leader-follower relationship characteristic of all primitive societies and signified in the early forms of royal titles: king not of the land but of the people—*rex Anglorum* or *rex Francorum*.

However, as the early kingdoms became more developed and stable, the people less mobile, and the frontiers fixed, with written laws and titles regulating the whole, so land itself became the basis of the social structure and hence of political obligation: the *rex Anglorum* (king of the English) became the *rex Angliae* (king of England).[1] One's prime duty was to the lord of one's estate, and the greatest of the estates was the kingdom. Such a system tended to cut across the nationality principle even though the sense of national identity was then inchoate. Kingdoms, duchies, and lesser estates were acquired by conquest, grant, or marriage, with the consequence that one's feudal lord was as often as not a foreigner. Thus throughout the twelfth century England was ruled by French-speaking kings and in the latter part of that century about half of all Frenchmen found themselves living in the French domains of the king of England. Meanwhile the Normans, the supreme "go-getters" of the time, the conquerors of England, southern Italy and Sicily, began to acquire political influence and vast estates in Scotland and Ireland—a type of enterprise paralleled by the movement of land-hungry German warriors and settlers into the sparsely populated Slavonic lands of the Baltic littoral.

Everywhere the land was tamed, and so were the people. Dynasticism, the rule of family and the politics of family aggrandizement, was the form of governance produced by a land-based economic and social system. For the remainder of the Middle Ages dynasticism held the field. It then encountered a force which had long been developing and which ultimately proved its undoing. The battle was not over until 1918, when the Austro-Hungarian Empire, the last great expression of dynasticism, fell before this force—or even, perhaps, not until 1991 when the Soviet Union, successor state to a great dynastic empire, suffered a like fate. This force we know as nationalism.

The essence of all nationalism is the emotional identification of the individual with the nation or the national idea, but the degree to which political consequences flow from this will depend upon a society's political culture and structure. A nascent nationalism may exist, but until it can be focussed in a kingdom or other form of polity it will remain largely the preserve of cultural or literary expression. The process can be seen in the early development of English nationalism.

In the eighth and ninth centuries England was divided into several warring kingdoms, the ruler of each of which could mobilize in his own dynastic interests the allegiance of his subjects, yet there was a sense of, indeed pride in, "Englishness" as reflected in the two major literary products of the time: Bede's *Ecclesiastical History of the English People* and the *Anglo-Saxon Chronicle*. The position was not unlike that of Greece in the age of the city-states, or the Arab world today, with a consciousness of a common cultural, linguistic and religious heritage, and the possibility, when facing an alien threat, of short-lived political cooperation. It was the unification of these kingdoms under the House of Wessex that allowed this rudimentary national feeling to develop further, for not only was there the psychological bonding of living under the same laws, fighting the same wars and engaging in the same political enterprise, but loyalty to the dynasty and pride in the nation could now merge. Nonetheless, the one great obstacle to the evolution of nation-states throughout the Middle Ages, and indeed in some cases up to the early nineteenth century, was the inherent contradiction between dynastic and nationalist principles and objectives.

Dynasticism by its very nature was transnational. Kings acquired alliances, and often territory, by marriage, or went to war in pursuit of dynastic claims. Moreover, owing to their links with other royal families, their friends, servants, advisers, and even their tastes and culture, were not infrequently of a foreign or cosmopolitan character. Yet their power-base almost invariably lay in some particular nation, and to ignore or alienate national sentiment was to incur unpopularity, even, perhaps, to the extent that the throne was lost to a rival claimant. For the most part, medieval nationalism was a force that could be exploited, and which it might be risky to ignore, but was not the governing principle of politics. This lay with the rivalries and ambitions of the magnates and the loyalties they could command, and operated as well on the international as on the domestic stage, as witness the claim of the Duke of Normandy to the throne of England in 1066, and that of the kings of England, from 1340 on, to the throne of France, both pursued on dubious dynastic grounds. In the case of the latter claim, the victories of the Plantagenets over the French—Crecy, Poitiers, Agincourt—were popular with the English of the time and have retained their place in the national mythology. Yet, had Edward III or Henry V been ultimately successful in their dynastic conquest of France, England would have become a mere appendage of the larger and richer kingdom, a fate which befell Normandy following the Norman conquest of England. Thus would the national principle have been undermined.

Medieval nationalism, in short, was itself feeling and reacting dynastically because dynasticism was the dominant political mode. That this was so is strikingly revealed in the career and outlook of Joan of Arc. She was engaged in what today would be called a campaign of national liberation, leading Bernard Shaw to describe her as "one of the first apostles of Nationalism."[2] Yet her attitude was essentially medieval in its focus upon kingship. Her loyalty was directed above all to her sovereign as God's regent upon earth, but she also held, and this was a sign of change, that he should be master in his own estate: France.

That in medieval western Europe nationalism was not subverted by dynasticism but was able to run, if sometimes uneasily, in harness with it, was owing to the ultimate success of the French and Scots in resisting the English crown's attempts at dynastic conquest, an outcome itself largely attributable to the growth of national feeling aroused in those sanguinary and protracted struggles. The long wars against the Muslims had a like effect in Spain, where national unity was achieved through an opportune dynastic marriage followed by the conquest of the remaining Moorish south. Henceforth strong national monarchies were free to develop in geographically consolidated areas where single languages, or groups of related dialects, provided the required degree of cultural cohesion. In central Europe, on the other hand, owing partly to its falling less naturally into regions delimiting state power, and partly to the archaic feudal structure of the Holy Roman Empire, dynasticism was successfully able to frustrate the fulfillment of the national principle until comparatively recent times.

## The Rise of Modern Nationalism

Medieval nationalism in the main related to the kingdom much as today's average student relates to his university or college: great loyalty, especially in the field of organized physical combat with traditional rivals, but no thought that the appointment of the institution's governors, or indeed its continuance, merger, division, or termination—although he might have strong opinions on such matters—were ultimately any concern of his. Nationalism could make no further headway until a class had arisen that was sufficiently self-confident and economically powerful to challenge the dynastic principle as a political, legal, and psychological force. This began to occur, particularly in some of the trading nations of northern Europe, in the latter half of the sixteenth century.

It is seen in the successful revolt of the Dutch against the Spanish crown and in the increasing restiveness of the political class in late Tudor and early Stuart England. The Reformation greatly helped the process, for it emphasized theocratic rather than dynastic values, with the result that dynastic authority was weakened. Monarchs remained generally dynastic in their outlook, but the more politically astute amongst them saw the wisdom of identifying with this growing national sentiment and placating the rising urban class which chiefly manifested it. Henry IV of France did this when he declared that Paris was "worth a Mass"; Elizabeth I of England did this in adopting a national brand of Protestantism and in expressing and symbolizing the nation's defiance of the might of Catholic Spain. In her last address to her subjects she said: "Though God hath raised me high, yet this I count the glory of my crown, that I have reigned with your loves."[3] Her whole method of governing, particularly in her approach to the marriage question, may be seen as a cunning balancing of nationalist and dynastic expedients with the aim of extracting the greatest advantage from each. Nonetheless, with a sure political instinct, she remained at heart a nationalist and thus secured her place in the national pantheon as perhaps the most popular and successful of English rulers.

The Stuart kings who followed her, with their dynastic notions of divine right, failed to understand the strong and irreversible nationalist tide which found expression in the cause of Parliament, and which gave a mortal blow to dynasticism in the English Civil War. Indeed, the party that won the war even replaced the divine right of kings with the divine right of the nation. Charles I was executed for having made war upon the people of England, deemed by the Puritans to be a sort of reincarnation of the Children of Israel. The intense nationalism of the ancient Jews proved to be a heady brew to a people steeped in the Old Testament, led Oliver Cromwell and John Milton, amongst many others, to see the English as being the chosen of God,[4] and had an influence which, passing through Puritanism across the Atlantic (a latter-day Red Sea), eventually formed a potent ingredient in the American national consciousness, as well as ensuring the development there of an essentially republican spirit and outlook. But even in England with its long tradition of monarchy, dynasticism had gone for good, as the brief and disastrous reign of its last exemplar, James II, demonstrated. British sovereigns ever since have been of a very different order from their medieval and Renaissance predecessors: reigning by parliamentary title, and as symbols and expressions of a national identity which alone conferred legitimacy upon them.

A sense of national identity seems to have been maturing and deepening in Europe through the eighteenth century. In the Protestant north it no longer had theological implications, except in the universal form that the God of Battles was always besought to favor the national side or cause, and was invariably rewarded with a *Te Deum* should victory be forthcoming. "Neo-Israelite" nationalism passed with the age of religious wars, surviving only at a deep level in the American consciousness, and in more pristine form with the Cape Dutch who, less affected by the Enlightenment, also found their circumstances to parallel the Biblical experience. In Europe, on the other hand, the growing sense of nationhood was undoubtedly encouraged by participation in the balance of power wars which intermittently convulsed the Continent throughout the century. These wars, protracted in today's terms, usually lasting seven years or longer, invariably began as "policy conducted by other means" but changed in character, inspiring that spirit of patriotic solidarity which is one aspect of nationalism, as the struggle wore on and particularly if the homeland were threatened. Thus in 1709, with Marlborough and Eugene at last poised to invade France, the French fought with a desperate resolve the Allies had not before encountered in eight years' campaigning, making Malplaquet the bloodiest battle of the century. In Winston Churchill's words, "[t]hey had a feeling that they were fighting not only for their King but for their country."[5]

A like development is apparent in the wars in which the Russians were engaged against Napoleonic France. From being professional, strategic, "dynastic," the Russian approach to the war was transformed, when the French marched on Moscow, into something altogether more basic and instinctive, indeed "nationalistic," a metamorphosis which is one of the most profound and brilliantly handled themes in Leo Tolstoy's *War and Peace*. These wars were like hammer blows in the slow forging of dynastic states into nation-states, but the mutation was rather in the psychology of the wider political class than in the narrow political structure. Except in England, where dynasticism petered out as Jacobitism (to win a posthumous literary victory in the realm of romantic lost causes), and in Holland, the dynastic order remained in control until the French Revolution.

The Revolution not only represented the overthrow of absolutism and aristocratic privilege, but released a spirit of nationhood so stirring and powerful (as captured and evoked by that most electrifying of national anthems, the "Marseillaise") that some have supposed nationalism itself to have been born at this time. French Revolutionary nationalism had, indeed, certain new features. It marked a cleaner break with dynasticism than had been the case with the British and the Dutch, breathing defiance to the whole dynastic order.

This did not come immediately. The monarchy posed a problem. The royal house was part of that order, yet for many was integral to the very idea of "France." Initially, though largely stripped of his powers, Louis XVI was seen by the more moderate revolutionaries as part of their nationalism, as "their" king. The dynastic title "King of France," implying that the whole country was a royal estate, was replaced by the older form, "King of the French," stressing the link between monarch and people. Anti-dynastic hostility was directed in the main against Marie Antoinette—"*la chienne autrichienne*"—foreign consorts being favorite targets of nationalist intolerance (as was found by Charles I's Henrietta Maria, Victoria's Albert in the war hysteria of 1853–54, Frederick III's Victoria, and Nicholas II's Alexandra).

But any hope that the monarchy could become a popular national symbol, as had happened in Great Britain, was fatally undermined not only by Louis' inadequacy for the role, but also by the émigré factor. To the nationalist, to flee one's country for any reason other than the imposition of foreign rule is to put self-interest before the nation's interest: it is the supreme betrayal. This had been done by many of the aristocracy, and by the king's youngest brother. When the king sought safety with his wife's family in the abortive flight to Varennes, he stood revealed not as a nationalist but as a dynast, and this sealed his fate. With the deposition and execution of the king, the struggle between revolutionary nationalism and dynasticism was internationalized. No crowned head could feel safe while the Revolution survived; nor could the Revolution feel safe while the dynastic order remained. "The coalised Kings threaten us," cried Danton; "we hurl at their feet, as gage of battle, the Head of a King."[6]

The nationalism forged in the Revolution was different in other ways, indeed different in kind, from any that had gone before. Like American Revolutionary nationalism, it was imbued with the ideas and ideals of the Enlightenment: Liberty, Popular Sovereignty and the Rights of Man. But it was more thoroughgoing and universal. American nationalism, which took time to supplant the individual nationalisms of the former colonies, did not at first embrace any but those of European stock. French Revolutionary nationalism went further. The French were to be the core nation of a universal republic. And the criterion for membership of that republic was to be one's philosophy of life rather than one's ethnic origins or racial background. Such a basis for a reorganization of world society might have worked had not the French, in Martin Wight's words, been "sublimely incapable of distinguishing between the universal Rights of Man and French culture."[7] Napoleon's armies entered the surrounding countries of Europe as liberators, but to those being liberated it came increasingly to look like political and cultural imperialism on the grandest scale.

It was ironic that at the same time as French political hegemony was being imposed upon continental Europe, the French cultural hegemony which had characterized the whole eighteenth-century dynastic order was coming under intellectual and artistic attack. Particularly was this so in Germany, where Johann Gottfried von Herder with his idea of "national genius" (*Volksgeist*), Johann Gottlieb Fichte with his doctrine of the need for inward-looking polities united by language and his desire that the German nation should be raised to a moral ideal, as well as the new interest in folklore, philology, and the roots of national culture, chiefly associated with the names of Jacob and Wilhelm Grimm, all helped create a consciousness of "Germanness," which was to provide German nationalism with its intellectual and cultural justification.[8] To these currents was added the emotive ingredient of Romanticism, a cultural movement which many young German writers and artists embraced with enthusiasm, and which was seen as releasing the imagination from the constrictive discipline, formality, and symmetry of French classicism. Some of the poets of the period, notably Johann Christoph von Schiller in Germany and George, Lord Byron in England, championed in their writings—and Byron in active participation—the cause of small, oppressed peoples. All of this made a great appeal to the youth of the time, as the nationalism of radical protest was to make to young people throughout its subsequent history.

Napoleonic imperialism acted as a catalyst to the growth of nationalism in Europe, partly because certain of its territorial arrangements (the Confederation of the Rhine, the Kingdom of Italy, the Grand Duchy of Warsaw) went some way to meeting national aspirations, and partly through arousing strong national and patriotic feelings in the common struggle against France. But few nationalist hopes were fulfilled in the peace. The conservative statesmen who gathered at Vienna were resolved in the main to restore the dynastic order of the eighteenth century. Kings and petty princes were put back on their thrones. Whole peoples were allotted to this ruler or that on the principle of rewarding the victors, or strengthening barriers against France, regardless of their sentiments or opinions. Nationalism, and its twin, liberalism, were to play no part in this world restored. The czar, in his Holy Alliance, even attempted to create an interdynastic community of Europe.

Forces such as nationalism and liberalism, however, could not be repressed indefinitely. The expansion of trade and industry, the development of communications, the drift from the countryside to the towns, all made for the growth of a middle class which increasingly chafed at the multiplicity of customs barriers and other feudal restrictions, and which aspired to political influence commensurate with its economic strength and educational attainments. The upheavals of 1830 and, still more, 1848, and the struggle for the Reform Bill in England in 1832, mark the efforts of this class to come into its own. And in western Europe success was achieved; the liberal nation-state was launched. In central, southern, and eastern Europe, however, those bastions of dynasticism, the great military monarchies of Austria, Prussia, and Russia, proved everywhere too strong. The result was a setback not only for liberalism, but also for nationalism. The Italians, the Hungarians, the Czechs, and within a few years the Poles, were thwarted in their bids for self-determination, and in Germany the efforts of the bourgeoisie to achieve a unified state under the aegis of the king of Prussia were rewarded with the contemptuous reply that he "would not pick up a Crown from the gutter."[9]

The Continental nationalisms of the first half of the nineteenth century, led by intellectuals and supported chiefly by the middle classes and the urban, student young, were a far cry from the "Rule Britannia," bellicose, xenophobic nationalism of Hanoverian England. They were *movements*, founded to achieve certain goals: constitutional government, national unity, and cultural awareness. English nationalism had no such need; it was never a movement, but a robust, all-pervasive patriotism, suspicious of outsiders, hostile to the traditional enemy, the French, and emotionally focussed upon that mythological entity called "England," or affectionately "Old England." Horatio Nelson touched a profound chord with his famous Trafalgar signal, "England expects . . ." A nationalism like that had matured for centuries within the state and was perfectly geared to the requirements of the state.

In contrast, most Continental national movements either had no state, or such states as they did have were not theirs by preference. Indeed, the view held by the early champions of the nationality principle was that whereas nations were naturally fraternal, dynasties and dynastic states were inherently martial and combative, and hence a prime source of wars. When nationality had triumphed, said Giuseppe Mazzini, "all cause of war would disappear, and in its place arise a spirit of brotherhood and peaceful emulation on the road of progress."[10] This naive view, which not only, like most utopian notions, tended to discount the dimension of power, but also ignored such insoluble problems as two peoples claiming the same territory, was never put to the test. When the next great advances in the furtherance of the nationality principle took place, the unifications of Germany and Italy, they were accomplished less by the will of the peoples, present though this was, than by the power and policies of governments, by, in fact, blood and iron. The "fraternal" nations of Europe, instead of taking over and transforming the states of Europe, were rather taken over and transformed by them.

The period 1870–1914 saw the apotheosis of the nation-state. Many factors must have gone into the process by which the state and its nation—or at least its "core" nation—became integrated to an unprecedented degree. Economies and communications, particularly railways, had become sufficiently developed to give the middle classes, and increasingly the urban working class, a national rather than a local or provincial scope for their lives, but not yet an international one; frontiers were still barriers which the vast majority never crossed. Moreover, the old feudal and religious certainties and deferences were becoming weaker, often leaving an emotional void, or psychological insecurity, which loyalty to the nation-state or to the national idea did much to offset. Add to these changes the steadily enlarging sphere of state activity and responsibility, the impact of official propaganda and indoctrination over an increasingly literate public, and the effects of conscription in all the major powers of Europe except Great Britain, and a good part of this wide-spread sociopolitical phenomenon might be accounted for. The state had come into most people's lives, and most people, in return, provided that they were not of an alienated, subject nation, found that their pride and emotions were bound up with it, its achievements, performance in war, and international standing.

This was a time, too, when each nation seemed to develop some characteristic which heightened its sense of identity, its individuality. Britain, long imperial, discovered imperialism. Russia was in process of making one of its long pendulum swings away from its Western and back to its Slavonic-Byzantine heritage. Germany took pride in its new empire's military pre-eminence, which many believed, in the thinking of the time, to prove a moral preeminence. France, long riven by the antithesis of its two national traditions—the Revolutionary-urban-secular and the conservative-rural-Catholic—found some measure of unity both in a patriotic desire for revenge for the humiliating defeat of 1870–71 and loss of Alsace-Lorraine (the allegorical statue of Strasbourg in the Place de la Concorde was thenceforth veiled in crepe), and in pride in the empire-building and brilliant cultural achievements of the Third Republic. Italy, almost as though unable to believe that unification had been achieved, and perhaps uneasily aware that without the help of foreign powers it could not have been done, erected to commemorate the Risorgimento a monument of towering ostentation in the heart of Rome. The Austro-Hungarian Empire remained an anomaly in all this, for although, as its name indicated, it now attempted to accommodate the status and nationalistic pride of its Magyar as well as its German race, it yet denied an equal role for the other, chiefly Slavonic, peoples constituting its population. The last of the great dynastic states, it even took pride in the fact, and in the venerable dynasty which, with incredibly rigid protocol, presided over it, as well as in its rich, if not always overserious culture; but unlike its fellow powers, some of which retained dynastic trappings, it did not even have the makings of a nation-state.

To the degree that the peoples of Europe identified with their respective states, so were they, particularly in the case of the major powers, affected by the fortunes of those states within the international system. Although governments in the more nationalistic countries had occasionally in times past been vulnerable to war-fever (as with the British in 1739 and 1853–54, and the French in July 1870), strong public feelings were now becoming a potent and permanent feature of international politics. Rulers and governments were still in charge of the diplomatic game, but increasingly they found themselves in the position of captains and teams playing in a vast stadium thronged with phrenetic supporters and equally passionate opponents. Pride and jealousy were excited to an unusual degree and the drive for overseas possessions provided a new field for rivalry and contention.

After the fall of Prince Otto von Bismarck in 1890, the remaining conservative restraint went out of the system, and diplomatic retreats and accommodations which hitherto had been part of the normal working of the balance of power process could either no longer be made by governments or made only at the cost of gravely weakening their own prestige and authority. The effect, in the years prior to the First World War, was a "peace" characterized by growing tension, by armaments programs that were supported, and sometimes demanded, by the publics, and by diplomatic crises any of which might have thrown Europe into war. No one class had a monopoly of this excitable, irrational mood. It penetrated to the bottom of society, as in the "jingoism" of the British music halls, and to the very top, as in the militaristic posturing and chauvinistic speechifying of the German Kaiser.

Kaiser Wilhelm II, intellectually superficial and psychologically insecure though he was, is of historical significance for reflecting, almost in caricature, that strange mixture of envy, aspiration and suspicion, infused with a *hubris* that had grown with the strength of the state, which then characterized the collective mood of large sections of the German people. But all the major nations of Europe shared in varying degrees, and each in its own way, the pride and arrogance of the powerful, for were they not the lords of the greater part of the earth?

The First World War was precedented in being a balance of power war, differing from its predecessors in its scale; it was unprecedented in being also a sort of general nationalistic orgasm. Such was the mental climate of the time—in the words of President Woodrow Wilson's envoy, Colonel Edward House, writing from Berlin in May 1914, "militarism run stark mad"[11]—that had not the heir to the Austrian throne been assassinated by a Bosnian Serb in Sarajevo on June 28th, then some other inflammatory incident would undoubtedly have sparked off the war a year or so later. For long an explosive force born of the pride, passions, and frustrations of great populations had been building up in Europe, and Sarajevo provided a release. Never was war entered upon with such patriotic enthusiasm.

The hopes of some socialist leaders that the working classes would not fight their proletarian brothers were immediately and cruelly dashed. In London the veteran Labour leader Keir Hardie, in attempting to make an anti-war speech in Trafalgar Square, was howled down. Nationalism, which had been the bane of the European "establishments" only two generations earlier, now came to their aid, indeed swept along all classes in one great unity of purpose. The governments that had launched the war all believed they had embarked upon a conflict which their side would quickly win and then, as in a prenationalistic age, conclude with a negotiated peace; they soon discovered that they had unleashed vast primal forces which they could not control, but which, in effect, controlled them. Any chance of a reasonable accommodation was out of the question; the war had to go on until one side gave up through exhaustion and loss of hope, and the settlement imposed by the victors could only be draconian and humiliating. In 1815 the dynasts had treated the vanquished with comparative leniency; in 1918-19 nationalistic vindictiveness, inflamed by the huge losses sustained, would countenance no such outcome.

## State Nationalism

The nationalism that found its ultimate expression in the First World War was a concomitant of the love affair with the state, which the emerging political class had had since the late sixteenth century. Beginning in Protestant northern Europe, the sovereign, centralized, cohesive nation-state was seen by this class as the most advanced and hopeful development for internal order, external security, and material prosperity. It was favored by the mercantile class as a means of curbing both feudal anarchy and dynastic privilege and taxing power; it was championed by Protestants and by an increasingly secular intelligentsia as a way of countering the residual internationalist claims and political influence of the Roman ecclesiastical imperium. Moreover, it was attractive to a post-rural, post-religious working class for giving them a focus and a role in what had become for many a rootless and insecure existence; and it was desired by all that growing body of middle-class people (like the German revolutionaries of 1848) whom education had fitted to serve in the highest positions of state, but who were, with rare exceptions, excluded in preference to those of privileged birth, or having superior social connections, from service in the average *ancien régime*. For the middle class, the modern state, particularly if it embraced liberal principles, provided an opportunity to achieve status and secure a comfortable living.

Out of the state nationalism which these social developments engendered, together with the growth of empires, and of navies to defend them, grew the cult of imperialism. In part this reflected pride in the possession of vast territories, proclaimed on the world map in the national coloring, giving even small countries like Holland, Belgium, and Portugal the status of world powers, and arousing (especially the British Empire which looked even more immense in Mercator's projection) great jealousy and envy amongst the Germans and Italians who had come too late upon the scene to acquire what they considered to be their fair share of the world. In part, too, imperialism reflected the fact that overseas possessions provided a field for politically unhindered commercial expansion and exploitation. They also afforded career opportunities, which were not always available at home, for service officers, administrators, and professional people generally, together with a lifestyle for the middle classes previously enjoyed only by the aristocracy. Even those serving in the lowest ranks of the imperial power—Rudyard Kipling's Tommy Atkins and his like—were rarely untouched by the experience of belonging, if only temporarily, to a ruling caste, and tended to become confirmed nationalists and imperialists. To the amazement of the "liberal intelligentsia" in Britain, popular support for Prime Minister Anthony

Eden's disastrous Suez venture actually grew as the crisis developed, but then few families in the country had not had members serving in Egypt, in one or other of the world wars, or in the seventy-year occupation, and resentment, even anger, that "the Gyppos" had seized "our" canal, revealed how deeply colonialist attitudes had penetrated and affected all levels of British society.

State nationalism in the Western world has long been the virtual preserve of the political right. Indeed, it is now an element in the definition of the right. This was not always so. When the dynastic order held sway, state nationalism was a revolutionary force. But with the eventual triumph of the nation-state it became a conservative force, designed to bolster the status quo. The political left, whose function it is to overturn the status quo, tends therefore to be uneasy about the state and deeply suspicious of the type of nationalism which sustains it. It is not at Labour but at Tory party meetings that the dais table is customarily draped with the Union Jack and the proceedings conclude with the National Anthem or "Land of Hope and Glory," just as in the United States it is more likely to be at the homes of Reaganite "Middle America" that the Stars and Stripes would be seen giving a patriotic signal from front porch or garden flagpole. Moreover, in most countries the right sees itself as the custodian of the military tradition, the left turning instead to internationalism, to disarmament, even, at times, to pacifism. Yet by "the state," which is at issue here, is meant the country as a political entity in the world, together with those attributes— army, navy, public pageantry, architecturally resplendent capitals, prestige abroad, and good order at home—which enhance its self-regarding nature. "The state" in its other chief sense, government control over its citizens and over the economy at the expense of market forces, does not usually find favor with the right. Indeed, in the capitalist West, other than in those societies where a tradition of feudal paternalism persists, the right is as condemnatory of the state in this sense as the left, in its attempts to promote economic justice, is usually in favor of it.

Support for the state in the first of these senses, and hence state nationalism, is frequently class-based or otherwise sectional. Those who constitute, or who deem themselves to constitute, the ruling class in a country, tend to see the state as theirs. It is as though they have arrogated to themselves the view of the state once restricted to absolute monarchs, and declared, *"l'état c'est nous."* This in part explains the association of state nationalism with the political right, the conservative element in society usually being the most powerful and wealthy. But it is also true of those classes, sects or parties which achieve power after a revolution. Thus after the Reformation in Scotland, the Presbyterian clergy saw the state proprietorially, with even the sovereign as one who should be their subject—a situation paralleled (except that they dispensed with the sovereign altogether) by their Shi'ite equivalents in contemporary Iran. In this last case, as in that of Cromwellian England, Revolutionary France, Bolshevik Russia, Nazi Germany, and Communist China, to name but the chief examples, the state was completely remodelled by the new ruling party, becoming their instrument and bearing little relation to its predecessor.

In some states, usually ones whose population lacks ethnic or ideological cohesion, as well as the focus and continuity that monarchy or other constitutional structures of long standing provide, the army has come to see itself as the embodiment or custodian of the national idea. This is true of certain Latin American republics, notably Chile and Argentina. In Argentina, following the overthrow of army power in the wake of the Falklands fiasco, one member of an army family— such families forming a closely knit society at the officer level—made the comment, astonishing to any Anglo-Saxon, "How can these people" (i.e., the citizens) "treat us so after all we have done for them?"[12] It is a pattern likely to be repeated in many a Third World state of recent origin.

In consequence of the First World War, state nationalism underwent both a decline and a revival. In liberal, democratic Europe, it lost much of its force, a reaction not only to the war but to the values and mental climate which were thought to have brought it about. The effect in the United States was less traumatic, but even there the naive stridency of that type of nationalism of which *Teddy* Roosevelt was the personification, even though American nationalism remains a powerful and vital force, was never quite repeated. But whereas in those countries which emerged victorious from the war this decline, to a greater or lesser degree from the high peak of pre-1914 nationalism, remains true to this day, in those which had suffered defeat, or somehow felt they had lost the peace, state nationalism returned with redoubled intensity under Bolshevism and Fascism.

Whatever else these two creeds in their various manifestations were, they had this in common: each was a fierce and virulent reaction to liberalism, its system of values, and the class which produced it and prospered by it. And just as liberalism saw the state primarily as the protector of the individual, the guardian of that order under which the rights and interests of the citizen were maintained, the new totalitarianism, in contrast, exalted the state and its ideological expression, the party, into a totem and a Moloch for whose sake alone the individual existed.

So complete has been the downfall of Fascism, and now Bolshevism, that we may be in danger of forgetting the potency of the social and psychological forces to which they owed their birth and rise, as well as of ignoring the psychological inadequacy of the Western idealization of private life. Periodically man becomes thoroughly bored with a humdrum and routine existence and has an overpowering urge collectively to do spectacular, even violent things. Western democratic liberalism, unless, despite itself, it becomes caught up in war, offers little opportunity for this to happen. But the type of regime usually thrown up by a great revolution, or one at any rate inspired by some impelling belief or cause, can be the means by which these myriad impulses become focused and directed. The result is the release of colossal human energy, invariably expansionist, whether into wilderness or, in more heavily settled regions, into neighboring countries, a phenomenon which Tolstoy called "the swarm life of mankind."[13] Nothing that human beings experience can compare with the intoxication which comes from feeling oneself to be part of some great heave of history, from an awareness that the whole community is on the move. It was what the French felt during the Napoleonic period, the Germans before the First World War and still more so under the Nazis, many Russians even under the tyranny of Joseph Stalin, the Iranians in the initial phase of their Islamic republic.

The patriotism which is commonly associated with such upheavals is often infused with ideological or religious fanaticism, and although the state is exalted to a degree never approached in liberal societies, it is the state as the instrument of something greater even than itself: the impulse to mould the world anew. This is a time when men look forward; all thoughts are of the future with the past usually renounced or derided. To win in such circumstances stimulates an exhilarating sense of destiny which for a time carries all before it; to lose fosters a bitterness, a frustration, which can have the direst political consequences. The Nazi movement grew in large part out of the injured pride and thwarted dreams of Europe's most powerful, dynamic, and expectant people. The role of state nationalism in such circumstances would appear to bear out the truth of José Ortega y Gasset's conclusion that the state "is a plan of action and a programme of collaboration. . . . It is pure dynamism—the will to do something in common."[14] It is when that will is lacking that the state, if it is not ethnically homogeneous, will be in danger of falling into its constituent parts. Such was the fate of the Soviet Union. The regime did not lack the coercive means to hold the state together, but confidence in the future had gone, and so had the will to continue.

## The Nationalism of the National Idea

The world of nations is primarily and essentially a world of the mind.[15] Yet so powerfully and intimately do nation-states impinge upon the lives of their citizens, influence their attitudes, and engage their emotions—whether by enlisting their loyalties or arousing their hatreds—that few there are who recognize the true nature of what is happening. In every nation-state there will slowly have evolved a view of itself, a "national idea," each new historical and cultural experience adding to, and perhaps subtly modifying, the whole. And upon the extent to which this idea is shared by, and influences, the total population, will depend the cohesion of the nation and hence the inner strength of the nation-state. It is therefore in the interests of the ruling political class, and of those writers and other artists and intellectuals who support it, or to whom it offers patronage, to develop and publicize the national idea, as Virgil with singular success gave universal currency to the idea of Rome. In many parts of the world this process has not even begun, and it is to the fact that their peoples have no shared view, no collective image, either of themselves or of the country of which they are citizens, that many new states owe their chronic weakness.

Sometimes, however, weakness arises in another way. If the national idea is seen too closely to serve the sectional interests of the ruling establishment, an alternative one may be adopted by a rival or dissenting class and given all the passionate loyalty to which nationalism is prone. Hence the extreme bitterness of most civil wars. Each side is patriotic but each has a vision very different from the other of the *patrie* and what it stands for. The "new Israel" that was the Puritan England was hardly likely to be the England of the Stuart court. Indeed, national ideas may well become polarized, and induce explosive mutual antagonism on the part of those who hold them, long after the social fracture which originally gave rise to them.

Throughout the nineteenth century and for most of the twentieth, France was riven in this way. On the one hand was the France of 1789, of rationalism and anti-clericalism, a tradition fostered by the radical intelligentsia of Paris; and on the other was Catholic, conservative, primarily rural France. This was a split which went right down to village level with the proverbial rivalry of schoolmaster and priest. But if a nation can be divided by ideas, so too can it be reunited. It was part of the political genius of Charles de Gaulle, perhaps the supreme statesman-nationalist of the twentieth century, if only because his goal of national unity and renewal was achieved in the face of almost impossible odds, to contrive a vision of France which subsumed all previous traditions. That vision embraced greatness and "*la gloire.*" To outsiders, and indeed to such anarchic insiders as the Parisian satire industry, it appeared somewhat ridiculous, but it was a means by which all the major figures of French history could contribute to the national identity, just as the regime which he founded in 1958 linked two traditions in that it was republican in form yet monarchical in spirit.

Benjamin Disraeli spoke of England's "two nations," by which he meant the rich and the poor, yet *pace* Karl Marx, even gross inequalities of wealth have rarely prevented a people from feeling loyalty to a national idea provided that this enshrined values with which they were in sympathy. Before the Civil War, Americans, although united over those principles which had led to their independence, could not complete their nationhood, come of age as a nation, so long as slavery constituted an untenable ethical ambiguity. After the Civil War the way was clear for the cohesion so long delayed, a cohesion paralleled by that of the state itself, with the very name "United States" thenceforth given a singular rather than plural meaning.

Even though the national idea may represent a coherent set of values, it needs to extend into the world of ideals, even of dreams, if it is to establish its full potency in the psychological bonding of a people. Thus central to every nationalism is the nationalist's country, ideally conceived. One can see this in the alternative names of certain countries. Thus "America" has come to have for Americans associations and resonances that are hardly conveyed by "United States." And for an Englishman, Scotsman and Welshman, "England," "Scotland," and "Wales" will strike deeper chords by far than the comprehensive and originally geographical term "Britain" or "Great Britain," to say nothing of the official designation of the state, usually abruptly shortened to "U.K." Indeed, the political conception of a nation tends to lack all mystique. The Bolsheviks tried to transcend nationalism by setting up the world's workers' own state, unique in having no geographical reference in its title. Yet although the Soviet Union made a strange psychological appeal as a utopia to some alienated proletarians and disaffected intellectuals in other lands, it was not to the defence of "the workers' paradise," but to that of "Mother Russia" that Stalin was impelled to rally the people in 1941. The ideal motherland, often referred to as "home," has an even greater hold upon the exile. "Jerusalem" features as such in the exilic writings of the Old Testament, and has played a comparable role in the maintenance of a Jewish identity throughout the long centuries of the Diaspora. To those who have stayed put after a political upheaval, the émigré has forsaken his nation; to the émigré himself, he has taken it with him. The émigré, or exile, is often the most intense nationalist of them all.

### Nations and *Ethnie*

Undergoing a common collective experience nearly always leads to the bonding of those involved. Going to the same school or college has this effect, as does service in the same regiment, and particularly in the same action or campaign. The history of the evolution of the state is also, therefore, the story of the development of a group consciousness of those living within its borders. They experience the same government, live under the same laws, and, when the state goes to war, share the same sacrifices, sense of purpose, and defeats or triumphs. Thus is the state nation formed, even at times out of those who might be expected to be resistant to its psychological pull. When, during the First World War, Sir Roger Casement, the Irish nationalist, visited prisoner-of-war camps in Germany with the aim of recruiting Irish soldiers of the British Army to the anti-British cause, he met with scant success, indeed with anger and hostility.

Yet the attempt was not ill-conceived; even while he was so engaged, plans were being made in Dublin for a rebellion against British rule. Most of the Irish proved in the end to be unassimilable, showing that an overpowering sense of historical identity, usually associated with an ancestral language and perhaps a distinctive faith or branch of religion, can be proof against the integrative effects of the state. Because "nation" has increasingly come to signify "state nation," an alternative term is required for the category just described. English has no appropriate word. The German "*Volk*" expresses the idea, but is too suggestive of German-ness. Hence some scholars have borrowed the French word *ethnie* (from ἔθνος—race, tribe, nation, people) to meet the need.[16]

Compared with nations, *ethnie* are primordial, or rather they correspond to nations in the original Roman sense. What makes them special is a distinct cultural character usually expressed in language, origins in the remote past, a long-settled homeland, and a sense of kinship. Some of the beliefs an *ethnie* holds about itself may be derived more from myth than reality: the idea of the Founder of the People, a

Father Abraham or an Aeneas, or the claim, made for the Romans, and for the medieval Celtic British, of descent from fugitives from Troy. Myth, in fact, not only plays an essential part in group identity, but is continuously created to preserve and enhance that identity. As any student of a nationalist movement knows, the ongoing mythologizing of history can produce a psychological unity of fearsome potency.

That *ethnie* have not been given the attention they deserve as components of world politics is largely owing to the modern state's rarely being an expression of them. Indeed, it often ignores or discounts their existence, preferring that they should be subsumed in its own state-nation. Moreover, the concept of ethnicity has usually been marginalized to minorities of alien background, it seldom being considered that in many states, as in the long-established nation-states of Europe, the indigenous people, too, have an ethnic side. With the notable exception of Japan, the modern industrial state has sought to distance itself from its ethnicity, seeing this as a relic of the primitive, or the rural, flying in the face of all notions of progress, modernity, mobility, and internationalism. The example of the United States has encouraged this outlook. The richest and most commercially successful of all great countries, not only was it not founded upon ethnicity, it was a living contradiction of it. The multi-ethnic state has thus been taken as a model by governments anxious to foster develop-ment, or increase the labor force, as when Britain and other European colonial powers encouraged immigration from their former overseas territories in the 1950s and 1960s, Western Germany admitted large numbers of Turkish guest workers over the same period, and Australia abandoned its white Australia immigration policy in 1973.

## Ethnic Nationalism

The imperviousness of many modern states to ethnic realities has led to a recrudes-cence of ethnic nationalism. This essentially may be taken as the self-assertiveness of the *ethnie*, although the form it takes and the ends it seeks will vary with historical circumstances. It will be convenient, however, to divide the phenomenon into "hard" and "soft" ethnic nationalism.

Hard ethnic nationalism is the most basic of all politics, reducible to the simple question: "Who gets what land?" But this, too, may be divided into, "Who settles what land?" and "Who rules what land?" An *ethnie* seeking land to settle, either because it has been driven out of its own, or through overpopulation, or because it believes it has an historic or even divine claim to pursue, can behave with great ruthlessness. Indeed, some of the most intractable political conflicts the world now faces have their origins in the intrusion of one *ethnie* into the territory of another. This is currently occurring in Bosnia, but perhaps the most prominent example this century has been the influx of Jews into Palestine. Any hope that the passions aroused and the implacable hatreds engendered will fade with the passage of time seems hardly borne out by the experience of Northern Ireland, now an "Israel" of nearly four centuries' standing. And this remains true despite the "peace" arrived at over Palestine in 1993 and in Northern Ireland in 1994: in each case this came about for tactical reasons and through exhaustion rather than through any significant change of heart. That this type of situation is not more prevalent is largely owing to the grim fact that few of the world's *ethnie* have acquired their present homelands without expelling, enslaving or slaughtering the previous inhabitants. And even when these survived in any numbers, and not just as anthropological curiosities, they not infrequently lost their language and their culture. Such genocidal happenings are usually a feature not of settled times, but of the breakdown of an *imperium* or other established system, or of an advancing frontier where civilized control tends to be weak.[17]

*Ethnie* in a "state of nature" find their own balance, but the imposition of empires or of state structures that in no way correspond to their strengths or settlement patterns will have a distorting effect, and one likely to grow as groups begin to live in areas they would fear to inhabit without the order ensured by the imperial power. The disappearance of an empire thus has the effect not unlike that of the staff departing from a zoo after leaving all the cage doors open. The widespread massacres which took place in Calcutta, Delhi, and the Punjab after the withdrawal of British power in 1947, and the "ethnic cleansing"[18] following upon the disintegration of Yugoslavia (which one might see as a delayed outcome of the fall of the Ottoman Empire) are examples of the bloody process by which a new ethnic equilibrium is established. A new political structure will inevitably follow: the creation of states and drawing up of frontiers to reflect the new reality.

Ethnic extremism may also be the response, sometimes paranoiac in its intensity and irrationality, to a perceived threat to the national identity. This may be seen in the form of a class of people deemed to be permeated with foreign influences, and only with their utter elimination can the purity and security of the *ethnie* be ensured against the surrounding enemies. By such drastic means, it seems, including the depopulation of the capital, Phnom-Penh, did the Khmer Rouge regime of Pol Pot attempt to maintain the integrity of the nation at the cost in lives of a large portion of it. A similar explanation lies behind Robespierre's Terror: no-one who was not a wholly committed revolutionary could be guaranteed not to have traitorous links with the enemy powers now ranged against France.

The impulse to preserve the ethnic identity sometimes takes the form of seeking to recover the "national soul" from the "pollution" of internationalist materialism. Thus Mahatma Gandhi preached the need to return to the spinning wheel and humble peasant values, echoing in this the philosophy of Tolstoy before him; Eamon De Valera sought a return to an Ireland that never really was except in the imaginings of late Celtic romanticism; and Welsh nationalists of the 1930s advocated, under a similar influence, the pastoralization of their country—a proposal not well received by the miners of South Wales.[19] The most striking manifestation of this hostile reaction to materialist values has been the populist anti-Western character of a revived Islam, the force behind the Iranian Revolution of 1979 and now actively undermining the more secular, pro-Western regimes in the Moslem world.

The most direct way of preserving the ethnic identity is by disallowing inter-mixture by natural means. Religion has historically been a prime factor in ensuring that marriage was confined to the community, and has largely made possible the continuous existence over many centuries of the Jewish people living in small groups among others. In the same way, the two major communities of Northern Ireland have preserved their separate identities by religious difference: marriage across the religious, and hence ethnic, divide is still rare, and at the lower levels of society can lead to ostracism or even danger. Usually, the force of public prejudice is a sufficient deterrent to mixed marriages where there is a strong ethnic conscious-ness but sometimes, and particularly when race is involved, these will be prohibited by law. Such was the policy enacted by the South African Nationalist regime during the *apartheid* period, as it had been earlier by Hitler's Reich.

These two regimes have been exceptional in modern Western history in fos-tering, indeed being expressions of, ethnic nationalism in an extreme form. Fascist regimes other than the Nazi may have been ultra-nationalist but they were not ultra-ethnicist. In the case of South Africa, this was born out of a fear of losing power to, or being submerged by, the much more numerous nonwhite population of the country. But in Germany there was no such fear, only a strong racial or ethnic pre-judice that exists at a deep level in many European societies. Massacres and expul-sions of Jews had occurred intermittently through European history, sometimes led or abetted by the authorities, but often spontaneous and popular. Until the Holocaust, the worst modern incidents were the Russian pogroms of the 1890s, occurring at the village level but officially encouraged and leading to the mass flight of Jews to Western Europe and America. Such racialism had rarely been expressed as declared government policy, at least in modern times, but in the Nazis a class that shared these sentiments at last came to power. In the bid for revolutionary power they possessed a trump card. The racial creed made a seductive appeal to those who were lowly placed, yet by nature "upwardly mobile." The humblest clerk, provided he was of good Aryan stock, now had the priceless advantage of "blood": from being a nobody under the Kaiser, he now became, in Hitler's system of racial values, one of the lords of creation.

Whereas "hard" ethnic nationalism insists on ethnic purity, achieved either by segregation (*apartheid*) or by the more drastic "ethnic cleansing" of expulsion or exter-mination, "soft" ethnic nationalism is content with sovereignty, or, if that is unobtain-able, with cultural autonomy or privilege within its own region. It is a product of the liberal democratic movements of the last century and came into its own with the peace settlement of Versailles. Not surprisingly, ethnic nationalist movements arising from minority *ethnie* within a larger state are invariably more self-conscious about their nationhood than is the more populous "core" nation within that state. Hence the vibrant political and cultural nationalisms of the Catalans, Basques, Bretons, Welsh, and Scots, to name but a few, whereas ethnic "English nationalism," except in marginal cultural ways, can scarcely be said to exist—perhaps because it does not need to.[20]

Thus far we have looked at varieties of nationalism over historical time and space. There is no more protean force in politics. It adapts itself to different circumstances, needs and goals. There are times when it appears to be a spent force, and then, to universal surprise, it springs back with redoubled fury. In the present writer's view, it is the *ethnie* that are the true realities of much of the world, and the world will ignore or discount them at its peril. Already they have torn to pieces several African and Middle Eastern states, and in cultures where kinship counts for everything and allegiance to an inherited, rather than indigenous, state-system little or nothing, the political superstructure looks more and more vulnerable. *The nationalism of nation-building may save something from the impending wreck, but time is running short and the omens are not propitious.*[21]

Upon the collapse of the Communist order in 1989–91, there were those who seem prematurely to have held that History had ended. On the contrary, it appears to be taking a new and alarming turn. Out of the anarchy and turmoil of the Dark Ages a feudal order of dynastic kingdoms at length arose. This in turn gradually gave way to a new order of nation-states, a process fired by nationalism and marked by the wars, revolutions and upheavals that characterized especially the period from the French Revolution to the Second World War and its anti-imperial aftermath. The twentieth century has seen the nation-state almost everywhere prevail. Indeed, it became the model which the former colonial world was bequeathed and expected to operate and prosper by. But no sooner had the idea of the nation-state achieved worldwide currency, than a new type of polity founded upon ethnicity, tribalism, and kinship, appeared to be struggling to be born. The bloody events in the former Yugoslavia; the genocide in Rwanda and virtual disintegration of other African states; the reappearance of a virulent anti-semitism in Russia; the hostility, sometimes murderously expressed, towards poor immigrants flooding, often illegally, into Western Europe and the United States; and the fierce demand for the recognition of their identities by hitherto quiescent minorities in certain old established nation-states; all these indicate that the race is on between ethnicism and state nationalism for the future and the soul of the world. Which of these two great social and political forces will triumph? Just as the dynastic state gave way to the nation-state, are we seeing the birth pangs of a new world order structured less upon nationalism than upon ethnicity? Is the ethnic state the state of the future? This is probably the most momentous political question facing the coming century, for upon its outcome the fate of millions will be decided.[22]

## Notes

1. The change of title from king of the people to king of the land came in England with the accession of John (1199), but in Scotland, with rare exceptions, not until the union of the crowns in 1603, hence "Mary, Queen of Scots." This indicates

the persistence of the archaic Scottish view of monarchy as a relationship between chief and kindred.

2. Bernard Shaw, *Saint Joan*, first paragraph of the preface.

3. J. B. Black, *The Reign of Elizabeth 1558–1603* (Oxford: Clarendon Press, 1936), p.194.

4. See John Milton on God's choice of "His Englishmen" to achieve divine purposes: *Areopagitica* in *Milton's Prose Writings* (London: Dent, Everyman edn., 1958), p. 177. See also William Haller, *Foxe's Book of Martyrs and the Elect Nation* (London: Cape, Bedford Historical Series, 1967), chap. 7, "The Elect Nation," especially pp. 237–41, 245, 249.

5. Winston S. Churchill, *Marlborough: His Life and Times* (London: Harrap, 1947 edn.), book 2, p. 562.

6. Thomas Carlyle, *The French Revolution* (London: Chapman and Hall, 1900 edn.), p. 609.

7. Martin Wight, *International Theory: The Three Traditions* (Leicester and London: Leicester University Press, 1991), p. 91.

8. A cheap edition of the *Nibelungenlied* was published in 1815 for the use of soldiers, see *The Fall of the Nibelungs* (London: Dent, Everyman edn., 1908), p. vii n.

9. K. R. Minogue, *Nationalism* (London: Methuen, University Paperback edn., 1969), p. 70.

10. Bolton King, *The Life of Mazzini* (London: Dent, Everyman edn., 1911), p. 310.

11. *The Intimate Papers of Colonel House* (London: Ernest Benn, 1926), vol. 1, p. 255. House predicted "an awful cataclysm" which no one in Europe, where there is "too much hatred, too many jealousies," could avert.

12. Cited in one of the many commentaries on Argentine society made in the aftermath of the Falklands War of 1982, but not now attributable.

13. The phrase occurs in book 9, chap. 1, of *War and Peace* but the idea is expounded particularly in chap. 1 of the first epilogue and at greater length in the second epilogue of the novel.

14. J. Ortega y Gasset, *The Revolt of the Masses* (London: Allen & Unwin, 1961), p. 124. Note also de Gaulle's observation "that only vast enterprises are capable of counter-balancing the ferments of disintegration inherent in [the French] people; that our country . . . must aim high and hold itself straight, on pain of mortal danger. In short, to my mind, France cannot be France without greatness.": Charles de Gaulle, *War Memoirs*. Vol. 1: *The Call to Honour—1940–1942* (London: Collins, 1955), p. 9.

15. Two of the most perceptive books on this theme are C. A. W. Manning, *The Nature of International Society* (London: Macmillan, reissued edn. 1975), and Benedict Anderson, *Imagined Communities: Reflections on the Origin and Spread of Nationalism* (London: Verso, 1983).

16. See Anthony D. Smith, *The Ethnic Origins of Nations* (Oxford: Blackwell, 1986), pp. 21–22, and E. J. Hobsbawm, *Nations and Nationalism since 1780* (Cambridge: Cambridge University Press, 1990), p. 160 and n. 24.

17. For examples of "Frontier" genocide, with further references, see Martin Wight, op. cit. note 7, Chap. 4, "Theory of Mankind: 'Barbarians,'" section on Realism, pp. 50–66.

18. This phrase—*"ciscenje"* in Serbo-Croatian—was first used in 1991 by Vojislav Seselj, a Serbian politician and extreme nationalist whose paramilitaries were responsible for driving people from their homes. Report from Belgrade by Louise Branson, *Sunday Times* (London), July 26, 1992, p. 23.

19. As one at a public meeting robustly put it, "So you want to turn us all into bloody shepherds!" (told to the writer by an eyewitness).

20. The English are the only indigenous people of the British Isles not to have produced a nationalist party, although some might argue that they produced the nationalist parties of all the rest.

21. The italics are the editor's.

22. I treat of the developing contest between nationalism and ethnicity more fully, and with particular respect to Africa, Europe and the United States, in "Nationalist Ideals and Ethnic Realities," chap. 6 of *Community, Diversity and a New World Order: Essays in Honor of Inis L. Claude, Jr.*, edited by Kenneth W. Thompson (Lanham, New York, London: University Press of America, 1994). That contribution may be regarded as a sequel to the present chapter.

# 5

# Cultural Foundations of Ethnonationalism

## The Role of Religion

MARTIN E. MARTY

### An Assessment of the Current Scene

A goal of this volume is to throw various lights on ethnonationalism, a surprisingly strong phenomenon at the end of this century. This implies understanding the role of "ethnos," the people or peoplehood in the aggregates that make up a nation, in some cases, or which is seen to be coextensive with the political boundaries of particular nations in others. The assumption is that some comparative study will help bring out features that might otherwise go unnoticed or uncomprehended. With this comparativism there is also an effort to isolate some variables, in this chapter, the role of religion.

Let me quote for openers one of the more eloquent assessments, this one by Harold R. Isaacs:

> We are experiencing on a massively universal scale a convulsive ingathering of people in their numberless grouping of kinds—tribal, racial, linguistic, religious, national. It is a great clustering into separateness that will, it is thought, improve, assure, or extend each group's power or place, or keep it safe or safer from the power, threat, or hostility of others. This is obviously no new condition, only the latest and by far the most inclusive chapter of the old story in which after failing again to find how they can co-exist in sight of each other without tearing each other limb from limb, Isaac and Ishmael clash and part in panic and retreat once more into their caves.[1]

Ethnonationalism—we have the "ethnos" feature here in mind—often with a religious base, has been present from the beginnings of recorded history. Such an expression is now intensified and rendered more lethal, thanks to new technology and weaponry. Once upon a time, the little quasi-national groups on one side of a hill could engage in tribal warfare with those on another until one would prevail or both would retreat—while the rest of the world went on, indifferent to or ignorant about the event. Today, however, ethnonationalism is a part of geopolitics; cheap weaponry and even nuclear destruction are part of the specter it creates.

At mid-century the favored elite symbols indicated convergence, centripetalism: the United Nations, United World Federalism, UNESCO, a World Council of Churches, ecumenism, interfaith agencies, internationalism, racial integration, "the family of man," "global village," "spaceship earth," even the nation itself, and religious syntheses (in Arnold Toynbee, Julian Huxley and Teilhard de Chardin) were dominant. At the end of this century the symbols point to divergence, centrifugalization: particularisms based on gender, class, region, ideology, and most of all, religion combined with ethnicity and race have come to dominate.

Not all ethnonationalism is "natural," it can be contrived. Max Weber addressed the definition and distinctions helpfully:

> Any aspect or cultural trait, no matter how superficial, can serve as a starting point for the familiar tendency to monopolistic closure. . . . Almost any kind of similarity or contrast of physical type and of habits can induce the belief that a tribal affinity or disaffinity exists between groups that attract or repel each other. . . . The belief in tribal kinship, regardless of whether it has any objective foundation, can have important consequences especially for the formation of a political community. Those human groups that entertain a subjective belief in their common descent—because of similarities or physical type or customs or both, or because of memories of colonization and migration—in such a way that this belief is important for the continuation of non-kinship communal relationship, we shall call 'ethnic' groups, regardless of whether an objective blood relationship exists or not. . . . Behind all ethnic diversities there is somehow naturally the notion of the 'chosen people,' which is nothing else but a counterpart of status differentiation translated into the plane of horizontal coexistence. The idea of a chosen people derives its popularity from the fact that it can be claimed to an equal degree by any and every member of the mutually despising groups.[2]

We note Weber's double use of the word "objective": he observes that there may be no objective foundation or objective blood relationship. People presume that there is one, or that it can be fabricated. Religion, as we shall see, can be a potent element in developing the mythic structures that stand behind ethnic groups and ethnonationalism.

Those who study religion in international affairs will instinctively correlate these political situations with cultural, including religious, phenomena. Religion is a more visible and potent factor in some situations than others. Wherever the word "Islam" or "Israel" shows up, the public begins to think of Shi'ite and Sunni Islamic fundamentalism versus Israeli movements like the Bloc of the Faithful, the Gush Emunim, or the tribalism of the Haredim. India is today torn between Islamic, Hindu, and Sikh fundamentalist-like movements that may jeopardize inherited constitutionalism. Canada is troubled by phonic and religious cultures between Quebec and the rest of the nation. In Northern Ireland the partisan boundaries match religious terminology: Protestant and Catholic. "Muslim Bosnia" is the standard name for one of the beleaguered areas of what was Yugoslavia, and the word Christian or Orthodox or Catholic gets associated with Serbian, Croatian, and other areas there.

Meanwhile in Nigeria, groupings marked by what used to be called "animisms" define themselves between and alongside rival Islamic and Christian proselytizing movements. In South Africa, the Inkatha party and the Zulu movements connect with symbols that are vastly different from those that give life to the ANC. And the old Dutch Reformed Church's former legitimation of *apartheid*, as well as English religious racism in white populations are well known. The role of intense religion is evident, also, for example, in the New Christian Right in the United States, or the spiritual definitions of African-, Native-, Asian-, or Hispanic/Latino- (to say nothing of sundry Euro-) Americans in the United States, and provides more close to home access to ethnonational elements. We leave to specialists the assessment of particulars on all these regions, including where religion does or does not play a major role; our task is anticipatory, inclusive, comparative, and synthetic.

### What We Make of the New Situation

It is as foolish to overestimate the religious factor in ethnonationalism and conflict as it is dangerous to underestimate it. Much of the sense of identity and purpose within groups would exist apart from anything approaching religion. There are ageless elements of human individual and group aggression, little understood (or at least productive of few shared explanations), which inspire bonding apart from sacred symbols. People may be expressing heritages of particularly violent simian ancestral strains, as some of the more extravagant ethologists claim; or they may be working out Oedipal impulses; or, as another option, merely seeking turf and territory. But there are some particular new features.

The issue of personal and social identity[3] has grown acute in postcolonial, post–Cold War circumstances. When the empire subjugated "you," you knew who you and your group were. You gained identity by facing off against the barbarians, the foreign devils. When they went home, you were left without that foil for self-definition and began to redraw the boundaries of the nations that they had artificially drawn and produced. The American could wake up any morning from soon after 1945 until 1989 and know who s/he was, because the "evil empire" over there was everything that a U.S. citizen was not. But when the Iron Curtain was torn and the Berlin Wall fell, new questions arose as people had to ask what defined geopolitical life. Of course, modern ethnonationalism existed where colonialism and imperialism were not the dominant factors, and tribalism lived on among peoples remote and not immediately affected by the Cold War. But the changed international situation has made these forces more vivid, more vital, more visible than before.

The question of identity links with questions about whom one trusts; where are the continuities in life; with whom can I bond for my security or the expression of my altruism; who protects me; who guides me through the mazes of life? The tribalist offers to simplify life by making ethnicity and meaning roughly coexistent and coextensive. And as the ideologies associated with imperialism and the Cold War were found to be ineffective or obsolete, it left millions without something in which to believe. They could at least reject cosmopolitanism, internationalism, and universalist impulses and draw themselves together in support of themselves, their tribes, their meanings.

Modern ethnonationalism with its religious dimensions is also expressive of moves toward filling power vacuums or rearranging polities. Where the ballot does not serve, the bullet may. This version of ethnicity includes aesthetic elements and belongs at least to the decor of life, if not to its substance. Folk song, popular dance, the stories told, the posters and images projected, have great appeal when they reinforce the tribe(s) to which one belongs. And ethnonationalism seems to be growing as part of a revolt against bureaucratization, remoteness, impersonality, and decision-at-a-distance. The ethnic group, the subnation, or even the nation, as the case may be, is close at hand, observable, possibly malleable to the purposes of ordinary participants.

For all these reasons ethnonationalism is and would be strong without religious reinforcement; but it has religious reinforcement or impulse in surprising abundance and variety today.

**The Surprise Factor: Why Religion, Why Is It Overlooked?**

A fissure runs through world cultures, nations, ethnic groups, and ethnonationalisms. On one side are those where religion is seen as a "private affair," a secondary factor, something that is waning and will presumably disappear. On the other are those where religion is manifest, visible, palpable, flaunted as a force in human affairs. Its institutions are massive; its hold and demands pervasive; its symbols are public and proudly displayed. The contrast would be most visible to someone who compared, for instance, the physics or biology department of a typical state-sponsored university in Europe or America with a circle of Islamic fundamentalist partisans in a city square in Algeria. In the case of inhabitants of the Western university world, they may be religious by moonlight, spiritual on their own time, pious in private. But in few overt ways could anything even reminiscently or vestigially religious be seen as integral to the processes that constitute academic investigation, research and teaching. In the case of the Algerians, hitherto relaxed and semi-secular Muslims have foregone further intrusion into the camps of modernity. They have redonned garb that signals Islamic culture, including the *chador* or veil. They are punctilious about attending to prayer and worship. They study the scriptures and take signals from its expounders, being unsatisfied with secular explanation.

Not only is there a fissure through cultures; ethnonationalism also has elicited or produced a situation in which there is little understanding by elites of the motivations of those who lead or follow in the path of the Other. To the ethnonationalist fired by religion, the modern university, clinic, broadcasting studio, legislature, or social circle is, through ignorance or malevolence, incapable of understanding the True Way. To the modern academic, clinician, laboratorian, politician, or broadcaster, the ethnoreligious group moved by a sacred scripture looks like a vestige of an earlier human condition or situation; a pocket of people who have just not gotten the signals of change; an embodiment of cultural lag that sooner or later will catch up with the forces of modernization and secularization. What has led to the second of these two, a characteristic stance that has excluded religion from common concern?

To most observers, the key would be the shaping of the modern university in the afterglow of the Enlightenment. For two centuries people moved by reason, science, and a belief in progress, helped develop reflexive ways of doing and interpreting life. To them religion was a set of practices or ideologies which must all but inevitably wane. For Auguste Comte, religion, like metaphysics, belonged to an earlier stage of humanity, and would be replaced. For Karl Marx it would wither away as the communist process and philosophy of history unfolded and triumphed. Max Weber, though an acute observer of religions everywhere, saw the modern scene as one of *Entzauberung*, disenchantment, rationalization and not a response to revelation. Sigmund Freud located religion in quasi-mythical layers of the troubled psyche.

Today critical analysts speak of this internally contradictory cluster as somehow sharing in "the Enlightenment project," which is presumed to be in trouble at the horizon of postmodern times. Critics from within have questioned the presumptions behind the face of reason. Science has produced mixed benefits. Progress was a God that failed. Many believe that this project is in trouble, but have not come up with alternatives, and tend to act on the effects where the founding assumptions have all but disappeared. Along with the belief that religion would go away and that nationalism, ethnicity, or some other force would by itself prevail, there was a less clearly voiced implicit belief that while religion survived, that which would endure would be necessarily concessive, adaptive to international and cosmopolitan forces, uprooted from tribalist bases. Its professors and confessors would be empathic, responsive, ecumenical, interfaithed, tolerant people. Conversation, dialogue, and openness would accompany the religion that survived.

What was overlooked in these projects, as postmodernists or critical rationalists now both like to point out, is that Enlightenment modernism was still another substantive philosophy of history. The rationalists acted as if they knew something about the secrets of the future, about outcomes. Also overlooked was the ideological tendency, often unrecognized by the secular observer. In the eighteenth century, the movements and their leaders knew the future: reason would prevail. In the nineteenth century, the Gods would die because social and psychological forces would make them unnecessary and irrelevant. In the twentieth century, the human Theater of the Absurd would convince people that religious explanations were all bad faith and illusion. Yet religion in its ever-adaptive ways (sometimes by going underground or turning private, as it does not in ethnonationalisms) outlasted most of the prophets and prophesies.

Who is surprised? Paradoxically and ironically: the leadership in the very agencies which are supposed to monitor human impulses. The academy, with its antennae, its social scientific fabric, largely has marginalized religion. In selective corners of it, in order to understand ethnonationalist movements, there has been considerable recovery of interest. But the academy, which should be the first to measure, was sometimes the last to learn how to account for the scope of ethnonationalist religion. The mass media of communication, often in the hands of people who did not share the ecologies where religion prospered, were dismissive of religion where it did appear. Commerce is secularly ecumenical: there are no denominational labels on stocks and most bonds. The modern hospital or clinic, even though its clients may be struggling with the most profound religious themes, ordinarily goes about its business the same way whether or not religious meanings exist.

Those who are making claims for their ethnonationalist tribes do not have the luxury of overlooking and underusing religion; nor do they understand how others can fail to see what motivates them. While it is not the only factor and not always the dominant one, religion is sufficiently integrally related to ethnonationalisms that it demands fresh inquiry.

### Religion: What It Is and Does in Ethnonationalism

A volume such as this one could hardly fail to scrutinize the religious dimension of ethnonationalism. Thirty years ago it would have been easier to neglect religion than it is now. That situation may have been the result of indifference to, or ignorance of, religion. The Western academy and media, where pluralism and secularization have blunted the force of religion or the comprehension of it, often overlooked the role it played under the noses of observers or in remote cultures. After the Iranian revolution in 1979, high operatives in the United States Central Intelligence Agency had to explain why they had been caught off guard by the Ayatollah Khomeini. The regular answer, paraphrased, was: "We observed all forces and elements that could have worked against our purposes. We watched banking, education, mores, costume, entertainment, technology, family-life, media, and more. The only thing we paid no attention to was religion, presuming that everyone knew that religion had no power in the modern world."

Today, while religion may be treated in isolation and as a segregated topic, anyone in government, the media, or the academy who wants to do full justice to ethnonationalism has to include observation of religion. But the ability to do so has been atrophied, or rendered difficult, by the complexity of the subject—beginning with definition. We know what weapons do; we can observe troop movements; it is not difficult to define boundaries like rivers; there is much experience in the understanding of constitutionalism and economics. But religion is diffuse, hard to grasp, hard to isolate; it may be epiphenomenal, which means attached to a force that would be there anyhow; or it may be the main motivating force. It may be explained away through reductionism: religion of the sort that inspires ethnonationalism is "nothing but" this or that—economics, psychology, sociology, status, magic and superstition, and who knows what else, are called into play as explanatory factors. Yet after all the reducing and explaining, something remains. What is meant by religion? What is it?

An open-textured way of bringing focus to the topic is to say: "Religion is what you would put into a multimillion word, sixteen-volume encyclopedia, as we did with *The Encyclopedia of Religion*." That is, some definitions of religion are so broad that they virtually are coexistensive with all human reality. Thus one can enhance and illustrate the phenomenology of religion by showing how professional football, the Miss America contest, bull-fighting in Spain, and Mardi Gras are religious; they certainly have religious dimensions. But each use of the term for illustrative purposes there confuses commonsensical uses.

At the other end, the definition can be too narrow: religion is what one finds in the phone book's Yellow Pages under "Churches and Synagogues," and is thus identified only with the institutions of organized religion. Many tribalists on the ethnoreligious scene may not even frequent institutions of the faith under whose names they move. Thus the Catholic Church in Northern Ireland often works to bring ecumenical concord and civil peace. Unchurched peoples named Catholic, who may seldom attend mass or other rites of the church, are described as both "religious" and ethnonationally militant.

Rather than attempt to construct my own definition of religion for present purposes, I will simply borrow some pointers used by Harold Isaacs, a pioneer student of tribalism. He defines religion functionally, by pointing to what it sets out to provide. I quote:

- a powerful personal-individual-emotional-subjective experience
- a powerful institutional-social-historical-objective actuality
- a way of dealing with the awesome forces of nature. . . .
- a provider of a set of explanations for the inexplicable . . . a source of meaning [Weber]
- a way of ordering the vagaries of misfortune and good fortune. . . .
- a supplier of significance for the insignificant . . .
- a source of solace . . .
- a source of authority, of commanding law to be obeyed . . .
- "a dramatization on a cosmic plane of the emotions, fears, and longings" stemming from each person's own relations with his/her father and mother . . . ([Freud,] Ernest Jones)
- as sanction and upholder of temporal authority, providing the halo of divine origin for earthly rulers, defining and defending norms, public morality and obligations, a bulwark against anarchy/evil, the indispensable bonding cement in the social order, God as "symbol of society" (Durkheim)
- as tool of power, blesser of banners of conquerors . . .
- or, contrastingly, religion as source of challenge to authority as . . . in the many millenarian revolutionary movements.[4]

Instead of defining religion, one may effectively point to phenomena which, by common consent, have come to be seen as possessing qualities that would, indeed, lead to their being included in a work called *The Encyclopedia of Religion*. This nominalist-of-a-sort approach means, for me, that one watches for:

*"Ultimate concern."* Paul Tillich's term for whatever it is to which humans are most attached, in which they are grounded; not all ultimate concern is necessarily religious, but all religion is expressive of ultimate concern. Tribalists who send their sons out as part of a human chain to walk across landmined areas so troops can move safely, believe that they serve the purposes of Allah and will be rewarded in Paradise so they are not deterred by the attractions of proximates. They are wrapped up in ultimacy, to the point of the sacrifice of life.

*Experience of the sacred.* One hears the voice of God or, more likely, reads or hears a scripture that is conceived of as an utterance of the divine; there is what Rudolf Otto called a sense of the *mysterium tremendum et fascinosum*, a mystery. "Take the shoes off your feet, for the ground on which you are standing is holy ground." The call of the ethnoreligious militant is to serve sacral purposes.

*Socialization.* While ultramodern religion, for example American style, and some earlier religion, including nonmonastic and noncommunal Buddhism, might make room for solitary spirituality, for "privatization," most experience of the sacred or devotion to ultimate concern leads people to build community. Some ethnoreligious movements employ the religious vision to deepen socialization; some begin as socialized religious responses which then impel action.

*Preference for mythosymbolic expression.* The connections between religion and myth are profound, and most religious reinforcement occurs through symbols. Religious people by and large prefer not to use abstract or scientific communication; they cherish mythic accounts of origin and destiny. Thus most ethnoreligious tribes, from animists in Africa to civil religionists in the United States, have some founding myths. ("Fourscore and seven years ago, . . ." Lincoln could have said "Eighty-seven years ago," and sounded like the drafter of an article for an encyclopedia entry on constitutionalism or war. He invoked rhetorical strategies that his hearers associated with the fabric of sacred scriptural voice.)

*Rite and ceremony.* Religious people are not the only ones to engage in ritualization, though some anthropologists see a religious dimension in all ritual and ceremonial activity. But religious people in almost all cases do engage in ritualization of the passages of life, the elements of their bonding. Even highly rationalized and humanistic religions like Unitarian Universalism and Ethical Culture find it valuable to provide rites after birth and for marriage or at the time of death. So ethnonationalist groups enhance their life together with ritual.

*Quasi-metaphysical appeal.* Some religions are frankly metaphysical and argue their case philosophically; others are more economical about philosophical claims. But most of them suggest that something is going on behind the scenes; there is a backdrop to history. Thus ethnonational groups, however small they be, are convinced that they are acting out divine purposes that can be known through scripture, charismatic leadership, or meditation.

*Behavioral correlation.* Everyone behaves; it would be silly to claim that religion alone stands behind moral expression in specifics and action in general. But religions all do make certain demands: they ask, do you believe thus and so? Then eat this and do not eat that; bring up your children thus; wear that; worship here; observe this season. Ethnonationalists when they are informed by religion make moral demands on insiders and prescribe action against outsiders.

Why do they act religiously? For at least these five reasons. First, they have a sense that they have had an encounter with the Other through revelation, disclosure, scriptural study, reason, nature, or rhetoric. What is disclosed is demanding, encompassing, total. It must be acted upon. Second, this Other is perceived as Spirit: transcendent, sacred, divine, uncanny, not easily accessible, not available to the outsider. Third, this Other imparts some sort of inside knowledge, gnosis, particularized interpretation of experience. Be equipped with this knowledge and one can engage in extraordinary action, can interpret success and failure alike. Fourth, the issuance of this knowledge connects with power. It legitimizes action and grants authority. Finally, the encounter with the Other implies a call for the individual or the collective to be agents of the sacred and the divine. They are elect people, selected for mission.

Religion on these terms, then, gives people an identity and sense of belonging and, in almost cases, a network to which to belong. The benefits of belonging may include encouragement for healing, inspiring, enabling, and providing interpretation. In ethnonationalism, religion tells why a group came to be, why one should respond to it and shun others, why there should be consequent action to the point of death. Conversely, religion is an instrument in separation. Over against the true believers there are the false; against the orthodox are the heterodox and the heretics; the Great Satan, the AntiChrist, the Western Imperialist, the Barbarian Muslim, the Jew—these and similar symbolizations of evil help the ones who belong remain loyal, the activists are inspired to act against those who stand in the way of the group and the divine.

Some religions fulfil these purposes better than others; one very broadly defined style or impulse has arisen late in the twentieth century, with many historical precedents. It deserves separate observation and analysis.

### The Power of Religion[s]: A Fundamentalist Outlook

If religion as such is an unexpectedly powerful agent on the ethnonationalist scene, one must ask which forms of religion do the most to reinforce tribalism? Obviously, historic religions have undergone great transformations as they moved into and through modernity and into the postmodern situation, as many of them have. Forces of secularization have often led to a diminishing or what Marx called a "withering" of religion. Much of Western Europe, site of historic Christendom, has seen church-religion become little more than a remembrance, something that has left cathedrals and monasteries, now empty, as monuments. Or after a passage through the Enlightenment, some of these religions saw the aggressive elements of faith to be moderated, and tolerance come to be appreciated and evidenced. But ecumenical, rational, reconciliatory, semi-indifferent, and tolerant religions are precisely those that, despite Enlightenment prophesies that they would prosper, have not done so. In open competition everywhere in the world, they are no match for aggressive, assertive, imperial, and harder-line religions.

Some of these spiritual impulses have few immediate tribal, ethnonational, or belligerent implications. As one example, within Christianity various sorts of pentecostalisms and charismatic movements have transformed the lives of their advocates and converts without in every case turning political. They are outbursts of what sociologists of religion like Emile Durkheim think of as "effervescences." They may be coping devices for the oppressed and poor, signals of hope in an otherwise hopeless world. They may serve as legitimators for people who are making new economic moves. They serve to ritualize the passages of life, the seasons of the year. They provide dignity and hope. Such religions and spiritual forces help individuals make sense of the universe around them, and fulfil or exhaust themselves on personal or small and local communal levels.

Alongside such exuberances, however, there are neoreligious forces that do motivate aggression; they do solidify tribalist groups and impulses; they do legitimate exclusion of the "other," the stress on "difference," the exaggeration of the flaws of non-members and of the virtues of adherents. They might be spoken of as "retribalist" religions. A code-name for many of them is fundamentalism,[5] a subject that has inspired considerable curiosity and scholarly inquiry, as well as media attention, in a world where many thought religions would decline and disappear. Fundamentalisms, movements bearing family-resemblances to fundamentalism, fundamentalist-like forces, demand and deserve analysis for their role in ethnonationalism, and we shall spend some time exploring them under whatever name.

(The use of the term 'fundamentalism' is sometimes controversial, so I shall spend a moment discussing and qualifying its use. The term was invented early in twentieth-century American Protestantism, after a series of pamphlets called *The Fundamentals*, a "World's Christian Fundamentals Association" founded in 1919, and an editorial by a Baptist editor in 1920. It was associated with intraProtestant battles over biblical criticism, evolution, apocalypticism, and general modernist trends. The hallmark became a doctrine of "biblical inerrancy," and for decades European dictionaries equated the doctrine with the term. For those reasons, non-Protestants and non-Christians have sometimes rejected the application of the term, seeing it to be "linguistic imperialism" by the West. Various substitutes have been offered, for example "Radical Reformist" or "Reformist Revolutionary" Shi'ite Islam, in the case of one phenomenon. It is sometimes mentioned that Arabic and Jewish dictionaries do not include cognates to the term fundamentalism. However, the use of the term by media, publics, and academics around the world, has grown. The term is exportable and used for comparative purposes, for example as in the case of "nationalism," "liberalism," "conservatism," or whatever. Scholars tend to be cautious in the use of the term, not ready to equate it with "militancy" or "extremism." But it is likely to survive as the designation for the kind of religion which can move from passivism toward the impelling of activism in ethnonationalism. Not all ethnonationalism is religious and not all religious ethnonationalism is fundamentalist. But the connections are sufficiently widespread that examination of the fundamentalist phenomenon is in place.)

Students of the current subject, religious ethnonationalism, have increasingly come to the observation that the "old-time religion" appearance and self-advertisement of these movements in Christianity, Judaism, Islam, Hinduism, Buddhism, and more, can throw one off the trail. They appear to their adherents as mere traditionalism, conservatism, or orthodoxy. However, the fundamentalisms are distinctively modern, dynamic, and innovative movements. Indeed, the term 'fundamentalism' was coined by some adherents precisely to set themselves off and apart from conservatisms, which were seen as too quietistic, too ready to let the world pass it by. The fundamentalist is a reactor, a participant in confronting modernity, an inventor of the new while retaining and refurbishing symbols of the old. It has been said that a true traditionalist does not know s/he is a traditionalist; once one is self-aware, thanks to a confrontation with "the other," it is necessary to work at traditionalism, to make new things out of it.

The ethnoreligious fundamentalisms, therefore, take rise only after modernity (under whatever description and name) and modernism as a religious adaptation to it have threatened members of a conservative movement. They must perceive modernity as a total threat to their personal and social identity; unless they respond, its pluralism, relativism, and "worldliness" may well be lures for their young and will be corrosive and potentially overwhelming to all. They must react. This is the point at which "old-time" elements, the "fundamentals" from purportedly pure pasts, pure scriptures, better moments, clearer laws, come to be invoked. Karl Rahner, a Catholic theologian, has spoken of "selective retrieval." Fundamentalists selectively retrieve "fundamentals" from a presumed past. They are practical, choosing those what will most help ward off threatening forces of the other and that will most keep their groups together. This means that they create boundaries, distance themselves from others, eliminate the compromisers, adapters and moderates, and magnify their difference from others.

When the group, cell, movement, or tribe has been fashioned, motivated, instructed, and reinforced, fundamentalist ethnonationalisms regularly express a sense that they have a mandate from God, from suprahuman or supernatural forces or powers or persons, to carry out a sacred will. With the mandates and commands come promises: be the agents of the divine in history and, no matter how much travail adherents undergo and however much frustration there may be, the participation will be rewarded—perhaps through ultimate earthly victory or through final, postdeath compensation. Such a religious ethos imparts a sense of knowledge about where history is going. It has a telos, a goal, an end. The militant moves in confidence with an awareness that he or she knows what that goal is, and something of how to attain it. So there are all-purpose explanations for what goes wrong, and morale-building elements to help set things right.

There are local variations, depending upon the religion and the poise of the followers. Thus American Protestant fundamentalists have little immediate hope of capturing the polity. They can influence it, through constitutional revision and local reform. American fundamentalisms may produce tribes, but they have rarely motivated armed conflict. They provide symbolization for patriotic "hyper-Americanism" and ordinarily identify with the secular political right, but rarely do they follow simple ethnic lines. Hispanics and Anglos may belong to the same movement; Alabamans and Arizonans who never meet each other, never form a circle, never shoulder weapons together, and thus are hardly ethnonationalists, can share a militant religious vision and win parts of a polity.

In other polities, such as Arabic Islamic states, where "church and state," "religion and regime," have never been "separated" as American constitutionalism separated them, religious ethnonationalists can more credibly picture taking over the polity. This they have done in Iran, the Sudan, and elsewhere. In Algeria, for example, secular-military regimes of nominal Muslims are on the defensive against now majority fundamentalist militant parties. Small groups of these threaten the semisecular ruling party of Egypt. If and when they prevail, these movements attempt to see to it, and sometimes succeed in their endeavors, to have the boundaries of the nation-state coincide with their religious rule. This greatly inconveniences ethnic and religious minorities; one thinks of the Kurds and Baha'i religionists in Iran as particularly threatened by nationwide ethnonationalism.

In other cases, subnational tribalists are agents of religious disruption. Yugoslavia was an artificial national fabrication; as it was free to disintegrate it became clear that Orthodoxy, Catholicism, and Islam had reinforced the peoples who had been forced into federation, so Yugoslavia broke apart. Similar circumstances prevailed in Lebanon, which officially held together but has been torn by warfare and has had great difficulty effecting a working peaceable polity. The Central Asian republics of the former Soviet Union and Afghanistan are further examples of the ways militant religion, often fundamentalist, tears at or sunders the larger nation. The battles between Muslims, Hindus, Sikhs, and other belligerent forces threatens secular constitutionalism in India. In summation: "ethnonationalism" may mean identification of one's tribe with religious truth even if that unit may not find its borders coexistensive with those of a whole nation-state. But it can also mean that a whole nation converts to a polity and policy expressive of such a religious element. Such forces are disturbing to, and disruptive of, republics, which by definition are aggregations of groups. In fundamentalism, the agents of God must, no matter how long it takes, prevail in their sacred cause. They will not be talked out of it, compromised, or mannered. Their moment will come; the Lord, by whatever name, has told them so.

## Prospects for the Future

For all the dreams that, after the Cold War and with the implosion of ideological systems such as Soviet Communism, there would be a period of relative peace, few look into the twenty-first century with equanimity or hope. During the Cold War a kind of rationality marked the irrationalism of weapons build-ups, espionage, propaganda, and expression of suspicion. That is, the Soviet Union and the United States, the two major players in everyone's conception of international confrontational games, were highly aware of the costs of adventurism. They knew that their nuclear capabilities rendered their freedom of movement on the global scene complex and limited. While they used their power around the globe, taking sides in conflicts everywhere, both seemed to know their limits and the risks of pushing the other too far. In retrospect, it may be that each overestimated the aggressive instincts of the other. They may have fallen victim to their own arms industries and paranoia: for that reason the Cold War will be seen as having had irrational dimensions. Yet calculation and an eerie sense of rationality characterized and qualified the moves of the superpowers.

Today, while there are still armaments and there is still wariness, and while internal upheavals in an unstable Russia or assertiveness in China, North Korea, or other polities may destabilize situations elsewhere, the eyes of people in statecraft, media, and the academy have turned and will continue to turn to the ethnonational and what I have called the tribalist scene. An observing world, looking on first at Lebanon and in recent years particularly at Afghanistan, the former Yugoslavia, the Arab-Israeli Middle East scene, Nigeria, Sudan, the republics of the former Soviet Union, and many other scenes, is more wary and watchful, more ready to feel powerless and frustrated, as smaller-than-national groupings of people set themselves over or against others.

The racial, ethnic, tribal, and religious memories and resentments are so deep, so incapable of being restrained, corrected, moderated, or put to positive use, that no moves by superpowers seem effective. The United Nations may do and has been doing policing in some of these areas, but the nations who provide troops cannot do so for decades or even centuries. Resources and resolve run out. The moment they retreat from the scene, repressed ethnonationalist and religious tribalism reassert themselves, with battles fought to a draw or until there is total victory of one side— even at the expense of "ethnic cleansing" that takes on the character of virtual genocide.

Over the course of the next century, new unforeseen forces will no doubt come upon the scene. One observer came up with the picture of "MacWorld," a network of economic forces that tend to impel interactions and produce transethnic impulses, which might compensate. It may be that prophets on the religious scene may be able to reach into heretofore overlooked elements of the various traditions as they give voice to universalism, ecumenism and reconciliation, impulses currently obscured. It could be that a "neo-Enlightenment" could arise to promote some measure of rationality in the interactions. The historian has seen too many surprises to say "never" about recoveries and changes in political and humanistic energies.

However, on the shorter range, say, through the next couple of decades, one can expect ethnonationalism, reinforced with or motivated by religious and mythical interpretations, to continue to cause tension and upheaval. It is likely that techniques of surveillance will be developed further in order to limit the terrorist possibilities of tribalist groups. It is almost certain that munitions makers, in rich nations as well as poor ones, will continue to find the supply of weapons to even those forces subject to international boycotts to be so profitable that the lethal threat will continue to grow. More than likely, mistrust of the possible agents of the tribalists will remain high, forcing invasions of privacy in many areas.[6]

One can chart the course of the occasional utopian-sounding book that foresees concord: each gains some notice and following, but after the publishing season in which it appears is over, all traces of what it envisioned and proposed tend to disappear. In universities there is some growth of studies in areas like *Religionswissenschaft*, "history of religions," comparative religion, and the like. Some of their advocates making the claim that academic pursuits will lead to a growth in empathy, tolerance, and reconciliation, or at least a minimization of bloodshed. But the hearts of the scholars do not seem to be in their endeavor to move beyond inquiry and understanding, conferences and consultations notwithstanding, and public expectation of results is minimal.

Now and then someone gives expression to the hope that some new Gandhi or Schweitzer or King, some exemplar of reconciliatory resources, will appear in various cultural contexts. The religious texts speaking of transcendent and transtribal concord are rich and available. They can stir conscience and promote moral vision. It would be foolish to abandon hopes for reaching into and beyond the self-enclosed and self-interested tribalisms and offering larger visions. But it also would be foolish to expect reconciliation and rationality to be strong enough visions and forces to counter the threats that disturb the peace as this century and millennium come to an end.

## Notes

1. Harold Isaacs, *Idols of the Tribe: Group Identity and Political Change* (New York: Harper & Row, 1975), p. 10.

2. Max Weber, "Ethnic Groups," in Talcott Parsons et al., *Theories of Society*, vol. 1 (Glencoe, Il: Free Press, 1961), p. 305ff.

3. On the identity theme, see Thomas Luckmann, *The Invisible Religion: The Problem of Religion in Modern Society* (New York: Macmillan, 1967), e.g., p. 97.

4. Harold Isaacs, op. cit. note 1, pp. 31–32.

5. Some elements of what follows parallel argument in Martin E. Mary and R. Scott Appleby, *Fundamentalisms Observed* (Chicago: University of Chicago Press, 1990.)

6. Editor's Note: The detention and interrogation of Abraham Ahmad, a thirty-one-year-old United States citizen of Jordanian birth, by British authorities at London's Heathrow Airport on April 20, 1995—the day after the bombing of the Alfred P. Murrah Federal building in Oklahoma City—instantiates powerfully Marty's observation. *The Milwaukee Journal Sentinel* of Tuesday, April 25, 1995, reported the following:

> Ahmad . . . says he thinks his Middle Eastern appearance and name . . . plus the fact that he was coming from Oklahoma City prompted authorities to detain him.
>
> "People automatically think that the person who did this is from the Middle East. But I didn't think that the FBI would think so," [said Ahmad]. . . . When British immigration officials discovered [that Ahmad] was from Oklahoma City, he was handcuffed and questioned for four or five hours. . . . The worst part of the ordeal, Ahmad said, was when the British authorities sent him back to America. They marched him—tired, hungry, handcuffed and ashamed—through [a] crowded airport.

He said he was flown under armed guard to Dulles Airport near Washington. After several hours, the agents in Washington told Ahmad that he was free to go.

# 6

# Cultural Nationalism and "Internationalization" in Contemporary Japan

KOSAKU YOSHINO

Whereas the development of nationalism has often been associated with the role of the state, it may also be argued that nationalism is formed through informal processes. Nationalism is essentially a dual phenomenon consisting of a formal state-supervised process and an informal process, by which is meant the absence of direct supervision by the state. Most previous studies of nationalism are limited in their scope in that they confine themselves to the process by which political and cultural elites produce national myth and ideology and by which the state inculcates such myth and ideology into the masses through formal education. This study explores the characteristics and workings of informal cultural nationalism, inquiring into the informal process by which ideas of national distinctiveness are "produced," "distributed," and "consumed" in the "market." The study draws its empirical material from Japan in the 1970s and 1980s, a period which saw a resurgence of cultural nationalism or reaffirmation of an active sense of Japanese uniqueness. Japan's cultural nationalism of this period, it will be found, is closely associated with its desires to "internationalize," paradoxical as it may sound.

This chapter begins with a brief mention of Japan's formal nationalism with the aim of showing why the perspective of informal cultural nationalism is relevant in contemporary Japan. Analysis will then be provided of the ways in which ideas concerning peculiarities of Japanese society and culture—generally referred to as the *nihonjinron*—have been produced, distributed and consumed in Japanese society. Particular attention will be given to the paradoxical relationship between "internationalization" and cultural nationalism. The case of businessmen in their role model as "social bearer" of this type of cultural nationalism will be examined.

Definitions of the terms nationalism, political nationalism, and cultural nationalism should first be made. Nationalism comprises both the sentiment among a people that they constitute a community with distinctive characteristics, as well as the project of maintaining and enhancing that distinctiveness within an autonomous state. Political nationalism emphasizes the nation's collective experience as a political reality by achieving a representative state for its community. Cultural nationalism regenerates the national community by creating, preserving or strengthening a people's cultural identity when it is felt to be lacking, inadequate, or threatened. Moreover, cultural nationalism regards the nation as a product of its unique history and culture, and as a collective solidarity endowed with uniquely shared attributes. It is thus fundamentally concerned with the distinctiveness of the historical and cultural community as the essence of a nation. Political and cultural nationalism often do coexist, but the two should be distinguished for their different purposes.

It should be made clear at the outset that this chapter does not aim to furnish an overview of contemporary Japanese nationalism, let alone a historical survey of nationalism in Japan. Nationalism works differently for different groups and for different individuals, and diverse processes are at work in forming the phenomenon of nationalism. Discussion in this chapter will be restricted to one of such processes.

## The State and Formal Cultural Nationalism

A perspective that pays attention to the distribution and consumption of ideas in the "market" is necessary for an analysis of contemporary Japanese society, where people's participation in cultural nationalism is no longer explicitly supervised by the state. Zigmunt Bauman makes a relevant point when he observes that "[a]s the interest of the state in culture faded (i.e., the relevance of culture to the reproduction of political power diminished), culture was coming within the orbit of another power the intellectuals could not measure up to—the market. . . . More and more the culture of consumer society was subordinated to the function of producing and reproducing skillful and eager consumers, rather than obedient and willing subjects of the state."[1]

Bauman is, however, on less firm ground when he argues that the area of culture, which has been "freed from direct supervision by the state," is "now reduced to things of no concern to political powers."[2] Although cultural nationalism in contemporary Japan may be generated in different ways from the time when culture was under the state's direct supervision, one should not totally neglect the state's interest in cultural nationalism.

Even today, the state's interest in cultural nationalism is evident. To give but one example, the Ministry of Education's guidelines on the content and goals of school curriculum, announced in 1989 and put into effect in 1992, reveals an ever stronger emphasis on nationalism. The guidelines reflect conservatives' demand for the removal of Occupation-imposed elements of the education system and a return to traditional values as a way of restoring appropriate attitudes among the youth. The main emphasis is on moral education from primary to high school, a move regarded by education authorities as a remedy for problems at school such as "school refusal syndrome" and bullying among pupils. Also, the state, for the first time in the postwar period, *requires* the *Hinomaru* flag to be displayed and the *Kimigayo* anthem to be sung at school ceremonies. The state also requires primary school curriculum on history to include forty-two selected historical figures including Admiral Tōgō Heihachirō, whose exploits in the Russo-Japanese War (1904–05) were used to promote militarism in textbooks during the Second World War. Despite the Education Ministry's claim that the system for authorizing textbooks is a process of quality control, the system actually entails control of content.

I do not know whether the role of the state has increased, for it may be that the state is only responding to the change in the public's perceptions of national identity, pride, and confidence. These are, in turn, closely associated with other factors such as thinking elites' rearticulation and reassertion of Japanese uniqueness, as well as the sentiment and activities of other educated sections of the population who respond to such thinking elites' writings, which are the main themes of this chapter. I also find it difficult to assess the effectiveness with which the state enhances national sentiment compared to social groups such as intellectuals, media people, businessmen, and so on. It is essential to observe here that although there is little doubt that some of the symbolic rituals of "old" nationalism often "function" to enhance national solidarity, nationalistic rituals also work in the opposite way.

Robert Bocock makes an interesting point when he notes that rituals "may also make some groups feel less part of the national group in that they are made conscious of the fact that they do not share some of the values which seem to lie behind the group's ritual," such as respect for established authority and military virtues. He goes on to point out, for example, that some groups in Britain find their sense of separateness from the "mainstream" society enhanced and their disrespect of established authority and military values reinforced when they witness rituals involving the Royal Family (e.g., Trooping the Colour, the Queen's Christmas Day speech, and the State Opening of Parliament).[3] The same is true with similar ritual occasions in Japan. There always have been, and still are, significant numbers of people whose opposition to nationalistic values are reinforced precisely because of the existence of these "nationalistic" rituals, such as the display of the "national" flag and the singing of the "national" anthem at school ceremonies, the "National Foundation Day," cabinet ministers' visits to the Yasukuni Shrine (where the war dead, including war criminals, are enshrined), and so on. For them, such rituals are nothing but a reminder of their opposition to nationalism. Restraints on any explicit expressions of nationalism are still very strong among substantial numbers of the Japanese.

It is well to observe here that precisely because state-initiated cultural nationalism centers around obviously nationalistic ideas and symbols—nationalistic in the classic sense—it fails to elicit voluntary and positive support from large sections of the population. Anti-war and anti-nationalist sentiment is still noticeably strong among the majority of the Japanese, who disdain sacrifice of their personal lives for the sake of the nationalistic projects of the state.

Strict adherence to the classic view of nationalism, which focuses on the state-initiated production of nationalist ideology and its dissemination through formal education, will result in failure to recognize a number of relevant issues of cultural nationalism in contemporary Japan. The following discussion presents another type of cultural nationalism in contemporary Japan, generated through a more informal, market-oriented process. We shall see that this type of informal cultural nationalism can be promoted paradoxically through an attempt to "internationalize" one's knowledge. "Internationalization" is an agenda that appeals favorably to many sections of contemporary Japanese society that would not wish to see a recrudescence of the "narrow-minded" nationalism of the prewar type. I will even maintain that, though one should not overgeneralize, those who make apparent efforts to "internationalize" can ironically end up being agents of informal cultural nationalism.

### Informal Cultural Nationalism

What I call informal cultural nationalism, has developed mainly in the 1970s and 1980s in relation to the vast amount of publications which Japanese "thinking elites" produced to define the uniqueness of Japanese society, culture and national character. This type of literature is commonly referred to as the *nihonjinron* (literally, discussions of the Japanese). Discussions of Japanese uniqueness appeared in popular editions of books, and occasional essays in newspapers and general interest magazines. Reflecting the competitive market for such works, writers came up with one buzzword after another to describe Japanese uniqueness in order to attract readers. The thinking elites, broadly defined, who participated in the *nihonjinron* were not confined to academics but included thinkers of various occupations such as journalists, critics, writers, and even business elites.

A detailed description of the content of the *nihonjinron* may be dispensed with here since it has been the subject of many other studies.[4] Suffice to summarize briefly the three main themes frequently discussed in the *nihonjinron*.

First, Japanese society is characterized by groupism or "interpersonalism," vertical stratification (intracompany solidarity), and dependence (other-directedness) in contrast to Western society, which has the opposite characteristics of individualism, horizontal stratification (class-based solidarity), and independence (self-autonomy). The *nihonjinron* describe the Japanese as a group-oriented people acting within the framework of a group (typically, a company). Such a Japanese group is hierarchically organized based on affective social relations between superiors (parent-role players) and their subordinates (child-role players).[5] The theory of vertical and group-oriented social structure finds emphasis in the psychological theory of *amae* (dependence), according to which the socialization process in Japan encourages dependence on very close emotional bonds, thereby enabling the persistence of group-oriented, vertical social structural features (such as quasi-parent-child relationships).[6] Some argue that the concept of groupism, often contrasted with individualism, does not accurately describe Japanese social reality, because groupism implies unilateral influence or control by society over individual behavior. These theorists argue that "interpersonalism" (*kanjinshugi*) is a more appropriate concept here in that it gives the highest value to interpersonal relationships, not to society as a moral constraint.[7]

Second, the *nihonjinron* frequently discuss unique Japanese patterns of communication, which are supposedly characterized by a lack of emphasis on logical and linguistic presentation in contrast to the Western patterns that attach utmost importance to the use of dichotomous logic and eloquence (linguistic expression). It is a popular theme in the *nihonjinron* that essential communication is performed nonlogically, empathetically and nonverbally such as, for example, through *haragei* (the art of communicating between persons without the use of direct verbal assertions, and is, incidentally, often a way of achieving a difficult consensus). The mutual sensitivity found in the social interaction of the Japanese is considered to obviate the need for explicit verbal communication.[8]

Finally, the uni-racial (*tan'itsu minzoku*) and homogeneous composition of Japanese society is widely assumed in the *nihonjinron*. These three themes are closely interrelated: the Japanese patterns of communication which discourage dichotomous logic and verbal confrontation are closely related to the high valuation of consensus and harmony in interpersonal relations, and empathetic, affective, and nonlogical communication are believed to be a product of a largely homogeneous society.

Given their pervasive impact on perceptions of the Japanese, a number of criticisms and interpretations of the *nihonjinron* appeared in the 1980s. One prevailing view has it that the *nihonjinron* constitute a nationalist ideology which elites have used to instill a sense of cultural superiority among the Japanese.[9] Just as ruling elite groups generated nationalism from above in prewar and wartime Japan, so it is claimed, similar elite groups produced literature on Japanese uniqueness in contemporary Japan with the intention of manipulating mass psychology in the direction of nationalism. Critics saw the *nihonjinron* as an attempt to attribute Japan's economic success and its apparent lack of serious social problems (e.g., crime, drugs, social divisions) to the unique virtues of Japanese society and national character. The *nihonjinron* were thus considered to present the view that Japan's economic and social success is a cultural victory of the Japanese.[10] However, it would be grossly simplistic to suppose, as many critics have done by holding the classic assumption associated with formal nationalism, that cultural and political elites *consciously* produced nationalist ideology in the form of the *nihonjinron* with the intention of manipulating mass psychology in the direction of nationalism.[11]

It is not the concern of this chapter to explain why professional thinkers produced theories of Japanese uniqueness. Rather, I should like to explore the effects, intended or unintended, which the thinking elites' ideas of Japanese uniqueness have had on the rest of the population in relation to the promotion of cultural nationalism. I shall scrutinize how these ideas of Japanese uniqueness have been "consumed" in Japanese society and how in this process such ideas have promoted cultural nationalism among ordinary people—ordinary in the sense of not being professional thinkers. In so doing, attention will be paid to the workings of informal "market"-based cultural nationalism compared with those of formal, state-initiated nationalism.

### The Consumption of Ideas of Japanese Uniqueness

In order to inquire into who "consumed" thinking elites' ideas of Japanese uniqueness, and why and how they did, I conducted field research in a fairly large provincial city with a population of several hundred thousand in central Japan in the late 1980s.[12] I focused on educators (school teachers and principals) and businessmen since the two groups have a profound influence on Japanese society at large; the former by way of formal socialization of youth, the latter by virtue of the fact that large numbers of the population are employed by companies.

The respondents' consumption of the *nihonjinron* stemmed from their practical concerns to understand and solve concrete problems in their own immediate surroundings.[13] Two types of concern were found to be prevalent among respondents: cross-cultural and organizational.[14] The *nihonjinron* provided those interested in cross-cultural contacts with supposedly useful ideas on cultural differences. The *nihonjinron* also attracted their readers by providing them with ideas and insights considered useful for their organizational concerns at the work place since in the *nihonjinron* Japanese social characteristics are frequently discussed in the context of employment practices, industrial relations and decisionmaking processes. These concerns were especially relevant to businessmen (of the two groups on which I conducted research). By businessmen I mean "company men" or "salarymen," including those of the managerial class, employed by large companies, not owners of small and medium-size businesses. A significantly larger number of businessmen than educators actively responded to and "consumed" the *nihonjinron*.[15] Although my research was restricted to the two groups, these concerns are certainly not specific to businessmen. For example, cross-cultural concerns can be expected to be shared by anyone interested in international contacts such as students and even tourists. Bearing this in mind, inquiry into businessmen's concern with the *nihonjinron* provides hints as to what types of people with what types of concern are likely to consume thinking elites' ideas of Japanese distinctiveness. We shall, therefore, deal with businessmen in their role model as the "social bearer" of informal cultural nationalism.

Before we examine businessmen's place in cultural nationalism, it may be useful here to compare what I call primary and secondary nationalism with regard to the channels through which national identity is disseminated among the population. By "primary" nationalism is meant original nationalism as concerned with creating national identity, in contrast to "secondary" nationalism which preserves and enhances national identity in an already long-established nation. In actuality, the boundaries between primary and secondary nationalism cannot be drawn with precision because of the difficulty of deciding when national identity has been established among significant numbers of a population, and what precise value should be appended to the term significant. Yet a working distinction might nonetheless be proposed.

Primary nationalism normally attaches utmost importance to formal education, which is often conducted, as was the case in prewar Japan, through the power of the state. The school is a powerful agent for injecting national spirit, and the state inculcates national values through formal education. Primary cultural nationalism usually occurs as part of nation-building which involves the process of absorbing individuals into the organic state, the politicized aspect of the national spirit. Primary nationalism in Japan was essentially formal nationalism.

Another important point about primary nationalism is the role of ancestral myth. The initial stages of the formation of national identity center around the discovery or rediscovery of the mythical history and ancestral culture of the nation, for which reason "historians" are given an important place. A sense of having a common and distinctive history and ancestral culture unites successive generations, and fosters a feeling of communal uniqueness. For example, the invention of the tradition of the emperor system in the early Meiji period was intended to combine traditional familism and State Shinto and thereby to stress the unbroken imperial lineage from time immemorial, as well as the unity of Japanese subjects based on the invented historical vision. Parallels are found from around the world.[16] In secondary nationalism, where a sense of belonging to a historical nation already exists, ancestral myth or historicist vision is less relevant. More relevant as a source with which to reaffirm a sense of difference for the contemporary audience is the nation's contemporary "social culture." The writers of the *nihonjinron* are "popular sociologists" or the type of thinking elites who are interested in discussing exactly this sort of social culture.

If we consider this point about different types of ideas of national identity, we may understand why primary nationalism attaches importance to formal education. Ancient history or ancestral myth has, in a sense, to be taught unilaterally to "ordinary" people through the medium of formal education. By contrast, contemporary social culture, an important source of national identity in secondary nationalism, is already empirically known to ordinary people, and the role of thinking elites here is to provide them with perspectives from which to think more systematically about their society and behavior. Thus, the readers of the *nihonjinron* did not respond positively to them in order to "be taught" about their society unidirectionally by the elite but, rather, because they wanted to endorse what they already knew and felt about their society and behavior. They regarded the *nihonjinron* as "social theories" they could use to consciously organize their thinking about their everyday patterns of behavior and thought.

It may be argued that the approach that assumes unilateral transmission of knowledge—and, therefore, explicit ideological manipulation—from above is inappropriate as a perspective on the workings of ideas in contemporary cultural nationalism. The case of the *nihonjinron* suggests that the workings of ideas concerning national identity can be more insightfully examined by paying attention to the informal, "market" process in which producers, distributors and consumers of ideas of national distinctiveness participate.

## The Reproduction of Ideas of Japanese Uniqueness

Let us now return to the case of businessmen. Edward Shils' classification of intellectuals may usefully be applied to characterization of businessmen's place in relation to the *nihonjinron*. Shils classifies intellectuals into "productive intellectuals," who produce intellectual works, "reproductive intellectuals," who engage in the interpretation and transmission of intellectual works, and "consumer intellectuals," who read and concern themselves passively with such works.[17] We have seen that businessmen were keen consumers of the *nihonjinron*. When leading members of the business elite publish their ideas of Japanese business and social culture on the basis of their own experiences, they become "productive intellectuals." One might think, for example, of Morita Akio's *Made in Japan* or Matsushita Kōnosuke's *On Japan and the Japanese*.[18] Interestingly, many of my respondents classified leading members of the business elite as thinking elites because they are both practically experienced and highly knowledgeable about Japanese society. Leading business elites are well aware through their frequent contacts with non-Japanese that the Japanese are the subject of conversation abroad, and they generally know how to "present themselves" to the rest of the world, thereby taking on the role of spokesmen for the majority of ordinary Japanese.

What is particularly important in the context of the present study is the role of Japanese business elites as "reproductive" intellectuals, who interpreted academics' theories of Japanese society and culture, rephrased them as popular "social theories" which ordinary people could presumably put to practical use, and disseminated them to the other sections of the population. This was an important channel through which the academics' *nihonjinron* were distributed to a wider readership. Many of my respondents familiarized themselves with academic works on Japanese distinctiveness (such as Nakane's "vertical society" theory) through reference to such theories in business elites' writings. S. N. Eisenstadt makes a relevant point when he remarks that "reproductive" intellectuals ("secondary intellectuals" in his own words) "serve as channels of institutionalization, and even as possible creators or new types of symbols of cultural orientations, of traditions, and of collective and cultural identity."[19]

Japanese companies have played an interesting part in disseminating the *nihonjinron* by publishing what may be called "cross-cultural" manuals, that is, handbooks, glossaries and English learning materials which describe the distinctiveness of Japanese patterns of behavior in the contexts of intercultural business negotiations, business and management practices, company employees' everyday lifestyle, "untranslatable" Japanese expressions, and so on. One might mention, for example, Mitsubishi Corporation's dual-language *Japanese Business Glossary*; Nippon Steel Corporation's dual-language handbook *Nippon: The Land and Its People* (which summarizes a wide range of subjects dealt with in the *nihonjinron* such as the nonassertive mode of communication, group behavior, communal mentality, management and employment practices, decisionmaking, and industrial relations); and Taiyō Kōbe Bank Ltd.'s *The Scrutable Japanese* (a handbook which portrays the lifestyle of Japanese company employees in English).[20] There are a number of other similar company publications such as *Skills in Cross-cultural Negotiation* by Nisshō Iwai Corporation and *Toshiba's Practical Cross-cultural Dialogues* by the personnel development department of Toshiba Co.[21]

In these cross-cultural manuals, the *nihonjinron* are popularized in such a way that their consumers may apply them to practical use. The general manager of the corporate communications office of Mitsubishi Corporation explains the aim of their handbook as introducing "unique Japanese business practices and expressions in a light but informative form."[22] Similarly, the president of Taiyō Kōbe Bank, commenting on the reaction to their handbook, remarks that "Japanese students were anxious to know how customs and practices unique to the Japanese were described in English."[23] Considering that the ability to use practical English and knowledge of cultural differences are regarded by many well-educated Japanese as two necessary conditions to be a *kokusaijin* (international person), most of these cross-cultural manuals are intended to serve both as English language leaning materials and guidebooks on cultural differences at the same time. This point is illustrated well in the following quotation from *Talking about Japan*, by Nippon Steel Human Resources Development Co. Ltd., in which the three main academic theories on the distinctiveness of Japanese behavior (*nihonjinron*) discussed earlier in this chapter, are summarized and presented in the form of English dialogues:

> *Mr. Suzuki (a Japanese businessmen)*: Most Japanese tend to avoid doing anything that sets them off from others. They worry about what others think and change their behavior accordingly.

> *Mr. Jones (an American)*: That's probably one of the reasons why people talk about Japanese groupism.

*Mr. S*: It's a factor. It's also why Japanese are poor at asserting themselves. We tend to speak and act only after considering the other person's feelings and point of view.

*Mr. J*: You can't say that for most Westerners. In America, we try to teach our children to be independent, take individual responsibility. . . . We also try to train them to think logically, and learn how to express their thoughts and opinions.

*Mr. S*: Yes, I know. . . . Foreigners often criticize us Japanese for not giving clear-cut yes or no answers. This is probably connected to our being basically a homogeneous society and our traditional tendency to try to avoid conflicts.[24]

It may be argued that this type of conversation manual predetermines the way one expresses one's ideas of Japanese society by providing the very language and concepts one uses. Furthermore, it influences the way one perceives Japanese society since language learners often parrot model sentences and absorb them uncritically. Many of these cross-cultural manuals published by companies were originally intended for, and distributed to, their employees and students (prospective employees), sensitizing them to the distinctiveness of Japanese patterns of behavior and socializing them to be "internationalized" Japanese.

We may argue that, whereas textbooks are a chief means of ideological transmission in state-initiated formal nationalism, cross-cultural manuals, such as the ones that have been mentioned, are an important tool for the dissemination of ideas in informal cultural nationalism. Also, whereas school textbooks are a means of childhood socialization, these manuals are used for adult socialization—to reinforce Japanese identity.

**Intercultural Communication and Cultural Nationalism**

Ironically, many of the producers and distributors of the *nihonjinron* may be thought of as "internationalists." It would be very inappropriate to call them nationalist ideologues. One avowed and widely shared motive for thinking elites' production of the *nihonjinron* was their concern to improve intercultural communication between Japanese and non-Japanese. Being cautious about any possible revival of the narrow-minded nationalism of the prewar type, many well-intentioned thinking elites sought, through their writings, to effectuate the emergence of large numbers of internationally minded Japanese who had knowledge about different cultures and could communicate well in intercultural settings. Such an interest in international understanding was widely shared by the educated Japanese. "Internationalization" (*kokusaika*) became a national agenda in the 1970s and 1980s, and "intercultural communication" (*ibunkakan komyunikēshon*) became a popular subject among students, businessmen or anyone interested in communicating with non-Japanese.

Cross-cultural manuals published by companies also grew out of their stated concern to reduce intercultural misunderstandings between Japanese and non-Japanese. Their strong concern with internationalization and intercultural communication is stated in their publications. For example, the president of Taiyō Kōbe Bank writes that the aim of their handbook is to "make a contribution, if modest, to the promotion of an understanding of Japan and the Japanese people at a time when comprehension is badly needed to ease mounting trade tensions [and also to] help Japanese students who are destined to live in an era of internationalization, by providing hints about how things Japanese may be expressed in good English."[25] Of particular importance here is the assumption held among Japanese thinking elites that the very peculiarities of Japanese patterns of behavior and thought are an obstacle to intercultural communication. This awareness of Japanese peculiarities was considered the first step to achieve better intercultural understanding. An interest in intercultural communication thus tended to lead to a strong interest in the distinctiveness of Japanese patterns of behavior and thought.

It is necessary now to elaborate on perceptions of Japanese identity as they are preconceived by the Japanese people. In general terms, national identity (and its substratum ethnicity) may be understood as a symbolic boundary process. Sandra Wallman understands ethnicity as "the process by which *their* difference is used to enhance the sense of *us* for the purposes of organization or identification."[26] We may say that, in the Japanese discussion of cultural differences, it is not "their" difference but "our" difference that is actively used for the reconstruction of Japanese identity. Japanese elites long perceived themselves and their culture to be on the "periphery" in relation to the "central" civilizations (first that of China and then of the West) and constructed and reconstructed Japanese identity by stressing their "particularistic" difference from the "universal" Chinese and Westerners. Japanese "uniqueness" as discussed in the *nihonjinron* is actually the "particularistic difference" of the Japanese.

Because of their perception of being on the periphery, Japanese elites tended to see it as natural to adapt themselves to the more "universal" ways of the West. The Japanese sense of uniqueness should, therefore, not be confused with ethnocentrism, which is the belief that one's own group is central, most important, and culturally superior to other groups. Explicit claims of Japanese superiority have been relatively uncommon. The image of the Japanese presented in the *nihonjinron* and held among the majority of the Japanese is fundamentally that of being very different without explicit claim of superiority. A "particularistic" sense of national identity is primarily a question of horizontal difference or difference of a kind.[27] By contrast, since the more universal aspects of human ability and activity are perceived to comprise the base of the "universal" civilization of the West, the dissimilitude between Westerners and others is likely to be perceived in terms of the difference in the ability to perform "universalizable" features of human activity. This may explain, at least partially, the vertical sense of superiority common in the West.

The *nihonjinron* and their popularized cross-cultural manuals offer abundant examples to suggest that Japanese patterns of behavior and use of language are so peculiar that one has to be born a Japanese to be able to grasp the intricacy of the Japanese language and the delicacy of the Japanese mode of thinking. For example, one writer observes that, though he knows of some Europeans whose Japanese is accurate and quite fluent, and though some Korean residents in Japan have won literary awards for their prose or fiction in Japanese, he knows of no foreigner who can compose good *waka* (or thirty-one syllable Japanese poetry).[28] This sort of remark may be taken as suggesting that the Japanese language "belongs exclusively" to the Japanese, in the sense that it can truly be appreciated only by the Japanese. Such a sense of Japanese uniqueness may aptly be described by using the metaphor "property," since possessiveness is its main attribute. Many Japanese express their sense of being unique as if Japan's peculiar cultural traits belong to, or are the exclusive property of, the Japanese people.

It should be observed here that highly particularistic perceptions of Japanese uniqueness are not entirely attributable to the *nihonjinron* of the 1970s and 1980s. Rather, to a much greater extent than previously, thinking elites' theories of Japanese distinctiveness have promoted an active consciousness of Japanese uniqueness among the educated public and also conditioned them to express Japanese identity in a particularistic manner. In this sense, the relationship between "consumers" and "producers" of the *nihonjinron* is not that of unilateral influence of the latter over the former but that of interplay between the two. Readers endorse what they have already felt about their society by reading thinking elites' ideas, and writers respond to and promote such interests of readers.

It was said earlier that an interest in intercultural communication tends to lead to an interest in the peculiarities of Japanese behavior and thought. If improvement of intercultural communication is attempted through emphasis on the particularistic difference of the Japanese, its unintended consequence can be the enhancement of cultural nationalism if those aspects of life held in common by different peoples are neglected. In fact, the large increase in the publications on Japanese uniqueness had the effect of emphasizing Japanese difference to the extent that the commonality between Japanese and non-Japanese was given short shrift. What started as a well-intentioned activity to facilitate intercultural communication thus had the unintended and ironic consequence of sensitizing the Japanese excessively to their distinctiveness, and thereby creating another obstacle to communication. One practical manifestation of this sensitizing process is the implicitly promoted assumption that foreign residents cannot understand Japanese people's supposedly unique mode of thinking and behaving. Such an assumption has tended to obstruct foreign residents' adaptation to social life in Japan. In this sense, an interest in intercultural communication (and internationalization) and cultural nationalism are two sides of the same coin. It is not that a favorable orientation towards nationalism has impeded internationalization but that, paradoxically, a concern with internationalization has made *internationalization* even more difficult. The distribution and consumption of the *nihonjinron* can be said to have been facilitated by readers' desire to internationalize their knowledge.

By using businessmen's activity as a case study, our discussion has shown the way in which the project of "internationalization" can ironically produce an unintended consequence of cultural nationalism. Although our discussion has been restricted to business people's activity, our findings can be expected to be generally valid for other fairly well-educated groups with an interest in intercultural communication.

## Conclusion

It should be mentioned in concluding this chapter that many of the themes dealt with here are by no means unique to Japan. Cultural nationalism is relevant in many other parts of the world, not merely countries of Asia and Africa but also of Europe and the Americas, though the ways in which it is generated may vary from one country to another and from one historical period to another. Cultural nationalism as a means of inventing, reinventing and enhancing a people's national identity has been an integral feature of the classical view of the modern international order. Moreover, cultural nationalism has the potential to produce diverse effects, for which reason it remains a far from negligible force in the contemporary world. Sometimes it may work to preserve the diversity of world cultures, in the face of homogenizing forces of dominant and assertive foreign cultural and civilizational powers. At other times, it may become a source of hindrance to international understanding through an excessive emphasis on national uniqueness. Indeed, it, itself, may even become a source of symbolic violence. Such multifacetedness is the nature of cultural nationalism.

Even though people may now talk optimistically about prospects for a supersession of nationalism and a rise of globalism and regional integration, these do not seem to entail the decline of cultural nationalism. Particularly characteristic of the development of cultural nationalism in many regions of the world, in the final decade of the twentieth century, is that, as the Japanese case has shown, a strong concern with cultural differences is promoted in the contexts of increasing globalization where cross-cultural contacts are becoming a matter of considerable concern in the lives of growing numbers of people. What is interesting is that the desire to cross national borders—whether in the form of multinational corporations, cultural exchanges, international tourism, or the creation of larger regional identities (such as "European" and "Asian")—is quite often accompanied by a heightened desire to be different in a world of "cultural nations."

## Notes

Note on Japanese names: Japanese names appearing in the text are given in the customary Japanese order of the family name first followed by the given name (e.g.,

Yoshino Kosaku). In the endnotes, the same order is used with a comma inserted after the family name (i.e., Yoshino, Kosaku) to avoid confusion since the names of Japanese authors of English books are normally known by the customary western order (i.e., Kosaku Yoshino).

1. Zigmunt Bauman, *Intimations of Postmodernity* (London and New York: Routledge, 1992), p. 17.

2. Ibid.

3. Robert Bocock, *Ritual in Industrial Society: A Sociological Analysis of Ritualism in Modern England* (London: Allen & Unwin, 1972), p. 98.

4. For detailed discussions of the content of the *nihonjinron*, see, for example, Ross Mouer and Sugimoto, Yoshio, *Images of Japanese Society* (London: Kegan Paul International, 1986); Peter Dale, *The Myth of Japanese Uniqueness* (London: Croom Helm, 1986).

5. See, for example, Nakane, Chie, *Tate Shakai no Ningen Kankei: Tan'itsu Shakai no Riron* [Human Relations in Vertical Society: A Theory of a Unitary Society] (Tokyo: Kōdansha, 1967); *Japanese Society* (Berkeley and Los Angeles: University of California Press, 1970).

6. Doi, Takeo, *Amae no Kōzō* [Structure of Dependence] (Tokyo: Kōbundo, 1971), translated as *The Anatomy of Dependence* by J. Bester (Tokyo: Kodansha International, 1973).

7. Hamaguchi, Eshun, *Kanjinshugi no Shakai Nihon* [Japan: The Interpersonalistic Society] (Tokyo: Tōyō Keizai Shinpōsha, 1982).

8. See, for example, Matsumoto, Michihiro, *Haragei no Ronri* [The Logic of *Haragei*] (Tokyo: Asahi Shuppansha, 1975); *Haragei* (Tokyo: Kōdansha, 1984).

9. The *nihonjinron* have been criticized from two other angles. First, criticism is directed at the lack of methodological concerns in the *nihonjinron* and at its heavy reliance on self-serving examples. Second, it is pointed out that these examples are used for ideological manipulation. It is claimed that the *nihonjinron*, which promote the "consensus model" or "group model" of Japanese society, work as dominant ideology or management ideology by emphasizing corporate solidarity and harmony rather than working-class solidarity.

10. See, for example, chapters by Kawamura, Nozomu and Sydney Crawcour in Ross Mouer and Sugimoto, Yoshio, eds., *Japanese Society: Reappraisals and New Directions*, a special issue of *Social Analysis* 5/6.

11. This may be demonstrated by the fact that the majority of my respondents read the *nihonjinron* in a very different manner from critics have supposed. Respondents' reading of the *nihonjinron*, especially academics' *nihonjinron*, was very critical because they interpreted it as representing a negative and self-denying view of Japanese peculiarities and, as such, discouraging the Japanese from having a sense of national pride. This is understandable considering that many had already been exposed to the self-critical discussions of Japanese peculiarities prevalent in the early postwar years and regarded the *nihonjinron* as a continuation of such literature.

This shows that critics' speculation about ideological manipulation does not necessarily hold true. On this, see Yoshino, op. cit. note 12, pp. 190–91.

12. For the details of this field research, see Kosaku Yoshino, *Cultural Nationalism in Contemporary Japan: A Sociological Enquiry* (London and New York: Routledge, 1992 [hbk], 1995 [pbk]).

13. That one's immediate group exerts a major influence on shaping one's orientation to a particular ideology has been pointed out by a number of sociologists, albeit in differing contexts (i.e., Nazism, democracy, communism). See, for example, Sidney Verba, *Small Groups and Political Behavior: A Study of Leadership* (Princeton, NJ: Princeton University Press, 1961), chap. 2; Karl Mannheim, *Freedom, Power and Democratic Planning* (London: Routledge & Kegan Paul, 1951), p. 181; Edward Shils and Morris Janowitz, "Cohesion and Disintegration in the Wehrmacht," *Public Opinion Quarterly* 12 (1948): 314; Gabriel Almond, *The Appeals of Communism* (Princeton, NJ: Princeton University Press, 1952), pp. 272–79.

14. For these and other types of concern, see Yoshino, op.cit. note 12, chap. 7.

15. Seventy-five percent of the businessmen actively responded to the *nihonjinron* compared to 28.6 percent for educators. See Yoshino, op. cit. note 12, p. 134.

16. See Yoshino, op. cit. note 12, chap. 3.

17. Edward Shils, "Intellectuals, Tradition, and the Traditions of Intellectuals: Some Preliminary Considerations," *Dædalus* 101.3–4 (Spring 1972): 22.

18. Morita, Akio, *Made in Japan: Akio Morita and Sony* (New York: Signet, 1986), translated as *Made in Japan: Waga Taikenteki Kokusai Senryaku* (My Own Experience of International Business Strategy) by Shimofusa, S. (Tokyo: Asahi Shimbunsha, 1987); Matsushita, Kōnosuke, *Nihon to Nihonjin ni tsuite* [On Japan and the Japanese] (Tokyo: PHP Kenkyūjo, 1982).

19. S. N. Eisenstadt, "Intellectuals and Traditions," *Dædalus* 101.3–4 (Spring 1972): 1–16.

20. Mitsubishi Corporation, *Japanese Business Glossary/Nihongo* (Tokyo: Tōyōkeizai Shinpōsha, 1983); Nippon Steel Corporation, Personnel Development Office, *Nippon: The Land and Its People*, 2nd edn. (Tokyo: Gakuseisha, 1984); Taiyō Kōbe Bank, *The Nihonjin/The Scrutable Japanese* (Tokyo: Gakuseisha, 1988).

21. Nisshō Iwai Corporation, *Ibunka Kōshōjutsu: Kokusai Bijinesu no Genba kara* [Skills in Cross-cultural Negotiation: From the Scene of International Business] (Tokyo: Kōbunsha, 1987); Toshiba Co., Personnel Development Department, *Toshiba's Practical Cross-cultural Dialogues* (Tokyo, 1985).

22. Mitsubishi Corporation, op. cit. note 20, p. 4.

23. Taiyō Kōbe Bank, op. cit. note 20, p. 2.

24. Nippon Steel Human Resources Development Co. Ltd., *Talking About Japan/ Nippon o Kataru* (Tokyo: ALC, 1987), p. 405.

25. Taiyō Kōbe Bank, op. cit. note 20, p. 4.

26. Sandra Wallman, "Introduction: The Scope for Ethnicity" in Wallman, ed., *Ethnicity at Work* (London: Macmillan, 1979), p. 3. Author's italics.

27. This does not mean that a sense of superiority is absent among the Japanese as in the case of their attitude towards Koreans and other minorities in Japan.

28. Watanabe, Shōichi, *Nihongo no Kokoro* [The Soul of the Japanese Language] (Tokyo: Kōdansha, 1974), pp. 105–6.

# Part II

## National Identity and the Struggle for National Rights

# 7

# Religion and Identity in Northern Ireland

MARIANNE ELLIOTT

During 1992–93, I acted as one of the seven commissioners of the Opsahl Commission: an independent inquiry into ways forward in Northern Ireland, which produced its report in June 1993.[1] The commission was a novel exercise in democracy, which sought to involve the people of Northern Ireland in the debate about its future. It received submissions from some 3,000 people and held public meetings and oral hearings throughout the region. The report made a number of recommendations which were subsequently endorsed in public opinion polls in Northern Ireland, Britain, and the Republic of Ireland.[2] Most of these recommendations stemmed from the people's sense of frustration and helplessness after a quarter of a century of violence and deadlock and their desire to have more control over their own future. To do so, they recognized, would also involve them taking responsibility for the situation, past and present. This recognition—that the source of the conflict lies inside rather than outside the province, with the people themselves— was the uncomfortable conclusion of most of those addressing the commission. There is no "quick fix" to Northern Ireland. This is why the Opsahl Commission recommended a series of "building blocks" to help the different communities build up trust, and the experience of working together before they could arrive at some common ground on Northern Ireland's long-term future.

The exercise showed that opinion has shifted considerably since the onset of the Troubles in 1969. But it also highlighted a continuing gulf of misunderstanding between Protestant and Catholic, however anxious the individual to reach accommodation. There is still a sense that the other community is a different people and ignorance is preventing any overall sense of a shared culture. Basic ignorance about what the other faiths teach is rampant. Thus cocooned within their respective communities and traditions, most people in Northern Ireland have had little experience of the other community outside their workplace. There is almost a total lack of neutral venues where their differences can be explored in safety. Northern Ireland is not a zone of conflicting polarities as many believe. There are too many shades of grey, too many people who "pick and mix" from a range of identities for that.[3] But there are certain fundamentals to the mainstream religions which their adherents rarely lose even when they cease to be practicing members. It is these core differences which this chapter seeks to analyze.

## I

The oral hearings of the Opsahl Commission closed with two schools assemblies in Derry and Belfast. In Derry, the subgroup discussing culture and identity produced the following motion: "Our culture and identity [are] influenced more by our religion than by any other factor." A number of Catholic sixth-formers subsequently voiced their bewilderment to their friend who had been part of the group at the choice of such a motion. On an earlier occasion, the same school group had told the commission that they opposed integrated education[4] not so much because their religion would be in any way diluted, but because their Irish culture would be.[5] Interestingly, it is the same consideration which inspires greater hostility towards educational integration among Sinn Fein supporters than among Catholics generally.[6] Throughout the hearings these core differences between Catholics and Protestants emerged time and time again: the centrality of religion to the identity of the one, of Irish history, language and culture to the other. The bogeyman for Catholics was the state and its representatives, that for Protestants the Catholic Church itself.

This fear of Catholicism as a powerful political system, the commission found at every level of the Protestant community. It is the one element which unites an otherwise very diverse, even divided community.[7] It is the main defining element of their Britishness and the perceived link with a Protestant power.[8] The commission was told repeatedly of Protestants' reluctance to call themselves Irish. It is a decline in Protestants' sense of Irishness which, whilst never high before the Troubles, plummeted sharply after their outbreak.

"Irishness" was perceived as something not only Catholic, but as highly politicized, something which had been "hi-jacked" by the republicans. It is this which dictates Protestant attitudes to the Irish republic, which they see not as a modern democracy but as the incarnation of their worst nightmare: a hostile Catholic state, out to destroy Protestantism itself. Protestants, we were told by a former moderator of the Presbyterian Church,

> see the political situation in clearly religious perspectives. . . . They see the attempt to bring about a "United Ireland" not only as an attack upon their political and constitutional well-being, but also as an attack upon their

**Table 7.1. Religion and National Identity in Northern Ireland**

|          | 1968 | | 1978 | | 1986 | | 1989 | |
|----------|------|------|------|------|------|------|------|------|
|          | *Prot.* | *Cath.* | *Prot.* | *Cath.* | *Prot.* | *Cath.* | *Prot.* | *Cath.* |
|          | % | % | % | % | % | % | % | % |
| British  | 39 | 20 | 67 | 20 | 65 | 9 | 68 | 8 |
| Irish    | 20 | 76 | 8 | 69 | 3 | 61 | 3 | 60 |
| Ulster   | 32 | 5 | 20 | 6 | 14 | 1 | 10 | 2 |
| N. Irish | — | — | — | — | 11 | 20 | 16 | 25 |

*Source*: Edward Moxon-Browne, "National Identity in Northern Ireland," in Peter Stringer and Gillian Robinson, eds., *Social Attitudes in Northern Ireland* (Belfast: The Blackstaff Press, 1991), p. 25.[9]

religious heritage and an attempt to establish in Northern Ireland the dominance of the Roman Catholic Church and people. . . . They see every aspect of the political, cultural, educational, medical, industrial, social and religious life of the Republic dominated, and often controlled, by the power and influence of the Roman Catholic Church.[10]

In such a rapidly changing society as that of the Republic of Ireland, people have genuine difficulty accepting the sincerity of such views of their state as "priest-ridden." The recommendation of the Opsahl Commission which received scarcely any mention in the otherwise vigorous and positive reception of the report in the Republic, was that on the Catholic Church in Ireland.

4.1. In the light of the widespread and deep fear and mistrust we encountered among Northern Protestants about the Catholic nature of Southern society . . . we believe that the government of the Republic of Ireland must move—and be seen to move—to make good the claim in the 1916 Declaration that it cherishes all the children of the Irish nation equally.

Recalling the Irish Hierarchy's declaration to the New Ireland Forum that it did not wish to have the moral teaching of the Catholic Church become the criterion of constitutional law or to have its principles embodied in civil law, and its reference to the need for a balanced examination of the role of the Church in a changing Ireland, we urge that this examination—and a public debate on it—should take place now. To this end we suggest the setting up of a wide-ranging public inquiry into the role of the Catholic Church in Ireland.[11]

This was in June 1993, and I have to say now that this recommendation may not have been the dead letter that once I thought. The joint Downing Street Declaration of the British and Irish governments on December 14, 1993, does signify a genuine reaching out by the latter to the Protestant people of Northern Ireland. It contains the following undertaking:

> The Taoiseach will examine with his colleagues any elements in the democratic life and organization of the Irish state that can be represented to the Irish government in the course of political dialogue as a real and substantial threat to their way of life and ethos, or that can be represented as not being fully consistent with a modern democratic and pluralist society, and undertakes to examine any possible ways of removing such obstacles.

No such inquiry was established. But in the aftermath of a number of scandals affecting the church during 1993–94 (notably the case of the pedophile priest, Brendan Smyth), a very wide-ranging public debate on the role of the Catholic Church in the Republic got underway.

Conscious of how antiquated their fears of "popery" sound, most Ulster Protestants have great difficulty defining their identity in public. In private they were more forthcoming. "There is the notion that you have to be Catholic to be Irish," we were told in Auchnacloy, a border town in County Tyrone, but this was the Catholic Church teaching the children biased history and hatred of anything British, and Catholic teachers in schools would force their views on the children since "Catholics are taking their lead from Rome and Rome is out to get rid of Protestants." Despite the Catholic Church's relaxation of directives concerning the religion of children of mixed marriages, even the leaders of the Protestant Churches think the Catholic Church has not made sufficient concessions in this area.[12]

It is not surprising, therefore, to find ordinary Protestants still convinced that the Catholic Church's views on the family, education, and mixed marriage are part and parcel of some great conspiracy to destroy Protestantism entirely. It is the church which urges its adherents to bigger families, and forces mixed-religion couples to bring up the children as Catholics (every Protestant commenting on this knew all about the Ne Temere decree of 1907 on Catholic marriage, though most Catholics had never heard of it).[13] There is more hostility to mixed marriages among Protestants than Catholics, even liberal-minded Protestants thinking it "something that's morally wrong." Similar hostility is expressed to attendance at any kind of service in a Catholic Church, only half of church-going Protestants claiming that they would do so.[14] Members of the Orange Order are required to "scrupulously avoid countenancing (by his presence or otherwise) any act or ceremony of Papist worship."[15] The Rev. Ian Paisley's frequent reference to "Jesuitical" conspiracies,[16] particularly in connection with the Republic's territorial claim over Northern Ireland, strikes a real chord. Although there are only 13,000 Free Presbyterians in Northern Ireland (i.e., followers of the fundamentalist Protestant church led by the Rev. Paisley), over a quarter of the Protestant electorate regularly votes for his party, the

Democratic Unionist party. While an estimated 100,000 Protestants belong to the male-only Orange Order—a staggering 38 percent of the Protestant male population—which requires its members to "strenuously oppose the fatal errors and doctrines of the Church of Rome."[17]

Given such views that the Catholic Church's ultimate aim is to destroy Protestantism, current demographic trends are contributing to an apocalyptic psychology among some Protestants. The 1991 census showed a rising Catholic population (41.4 percent, up from 34.7 percent in 1971, against 54 percent Protestant), with Catholic majorities in almost every local authority west of the Bann, south Down and north Antrim. Whilst in Belfast, whose City Council is the most notoriously anti-nationalist in the province, there has been an increase in the number of Catholics from 32.2 percent in 1971 to 42.5 percent in 1991.[18]

Protestants in these areas and along the border with the Republic have felt most beleaguered. The IRA's border attacks were seen as "ethnic cleansing," and Protestants perceived to be "selling out" to Catholics were condemned by their co-religionists. Since Protestants generally still think of the Catholics as a "fifth column," awaiting their moment to remove the constitutional link with Britain, the threat these figures seemed to hold out of a future end to a Protestant majority was a factor in the escalating numbers of murders of Catholics by loyalist terrorists in the two years prior to the 1994 ceasefires.[19]

All social surveys show Protestants to be less tolerant of Catholics moving into their neighborhood than the reverse. The experience of the Waterside district of Derry (Londonderry), and Protestant North and West Belfast is perceived as a portent of things to come. In Londonderry, most Protestants have moved out of the city and into the Waterside in the last twenty years, consciously ghettoizing themselves from a city now deemed Catholic—a microcosm of how they would see themselves in a united Ireland.[20] In Belfast the commission was told that the Protestant population of the Shankill in West Belfast had dropped from 76,000 to 27,000 and in North Belfast from 112,000 to 56,000 over the past twenty years. There is "a sense of siege, of retreat, almost of defeat," commented one community worker from the Shankill.[21] They see neighboring Catholic areas bursting at the seams while their own community is declining. Since the onset of the Troubles coincided with the virtual collapse of heavy industry in Northern Ireland (where the workforce was predominantly Protestant), the Protestant working class is experiencing new levels of unemployment and deprivation, where once they were a largely Catholic phenomena. Given the anti-discrimination legislation introduced in the last two decades, much of it to redress undoubted discrimination against Catholics, Protestants see all the economic gains as having been on the Catholic side, and they consider bogus the statistics which show Catholics still twice as likely to be unemployed.[22] It is, after all, in Catholic culture to complain. The sentiments expressed in a satirical song at the beginning of the Troubles still find echoes today.

Come all you boys that vote for me, come gather all around.
A Catholic I was born an' reared an' so I'm duty bound
To proclaim my country's misery and express our Papist hope,
To embarrass all the Orangemen an' glorify the Pope.
Chorus: Sing fol dol do dee, its great to be in the Nationalist game,
We don't attempt solutions, we have only to complain.[23]

## II

Catholics are baffled and embittered by such attitudes. Surely it is they who have been the victims in the past? They see themselves as being most reasonable, making all sorts of overtures for good community relations, and point to the local councils with nationalist majorities having adopted power-sharing as policy. They find puzzling Protestant rejection of things Irish and their general ignorance of what Catholics believe. "It's funny how little they know about us," commented one Catholic in south Armagh. "They have a picture of the south as a wee red-haired fella with a freckly face pulling a donkey loaded with turf . . . and that the people are all ruled by the church and things like this."[24]

This comment highlights a general Catholic belief in a continuing Protestant tendency to see them as an inferior breed. Yet there has always been an inferiority/ superiority dichotomy in Catholic thinking, the belief that they hold the high moral ground, inducing a sense of pity of Protestants whose culture they see as more sterile and impoverished than their own. At its more extreme, this inferiority/superiority syndrome induces self-righteousness and moral elitism. Republicans are particularly skilled at exploiting Catholics' shared memory of disadvantage, and any effort to break away from it risks the accusation of selling out. John Hume, leader of the Social Democratic and Labour Party (SDLP), has little time for such "whining" among his own community, suggesting that it suits many to persist in this kind of "grievance mentality," rather than attempting to remedy the cause of their complaint.[25] It is because of such shared memory of disadvantage that Catholics are so unwilling to accept that Protestant fears might be genuine. Fear of Catholic Church power is simply a cover for pure bigotry; Protestant determination to cling to the union with Britain is a ploy to maintain their "ascendancy" over the Catholics.[26] The use of the word ascendancy by Catholics when speaking of their Protestant fellow countrymen is instructive. Originally defined in the eighteenth century to describe exclusive Protestant rule of Ireland, it is a word embedded in the Catholic psyche. It acquired a new resonance after the creation of the Northern Ireland state in 1921, and the embers of resentment are easily ignited. It is such memories which unites SDLP and Sinn Fein supporters (though they agree on little else) against anything savoring of restored majoritarian Unionist rule.

Now although I think such Catholic perceptions of Protestant motivation are no longer accurate, and the commission was made aware of a certain grudging admiration among Protestants for many aspects of Catholic culture, notably a greater ability to organize at the community level, nonetheless, historically the tendency to see Catholics as an inferior breed is accurate enough. Protestants think they are culturally more inclined to the useful scientific subjects, whilst Catholics prefer "soft" subjects like history and the arts,[27] hence the perceived economic backwardness of the South, with which Protestants normally associate the northern Catholics. Much of this they attribute to "priestly tyranny," keeping the Catholics in ignorance and superstition. Catholics were encouraged by their priests to believe in fairies, Dr. Bob Curran's Protestant grandmother told him when he was a child in the Mourne Mountains. "As long as they believed in the supernatural (fairies, cures, visions and miracles) the priests had them in their grip. Catholics would believe anything which you told them—not like Protestants who were altogether much more sensible."[28]

Such attitudes to the Irish are part of British culture, which can be documented from at least the time of Gerald of Wales in the twelfth century.[29] At the time of the Reformation, the image was transferred to the Irish Catholics generally. In Ulster in particular, the absence of a Catholic gentry, and later a Catholic middle class, seemed to fulfil the stereotype, for most Catholics have remained largely lower-class and rural.[30] Travellers in eighteenth and nineteenth-century Ulster were struck by the lengths to which Protestants would go to avoid being confused with the Catholic Irish. In 1812, John Gamble recorded an encounter with an innkeeper named O'Sullivan near Larne: "[H]e was very anxious to assure me that he wasn't Catholic, despite the name, but descended from a Huguenot"—"a zealous Protestant would as soon call his son Judas as Pat."[31] But nothing caused more irritation to Catholics in past centuries than to be lorded over by Protestants who were sometimes intellectually and socially their inferiors. For the centrality of status in Gaelic culture had transferred itself to that of the Irish Catholics in early modern times. One of the aspects of the eighteenth-century penal laws most resented by Catholics, was the ban on Catholics owning or carrying arms, thereby denying their middling and upper ranks the external status symbols of a gentleman.[32] A natural deference to their social betters had also been a trait of Gaelic society, and in many cases it was transferred to the new landlords (it was the settlers who were resented, more for their lowly social status than their religion). Likewise, this natural deference was misinterpreted as the sign of a slavish mind and entered Protestant folk stereotype of Catholics, defying even the recent emergence of a Catholic middle class, noted earlier:

Come all you loyal Ulstermen, rejoice that we're together,
We Catholics in the Middle Class have never had it better . . .
And if some have not got houses or employment we don't grumble,

Why don't they beg and grovel, can't they follow our example . . .
My son will go to Clongoes Wood[33] and stay there till he's twenty,
And learn there how to scrape and bow and pass himself with gentry.[34]

### III

The kind of mutual incomprehension of the other community's core values that has been outlined owes not a little to the way in which they are expressed. "The talks failed for lack of language," wrote Professor Edna Longley of the breakdown of interparty talks on the future of Northern Ireland in November 1992.[35] Certainly, Catholics and Protestants appear to have different thought-patterns in Northern Ireland. Social science surveys have found social attitudes consistently different, even if they share a general religious conservatism.[36] The self-image of the Northern Protestant is that of a straight, uncomplicated, trustworthy, direct, plain-speaking individualist, as opposed to the dissembling, untrustworthy, Jesuitical Catholic.[37] "The SDLP speak with a forked tongue," a group of Protestants from Castledawson in County Londonderry told the Opsahl Commission. "The Republic can always wriggle out of things," we were told by another group in Auchnacloy. "Northern Protestants believe that Catholics do not say what they mean," the Rev. Sydney Callaghan told the commission, "that they are profligate with words, past masters of the art of the fine point, the innuendo and the half-truth."[38] Whereas the Unionists tend to see hidden agenda and seek a cautious, step-by-step approach, the Nationalists think in terms of frameworks and big solutions.

Ingrained cultural differences have meant that the two have constantly by-passed each other in every attempt at compromise, and the differences in outlook have fed into many other areas of the Northern Ireland crisis, most notably law, justice and security. There is a collective sense among Catholics that their whole community is treated unfairly in these areas: "the army asked me what religion I was and I felt intimidated," commented a Catholic from Keady in south Armagh. "When I see a member of the security forces I feel intimidated and guilty, even though I haven't done anything," a Catholic sixth-former told the Opsahl Commission's Schools Assembly in Belfast. And from all over the province, the commission heard evidence that those with Catholic-sounding names are more likely to be harassed by the security forces and stopped at checkpoints.[39] In this context, the following observation is most insightful:

> In the different religious/national traditions there have developed different visions of righteousness, radically different versions of justice. In a significant part of the Ulster Protestant tradition justice tends to emphasise honest dealing, getting one's deserts, acting rightly, fair procedures and the punishment of the guilty. Communal justice is not so central.

In the Irish Catholic tradition, there has developed a victim theology whereby the community sees itself as the victim and making sure the oppressor gets his deserts. . . . Peace comes after justice and justice is the right framework. Reconciliation in this perspective is seen merely as giving the other a place in our framework, not together trying to create something new.

This radical difference in perspective between the two communities is one of the reasons why they have such difficulty understanding each other.[40]

In this regard, Paul Burgess' analysis also presents a disturbing finding, namely, that the major Protestant and Catholic communities do not share a common morality. Hence the moral ambivalence and double standards which pervade Northern Irish society, and permit otherwise peaceable people to perceive terrorist acts by one side as morally less reprehensible than those by the other. Burgess' survey shows that sectarian stereotypes are acquired from an early age through the segregated schools, often unconsciously transmitted by teachers (though more influentially, by parents) themselves. This is why the government's well-intentioned "Education for Mutual Understanding" program has failed. With limited, frequently non-existent, contact between schools of different denominations, it is taught by teachers who have not been specially trained and inevitably carry their own cultural baggage in the politically partisan nature of education in Northern Ireland. "I have seen these so-called inter-school contact programmes," one Catholic teacher told Burgess. "We take our lot to the swimming pool along with the neighboring Protestant school. What actually happens is our kids stay up one end of the pool while they stay down the other."[41] Little wonder, then, that the program evokes cynicism and a sense of futility among the schoolchildren at whom it is directed. "It is not us, but our parents and teachers who need EMU," commented one sixth-former at the oral hearings of the Opsahl Commission in Dungannon, Tyrone in February 1993.[42]

Sectarian consciousness is pervasive in Northern Ireland. It is not the monopoly of one community or the other, and is often far removed from what we commonly call bigotry. It can be instinctive even to the most liberally minded, and provides fertile ground for the kind of insider humor about prejudice and difference which most Northern Irish people engage in from time to time. It is there because difference has been institutionalized, locked, sometimes imperceptibly, into the social fabric of people's lives. It is a difference preserved and exaggerated by the very high levels of segregation in Northern Irish society. Some 83 percent of Catholics and Protestants questioned in 1992 said most or all of their relatives are of the same religion. Educational, sporting, as well as other social activities, and now increasingly housing, are confined within one community.[43] The Opsahl Commission was told repeatedly of once mixed communities having become predominantly one religion as a result of the Troubles. It learned of working-class males, in particular, who were deterred by fear from moving outside the safety of their own areas, even to take up much-needed employment; it was acquainted with the problems of attending integrated schools which might involve travel through areas dominated by the other community.[44] One of the most notable aspects of the rapid thaw in atmosphere following the 1994 ceasefires, was a visible increase in public mobility, particularly in the Belfast area.

In March 1993, a leading Northern Ireland journalist, David McKittrick, analyzed unpublished data from the 1991 census and produced statistics for such increasing segregation which startled even those who knew it was occurring. He concluded that:

- Some 50 percent of Northern Ireland's 1.5 million populace lived in areas which over 90 percent Protestant or Catholic.
- Less than 110,000 people lived in substantially mixed areas, and even here there may be internal separation by the numerous "peace lines" (twenty-foot high walls physically separating Catholics and Protestants).
- In the last twenty years the number of wards exclusively Catholic or Protestant had increased from 43 to 120 and 56 to 115 respectively.
- In Belfast 35 of its 51 wards were over 90 percent one religion.

A community worker on the almost exclusively Protestant Shankill Road in Belfast neatly summarized the lifelong cycle of segregation thus:

Young people start off in primary school: they are segregated. They go to secondary school: they are segregated. They leave school, no hope probably of getting a job . . . so they go to a youth training program. There are separate YTPs for Catholics and Protestants. . . . Because they don't have any money they are stuck in their own areas, so they don't get to see other people with other religions or other cultures.[45]

It is this lifelong separation of the communities which has caused stereotypes to take the place of understanding in Northern Ireland. When the two communities do mix in the workplace, good relations are maintained by polite fancy footwork, tiptoeing around potentially controversial topics. "Sectarianism . . . is the ghost at the feast of much of polite society in Northern Ireland," Ken Logue told the Opsahl Commission. It "depends essentially on a popular culture which invokes religion as a boundary marker between the two communities." It can operate without any overt signs of such sectarian consciousness. The stereotypical cues of appearance, name, school, cultural values, and speech are the unspoken language of everyday discourse.[46]

## IV

Authoritative research into the historical background to this gulf of misunderstanding, is yet to be done. The Ulster Catholic in particular must be one of the most under-researched figures in Irish history. To grow up as a Catholic in Northern Ireland—particularly in working class areas—is to grow up convinced that you occupy the high moral ground, as a descendant of the true Gael, your ancestors were deprived of their land and persecuted for their religion. Protestants are perceived as not entirely Irish, and Catholicism itself as possessing some kind of organic unity with Irishness, the very landscape suffused with both. "It is perhaps inevitable that our poetry should be provincial," wrote the Ulster Protestant poet Roy McFadden in 1946, ". . . concerned with appearances, seeing the tree and the field without the bones beneath."[47]

Although the Catholic tendency to think in terms of "native" and "planter" is on the wane, particularly among the young, traditionally, Catholics have believed that they are "the Irish properly so-called, trodden and despoiled." The words are those of Theobald Wolfe Tone, generally held to have been the founder of modern republican nationalism at the end of the eighteenth century. But this perception has been part of the Irish Catholics' "origin legend" since the seventeenth century.[48] The satirical song of the current Troubles, cited earlier, points to the centrality of this belief in northern nationalism.

Our allegiance is to Ireland, to her language and her games,
So we can't accept the border boys, as long as it remains,
Our reason is the Gaelic blood that's flowin' in our veins,
An' that is why our policy is never known to change.[49]

Protestants of all social categories are ambivalent about the cultural meaning of Irishness. On the one hand, they reject it as subversive, used, as it undoubtedly has been, by extreme nationalists to exclude Protestants from the Irish fraternity. On the other, they resent this narrow political focus and some are taking action to redress it. Indeed, many Protestants are now showing a particular interest in Irish history and the Irish language, once unknown to Protestant schools.[50] "Nationalists have defined Protestants out of being Irish," Dr. Chris McGimpsey of the Ulster Unionist party told the commission. "Nationalism is seen to be exclusively defined in terms of a 32 county state and a united Ireland. Many Protestants feel very Irish. Linking Irishness to a specific ideology has done tremendous damage."[51]

The truth of this claim of the "faith and fatherland" reading of Irishness is indisputable. A 1905 *Irish History Reader*, published by the Christian Brothers included the following instructions:

The teacher should dwell with pride, and in glowing words on Ireland's glowing past . . . her devotion through all the centuries to the Faith brought by her National Apostle. . . . [Pupils'] interest should be aroused in that widespread movement, the creation of earnest men, that has already effected so much for Ireland in the revival of her native language, native music, and native ideals; they must be taught that Irishmen, claiming the right to make their own laws, should never rest content until their native Parliament is restored; and that Ireland looks to them, when grown to man's estate, to act the part of true men in furthering the sacred cause of nationhood.[52]

Ulster Protestants were more likely to reject a common Irish identity in past centuries. The following early nineteenth-century warning of the combined political and religious threat awaiting Protestants who flirted with separatism and nationalism was a common one:

From experience of th[is] event [the 1798 rebellion] . . . Irish Protestants ought to be convinced that the political separation of their country from Britain by a popular insurrection must involve their extinction and that consequently an infrangibly determined adherence to their British connexion is necessary for their safety.[53]

There is not much sense here of an ethnic Britishness among Protestants to match the ethnic Irishness of the later Gaelic revival. This is because their identity as a Protestant people was already well established, a religious identity that did not require racial underpinnings except in very specific periods of threat. The racial undertones of nationalist theory in nineteenth- and twentieth-century Europe have made it more difficult for Ulster Protestants to explain their identity in purely religious terms, however accurate it is in reality. But Britishness is more a declaration of political affiliation than an accurate label for that identity. A recognition of its inadequacies is one of the reasons for the collective loss of confidence among Northern Ireland's Protestant community.

There is already a search underway among some Protestants for an equivalent origin legend to that of the Gaels for the Catholics. The argument is that Ulster has always been a distinct nation; that Protestants are not Johnny-come-latelys, but descendants of the ancient Celtic people of Ulster, the Ulaid, the people of the Ulster Cycle and the heroic tales of Cuchullain—the central theme of which is the struggle of the Ulster people against the rest of Ireland. As such, it provides an alternative origin legend for those arguing today for an independent Ulster against the territorial claims over the province made by the Republic's Constitution. In other words, it is the Protestants who are the natives, not those of Gaelic stock. It is interesting that this origin legend should extract similar romantic views from the past for incorporation into a future state as the Gaelic revival did for the future Irish state, notably, a rejection of materialism and an idealization of life on the land. An extension of this version of pre-history is to see the Scottish settlers who came over at the time of the Ulster Plantation as descendants of the ancient Ulaid, who had been pushed into the Northeast, then to Scotland, returning in the seventeenth century to reclaim what was rightfully theirs.[54]

In fact, the Gaels, like the Ulaid before them, were simply a warrior elite which absorbed indigenous peoples. It is impossible to trace lineage back beyond the eleventh and twelfth centuries, though the learned classes were kept busy creating bogus lineages into early modern times. It is unlikely that anyone in modern Northern Ireland can trace an unbroken lineage to either the ancient Celts or Gaels. There is one important rider to all of this, however: the Gaels did succeed in imposing their culture not only over the whole of Ireland, but also over Scotland. So that the 25,000 Scots mercenaries (Gallowglasses) operating in Ulster by the sixteenth century were Gaelic in culture—their language and religion (Catholic) were those of their hosts.[55] What differentiated the Scottish settlers at the time of the Ulster Plantation from the resident populace and families of Scots descent, was their religion, not their race. It simply cannot be proven that the settlers were Celts. Gaelic-speaking is not evidence—the Gaels and the Celts were different peoples.

This is a mirror-image of the organic link thesis between Catholicism/ Irishness/ territory, which has dominated Catholic and nationalist readings of the past since the seventeenth century, and which still surfaces in the popular tendency to see Protestantism as alien to Irish culture. The process whereby this image of the Catholic Gael was constructed has long been recognised by scholars. Less noticed, but equally important in the identikit of the Ulster Protestant, was the similar cultural creation of the the Ulster Scot. In this, the Ulster Plantation of the early seventeenth century introduced a hardy breed of Scots. Endowed with the Calvinist work ethic and no-nonsense independence of spirit, they turned the province into the economic success story which it was when the myth was fully developed in the nineteenth century and gave to Ulster that distinctive quality which separates it from the rest of Ireland.[56] All of this ignores the distinctiveness of Ulster long before the Plantation; the impact of Catholic Scots (not least in the Plantation itself, where some 20 percent of the settlers were Catholic); the preexistence of linen production which would provide the base for the economic miracle; the high proportion of intermarriage and the general cultural mix which have gone to make the Ulster Catholic more like the Ulster Protestant than his co-religionists elsewhere in the country.

This does not deny the fact, however, that even in the seventeenth century, one was already deemed English/Scots or Irish according to one's religion. Not until the very end of the eighteenth century did some Irish Protestants call themselves Irish. Until then, to be Protestant in Ireland was to be English. This, of course, was not a term readily adopted by the Ulster Presbyterians, who used terms such as Scots, Hiberno-Scots, and, on those occasions when a common Protestant identity was assumed in the face of a Catholic threat (for example, the 1690s, 1820s–40s, and during the Troubles), British.[57] It was this reluctance by the Ulster Presbyterians to think of themselves as Irish which prompted Wolfe Tone's famous "common name of Irishman" plea, though even he never lost that instinctive Protestant dislike of

Catholicism as a system. Also notable, was his other call to give Catholics rights and liberty in order to make them think more like Protestants—a foretaste of Terence O'Neill's infamous, though equally well-intentioned remark: "Give them jobs and houses and they will live like Protestants."[58]

Contemporary Protestant rejection of Irishness thus has a long history, and it occurred long before it was taken over by an equally exclusive nationalism at the turn of the nineteenth and twentieth centuries. In many ways, it is not historical to expect Ulster Protestants to readily accept an Irish identity, though many have. As long as Irish culture has an identifiable link with Catholicism, it will continue to be suspected by the bulk of Protestants, for it is dislike and fear of Catholicism which have informed their religion and shaped their identity for the last four centuries.

V

There can be no doubt, then, that twenty-five years of violence have polarized people in Northern Ireland to a greater extent than before. Peace, as witnessed during the republican and loyalist ceasefires after August and October 1994, could transform the situation.[59] But it will not do so overnight, nor will it of itself remove the underlying causes of the Troubles. Poverty, discrimination, massive unemployment, and a dependency culture[60] are all too real. Yet it is division grounded in these that increasingly is being recognized by the people of Northern Ireland themselves as the underlying cause of the Troubles. The events of the past twenty-five years have been a deeply humbling experience.

The experience of the Opsahl Commission has shown that there is a greater willingness among the people to admit and explore the prejudices which have divided them than ever before. It, and other recent commentaries, also show a fracturing of the old quasi-monolithic Catholic/Protestant identities; a fracturing which, particularly within the Protestant community, created a deep sense of decline and despondency, and was the backdrop to the escalation of Protestant paramilitarism before the two ceasefires. That fracturing, though, may be the necessary precondition for a recognition of what unites rather than what divides the communities.

There is a small but significant increase in the number of people who accept a common Northern Irish identity (table 7.1), and the Opsahl Commission revealed a growing desire among nationalists to be given a more legitimate role within Northern Ireland (see appendix), whereas once only reunification of the island would have satisfied them. It is not yet an equality which many Protestants would easily accept. Nevertheless, even here there is a recognition that religious misunderstandings and prejudices have artificially divided sectors of the populace (notably in deprived working-class areas) that had more in common with one another than with other social sectors within their own community, or with the Irish or British governments with which they had traditionally identified. The Opsahl Commission (1993), the Downing Street Declaration (1993), the republican and loyalist ceasefires (1994), the "Frameworks" proposals (1995), and a host of other local, national and international initiatives, are products of an ongoing peace process which started on the ground in Northern Ireland in 1992. At the heart of all these developments is a recognition that the problems in Northern Ireland will only be resolved from the bottom up, by its people learning to live and work together, prior to any decision about long-term constitutional structures.

**Appendix: British-Irish Opinion Poll Findings on the Recommendations of the Opsahl Commission**

(The main results of the opinion polls, June 1993, are reproduced in the 2nd edition of *A Citizens' Inquiry*, note 2.)

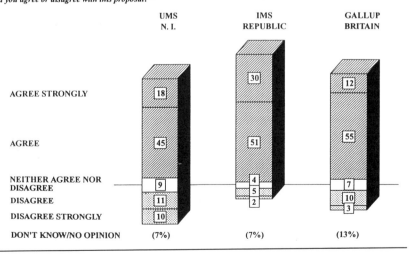

**MAJORITIES BACK INTER-COMMUNITY EQUALITY IN FUTURE N.I. GOVERNMENT**
**(Base: All Adults 18+)**

*"The (Opsahl) commission proposed a new government of Northern Ireland, based on the principle that each communtiy should have an equal voice in making and executing laws or vetoing them and an equal share in administrative authority. Would you agree or disagree with this proposal?"*

|  | UMS N. I. | IMS REPUBLIC | GALLUP BRITAIN |
|---|---|---|---|
| AGREE STRONGLY | 18 | 30 | 12 |
| AGREE | 45 | 51 | 55 |
| NEITHER AGREE NOR DISAGREE | 9 | 4 | 7 |
| DISAGREE | 11 | 5 | 10 |
| DISAGREE STRONGLY | 10 | 2 | 3 |
| DON'T KNOW/NO OPINION | (7%) | (7%) | (13%) |

## Notes

1. T. Opsahl, P. O'Malley, M. Elliott, R. Lister, E. Gallagher, L. Faulkner, and Eric Gallagher, *A Citizens Inquiry: The Opsahl Report on Northern Ireland,* ed. Andy Pollak (Dublin: Lilliput Press, 1993).

2. *Northern Ireland and the Opsahl Proposals: A Tri-partite Poll* (Dublin: Irish Marketing Surveys, June 1993), summarized and extracted in *A Citizens' Inquiry,* 2nd edn., pp. 435–44.

3. Opsahl Commission, submission no. 531, Prof. Edna Longley. The Opsahl Commission submissions have been deposited with the Linenhall Library in Belfast.

4. Schools in Northern Ireland are generally divided by religion. Integrated schools account for only 1 percent of school-age children (i.e., 14 out of a total of 1,336 schools, most of them at primary level). But the integrated movement is very recent and is gaining ground. It is still vigorously opposed by the Catholic hierarchy, inspires caution within the leadership of the Church of Ireland and Methodist Church, but is welcomed by the Presbyterian Church. Growing numbers of laity, however, are positively inclined.

5. Opsahl Commission, oral hearing Dungannon, February 5, 1993, Omagh Christian Brothers School. Catholics in Castledawson told the commission likewise.

6. John Whyte, *Interpreting Northern Ireland* (Oxford: Oxford University Press, 1990), p. 47.

7. See also Rosemary Harris, *Prejudice and Tolerance in Ulster: A Study of Neighbors and "Strangers" in a Border Community* (Manchester: Manchester University Press, 1972), p. xi.

8. This emerged particularly during the Opsahl Commission, Derry Schools Assembly, discussion group on "Culture and Identity."

9. I am grateful to Dr. Moxon-Browne for granting me permission to reproduce his findings. See also an analysis of similar findings in Whyte, op. cit. note 6, pp. 67–69.

10. Opsahl Commission, submission by the Rev. Robert Dickinson; also presentation by The Witness Bearing Committee of the Reformed Presbyterian Church of Ireland, oral hearing Shankill Rd., February 18, 1993.

11. *A Citizen's Inquiry,* op. cit. note 2, p. 120.

12. *Sectarianism: The Report of the Working Party on Sectarianism: A Discussion Document for Presentation to the Inter-Church Meeting* (Belfast: Irish Inter-Church Meeting, 1993), p.133.

13. Opsahl Commission, Auchnacloy focus group; see also classic Protestant statement in a letter signed "L.S. Coleraine," *Belfast Newsletter,* March 13, 1989, also one signed "Ulster Loyalist," *Irish News,* April 11, 1992.

14. Peter Stringer and Gillian Robinson, eds., *Social Attitudes in Northern Ireland: The Second Report 1991–1992* (Belfast: The Blackstaff Press, 1992), p. 141.

15. *Sectarianism,* op. cit. note 12, p. 147.

16. See, for example, his comments on President Mary Robinson's controversial visit to West Belfast in his interview with Jim McDougal, *BBC Radio Ulster*, "A Week in Politics," August 1993.

17. *Sectarianism*, op. cit. note 12, pp. 144–45.

18. *The Irish Times*, November 14, 1992, report based on the 1991 census.

19. Fionnuala O'Connor, *In Search of a State: Catholics in Northern Ireland* (Belfast: The Blackstaff Press, 1993), p. 145; Opsahl Commission, submission no. 402, The Witness Bearing Committee of the Reformed Presbyterian Church of Ireland, on how Catholics were feared by the majority Protestant community as "subversive aliens."

20. Opsahl Commission, Waterside focus group; also *Irish News*, April 11, 1992.

21. Opsahl Commission, submission by Jackie Redpath and oral hearing, Shankill Rd., February 18, 1993.

22. Opsahl Commission, oral hearing, Shankill Rd., February, 18, 1993, particularly the Rev. Jack Magee and Roy Montgomery; Fintan O'Toole, "On the Other Foot," *The Irish Times*, November 30, 1993.

23. Linenhall Library, Belfast, NI Political Collection: "A New Song for Nationalist Heroes."

24. Opsahl Commission, Keady focus group.

25. O'Connor, op. cit. note 19, p. 93.

26. Opsahl Commission, op. cit. note 24; also O'Connor, op. cit. note 19, pp. 370–71.

27. Terence Brown, "British Ireland," in Edna Longley, ed., *Culture in Ireland: Division or Diversity?*, Proceedings of the Cultures of Ireland Group Conference (Belfast: Institute of Irish Studies, 1991), pp. 71–72.

28. Opsahl Commission, submission no. 325, Dr. Bob Curran; "Culture Gap Divides Ulster from Eire," *Belfast Newsletter*, April 14, 1988; ibid., October 7, 1987—see Rev. Ian Paisley's comments on a Roman Catholic-Methodist conference; A. D. Buckley, "Uses of History among Ulster Protestants," in Elizabeth Tonkin, et al. eds., *History and Ethnicity*, (London: Routledge, 1989), p. 187.

29. Anne Laurence, "From the Cradle to the Grave: English Observation of Irish Social Customs in the Seventeenth Century," *The Seventeenth Century* 3.1 (1988): 63–84; D. W. Hayton, "From Barbarian to Burlesque: English Images of the Irish c. 1660–1750," *Irish Economic and Social History* 14 (1988): 5–31.

30. Marianne Elliott, *A History of the Catholics of Ulster* (forthcoming); S. J. Connolly, "Catholicism in Ulster, 1800–1850," in Peter Roebuck, ed., *Plantation to Partition* (Belfast, 1981), pp. 157–71.

31. John Gamble, *A View of Society and Manners in the North of Ireland, in the summer and autumn of 1812* (London, 1813), pp. 63, 83–84.

32. Marianne Elliott, *Wolfe Tone: Prophet of Irish Independence* (London and New Haven: Yale University Press, 1989), p. 112.

33. Clongowes Wood, prestige Catholic Boarding School in the Irish Republic.

34. Belfast, Linenhall Library, NI political collection: "Song of the Middle Class Catholic."

35. Opsahl Commission, submission no. 531, Prof. Edna Longley.

36. *Social Attitudes in Northern Ireland*, 2nd Report, p. 36; "Divided Localities," *The Guardian*, March 19, 1993; only 23,933 out of 342,059 pupils were reported as attending integrated schools in January 1992.

37. See my *Watchmen in Sion: The Protestant Idea of Liberty* (Derry: Field Day Pamphlet, No. 8, 1985).

38. Cited in *A Citizen's Inquiry*, op. cit. note 1, p. 37.

39. Opsahl Commission, submissions by Gabriel O'Keefe and Dr. Brian Gaffney; also oral hearings, February 4 and 6, 1993.

40. Opsahl Commission, submission by Pax Christi Ireland.

41. Paul Burgess, *A Crisis of Conscience* (Hants., U.K.: Avebury, 1993), particularly chap. 7.

42. Opsahl Commission, oral hearings Dungannon, February 5, 1993, discussion of submission no. 422, Cookstown High School.

43. *Social Attitudes in Northern Ireland*, 2nd Report, p. 36. The Opsahl Commission was also made aware of the polarization in charitable and voluntary organizations, Nick Acheson (submission no. 360 and oral hearing, Belfast, February 17, 1993).

44. See for example, Opsahl Commission, submissions nos. 340, North Belfast Women; 466, Community Development Trust; 540, Elizabeth Groves; 142, CBI Northern Ireland. But the most revealing comments and information on this issue came in the oral submissions of these four parties, Belfast, February 1993.

45. *The Independent* (London), March 22, 1993; David McKittrick, "Apartheid Deepens on Streets of Ulster," *The Independent on Sunday*, March 21, 1993.

46. Opsahl Commission, submission no. 472, Ken Logue; also his oral presentation, Shankill Rd., Belfast, February 18, 1993.

47. Quoted in Patrick G. Curley, "Northern Irish Poets and the Land since 1800," MA thesis, Queen's University Belfast (1977), p. 88.

48. Marianne Elliott, op. cit. note 32; Thomas Bartlett, *The Fall and Rise of the Irish Nation: The Catholic Question 1690–1830* (Dublin: Gill and MacMillan, 1992), p. 295; Bernadette Cunningham, "The Culture and Ideology of Irish Franciscan Historians at Louvain, 1607–1650," in Ciaran Brady, ed., *Ideology and the Historians* (Historical Studies XVII) (Dublin: Lilliput Press,1992), pp. 11–30; Opsahl Commission, submission no. 132, Centre for Research and Documentation; also oral hearing, February 19, 1993.

49. Linenhall Library, Belfast, NI Political Collection: "Song of the Middle Class Catholic."

50. Opsahl Commission, submission no. 422,Cookstown High School, Lower Sixth Form; also Schools Assembly, Belfast; I am grateful also for information from Aidan McPholan of the Ultach Trust in Belfast.

51. Opsahl Commission, Oral Hearing, Newtownards, January 21, 1993.

52. Belfast Public Library, Bigger Collection, *Irish History Reader* (Dublin: Gill and Son, 1905); see also the Ulster Folk and Transport Museum, School Textbook Collection.

53. Quoted in R. R. Adams, *The Printed Word and the Common Man: Popular Culture in Ulster 1700–1900* (Belfast: Institute of Irish Studies, 1992), p. 143.

54. *Cruíthne: The Reawakening of an Ancient Kindred* (Ulster Motherland Movement publication, Portadown, NI, undated); see also Ian Adamson, *The Identity of Ulster: The Land, the Language and the People* (Belfast: Pretani Press, 1982); J. Michael Hill, "The Origins of the Scottish Plantations in Ulster to 1625: A Reinterpretation," *Journal of British Studies* 32.1 (January 1993): 24–43, for a more learned claim that many settlers were "Celtic . . . ethnically."

55. Ciaran Brady, "The Failure of the Tudor Reform," in C. Brady, M. O'Dowd, and B. Walker, *An Illustrated History of Ulster* (Belfast: Institute of Irish Studies, 1990), p. 90.

56. See Raymond Gillespie, "Continuity and Change: Ulster in the Seventeenth Century," in P. Roebuck, ed., *Plantation to Partition: Essays in Ulster History in Honor of J. L. McCracken* (Belfast: Blackstaff Press, 1981), pp. 124–26; Ian McBride, "Ulster and the British Problem," forthcoming paper—my thanks to Dr. McBride for sharing his thoughts on this topic with me.

57. S. J. Connolly, *Religion, Law and Power: The Making of Protestant Ireland, 1660–1760* (Oxford: Clarendon Press, 1992), pp. 118–19.

58. Quoted in Eric Gallagher and Stanley Worrall, *Christians in Ulster, 1968–1980* (Oxford: Oxford University Press, 1982), p. 17.

59. The republican ceasefire broke down in February of 1996.

60. The Northern Ireland economy receives British government subsidies totalling some £1.5 billion per annum; a further £0.5 billion is expended on the police and army and £500 million has been paid in compensation to businesses etc., in the course of the Troubles.

# 8

# Israel and Palestinian Statehood

## GALIA GOLAN

> It is the fate of the Arab and Jewish national movements to fight
> until one or the other prevails.
> —Neguib Azoury, Christian Arab,
> at one time an assistant to the Turkish ruler of Jerusalem, 1905

> It is our destiny to be in a state of continual warfare with the
> Arabs and there is no alternative but that lives should be lost.
> —Arthur Ruppin, Zionist leader, Jerusalem, 1936.

When this chapter was conceived, these statements might have been taken as sadly but prophetically true. They reflected not just a mood but a deep appreciation of the central issue of what later became known as the "Arab-Israeli conflict." That is, basically, the clash between the aspirations of two peoples for self-determination on the same piece of land, in the geographically identical "national home." Yet the agreement signed on September 13, 1993, between the Government of Israel and the Palestine Liberation Organization (PLO) may well have supplanted the tragic "fate" or "destiny" referred to by these earlier participants in the struggle. It did so, not so much in the specific clauses and articles of the agreement, but rather, in the underlying document and principles which accompanied it: the mutual recognition of Israel and the PLO.

This was not just the recognition of a government and an organization. It was historic because it was recognition of the legitimacy of the claims of both peoples to national existence. For Israelis, it was the fulfillment of the dream—partially fulfilled sixteen years earlier when Egyptian president Anwar Sadat spoke in the Israeli Knesset in Jerusalem—of acceptance of the State of Israel in the region. Yet it was also, for Israelis, official recognition of the nationhood of the Palestinian people, with all the rights and aspirations of a national movement. Finally.

## I

It has been argued that it was perhaps the fatal error of the Jewish national movement that its founders and early advocates did not express such recognition, that they ignored the presence of Arabs in the homeland they sought to rebuild for the Jews. In fact, this was not entirely the case. That there were Arabs living in the land was unquestionably a most important issue in the minds of the Jews. Literature and documents from the pre-state period are filled with discussions, soul-searching, arguments and recriminations over the issue. The problem, though, at least in part, was the failure to come to terms with the issue on a political basis, as a matter essential to the fulfillment of Jewish self-determination, and one that had to deal not only with "the Arabs" in Palestine or even the Arab national movement, but with the relationship to and national aspirations of the *Palestinian* people.

At one end of the pole there were the views of Brit Shalom, the one group which did see an understanding with the Arabs as the central and primary matter to be resolved if Jewish self-determination were to be accomplished. In time, seeking, as their spiritual leader Martin Buber put it, to "do no more injustice to others than we are forced to do in order to exist," they envisaged a bi-national state of two equal peoples in Palestine.[1] At the other end of the spectrum were the Revisionists, forerunners of today's Herut party (the dominant member of Likud), who subscribed to the idea that an "iron wall" must be built around the Jews to protect them until the Arabs, coming up against this wall, would finally accept the situation.[2] If mutual understanding and justice were the key words for Brit Shalom, strength and steadfastness were the guideposts for the Revisionists.

Still, the overriding attitude, particularly of the dominant Labor movement, was that the Arabs would benefit from the development the Jews were bringing to the country. Together, both peoples would be freed: the Arab peasant from the *effendi* landowners, the Jewish laborer from his "*galut*" (exile) mentality.[3] Workers solidarity would lead to cooperation and, as a Jewish majority developed into a (socialist) Jewish state, regional and local autonomy (self-rule) would provide national expression for the Arabs. This view tended to see local Arabs as part of the broader Arab national movement and, therefore, flirted with the idea that eventually a regional Jewish-Arab federation might be created, in which the Jewish state would be one autonomous part.

This idea grew out of the hope for an alliance between Arabs and Jews, first against the Ottoman Empire and later against the British. But it also fed into the perception that the local Arabs were part of a broader Arab world that would eventually provide them with a number of Arab states in which to express their national aspirations. For the Jews, only Palestine would provide this opportunity. Thus Ze'ev Jabotinsky argued:

> The Arab nation, which has about thirty-five million people, has [an area equal to] half of Europe, while the Jewish nation, which has about ten million people, wanders throughout the world and has no place of its own.[4]

David Ben Gurion tended to see this as the key to a solution:

> As a starting point one should take the assumption that the question is not between the Jews of Palestine and the Arabs of Palestine—which in this limited area there is indeed a contradiction which it is hard to reconcile— but one should see the Jews as a global unit, and the Arabs as a global unit. And I believe that between the national aspirations of the Jewish nation and the national aspirations of the Arab nation, there are no contradictions, because we are only interested in this land, and the Arabs are interested not only in this land but in the whole territory of the Middle East. And whatever will happen in Palestine will not change the global status of the Arab nations.[5]

My purpose in bringing up these early approaches is not to discuss the mistakes or efforts of the protagonists and thinkers of the pre-state Jewish movement. Much has been written and said of this complex and difficult period; my presentation here is clearly a simplification of the matter. It is my intention, rather, to highlight certain positions which may provide a clue to the attitude of many in Israel today with regard to a Palestinian state.

Two tenacious but interconnected conceptions ground the "Arab-Israeli conflict," namely, that there is not a Palestinian people, as such, and that the Palestinian Arabs are but part of the larger Arab world. From this has grown the idea that the conflict is entirely one between states, denying the centrality of the "Israeli-Palestinian" issue, much less any responsibility for the solution or, in some cases, even recognition that there is a "Palestinian" problem. At best, this last might be perceived as a refugee problem, and even as such, one for which Israel bears no responsibility (because the Arabs "chose" to flee in expectation of returning to a conquered Israel, the argument goes).

Denying the Palestinians as a people negates the corollary of a *right* to self-determination; seeing them as part of the whole Arab nation (composed of numerous Arab states) eliminates any *need* for self-determination, at least in any area beyond the existing Arab states. Moreover, the "global" view of the Arabs, as suggested by Ben Gurion, projects an image not only of large numbers but of great strength—a concept which has persisted despite the asymmetry, particularly since 1967, of the Israeli and Palestinian situations.

This attitude towards the Palestinians has not been unique to Israelis. United Nations Security Council Resolution 242 clearly dealt with the conflict as one between states, referring to the Palestinian issue only in the context of a refugee problem. Even the Palestinians' major champion in later years, the former Soviet Union, initially withheld support from the PLO, and denied it the status of a national liberation movement until the end of 1969, precisely out of the same approach to the conflict.[6] Indeed, throughout the interwar negotiations, the two-power Soviet-American and four-power (plus Britain and France) talks between 1967 and 1972, the Palestinian issue was treated solely as a refugee problem by all of the great powers.[7]

To some degree, the adoption of this view of the conflict was a useful tactic to later Israeli leaders, especially in the post-1967 period. It permitted one to avoid the very basic questions of justice, rights, claims to the land, and so forth, connected with the very founding of the state of Israel. For the ideologically motivated right-wing, such questions may not have existed at all, for all of Palestine was viewed as the Land of Israel given by God to his Chosen People. For the majority of people and politicians without this heavy ideological and/or religious orientation, the matter was dismissed on the grounds that the Arabs of Palestine had been offered a state in the 1947 Partition Plan (Security Council Resolution 181) and had rejected it in favor of trying to evict the Jews altogether. And so it could be said that the "Palestinians" had forfeited their rights, though in fact the Partition Plan argument was more often construed as proof that there was not a "Palestinian" national movement or aspirations.

Thus one was left with the argument that Israel's problem lay with its rejection by the Arab states—a politically more potent position given the strength of the Arab world, whether in firepower, oil-based wealth and influence, or international alliances. This was tactically more useful, not only because it eliminated the need to confront basic questions of justice and rights, but also because it played on genuine fears amongst the Israeli public, including the almost instinctive fears of being a persecuted minority in an alien, anti-semitic environment. At various times, particularly during the latter period of right-wing Likud rule in Israel, it also served to postpone the need for concessions, that is, genuine negotiations, because the Arab states were intransigent. Put simply: if dealing with the Arab states was the priority, and they were unwilling to deal with Israel, no deal had to be made, and the responsibility lay with them. This approach had the advantage, in certain periods, also of providing a basis for American support in the Cold War context of Soviet versus American power in the region. Here too, the Arab states, not the Palestinians, formed the center of concern.

There was, of course, also a basis in fact for focusing on the Arab states. It was indeed the states that had waged wars against Israel, it was the states that had the strength to threaten Israel's existence, it was the states that perpetuated economic boycott and hostile propaganda against Israel. In this regard, the leadership of the country was quite justified in its concentration on the Arab states. But in doing so, it failed to acknowledge the link, however partial, between the Palestinian issue and the hostility of the Arab states; it also failed to confront the day-to-day issue on the ground: the occupation and the effect of this on Israeli society.

Yet in time it was this last, the day-to-day issue on the ground, to wit, the occupation and its effect on Israeli society, that would finally and gradually bring about the critical change. It was not, for example, some kind of collective guilt because of the occupation. Most Israelis would not willingly admit to the term occupation but, rather, tended to find refuge in the idea that the Arabs began the war, and lost.

Therefore, the argument would claim, as in the results of any other war, they now found this particular land under our rule.[8] And further, Israeli rule was far more liberal and gentle than Israelis could have expected to be granted by the Arabs had the situation been reversed. Actually, according to the argument of some, Israeli rule in the territories had improved the lot of the Arabs there, for instance, the opening of universities, a rise in the standard of living, and so on.

Moreover, with or without the above rationalizations, an entire generation in Israel grew up with these lands in our possession. Maps in every school room bore no sign of the border which had existed prior to the June 1967 war. The "green line," that is the armistice lines of 1949 which had been the unofficial but generally recognized border of the country for almost nineteen years, existed only in the political parlance of the day. Even without annexation, the Likud government that came to power in 1977 sought to make these territories psychologically, as well as physically, part of the country, decreeing that all official references, including the state-owned television and radio, employ the biblical Hebrew names of these areas, Yehuda and Shomron. As a result, for a generation of Israelis—often regardless of their political views—it was not a question of "returning" the territories to the Arabs but, at best, "giving" them to their occupants. Psychologically, this would be perceived as a "concession," perhaps politically necessary, but not the recognition of a "right."

The Likud government went much further than psychological annexation. It tried, unofficially, to incorporate these lands into Israel by means of a massive settlement of tens of thousands of Israelis there. These settlers carried with them an infrastructure of services, facilities, and laws exclusive to them, as distinct from the Arab inhabitants around them. By offering extraordinary financial inducements and benefits, the Likud government sought not only to people the area with Jews, so as to make any kind of territorial separation between Jews and Arabs (partition) impossible, but also to create a large settler constituency with a vested interest in holding onto these territories. By 1993, this policy had brought the total of Jewish settlers in the territories to approximately 110,000, the overwhelming majority of whom had gone there for economic, rather than ideological, reasons.

The policy of settlement had actually begun under the Labor government, soon after the 1967 war. Under Labor, though, this had been a very limited attempt to place people in selected, unpopulated, sites which the government believed should remain in Israel's hands for security purposes (or water supplies), in the event that the territories were returned. There had been exceptions to this criterion under Labor, for example, the settling of Jews in a part of the heavily populated city of Hebron. Nonetheless, the overall conception avoided massive settlement, with a view to returning most of the land in exchange for a peace agreement at some point in the future. Just how much land would be returned was the subject of much ambiguity and discussion within the Labor party. The criterion of security was generally claimed, but increasingly demographic considerations were toted as the overriding factor, that is, a plan which would not end with the addition of thousands or hundreds of thousands of Arabs to the population of Israel.

This demographic argument had a certain attractiveness; it was based on real-politik and yet appealed to often visceral fears: holding onto the territories would mean continued life with 1.7 million Arabs in addition to the nearly 1 million Arab citizens of Israel. It was not meant to be racist but defensive, and most of all nationalist. Inclusion (through annexation) of such a large number of Arabs would, according to the demographic argument, create a security risk and, more important, lead over time to a bi-national state. The Arab population in time would be equal to, if not larger than, the Jewish; not only would the Jewish nation-state be obliterated, but Jews might once again become a minority, this time in their own land. Nor was this argument meant to be immoral.

The loss of the Jewish character of the state was juxtaposed to the equally undesirable option of the loss of the democratic nature of Israel. To maintain Israel as the state of the Jews, one would have to continue to deny citizenship and political rights to the Arab population of the territories. For the Labor party, preservation of Israel as a Jewish, democratic state became the rationale for territorial compromise. The party platform's rejection of rule over another people, namely the 1.7 million Arabs on the West Bank and Gaza Strip, could be interpreted by some as a moral argument, but for the many this was a question of internal security, with nationalist and even racist overtones. Even the Likud avoided annexation because of the demographic issue, and only a minority advocated solving the problem by transferring the Arab population out of the territories and then annexing them.

It certainly is not my contention that the people of Israel are devoid of moral principles or a sense of justice. Indeed, the value of justice, particularly social justice, is deeply implanted in Jewish life and Israeli culture. A dramatic sign of the persistence of these values was the phenomenon of 400,000 Jewish Israelis coming out to demonstrate against the compliance of Israel in the Lebanese Christians' massacre of Palestinians in the Beirut Sabra and Shatila refugee camps. Roughly one tenth of Israel's Jewish population came to this demonstration in 1982 to demand (successfully) a governmental inquiry into the role and responsibility of Israel in that tragedy.

Yet the average Israeli does not view the Palestinian problem as a moral issue. As already pointed out, there is little sense of responsibility for the Palestinians' position today (they were offered a state in 1947 and rejected it; they chose to flee, so they are refugees; they attacked in 1967, so they lost the territories). Rather, average Israelis see *themselves* as the wronged party (all we wanted to do was live peacefully in our own country, they rejected us and tried to push us into the sea; they will not let us live in peace). The roots of this attitude lay deep in the perception of Jews as perpetual victims: wandering the world unaccepted by any country, harassed and tortured by pogroms, wars, terrorism. The anti-Semitism of the Christian world becomes transformed into the hatred of the Arab world, which, in turn, becomes transformed into the immutable hostility of Islam toward the Jews. And every act of enmity, from economic boycott to terrorism, reinforces this view, irrespective of Israel's military might or victories in war. Indeed, for the average Israeli, the Palestinians are not the powerless two million under occupation, and not even the additional two or three million dispersed elsewhere. They are an extension of the 100-million-strong Arab world, and this world possesses missiles and tanks and planes, and oil.

## II

Still, a change has taken place. These underlying attitudes may remain much (not totally) the same, but something in the conclusions Israelis are drawing with regard to the future is undergoing transformation. This is evidenced by the 65 percent support evinced by Israeli urban, Jewish adults for the accords signed with the PLO.[9] It is evidenced by the reluctance of the mass of Israelis, even of Likud supporters, to come out and demonstrate against the accords.[10] It also is evidenced by public opinion polls, even before the signing of the accords. For example, on the critical issue of territorial compromise, generally accepted as a sign of Israelis' willingness to reach a compromise solution, a survey conducted in January 1993 found that 60 percent of the Jewish, adult, urban public were willing to return territories (all or part) in exchange for peace.[11]

Of even greater significance than this three-fifths majority is the fact that it represents a trend taking place in Israel. A number of studies conducted over the years indicate a growing tendency to compromise among the Israeli public, or what has been called "creeping dovishness."[12] An ongoing poll, conducted since 1967 by the Guttman Institute for Applied Social Research in Jerusalem, has found a decline in opposition to the return of the West Bank, from 86 percent immediately after the Six Day War to 45 percent by 1993.[13] Similarly, surveys conducted by Dahaf Research Institute since 1984, in which respondents were asked to indicate their preference between annexation of the West Bank and Gaza or giving up these territories, found that those choosing to give them up had increased from 29 percent in 1984 to 55 percent by 1993.[14] And the national security studies conducted since 1986 by Asher Arian for the Jaffee Center for Strategic Studies show a jump from 39 percent favoring return (partial or total) of all the territories in 1986 up to the 60 percent of January 1993[15] (figure 8.1).

Looking more closely at the fluctuations and changes in these statistics over the years, Professors Michal Shamir and Jacob Shamir point to two types of events that appear to have had an effect on the attitudes of the Israeli public. According to their analysis, there have been increases in dovishness both at times of perceived progress in relations with the enemy (following the disengagement agreements between Israel and Egypt, Israel and Syria; the interim agreement with Egypt, 1974–75; and the peace treaty with Egypt in 1979) and, apparently, in response to terrorism—the attack on Israeli headquarters in Lebanon, December 1983, as well as, though more gradually, the *intifada* which began in December 1987.[16] While, according to Shamir

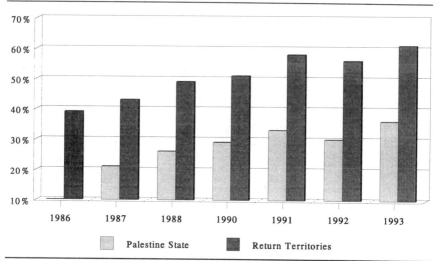

**Figure 8.1.** Israeli Attitudes, 1986–1993

and Shamir, there was an increase in dovishness prior to the outbreak of the *intifada*, this trend sharpened following the *intifada*'s onset, continuing each year of the uprising.[17] All the other surveys provide similar evidence as to the impact of the *intifada* on Israeli public opinion.[18]

The effects of the *intifada* were obvious to most Israelis even without the statistical evidence now available.[19] The major point that the *intifada* brought home to the Israeli public was the fact, for some surprising, that the status quo could not be sustained. It became clear, as a matter of empirical fact, that there was no such thing as a status quo but, rather, that the occupation had created a dynamic of increased violence and rebellion. While it did not have the nationally threatening effect of all-out war, the *intifada* did produce a reduction in the feeling of personal security. This was compounded by the increasingly apparent inability of the government to suppress the *intifada*, as well as by frustration over the inability of the mighty Israel Defense Forces (IDF) to protect itself from what were most often rock throwing women and children in the territories. There also was anger over the use of the IDF for such humiliating, and for some, morally painful, tasks. An unprecedented number of protest groups arose amongst the Jewish public, most notably among women, in response to this unarmed civilian uprising. Characteristically, these included a group of parents of young men about to be or recently inducted in their obligatory army service. Moreover, the international isolation of Israel as a result of the attention given Israeli efforts to suppress the *intifada* did little to raise the morale or pride of the Israeli public.

Yet, the most salient effect of the *intifada* was its stimulation of a certain realism among Israelis, and what might be called "fed-up-ness."[20] It was not, for the general public, a matter of now understanding or perhaps even sympathizing with the Palestinians; nor was it a recognition of their rights. It was, instead, a sense that matters could not continue as they were. Something had to be done; some solution had to be reached—to bring an end to *our* insecurity, the shedding of *our* blood, and the constant threat to *our* children in the army. For many, there was extreme discomfort with what *we* were doing, a discomfort which included a certain cognitive dissonance: *we* can't be doing this to other people. In addition, there was a growing realization that the world around us was changing, with the falling of the Berlin Wall and the end of the Cold War—what appeared to be a worldwide move toward resolution of conflict—and with this a sense of "inevitableness" regarding the outcome of our own conflict, whatever our own preferences.[21]

These responses, which produced the "creeping dovishness" noted earlier, are clearly evident in the survey data obtained by various independent sources over the past five years. For example, preference for the status quo as an option for the future of the territories, rather than annexation or return, was relatively high prior to the *intifada*, fluctuating between 40 and 50 percent, but a steady decline in this response began at the end of 1987, reaching a low of 25 percent by 1993.[22] Another survey, which presented more detailed options, showed a decline to 9 percent in 1990 and 6 percent by 1993.[23] A move away from the status quo option may have been connected with the greater realism reflected in people's expectations.

After the beginning of the *intifada*, there was an increase in the percentage of people who believed that Israel would eventually have to withdraw from part or all of the territories, and that there was greater likelihood of the creation of a Palestinian state (from 40 percent to 60 percent during the *intifada*).[24] About 80 percent of the respondents in a 1993 survey thought that Israel would be negotiating with the PLO within the next five years.[25] At the same time, perhaps making the pill easier to swallow, and possibly caused by the changes on the international scene, there was a slight change in the way Israeli's perceived Arab hostility. Looking at voters from all the political groupings in Israel (left, Labor, Likud, right), Shamir and Shamir found an across-the-board decrease, from 1987 to 1988 and 1990 to 1991 in the perceived Arab threat.[26] Arian's studies had the decline occurring later, accompanied by a steady increase from 1986 to 1993 in the belief that peace with the Arab states was possible[27] (figures 8.2, 8.3). That this was coupled with a certain concern or pessimism about Israel's future strength is suggested by other findings. According to Arian's studies, the percentage of Israelis who believed that Israel could win a war against the Arab states was down some 20 percentage points, from 77 percent in 1987 to 57 percent in 1993.[28] Still a relatively high percentage, this nonetheless marked a sharp drop in public confidence, possibly connected with the intervening Gulf War and its SCUD missile attacks on Israel.[29]

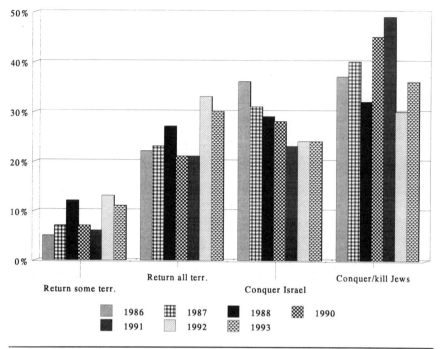

**Figure 8.2.** Arab Aspirations, 1986–1993

Greater realism in the Israeli public also produced a greater willingness to compromise. The percentages of those willing to give up the territories has risen significantly. Although the vast majority of Israelis continued to reject the option of a Palestinian state as the preferred solution, there was a slight increase in the number of respondents choosing that option. Prior to the *intifada*, choice of a Palestinian state as a permanent solution was around 8 percent. According to Arian, this choice was preferred by 9 percent in 1990 and rose to 13 percent by 1993.[30] Far more important, though, the percentage of those *agreeing* to the creation of a Palestinian state as part of a peace accord rose quite significantly (figure 8.1). Shamir and Shamir observe that prior to the *intifada* agreement to such a state was around 20 percent; during the *intifada* willingness for a Palestinian state to be created increased steadily to 30 percent in 1993.[31] Arian places acceptance at 36 percent in 1993. And, as we have seen, some 60 percent of the public believed there will be a Palestinian state, regardless of Israelis' preferences.

With the approach of the Israeli-PLO agreement, one week before the historic signing, a poll taken by the Guttman Institute showed a marked increase in Israelis' dovishness.[32] The crucial question of giving up territories, at least in part, drew a startling 71 percent. And in answer to the question "Are you for or against the crea-

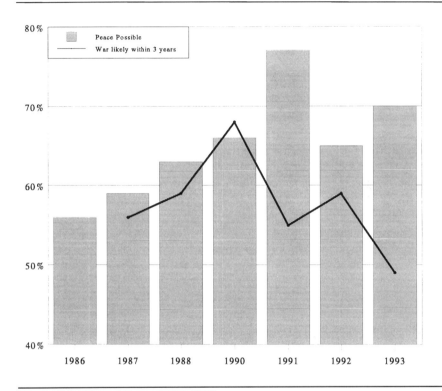

**Figure 8.3.** War and Peace, 1986–1993

tion of a Palestinian state in the territories?," the response in favor was 40 percent. While far from the 65 percent support given the Israeli-PLO accord signed one week later, and still less than a majority—60 percent responded against a state—this was nonetheless indicative of the relatively dramatic shift that has been taking place in the attitudes of the Israeli public over the past few years with regard to the Palestinian people.

With the September 1993 agreements, Israel recognized the Palestinians as a people and their national liberation organization, the PLO. With regard to the national rights of this people, however, Israel has committed itself thus far to only one form of expression: autonomy. The matter of the final status of the territories was put off until negotiations beginning in 1995. But the fact that autonomy is officially considered only an interim arrangement leaves the door open to the state solution, and indeed both the public and political elites in Israel expect a Palestinian state to emerge.

## III

Prime Minister Yitzhak Rabin and the Labor party have officially gone on record numerous times as opposing the creation of a Palestinian state.[33] Labor's preference would be to return part of the West Bank, in particular the Arab-populated areas, to Jordan, though in recent years the party platform has spoken of returning territories to a Palestinian-Jordanian entity.[34] Labor's preference for dealing with the Jordanians, what for years was called "the Jordanian option," dates back to the pre-state period.[35] In the 1940s, indeed even before, the Jews had much greater success in speaking with Jordanian officials, including King Abdullah, than with local leaders. Of course, such dealings suited the tendency to deal with states rather than a people, and to this day the Labor party would prefer to deal with King Hussein, with whom a direct relationship, and one of trust, has developed over the past few decades.

The rationale for this position appears to be based on security considerations. In order to prevent a military threat to Israel, the West Bank must be demilitarized, as it virtually was when it belonged to Jordan prior to the Six-Day War. As the argument goes, a whole state cannot be expected to be demilitarized, but, as part of a larger entity, the West Bank could be. Former Israeli foreign minister Abba Eban has commented in the past that he could not understand why his party preferred one large, strong state, to wit, a Jordanian-Palestinian entity, over two small ones in the same area.[36] The response to that, and the sentiment of many in Israel, is that a small, demilitarized Palestinian state on the West Bank would be a weak country, vulnerable to invasion or takeover from an Arab country such as Syria.

It is well to observe here that Israel has long prevented the movement of outside troops into neighboring Jordan, through threat of war. In September 1970, an Israeli threat to attack was a central factor in the swift retreat of Syrian forces which had entered Jordan on the side of the Palestinians in the civil war there; during the Gulf crisis of 1990–91, Israel made it clear that it would respond if Iraqi troops were permitted to enter Jordan. Presumably, Israel would be equally vigilant with regard to a Palestinian state.

The objection of most Israelis to the creation of a Palestinian state on the West Bank of the Jordan is based, justifiably or not, on security considerations. This is due to the small size of pre-1967 Israel, particularly its narrow middle which is no more than fifteen miles wide between the West Bank and the Mediterranean Sea. Objection to a Palestinian state is not due to an implacable attachment to a particular piece of land, that is, an ideological adherence to the Land of Israel (Greater Israel) concept. Research conducted by Shamir and Shamir found that only a small percentage, (10 percent) considered the concept of Greater Israel to be the most important value or even a priority for Israel, while the division within the public regarding territorial concessions showed a majority in favor of giving up territory.[37] This would indicate that something other than the ideological factor lay behind the position of most Israelis; most other indications suggest that the key factor in people's thinking is security.

Some form of demilitarization of the West Bank, whether as an independent state or as part of Jordan, would appear to be an absolute requirement from the Israeli point of view.[38] And in view of Labor's position, the idea of a Palestinian-Jordanian confederation, already endorsed by Yasir Arafat, might provide the solution. Israeli and PLO understandings of such an entity differ, however, on one crucial point: For the PLO, this must be a confederation of two at least initially independent states; for Israel, at this point in time, even a briefly independent Palestinian state is unacceptable. Yet, given the already evident change in the public's attitude toward the creation of a Palestinian state—the jump to 40 percent support—it is entirely possible, indeed even likely, that agreement to such a state will have majority support by the time negotiations are concluded for the determination of the final status of the territories.

Much will depend upon events in the coming interim period, in particular the degree to which the Palestinian leadership is able to limit violence from extremists within the territories. To some degree, this will depend not only on political and security measures, but also on the possibly still more crucial economic situation. Poverty and unemployment are the feeding grounds for discontent leading to extremism and violence. Indeed, whether in the interim period or in a Palestinian state itself, the economic factor will be of overriding importance.

In viewing the prospects for a state, one must bear in mind not only the requirement of demilitarization, as well as other security arrangements,[39] but also the links between the West Bank-Gaza economy and that of Israel. Coordination and cooperation will be necessary to deal with the 120,000 Palestinians who had been accustomed to finding work inside Israel or the thousands of Israelis who might seek tax-free purchases across the border in Palestine. In other words, labor and fiscal policies will require some cooperation, as will questions of transportation and communications. Water policy is already under discussion; the security of water supplies to Israel from sources in a Palestinian state is a major issue.[40] All of these matters, from the economy to water, also have regional aspects which may provide more durable solutions and incentives for cooperation.

## IV

In Israeli political discourse on the right, the Palestinians' right of return (solution of the refugee issue) is often presented as the crowning argument against a Palestinian state. In point of fact, the creation of a Palestinian state would provide a solution to this matter inasmuch as it would furnish the entity to which Palestinian refugees of 1948 might "return." Israeli concern on this issue revolves around the fear that conceding the right of return would lead to an influx of Palestinians into Israel, thereby changing the demographic character of the state—in effect marking the end of a Jewish state. PLO official Nebil Sha'ath has suggested that the right of return be acknowledged in principle but that implementation be determined in negotiations on the basis of Israel's requirements.[41] The result as predetermined would be the settlement of Palestinians from their Diaspora in the Palestinian state, with only exceptional cases of Palestinians returning to Israel. In their joint discussion of a Palestinian state, Mark Heller and Sari Nusseibeh contend that the PLO's 1988 acceptance of UN resolution 181, which called for the creation of a Jewish and an Arab state in Palestine, provides the basis for such an application of the right of return.[42] In keeping with UN resolutions (194 of 1948 on the refugee issue), consideration must be given to compensating Palestinians for lost properties and assets, although there are also Israeli demands for similar consideration to be given Jews forced to flee certain Arab countries following the creation of Israel.

The future of the Israeli settlements in the West Bank and Gaza is another problem that will have to be resolved in the negotiations preceding a Palestinian state. The interim accord basically excludes these settlements from the autonomy arrangements, and the Labor party platform envisages the settlements remaining, with Israeli protection, under any Palestinian-Jordanian entity that emerges. It is not clear that Palestinian sovereignty would not be violated by such an arrangement. It seems more likely that the Palestinians would agree to the settlements remaining, if at all, only if subject to Palestinian law. The matter cannot be easily resolved and, indeed, the Likud created these settlements precisely as a means to complicate, and ultimately prevent, the return of any territory and the subsequent creation of a Palestinian state.

The Israeli government under Labor might be expected to seek ways of leaving the settlements in place, so as to avoid both the stigma of responsibility for uprooting Jews from their homes, and the risk of forced evacuation conducted by Israeli forces. The folklore of Labor Zionism, with its pioneering ethic and return to the land ideal, disdains the dismantling of any Jewish settlement. And forced evacuation, which might occasion physical, possibly even armed, resistance from the albeit small number of fanatic, ideologically motivated settlers, would be still more repugnant.

The settlers as such do not have much support from the Israeli public. Actually, one of the phenomena which emerged quite strongly in the June 1992 Israeli elections was the anger of many in the electorate who viewed the settlements as a drain on the Israeli economy and, therefore, at least partially responsible for the unemployment, housing problems and inadequate infrastructure (roads, schools, etc.,) within Israel. Many even expressed the belief that the settlers were merely speculators who went to the territories with the expectation of being handsomely bought out by the government in case of a future peace agreement.[43] However, the majority of settlers probably went to the territories not out of speculation, nor out of ideological motivation, but rather in response to the material incentives offered by the government for housing and living conditions which would have been totally beyond their grasp inside Israel. Thus while the Israeli government might seek an arrangement leaving the settlements where they are, it may well undertake an effort quietly to induce voluntary departures by means of compensation and relocation.[44]

The most difficult issue to resolve, perhaps the most intractable of all, is the status of Jerusalem. It was in fact only the Palestinian decision to put off discussion of this issue, in exchange for Israel's dealing directly with Arafat, that prevented a collapse of the Israeli-Palestinian peace talks in August 1993. While the Palestinians lay claim only to the eastern part of Jerusalem, which they envision as the capital of their state, and is indeed the center of West Bank commercial, cultural, and political life, Israel is determined to maintain the unity of the city, as the Jewish capital, with exclusive Israeli sovereignty.

These two elements, unity and sovereignty, are inseparable in Israeli eyes. Public opinion polls, as well as the political statements of all the major Israeli parties, attest to this. There are few official Palestinian references to the issue of unity, but there does not appear to be a demand, nor even a wish, for a return to the physical division of the city which existed from 1949 until 1967. On this, at least, there would appear to be Israeli and Palestinian agreement. It is the claim to sovereignty over the eastern part of the city, with its Jewish as well as Arab population, history, religious sites, and symbolism, that constitutes the problem.

With regard to Jerusalem, sentiment and symbolism are often stronger than legalities and technicalities, but it may well be through the latter that a solution emerges. Quite a large number of proposed solutions have been suggested—ranging from single sovereignty with a shared municipality, to shared sovereignty with dual municipalities, to divided sovereignty with separate municipalities, to a borough system or neighborhood self-rule with or without sovereignty, or obfuscated sovereignty.[45] Acceptance of any one of these or other arrangements for Jerusalem will require a certain dissociation of the parties concerned from the emotional, religious, and symbolic considerations imposed upon them not only by their constituencies but also by powerful forces abroad—Jews and Moslems alike. Negotiation concerning the future of Jerusalem, difficult as it will undoubtedly be, will nonetheless be necessary. It is possible, however, that both Israelis and Palestinians will in time realize the necessity of reaching some agreement on the issue, inasmuch as it may well represent the last hurdle on the one-hundred-year course leading to Israeli-Palestinian peace.

### Notes

The sources of the epigraphs that open the chapter are: Neguib Azoury, *Le reveil de la nation Arabe* (Paris, 1905), p. V; and a citation in Susan Lee Hattis' doctoral dissertation *The Binational Idea in Palestine During Mandatory Times* (Geneva, 1970), p. 167.

1. From Martin Buber, "The National Home and National Policy in Palestine," October 1929, reproduced in Paul Mendes-Flohr, *A Land of Two Peoples: Martin Buber on Jews and Arabs* (New York: Oxford University Press, 1983), p. 86.

2. For the theoretical underpinnings of this view, see the discussions of Ze'ev Jabotinsky's views in Baruch Kimmerling, *Zionism and Territory* (Berkeley: Institute of International Affairs, 1983) or Shmuel Almog, ed., *Zionism and the Arabs* (Jerusalem: The Historical Society of Israel, 1983).

3. For a comprehensive secondary source, see Walter Laqueur, *A History of Zionism* (London: Weidenfeld and Nicolson, 1972). Selected primary sources may be found in David Hardan, ed., *Anthology of Contemporary Jewish Thought*, vol. 5 (Jerusalem: World Zionist Organization, 1975). See also Shlomo Avineri, *The Making of Modern Zionism: The Intellectual Origins of the Jewish State* (London: Weidenfeld and Nicolson, 1981).

4. Jabotinsky speech in 1914, *The World of Ze'ev Jabotinsky: A Collection of His Speeches and the Essentials of His Doctrine* (Tel Aviv: Defusim, 1972), p. 220 (in Hebrew).

5. Ben Gurion's comments to an Arab historian in 1936, cited in Kimmerling, op. cit. note 2, pp. 199–200.

6. See Galia Golan, *The Soviet Union and the Palestine Liberation Organization* (New York: Praeger Publishers, 1981).

7. See William Quandt, *Decade of Decisions: American Policy Toward the Arab-Israeli Conflict 1967–1976* (Berkeley: University of California Press, 1977) and L. L. Whetten, *The Canal War: Four Power Conflict in the Middle East* (Cambridge, MA: MIT University Press, 1974) for accounts of these negotiations. Both the US and the USSR were beginning to accord attention to the national aspects of the Palestinian issue during this period, but public references beyond the refugee question began to appear only in the 1970s. The Soviets themselves began to refer to the "national rights" of the Palestinians only after the Yom Kippur War of 1973. (Galia Golan, *Yom Kippur and After: The Soviet Union and the Middle East Crisis* [Cambridge: Cambridge University Press, 1977], pp. 139–40.)

8. There was also the ideologically based view of a relatively small minority that Israel had merely "liberated" lands of the Land of Israel (Eretz Israel), i.e., lands that belonged to it and the "Chosen People" in any case.

9. CNN poll taken together with a number of polling agencies in Israel on September 14, 1993. An Israeli poll taken just before the signing had urban, adult Jewish support at 62 percent. Inclusion of Arab citizens of Israel and nonurban kibbutz and moshav members is estimated to have raised this percentage by three or more points.

10. See article in right-wing press admitting this phenomenon: Michal Yudelman, "Rightist March out of Step with Likud Drummer," *Jerusalem Post*, September 24, 1993 ("It is significant that the first cracks in the Likud's anti-Pact armor were

caused by members who are most in touch with the public."), and "Chorus of Criticism for Natanyahu," September 26, 1993.

11. Asher Arian, "Israel and the Peace Process: Security and Political Attitudes in 1993," Jaffee Center for Strategic Studies, Tel Aviv University (February 1993), p. 8.

12. Jacob Shamir and Michal Shamir, "The Dynamics of Public Opinion on Peace and the Territories," Final Research Report submitted to the Israel Foundations Trustee and the Israel Academy of Sciences (September 1993), p. 10.

13. Ibid., p. 5.

14. Ibid., p. 12.

15. Arian, op. cit. note 11, p. 8.

16. Shamir and Shamir, op. cit. note 12, p. 8.

17. Ibid., p. 10.

18. See also a study by Hanna Levinsohn and Elihu Katz, "The Intifada Is Not A War: Jewish Public Opinion on the Israel-Arab Conflict," in Akiva Cohen and Gadi Wolfsfeld, eds., *Framing the Intifada: People and Media* (Norwood, NJ: Ablex Publishing Corporation, forthcoming).

19. See Galia Golan, "Arab-Israeli Peace Negotiations: An Israeli View," in Stephen Spiegel, ed., *Arab-Israeli Search for Peace* (Boulder: Lynne Rienner Publishers, 1992), pp. 37–48.

20. A term which I, like many others, have been using for a number of years (see Levinsohn and Katz, op. cit. note 18, p. 58, cited in Shamir and Shamir, op. cit. note 12, p. 72). It is not the same as war-weariness or exhaustion, as some abroad have translated it. Rather it is more akin to the feeling of simply having had enough!

21. Levinsohn and Katz coined the phrase "inevitableness," along with "fed-up-ness," in their discussion of the change in Israeli attitudes.

22. Shamir and Shamir, op. cit. note 12, p. 11.

23. Ibid., p. 11 using the Dahaf data; Arian, op. cit. note 11, p. 9 has the lower percentages with the longer list of options.

24. Shamir and Shamir, op. cit. note 12, p. 72 citing Levinsohn and Katz.

25. Ibid., p. 72.

26. Ibid., p. 92.

27. Arian, op. cit. note 11, pp. 2–3. His study showed a very high percentage of perceived Arab threat together with a slight trend in the other direction.

28. Ibid., p. 15.

29. Arian's data for 1991, the year of the Gulf War, do show a sharp rise in Arab threat perception but also a sharp rise in the belief in the possibility of reaching peace with them, presumably reflecting optimism over America's enhanced role. (Ibid., pp. 2–3.)

30. Ibid., p. 9.

31. Shamir and Shamir, op. cit. note 12, p. 73.

32. Poll taken September 7–8, 1993, commissioned by the American Jewish

Committee, published in part in the *Jerusalem Post*, September 13, 1993. My thanks to Dr. Hanna Levinsohn of the Guttman Institute for providing me with the complete results.

33. See, for example, *Ha'aretz*, September 22, 1993.

34. Labor's preference would presumably be the "Allon Plan" which would leave Israel territory along the ridge which runs through the West Bank, with certain areas such as the Jordan valley and Gush Etzion south of Jerusalem in Israeli hands. Labor's preferred map has never been officially pronounced, although the Labor party platform excludes a number of areas from return.

35. This by no means resembles the Israeli right-wing's idea of "Jordan is Palestine," which argues that inasmuch as the majority of the population in Jordan is Palestinian, King Hussein should be replaced and Jordan should be declared the Palestinian state—leaving the West Bank for Israel.

Editor's Note: Israel and Jordan signed a peace treaty on July 25, 1994.

36. Abba Eban made this remark on a number of occasions, for example, in a speech delivered at Tzavta in Jerusalem in 1981.

37. When asked to rank the values most important for Israel, only 10 percent placed Greater Israel (Eretz Israel) in first place, as distinct from peace (39 percent), the Jewish nature of the state—a Jewish majority (31 percent), and democracy (20 percent). (Shamir and Shamir, op. cit. note 12, p. 113.)

38. For two good discussions of this and other problems associated with the creation of a Palestinian state, see Mark Heller and Sari Nusseibeh, *No Trumpets, No Drums: A Two-State Settlement of the Israeli-Palestinian Conflict* (New York: Hill and Wang, 1991); JCSS Study Group, *The West Bank and Gaza: Israel's Options for Peace* (Tel Aviv: Jaffee Center for Strategic Studies, 1989); Ann Mosely Lesch et al., *Transition to Palestinian Self-Government: Practical Steps Toward Israeli-Palestinian Peace* (Bloomington: Indiana University Press, 1992).

39. For various proposals, see Ze'ev Schiff, "Security for Peace: Israel's Minimal Security Requirements in Negotiations with the Palestinians" (Washington, D.C.: The Washington Institute for Near East Policy, 1989); Valerie Yorke, "Imagining a Palestinian State: An International Security Plan," *International Affairs* 66.1 (January 1990): 115–36; Joseph Alpher, "Security Arrangements for a Palestinian Settlement," *Survival* 34.4 (Winter 1992–93): 49–67.

40. See, in particular, Peter Glieck, *Water and Conflict* and Miriam Lowi, *West Bank Water Resources and the Resolution of Conflict in the Middle East*, (Cambridge, MA: American Academy of Arts and Sciences and the Univeristy of Toronto, 1992).

41. For example, in his speech to a conference held at Columbia University March 11–13, 1989.

42. Heller and Nusseibeh, op. cit. note 38, p. 95. This book contains excellent treatment of the various issues connected with the creation of a Palestinian state, providing the outlines of reasonable solutions to most of the problems.

43. As the Sinai settlers had been when peace with Egypt was achieved.

44. It is estimated that approximately $2.5 billion ($100,000 per family) would be needed to relocate the 25,000 settler families in comparable housing inside Israel. It also is estimated that supporting the settlers in the territories costs the Israeli government today approximately $1 billion a year. (Arie Caspi, "The Low Cost of Withdrawal," *The Jerusalem Report*, April 21, 1994.)

45. This last was suggested by Heller and Nusseibeh. Some of the Israeli proposals can be found in the JCSS Study Group, op. cit. note 38, or Meron Benvenisti, "The Jerusalem Question: Problems, Procedures and Options" (Jerusalem: The West Bank Data Base Project, 1985); and Naomi Chazan, "Negotiating the Non-Negotiable: Jerusalem in the Framework of an Israeli-Palestinian Settlement" (Cambridge, MA: American Academy of Arts and Sciences, 1991), which summarizes many of the proposals.

# 9

# Palestinian Statehood

## MUHAMMAD HALLAJ

### Introduction

On September 1, 1993, when Palestinian and Israeli negotiators returned to Washington, D.C., for the eleventh round of talks in the peace process begun in Madrid in October 1991, they broke new ground. For the first time in nearly two years of talks, Israeli and Palestinian delegates gathered to undertake an unprecedented assignment: to fine tune and formally conclude an agreement secretly negotiated in Norway over a period of several months by their principals, the Israeli government and the Palestine Liberation Organization (PLO), and made public only a few days earlier. While the negotiating teams met in Washington, the Israeli government and the PLO went through their respective constitutional processes to ratify the agreement, to agree on a jointly acceptable announcement of mutual recognition, and to build domestic and regional consensus in support of their agreement.

The agreement gives the Palestinians a measure of self-rule in the West Bank and Gaza, and something akin to independence in the Gaza Strip and the ancient West Bank town of Jericho. This is an interim arrangement, pending the conclusion of a more comprehensive accord on the ultimate status of the Palestinian territory seized by Israel in the Arab-Israeli war of 1967.[1] Palestinian supporters and Israeli opponents of the agreement described it as the first step on the road to Palestinian statehood. It is too early to tell if the agreement is a step to statehood or a detour that will eventually carry the Palestinians away from national independence. The agreement includes provisions for Israeli control as well as Palestinian self-government that, contingent on which of the two categories of provisions that ultimately prevails, could deflect future Palestinian-Israeli relations in one direction or the other.

The fact remains, however, that the agreement is a landmark in the history of the conflict and Palestinian-Israeli relations. First, it is the first time since the conflict began in 1948 that representatives of Israel and the Palestinians reached a directly negotiated written agreement on anything. Second, it was negotiated by high-level representatives of the PLO and the government of Israel, a startling and major shift in Israel's policy of not dealing with the PLO. Finally, it underlines the frequently ignored fact that the conflict is no longer about Israel's existence but about Palestinian national rights.

The Palestinian-Israeli conflict has endured for so long not because the parties have found nothing to agree on; the real problem has been their inability to agree on what the conflict is really about, as well as their inability to agree on what needs to be done to resolve it, at the same moment in history. The agreement concluded between Israel and the PLO is the closest that the parties have ever come to a convergence of views concerning the conflict.

Although the "Gaza plus" agreement does not signal Israel's abandonment of its traditional opposition to Palestinian statehood, it opens the way to the emergence of an environment receptive to that option. For the first time, there exists the possibility of Israeli-Palestinian convergence on the two-state solution. Palestinian statehood, within the context of a two-state solution to the question of Palestine, has been the most widely accepted and at the same time the most vehemently opposed prescription for the resolution of the Arab-Israeli conflict. This was the case at the beginning, and it has not yet ceased to be the case.

In 1947, when the international community first grappled with the Arab-Jewish struggle over Palestine, the United National General Assembly endorsed the two-state solution, and the Arabs fought to prevent its implementation. They had compelling reasons for doing so,[2] since what they were asked to do was share their historic homeland, rather generously, with a minority of relatively recent immigrants. Their rejection of partition gave the conflict the durability that has made it one of the most stubborn regional conflicts in modern times. Subsequently, the tables were turned, and even though the two-state solution continued to be the most widely supported prescription for the resolution of the Arab-Jewish conflict over Palestine, Israeli opposition replaced Palestinian and Arab rejection as the obstacle to its termination. At the beginning, it was the demand for the establishment of a Jewish state, and Arab opposition to that demand, which triggered the conflict; now it is the establishment of a Palestinian state, and Israel's opposition to that demand, which keeps the conflict going.

In some respects, the Palestinian and Israeli positions have been mirror images of one another. In 1947, Israeli acceptance of the partition of Palestine was ideologically and emotionally repugnant, though deemed necessary, in the context of "Zionist pragmatism," and thus was accepted grudgingly as a political compromise, perhaps a temporary one. Jewish acceptance of partition in 1947, wrote Simha Flapan, "was an example of Zionist pragmatism par excellence. It was a tactical acceptance, a vital step in the right direction—a springboard for expansion when circumstances proved more judicious."[3] Today, the Palestinians accept partition in essentially the same spirit, that is, as a pragmatic solution, although most of them seem to understand it as an ultimate outcome. On both sides, the shared realization that partition gives as well as denies[4] has occasioned ambivalence about it, and partially accounts for the Palestinian rejection of Israeli statehood in 1947, as well as Israeli rejection of Palestinian statehood in 1993. In a very real sense, partition has been acceptable to the disprivileged and unacceptable to the privileged party. Moreover, in the case of the Palestinians in 1947, this realization led to the belief that Zionist ideology necessarily makes the Jewish state expansionist, and in the Israeli case in 1993, it fostered the belief that a Palestinian state would be necessarily irredentist. What makes the matter serious is that both beliefs are not lacking in validity, and must be woven into the texture of any sound explanation pertaining to why the partition of Palestine, accepted by both parties at different times, has always been a source of conflict rather than a meeting ground for them.

Decades of conflict over Palestine make it abundantly clear that neither side accepts partition as a fair solution, and that the only way out is that both of them accept it as a political compromise with which they can live. The best that can be expected is that the Palestinians and the Israelis accept partition, not necessarily as justice, but as a prescription for living with tolerable injustice. And they need to converge on this position at the same moment in history. The Palestinians, after a period of rejection, followed by a period of hesitation, have made such a transition. Israel has not yet done so, although its acceptance of the Palestinians' right to present their demand for statehood at the ultimate status phase of the peace talks, and its accord with the PLO, do indicate that it may be moving in that direction.

## The Evolution of Palestinian Political Thought

Although the Palestinians are often stereotyped as maximalists and inflexible, they have been highly flexible and accommodating. Since 1947, when the United Nations (U.N.) triggered the First Palestine War with its recommendation to partition the country, Palestinian political thinking has undergone dramatic shifts in the direction of greater accommodation. These shifts have made Palestinian-Israeli peace possible because they made the conflict manageable—a dispute about coexistence rather than a conflict over existence. The shifts are reflected in the following three phases of Palestinian thought on how the conflict with Israel should be reconciled.

### *Liberation and Return (1948–1968)*

For twenty years after the Catastrophe of 1948, the Palestinians thought of the partition of Palestine and the establishment of Israel, accompanied by their subsequent condition as refugees, as a gross miscarriage of justice. They understood their experience, described as a journey through the cosmic absurd[5] by a Palestinian writer who shared it, as one of foreign occupation and "ethnic cleansing." The remedy they sought was the reversal of the injustice. Their thinking on how the conflict should be resolved was summarized in the twin slogan: *Liberation and Return.*

For the Palestinians, the injustice required reversal. *Liberation* was the antidote to the occupation of the land, and *Return* was the antidote to the uprooting and dispersal of the Palestinian people. It was a moral position rather than a political program, and it required the dissolution of the new Jewish state. Thus, in 1964 when the Palestine Liberation Organization was established, included in the Palestine National Charter was the statement: "Palestine, within the frontiers that existed under the British mandate, is an indivisible territorial unit"[6] (article 2). The Palestinian position was frequently, and correctly, described at the time as wanting to "turn back the clock" of history. This was the period of "Palestinian indignation," and it produced a cry of anguish rather than a political proposition.

## *The Democratic Secular State (1969–1973)*

It took the Palestinians two decades to overcome the traumatic experience of homelessness and to begin to come to grips with the new realities that had emerged in Palestine. In 1969, they made the first attempt, since the Catastrophe of 1948, to reconcile their rights with the fact of the presence of a Jewish society in Palestine. The result was that the Palestinians made the first major shift in their attitudes toward the conflict with Israel, and the first political proposal for ending the Arab-Jewish struggle over Palestine. They still rejected partition and the existence of a Jewish state, but they expressed willingness to coexist with a Jewish society. They called for the reconstitution of Palestine as a binational republic, at the time described as "democratic secular" or "nonsectarian" state, in which Arabs and Jews could share the same homeland with equal rights and obligations. This rethinking of the future of Arab-Jewish relations in Palestine began to appear in official Palestinian pronouncements in 1969. In that year, the Palestine National Council (PNC) adopted, in its fifth session on February 4, a new statement of objectives concerning the Palestinian struggle, which defined it as an effort "to set up a free and democratic society in Palestine for all Palestinians, including Muslims, Christians and Jews."[7]

The Palestinians thought of the democratic nonsectarian state as something more, and more commendable, than a political compromise between conflicting claims. They saw it as a vision for historic reconciliation between Arabs and Jews. One of the most eminent Palestinian intellectuals and political activists of that period, Fayez Sayegh, explaining the difference between the vision and the compromise, put it this way:

> What is needed [he wrote] is a principled and courageous vision. The required vision must do precisely what a "compromise" cannot. A compromise takes its departure from the actual positions of the contending

parties and seeks to find a solution somewhere between them. The needed vision transcends those starting points and looks for a solution above them both. Men who cannot or will not surrender to one another may be inspired to surrender together to a higher vision—and in that surrender find freedom and fulfillment, as well as reconciliation.[8]

The Palestinians perceived the democratic-secular-state solution to be more in tune with the spirit of the times, of pluralist societies; more capable of fulfilling the aspirations and satisfying the emotions of both peoples since it did not deny either of them access to a part of the land they cherish. They called it "the civilized solution" to the conflict. However, the proposition entailed the dismantlement of the Jewish state of Israel as a polity, even though it recognized the legitimacy of a Jewish society in Palestine. For this reason, it was not something in which the Palestinians could engage Israel's interest. And because it entailed drastic changes in the status quo, it failed to evoke the interest of even the most ardent supporters of Palestinian national rights. It intrigued some intellectuals, but it failed to inspire political leaders.

In 1974, when Yasser Arafat addressed the United Nations General Assembly for the first time, he regretfully shelved the democratic nonsectarian state, calling it the "Palestinian dream."[9] The Palestinians never ceased to believe in the superiority of the democratic-secular-state formula, but since the mid-1970s, recognizing the necessity of political compromise, they ceased to advocate it as they made another major shift in their political thinking.

*The Two-State Solution (1974–present)*

After the Arab-Israeli war of 1973, a second major shift in Palestinian thinking and policies occurred. For the first time, a Palestinian consensus began to emerge in favor of a settlement based on partition and the two-state solution.

Three related events necessitated this shift in Palestinian thinking. First, there was the 1973 Arab-Israeli war. By fighting Israel to what they considered to be a stalemate, for the first time ever, the Arabs hoped that Israel would be more inclined to free the territories it seized from them in the war of 1967, making a negotiated settlement possible. Second, there was King Hussein's "United Arab Kingdom" proposal of 1972.[10] The Palestinians, still outraged by Jordan's expulsion of the Palestinian resistance in 1970–71, opposed the return of the West Bank to Hashemite rule in any form. King Hussein's proposal to reincorporate the West Bank as a region in a united kingdom under his rule focused Palestinian attention on the future of the West Bank and Gaza, and it triggered demands, particularly from inside the occupied territories, to preempt Jordan's claim to them. Finally, there was the great expansion of the PLO's international relations and its enhanced legitimacy. The PLO was taken more seriously by the international community as the Palestinian people's national liberation movement, and it came under pressure to rise up to the challenge by advancing a policy more likely to receive a favorable response from the international community. The supporters of Palestinian national rights were committed to the establishment of a Palestinian state in the West Bank and Gaza, and the PLO found it necessary to solidify that support by responding to the will of the international community.[11]

These were the immediate influences that led to the Palestinian move toward the two-state solution. Alain Gresh, in his pioneering study of the evolution of Palestinian policy, saw an even earlier beginning. The Arab defeat in the war of 1967, he wrote, killed the pan-Arab dream, brought Israelis and Palestinians face to face without Arab intermediaries, and fostered the restoration of the Arab-Israeli conflict to its original form as an Israeli-Palestinian conflict. The Palestinian national movement, "freed from external controls, came face to face with its responsibilities. It had to spell out its goals and objectives, in particular the state and territories to which it laid claim."[12] This process led to the eventual Palestinian acceptance of partition and the two-state solution.

In its twelfth session in June 1974, the Palestine National Council adopted a political program which opened the way to Palestinian acceptance of coexistence with the state of Israel. The ten-point program still identified a democratic-secular state in all of Palestine as the strategic objective of the Palestinian struggle, but it also legitimized an interim national authority in whatever portions that were freed from Israeli control.[13] The PLO did not accept the state of Israel, but it took the first hesitant step in that direction. In subsequent years the PNC increasingly made that acceptance more explicit, until in its nineteenth session, in November 1988, it made the first authoritative declaration of Palestinian acceptance of peace and peaceful coexistence with the state of Israel. At the same time, the PNC proclaimed the independence of the State of Palestine. This claim to independence was based on United Nations Resolution 181, which recommended partition in 1947. The PNC made it clear that the partition of Palestine and the establishment of Jewish and Arab states as successor states was the solution acceptable to, and sought by, the Palestinian national movement.[14] Unlike the democratic state idea, this program signified Palestinian acceptance of the existence of a Jewish state in Palestine.

Given widespread stereotypes about the Arabs and the PLO, their presumed inflexibility and tendency to exhibit moderation largely for external consumption, three crucial points about the evolution of Palestinian political thinking should be made here.[15]

> 1. The PLO, usually pictured as a radicalizing influence on Palestinians and Arabs, played an important role in leading the Palestinian people away from maximalist demands and towards more accommodating and conciliatory policies, and took the risk of alienating public opinion as it did so. In the late 1960s, its advocacy of the democratic-secular state alienated Arab and Muslim opinion by accepting the legitimacy of

Jewish presence in Palestine, and in the mid 1970s it provoked a mini–civil war (with the Rejectionist Front) by adopting the 10-point political program.

The PLO also made efforts to reeducate the Palestinians to its point of view. When it adopted the democratic-secular state idea, PLO schools began to teach Hebrew to Palestinian children to prepare them for the eventuality of coexistence with a Jewish community in Palestine.

2. Changes in Palestinian political thinking in the direction of more accommodationist solutions to the conflict with Israel occurred at moments of perceived Arab and Palestinian strength, and in that sense signified an authentic commitment to new thinking. The democratic-secular state proposal came as the Palestinian resistance movement was euphoric over its emergence, after the battle of Karameh in March 1968, as the antidote to the despair which engulfed the Arabs after the defeat of 1967. And the shift to the two-state solution came shortly after a new wave of euphoria swept over the Arab world after the war of 1973. It makes little difference whether the Arabs had valid reasons to be euphoric. The fact is that they interpreted these events as unmistakable signs of renewed national vigor, and it was at such moments that the Palestinians made their principal conciliatory gestures. It is also significant that the PLO's move to recognize Israel and to adopt a political program which authoritatively accepted a negotiated settlement based on partition came in 1988, again at a time when the Palestinian *intifada* revived hopes that Israel's occupation had been shaken and rendered "unsustainable."

3. The PLO contributed to making the conflict manageable not only by shifting Palestinian thinking away from maximalist demands, but also by modifying the means of securing Palestinian rights, by emphasizing diplomatic means at the expense of armed struggle, and eventually by a phased process which would begin with modest changes in the status quo. The "Gaza plus" interim agreement is the culmination of this process of taming Palestinian struggle to make it compatible with Israeli concerns.

The changes in Palestinian thinking on how to resolve the conflict with Israeli have been real. It serves no good purpose, neither is it fair to the Palestinians nor in the interest of peace in the Middle East, to argue, as many did when the PLO finally "uttered the magic words" (recognition of Israel, acceptance of Security Council Resolution 242 as a framework for a settlement, and renunciation of terrorism) in 1988, that the move toward recognition of Israel and acceptance of a negotiated settlement were merely ploys—because the leopard does not change its spots, as it was fashionable to assert at the time. Changes in Palestinian political thought, and the circumstances under which they occurred, challenge the racist notion, all too common in the West, that the Arabs "understand the language of force," a notion which unfortunately resurfaced after the Gulf War of 1991, when again it was used to explain Arab acceptance of the Madrid peace conference.

### Israel Moves the Other Way

As the Palestinians moved in the direction of accepting partition, Israel moved in the opposite direction. The emerging international consensus in favor of the establishment of a Palestinian state in part of Palestine, and growing Palestinian (and therefore Arab) acceptance of partition, threatened to call Israel's bluff as the traditional advocate of compromise, whose presumed willingness to live and let live was frustrated by Arab rejectionism. The Arab move toward coexistence in the context of the two-state solution increasingly isolated Israel and undermined its opposition to Palestinian statehood.

To preempt Palestinian statehood and to take the wind out of the sails of mounting international clamor on behalf of Palestinian self-determination, Israel mounted a two-pronged attack: to discredit Palestinian nationalism and to thwart the fulfillment of Palestinian aspirations. The first objective was pursued through a massive invasion of Lebanon in 1982, which was designed to cripple the PLO and to render it politically as well as militarily irrelevant. Israel also secured from the U.S. government a pledge not to recognize or deal with the PLO unless it met certain conditions, which were known to be unacceptable to the Palestinians at the time, including the unilateral recognition of Israel, disavowal of armed struggle, and the acceptance of Security Council Resolution 242 as the basis for a negotiated settlement. At the same time, it successfully mounted a worldwide campaign to brand the PLO, and the Palestinians in general, with the stigma of terrorism.

The second objective pursued by Israel was the speeded up de facto annexation of the Palestinian territory it seized in 1967, with the purpose of making the two-state solution impractical. In January 1982, an Israeli official signalled to a foreign journalist why Israel was building a road network, the so-called Trans-Samarian Highways, to connect the Jewish settlements in the West Bank to Israel and to integrate them more firmly: "Give us three or four or five years," he said, "and you'll drive out there and you won't be able to find the West Bank."[16]

In the 1980s, Meron Benvenisti popularized the notion that, regardless of whether one accepted or opposed the Israeli occupation of the West Bank and Gaza Strip, Jewish settlement in the territories had transformed the Palestinian-Israeli conflict from a national conflict requiring Palestinian independence to a less demanding ethnic dispute. The potential of Palestinian "communal power," wrote Benvenisti, "will be realized only when they identify short-range achievable communal objectives—political, economic, and social—within the realm of the possible under Israeli rule. Indeed, they must move in the system, albeit without granting it ultimate legitimacy."[17]

The Palestinians, on the other hand, were intent on proving the opposite. The *intifada*, or Palestinian uprising, which exploded in December 1987, developed into a Palestinian effort to counter Israel's policy of de facto annexation with de facto independence from Israeli rule. One of the major objectives of the *intifada*, as it evolved from street confrontations with Israeli troops to a process of nation-building, was to disengage from Israel and to force it to loosen its grip on the Palestinians and their land.[18] The struggle began to bear fruit in July 1988 when King Hussein renounced Jordan's claims and severed legal and administrative links with the West Bank, recognizing its Palestinian destiny.[19] Moreover, the world community came increasingly to perceive the status quo as "unsustainable," a view which led to mounting pressures on Israel to find a political solution to the conflict with the Palestinians.

A symbolic fulfillment of the *intifada*, and to give impetus to its goal of freeing the Palestinians from Israeli rule, was the proclamation of Palestinian independence and the establishment of the State of Palestine by the Palestine National Council on November 15, 1988.[20] The collision of Israeli power and Palestinian nationalism occasioned a new level of political stalemate, which fostered the conclusion— reached by the international community, including many Israelis and Arabs—that "The status quo bodes ill for Israel."[21] Something was needed to move the conflict off dead center. Taking advantage of regional and global circumstances which he judged to be opportune, particularly the end of the Cold War and the destruction of Iraq, as well as the consequent collapse of the Arabs' ability to confront Israel, U.S. President George Bush told Congress, in March 1991, that the time had come to put an end to the Arab-Israeli conflict.

**The Madrid Peace Process**

Ever since Israel seized the rest of Palestine in 1967, U.S. policy toward the future of these territories has been ambivalent. It endorsed both and neither of the Palestinian and Israeli objectives. It supported Security Council Resolution 242, whose preamble stated the principle of the "inadmissibility of acquisition of territory by war," but it also accepted an interpretation of the resolution which conflicted with that principle by arguing that the resolution permitted territorial "adjustments." President Jimmy Carter flirted briefly with the idea of a "Palestinian homeland," but President Ronald Reagan, in his initiative of September 1, 1982, rejected both Palestinian statehood and Israeli sovereignty over the West Bank and Gaza.

U.S. policy opposed Israeli annexation of the West Bank and Gaza but tolerated Israelis annexationist practices. It supported Palestinian self-government but opposed independence. It recognized Jerusalem as part of the occupied territories but understood Israel's refusal to negotiate its future. It supported U.N. Resolution 194 of 1948, which recognized the right of return for Palestinian refugees, but opposed Palestinian demand for the right of return.

The peace process put together by President Bush and his Secretary of State James Baker III, which was inaugurated in Madrid in October 1991, remained faithful to this American policy of being for and against everything. At the same time, it stipulated the exclusion of the international community, which held more consistent views on what should be done to resolve the conflict. The result has been a peace process which lacks a compass and tolerates practically any outcome, one which meanders aimlessly without a clear destination.[22]

Israeli policy of taking advantage of Washington's waffling to evade the imperatives of Palestinian nationalism is shortsighted. It may promote immediate purposes at the expense of historic interests. Even if it manages to coerce the Palestinians into acquiescing to an agreement which leaves them, in fact, a surplus people in the Middle East, it will be merely postponing the day of reckoning, perhaps to a time in the future when global and regional conditions may not be as favorable to peace as they are now. The Palestinians will not perish or vanish, and their national consciousness is too highly developed to permit perpetual denial of their right to self-determination. The second half of the twentieth century has proven that nationalism is still as unsuppressible as ever. This is so because of what Ann Lesch has called the "uncompromising reality" of life in a world of nation states. "In a world of nationalism," she wrote, "one can attain relative normality only by having one's own nationalism manifesting itself in one's own homeland."[23]

### The State of Palestine: Conceptual and Political Parameters

For the first time since the Palestinian-Israeli conflict began, it has become amenable to a political settlement. This is because, for the first time, the parties have converged simultaneously on the two-state solution. The process has not yet reached the point of no return, because this convergence is still rather tentative and is opposed forcefully by significant constituencies in both camps. It needs all the help it can get to survive and mature. To give it the opportunity it requires, conceptual and attitudinal adjustments, as well as political compromises, are essential. The needed conceptual adjustments include the following:

1. The authenticity of the Palestinian desire for accommodation must be recognized. It is self-defeating, as well as unfair, to deal with the Palestinians as if they were felons applying for parole, and it is counterproductive and risky to continue to assume that Palestinian compromises are nothing but grudging capitulation to the extant equation of power. There is no question that the imbalance of power is one of the incentives for compromise, on both sides, since more than four decades

of conflict have demonstrated the Arabs' inability to defeat Israel, and Israel's inability to vanquish and subdue the Arabs. Israel's military capabilities and diplomatic clout on the one hand, and the massive and deeply rooted Arab presence in and around Israel/Palestine on the other, make a historic stalemate inevitable. As Mark Heller and Sari Nusseibeh have observed, this also is true of the Israeli-Palestinian contest. "There is nothing to indicate," they wrote, "that either Israel or the Palestinians will, in the foreseeable future, have the power to impose their maximal aspirations on the adversary. . . . The only thing that can be said with certainty is that a resolution of the conflict is impossible unless the minimal needs and desires of both sides are reasonably satisfied."[24] A compromise is the only way out.

This means that Israel would be mistaken if it continues to seek the kind of peace that would reflect the relationship between victor and vanquished. Palestinian statehood, which requires the surrender of the Palestinian territory taken by Israel in the war of 1967, may exact from Israel more than the military imbalance of power would now demand. But it is what the historic moment summons, which matters if the opportunity for a historic reconciliation is not to be lost.

2. Palestinian rights should not be understood and dealt with as residual rights to be recognized and conferred if, and to the extent, that the requirements of other parties to the conflict permit. The Palestinian people cannot remain a "surplus people." That would only perpetuate the problem. The solution necessitates the rectification of this anomaly rather than its maintenance.

A workable and enduring solution requires that the Palestinian people be recognized and dealt with as partners in the community of Middle East nations instead of as an intrusion to be minimized, or a nuisance to be abated with minimal adjustments to the status quo. Palestinian statehood should be accepted not grudgingly as a measure of damage control, but generously in the spirit of conciliation, and willingly as a shared dream of peace, prosperity and stability in the region. It would be a mistake for Israel to continue to seek a solution whose overriding purpose is to find the absolute minimum of concessions to the Palestinians that it can get away with. The argument made by Heller and Nusseibeh regarding the "asymmetry" of the Israeli and Palestinian conditions, valid as it may be, can impede rather than facilitate a compromise, if carried to its ultimate conclusion.[25]

3. Israel must stop reacting to Palestinian statehood in the West Bank and Gaza as the expression of Palestinian radicalism, to be feared and avoided at all costs. It should deal with it as it really is: the expression of Palestinian compromise and accommodation, and the outcome of

Palestinian commitment to coexistence and conciliation. Israel's tendency to periodically redefine "Palestinian radicalism" in a way which ultimately discredits all Palestinians is a dangerous game. Not long ago, Palestinian "moderates" were people who accepted a Palestinian state in the West Bank and Gaza living in peace alongside the state of Israel; today Israel has redefined the same people as radical elements among the Palestinians. This game nibbles at those in the mainstream until they are all gone, and it is not in the interest of coexistence and regional peace.

4. Palestinian rights must not be judged strictly from the perspective of what is good for Israel, or other states in the region. And they must not be defined and circumscribed by the aspirations of the other peoples of the region. This is not to say that such considerations are immaterial or that Israeli interests and Palestinian rights are mutually exclusive. In his pioneering study of the impact of Palestinian statehood on Israel's strategic interests, Mark Heller shows that the two are not incompatible.[26] But it is not enough to concede the principle and ignore its political implications, namely, that the Palestinian people need to survive and prosper as a national society, and not just cease to be a nuisance to Israel. They need living space to rehabilitate displaced persons, political status to ensure responsible and effective Palestinian government, and balanced relations with the other peoples of the Middle East are requirements of Palestinian rights, which must be based on equity and not just the tolerance or ambitions of other parties.

5. Palestinian-Israeli peace must be understood as a process of reaching reasonable compromises to end a struggle between enemies who have compelling reasons to be enemies, not as a process of reconciling estranged lovers. Otherwise, the system of peace-making can be overburdened with unreasonable demands and unrealistic expectations. At least at this time, a compromise should be good enough, and conversion should be left to future history.

Within this conceptual framework, the rest would be relatively easy. The problem of how to make the transition from belligerency to peace becomes essentially a technical one which, freed of its emotional burdens, becomes more manageable. In mandatory Palestine, the theater of Palestinian-Israeli struggle, both Palestinians and Israelis agree (except in the case of Jerusalem) on what is Israel and what is not Israel. Heller and Nusseibeh's observation about the 1949 armistice lines, or the June 4, 1967 boundaries, being the most logical boundaries between Israel and Palestine is nearly universally supported. These boundaries do not preclude minor and mutually agreed upon adjustments to rationalize the borders, and to lessen their impact on frontier communities on both sides. The Palestinians no longer consider such adjustments "unthinkable." As early as 1978, Walid Khalidi, at the time widely rumored to be the most likely candidate for a future Palestinian prime minister, wrote that "[t]he frontiers of 1967 with minor and reciprocal adjustments are the most realistic under the circumstances."[27]

A symbolically armed Palestinian state, primarily for the purposes of internal security, and perhaps for psychological reasons, is not something that most Palestinians would find objectionable. Khalidi's proposal that, for internal security needs and in order that it would not become "the laughing stock of the Arab world," the Palestinian state should have a half or even a third of the level of Jordan's armament is something most Palestinians would be willing to live with.

Even the question of Jerusalem, widely advertised as the Gordian knot and the obstacle over which all efforts to make Israeli-Palestinian peace are likely to flounder, is not insoluble. Numerous models of a Jerusalem that could be the political capital of both Israel and Palestine, and at the same time a united city providing free access for religious, cultural, and emotional satisfaction by all have been sketched by both Israeli and Palestinian writers—including Heller and Nusseibeh, and Khalidi, in their already cited works. Others also have offered suggestions, the gist of which is that East Jerusalem and West Jerusalem could be the respective seats of government for Palestine and Israel, with a shared municipality that would make unnecessary the division of the city.

Adnan Abu Odeh, the Jordanian ambassador to the United Nations and a longtime confidante of King Hussein, who is of Palestinian origin, makes the important point that if one distinguishes *Jerusalem the holy city*, which stirs the emotions of people, from the much expanded *political Jerusalem* that now encompasses much of the West Bank territory, the problem becomes much more manageable. It is the exploitation of the Jerusalem issue for territorial aggrandizement which aggravates it and makes it appear "intractable." If the issue is redefined more appropriately as one concerning the holy places and the freedom of access to them, it can become a uniting influence instead of the divisive element that it has been.[28]

Other questions which need to be dealt with within the context of a Palestinian-Israeli agreement become manageable technical issues once the necessary conceptual adjustments have been made. This is not to say that they would cease to present difficulties, but they would become amenable to compromise solutions. These include the questions of Palestinian refugees, the presence of Jewish settlers, water rights and use, regional relationships and others.

Regarding the issue of refugees, on which the parties appear to adhere adamantly to opposing views—with the Palestinians claiming the right of return under United Nations General Assembly Resolution 194 of 1948 and the Israelis opposing it—compromises can be worked out involving partial repatriation in exchange for giving Jewish settlers in the West Bank and Gaza the option of remaining in the Palestinian state, and partial resettlement in and perhaps outside the Palestinian state in exchange for compensation. Many have offered ideas about how the refugee and settlement issues can be transformed from impediments to facilitators of an agreement.[29]

The main point being made about all of the issues involved in a settlement is that once the struggle becomes one over coexistence, rather than existence, compromises which now appear unthinkable become possible.

## Conclusion

In June 1988, Bassam Abu Sharif, senior advisor to PLO Chairman Yasser Arafat, circulated a Palestinian position paper during the Emergency Arab Summit Conference which convened in Algiers, June 7-9. It was meant primarily as a message to the Israeli people that the Palestinians were now ready for reconciliation. The Palestinians, he said, understood and accepted both the principle and the fact that "no one can build his own future on the ruins of another's." The PLO's *raison d'etre*, he wrote, "is not the undoing of Israel, but the salvation of the Palestinian people and their rights, including their right to democratic self-expression." He assured the Israelis that "no one can understand the Jewish people's centuries of suffering more than the Palestinians," and that the Palestinians would "welcome any reasonable measure that would promote the security of their state and its neighbors."[30]

The question, of course, is how to translate these pledges and sentiments into political compromises and agreements. Certainly not by allowing the past to paralyze the search for a better fixture. As Israel's [former prime minister,] Shimon Peres, who was a main player in the ongoing effort to find a mutually acceptable compromise once observed, in criticism of the opponents of compromise, "people prefer remembering, rather than thinking."[31] If Israelis and Palestinians continue to seek guarantees against the past, instead of a vision for the future, they will remain captive to the conflict which for more than forty years has been exacting a heavy toll in life, liberty and happiness. They both now speak of the need to take risks and chances for peace. When slogan becomes commitment the unthinkable becomes thinkable, and the impossible becomes possible.

It was the preference for remembering rather than thinking that encouraged gimmickry and political witchcraft in previous thinking about how to cut through the Gordian knot. It is the readiness to reach beyond the inhibitions of the past which gives the Palestinian-Israeli agreement on interim arrangements for the West Bank and the Gaza Strip, the so-called "Gaza-Jericho" accord, the promise of being the first step in the right direction. The implied recognition, reflected in the text of the accord, that the issue is Palestinian national rights corrects a notion which is no longer valid, namely, that the conflict is about Israel's existence and survival. This notion has caused previous attempts to resolve the conflict to go astray, and led to dead-end outcomes. Now, possibilities have been opened that did not exist heretofore.

**Notes**

1. Text of the agreement in *The New York Times*, September 2, 1993, p. A6.
2. Henry Cattan, *Palestine, the Arabs and Israel: The Search for Justice* (London: Longman Group, 1969), pp. 25–30.
3. For this interpretation of Jewish acceptance of partition in 1947, see Simha Flapan, *The Birth of Israel: Myths and Realities* (New York: Pantheon Books, 1987), p. 33.
4. Muhammad Hallaj, "The Palestinian Dream: The Democratic Secular State," in Rosemary Radford Ruether and Marc H. Ellis, eds., *Beyond Occupation: American Jewish, Christian, and Palestinian Voices for Peace* (Boston: Beacon Press, 1990), pp. 222–30.
5. Jabra I. Jabra, "The Palestinian Exile as Writer," *Journal of Palestine Studies* 8.2 (Winter 1979): 79.
6. Text of the Charter in International Documents on Palestine, 1968 (Beirut: Institute for Palestine Studies, 1971), pp. 393–95.
7. Text of the resolution in International Documents on Palestine, 1969 (Beirut: Institute for Palestine Studies, 1972), pp. 589–90.
8. Fayez Sayegh, "A Palestinian View," *The Arab World* (February 1970): 18.
9. Text of Arafat's speech in International Documents on Palestine, 1974 (Beirut: Institute for Palestine Studies, 1977), pp. 134–44.
10. Text of King Hussein's "United Arab Kingdom" proposal in International Documents on Palestine, 1972 (Beirut: Institute for Palestine Studies, 1975), pp. 289–93.
11. For expressions of international support of the PLO and Palestinian rights, see United Nations General Assembly Resolutions 3210 of October 14, 1974, and 3236 of November 22, 1974.
12. Alain Gresh, *The PLO, The Struggle Within: Towards an Independent Palestinian State* (London: Zed Books, 1983), p. 3.
13. For text of the 1974 political program, see International Documents on Palestine, 1974 (Beirut: Institute for Palestine Studies, 1977), pp. 449–50.
14. Text of the 19th PNC statement and the November 15, 1988, Declaration of Independence in *Journal of Palestine Studies* 28.2 (Winter 1989): 216–33—Document B3.
15. For a survey of changes in official Palestinian thinking on the conflict with Israel, based on analysis of political programs adopted by successive sessions of the Palestine National Council, see Muhammad Muslih, *Toward Coexistence: An Analysis of the Resolutions of the Palestine National Council* (Washington, DC: Institute for Palestine Studies, 1990). For an earlier but more detailed study, see Gresh, op. cit. note 12.
16. Ned Temko, "The Struggle for the West Bank," *The Christian Science Monitor*, January 4, 1982.

17. Meron Benvenisti, *Demographic, Economic, Legal, Social and Political Developments in the West Bank*, The West Bank Data Base Project, 1986 Report (Washington, DC: American Enterprise Institute, 1986), p. 95.

18. A 1989 report by the Jaffee Center for Strategic Studies of Tel Aviv University said that because of the *intifada* "the status quo appears to be working to the advantage of the Palestinians' unilateral statebuilding effort." *The West Bank and Gaza: Israel's Options for Peace* (Tel Aviv University, 1989), p. 43. For a study of the influence of the *intifada* on Israeli opinion, see Mark Tessler, "The Intifada and Political Discourse in Israel," *Journal of Palestine Studies* 19.2 (Winter 1990): 43–61. For general works on the *intifada*, also see Zachary Lockman and Joel Beinin, eds., *The Palestinian Uprising Against Israeli Occupation* (Boston: MERIP, 1989); Jamal R. Nassar and Roger Heacock, eds., *Intifada: Palestine at the Crossroads* (New York: Praeger, 1990); and Geoffrey Aronson, *Israel, Palestinians and the Intifada: Creating Facts on the West Bank* (London: Kegan Paul International, 1990).

19. Text of King Hussein's speech announcing the decision to sever links to the West Bank in *Journal of Palestine Studies* 18.1 (Autumn 1988): 279–83.

20. Text of the Palestinian Declaration of Independence in *Journal of Palestine Studies* 18.2 (Winter 1989): 213–16—Document B2.

21. Jaffe Center for Strategic Studies, *The West Bank and Gaza: Israel's Options for Peace* (Tel Aviv: Tel Aviv University, 1989), p. 155.

22. For a survey of the Washington peace talks, see Camille Mansour, *The Palestinian-Israeli Peace Negotiations: An Overview and Assessment, October 1991–January 1993* (Washington, DC: Institute for Palestine Studies, 1993).

23. Ann Mosely Lesch, *Transition to Palestinian Self-Government: Practical Steps Toward Israeli-Palestinian Peace* (Bloomington: Indiana University Press, 1992), p. 18.

24. Mark A. Heller and Sari Nusseibeh, *No Trumpets No Drums: A Two-State Settlement of the Israeli-Palestinian Conflict* (New York: Hill & Wang, 1991), p. 56.

25. Ibid., pp. 62–63.

26. Mark A. Heller, *A Palestinian State: The Implications for Israel* (Cambridge, MA: Harvard University Press, 1983).

27. Walid Khalidi, "Thinking the Unthinkable: A Sovereign Palestinian State," *Foreign Affairs* 56.4 (July 1978): 701.

28. Adnan Abu Odeh, "Two Capitals in an Undivided Jerusalem," *Foreign Affairs* 71.2 (Spring 1992): 183–88.

29. For an article on Palestinian views on the right of return, see Rashid Khalidi, *Journal of Palestine Studies* 19.2 (Winter 1990).

30. Text of the paper in the *Journal for Palestine Studies* 18.1 (Autumn 1988): 272–75.

31. Quoted in *Newsweek*, September 13, 1993, p. 26.

# 10

# Whither the Kurds?

GEORGE S. HARRIS

Ethnic groups have come into their own in many parts of the world in the waning years of the twentieth century. But will the Kurds? The most that they have managed thus far has been for the fragment in northern Iraq to reach de facto autonomy. The permanence of even that achievement remains in doubt, as is the future of the substantial Kurdish populations of Turkey and Iran, which have not gone nearly as far. Yet it appears certain that Kurds will continue to seek greater political, social, and cultural rights.

Kurdish history is replete with promising beginnings. It might have been expected that a people numbering some 20 million and speaking a tongue different from that of their neighbors would long since have achieved nationhood. An understanding of why Kurds have not won more autonomy or independence may help explain whether such factors will continue to frustrate Kurdish aspirations.

## Obstacles to Unity

Geography is central to this story. The Kurdish heartland is in the main a landlocked mountainous refuge area. But while the mountains have offered protection from external enemies, at the same time, they cut the Kurdish area into disconnected parts. In the past, transportation routes generally skirted this arc north of Mesopotamia from near the Mediterranean to the headwaters of the Tigris and Euphrates rivers to the edge of the Iranian plateau. Even today the paucity of good, all-weather roads within the region discourages homogeneous political evolution. And culturally, this fragmentation has been reflected in the evolution of Kurdish into several mutually unintelligible dialects, even written in different scripts. Although language is the surest touchstone of Kurdishness, these dialectical differences militate against unity. Conditions in much of the Kurdish region favor animal husbandry. That promotes the persistence of social organization characterized by transhumant life in tribes. This type of kinship organization has many strengths, but it discourages the pursuit of overarching ethnic objectives, because tribes commonly feud with each other over grazing rights and marriage partners.

Tribal organization is clearly being eroded under pressure of modern existence. Particularly in Turkey, the rapid hemorrhaging of Kurds out of their core area to the cities of western Anatolia adds to the weakening of tribal identity. Some of these deracinated elements have embraced radical social doctrines, which reject the tribal system as feudal. Accordingly, in addition to attacking Turkish authority, a major target of Abdullah Ocalan's Workers party of Kurdistan (PKK) in Turkey has been the tribal power structure.[1]

Religious behavior also divides the Kurds. Although the overwhelming majority are Sunnis of the Shafii rite, there are also significant numbers of Shia Kurds as well as some Yezedis and Christians. But even more politically divisive has been their involvement in competing Islamic mystical orders. Notably, the Barzani family is associated with the Nakshibandi, while Jalal Talabani comes from a family deeply involved in the Qadiri order. In fact, this religious-cum-tribal organization increases the likelihood that the aspirations of any leader would meet opposition from traditional rivals.[2]

Beyond internal fragmentation, an even more serious obstacle to national unity has been the division of the Kurdish core area between Turkey, Iraq, and Iran, with smaller communities in Syria, Armenia, and Lebanon. The borders drawn after the First World War assured the collective opposition of the states in which Kurds reside, should they try to assemble a common front to seek greater autonomy. At the same time, the need for international support encourages Kurds in one country to cooperate with neighboring governments, even if those regimes repress Kurds at home.

A further impediment has been the fact that Kurds form but a minority in all of the countries of their residence. In Turkey, where today somewhat over ten million people of Kurdish origin reside, they are outnumbered five or six to one by the Turkish majority, although that ratio is diminishing as the birthrate of the Kurdish population exceeds that of the surrounding Turks. The some six million Kurds in Iran and the four million in Iraq form about 10 percent and nearly 25 percent respectively of the population of these states.[3]

These circumstances strongly color the history of the Kurds in the twentieth century. But in addition, the particular problems they have faced in each state of residence have affected their chances of achieving greater self-rule.

### In Iraq

Iraq is where the Kurds have gone farthest toward determining their own fate. One can account for their greater success in a number of ways. But the factors which have had the greatest influence are ones for which the Kurds themselves are not directly responsible.

Key to the relative success of the Kurds in Iraq has been the fluctuations of power in the Baghdad regime and the number and strength of the distractions that have diverted it from stamping out Kurdish insurrection. When their attention could be focused single-mindedly, Baghdad regimes have normally had the military muscle to impose more or less complete control. But the eight-year war with Iran and the disastrous Gulf War against the international coalition, led by the United States in particular, drained Baghdad's power. Moreover, the draconian measures against the Kurdish population, at a time when the world community was aroused by Saddam Hussein's bellicosity, sparked a humanitarian intervention that today affords the Kurds of Iraq protection and a measure of autonomy. It is uncertain how these Kurds will fare when the international hand is removed.

Second, the Kurds in Iraq benefited from being concentrated in a single area with depth for retreat and maneuver. In that they differ from the Kurds in Iran, whose long, narrow area is open to penetration by outside forces. It contrasts with the distribution of Kurds in Turkey in both the west and the southeast of that country, leaving no one compact area embracing a majority of the Kurdish population. As a result, local insurgent leaders in northern Iraq have had greater ability to remain in their homeland.

Finally, the Kurds of northern Iraq might not have been positioned to take advantage of international support if they had not been the beneficiary of a long-standing tribally led insurrection. Even though the tribe does not promote an all-inclusive movement, the chieftain structure did offer leadership of armed fighters. And tribal rebellion was a familiar mechanism, tapping into strong and relatively unquestioning loyalties.

The fact that tribal rebellions had gone on in every decade this century in northern Iraq also was significant. Though repeatedly unsuccessful, the persistent efforts to resist Baghdad's control contributed to the fame and stature of the Barzanis. That broadened the movement, as well as offering outsiders a known address to which aid could be provided.

Traditionally restive, the Kurds of northern Iraq resisted British rule after the First World War. When the Iraqi monarchy backed by the British sent the army to suppress continuing Kurdish agitation in 1945, Mulla Mustafa Barzani, now the leader of this tribe, fled with a group of followers to Iran. On the collapse of the Kurdish Republic of Mahabad in 1946, he and his band made their way to the USSR where they were maintained by the Soviet government.[4]

Mulla Mustafa's departure assured that northern Iraq would be relatively quiet until Abdul Karim Qasim overthrew the Iraqi monarchy in 1958. At that time, the Barzani chief returned to Iraq with his followers. But Qasim followed the traditional policy of divide and rule against the Kurds. Granting legal status in 1960 to the Democratic party of Kurdistan (KDP)—of which Mulla Mustafa was titular head—

he at the same time encouraged the Zibari and Baradost tribes to pursue their traditional rivalries with the Barzanis.

In response, Mulla Mustafa led a revolt in June 1961. But at first he was not even supported actively by the small group of city-bred, detribalized Kurdish radicals who had been the guiding light of the KDP. They objected to his traditionalist approach and favored radical socialist solutions instead. Thus throughout 1962 the radicals maintained a separate identity, eventually establishing their own rival front in which Jalal Talabani was a leading figure in the rugged area around Sulaimaniya to the southeast of Barzani's territory.[5]

Unhappiness at Qasim's failure to end the Kurdish revolt may have been one factor in motivating powerful army factions to oust him in February 1963. But the new Baath party regime which ran Iraq for the next nine months was also unable to settle itself firmly enough in power to reestablish full control of the Kurdish area. Significantly, it was internal weakness of the Baath regime rather than Kurdish arms that won the day.[6]

The Arif brothers who dominated Iraq for the next five years used the traditional mix of conciliation and coercion to deal with the Kurds. Their offer of a ceasefire in February 1964 reinvigorated long-standing differences between the Barzanis and Jalal Talabani. When the latter accused Mulla Mustafa of selling out by ending the fighting without a specific promise of autonomy, Barzani expelled the Talabani group by force.[7]

This period saw the emergence of a new factor: the involvement of Iran in supporting the Kurds as a counterweight against the Baghdad regime. The flow of Iranian weapons into northern Iraq evened the contest somewhat, leading to a stalemate, in which Kurdish forces could not descend from the hills while the army was bound to the main roads where armor could deploy. Unable to prevail militarily, Arif offered a 12-point peace program in June 1966. It provided for elections, amnesty, reparations, and some form of decentralized administration. But before this could work, the Arif regime collapsed following the Arab defeat in the 1967 Six Day War with Israel.[8]

The incoming Baath regime had to consolidate its grasp on power before pursuing a military option. Hence the new rulers offered Mulla Mustafa a 15-point peace plan in March 1970, providing considerable autonomy for northern Iraq. It also granted the Kurds assured representation in the executive and legislative bodies of the central government, and pledged the rapid economic development of the Kurdish region. Moreover, this compact authorized the Kurds to keep their heavy weapons for a four-year transitional period.[9]

The 1970 agreement marked the high point in autonomy won by the Kurds. From this pinnacle, Kurdish fortunes declined precipitously, as the Baath regime overcame its internal divisions under Saddam Hussein, who was emerging as the dominant force in Iraq. At the same time, the Baghdad regime was able to end its isolation in the Arab world and to strengthen its ties with Moscow by signing a 15-year Treaty of Friendship in April 1972.[10]

Meanwhile, Mulla Mustafa could do little to bolster his forces. The shah kept the Kurds supplied only enough to take a toll on Iraqi forces, but not to the point of asserting independence. American support, extended at the shah's request, was limited to $16 million in military aid, a drop in the bucket in relation to what the Kurds would have required to hold off Iraqi forces and shoot down the advanced warplanes which the USSR had supplied to Baghdad.[11]

By 1974 when the Baath regime judged that the time was ripe for a renewed offensive, the tide of battle quickly turned against Barzani. For the first time he faced a fully determined, well-equipped military operation. And his Iranian ally was unwilling to commit regular forces to the combat. Instead, the shah accepted Hayri Boumediene's offer of mediation in March 1975 to work out a comprehensive settlement with the Baghdad government.[12]

The resulting Algiers Accord effectively ended the Barzani insurgency. Facing a hostile Turkey to the north, Mulla Mustafa, his sons, and a number of his supporters fled to Iran. He then proceeded to Washington for medical treatment, where he died in 1979. Cut off from the outside world, those Kurds left in northern Iraq surrendered *en masse*. Within days Baghdad reimposed its control.

Saddam Hussein then sought to clinch his hold for all time. He transferred thousands of Barzani tribe members to southern Iraq; he had Arabs brought into the Kirkuk oil field region on the border of the Kurdish area. In addition, a strip along the Iranian border was depopulated and security forces were beefed up. To dampen opposition, he formed a sham "Kurdistan Autonomous Region" in Dohuk, Irbil, and Sulaimaniya provinces, but gave it no decisionmaking authority.[13]

Iran's clerical revolution in 1979 and the start of the Iraq-Iran war the following year revived Kurdish activity in Iraq. Iran again offered help to the Kurds against Saddam's regime. This Iranian activism came as Baghdad was seeking to draw down its security forces in northern Iraq to use in the fight against Iran. In the effort to assure the loyalty of the Iraqi Kurds, therefore, Saddam Hussein offered the KDP concessions. And when Barzani's sons Idris and Masoud refused, he turned to Jalal Talabani and his Patriotic Union of Kurdistan party (PUK). This divide-and-rule tactic kept the PUK and the KDP apart, although Saddam Hussein eventually backed away from an accord with either.[14]

The Kurdish area in Iraq was only a sideshow in the Iran-Iraq war, but Iran did succeed in occupying some small border strips in the vicinity of Haj Omran during almost all of this war. From this base, the Iranians established continuing contact with the Barzanis and eventually with Jalal Talabani, a collaboration which the Baath regime would not forgive.

In response, Saddam Hussein launched the so-called "Operation Anfal" (the term for Qur'anically permitted spoils of war). It involved vigorous efforts to eliminate opposition by abducting and killing Kurds as well as razing their villages, especially along the Iranian and Turkish borders. After Iran occupied the border town of Halapja with help from the local Kurdish population in March 1988, Iraq used poison gas against the inhabitants.[15]

The brutality of this attack had lasting effects. It prepared the local population to panic when such weapons were again used and it reinforced the inclination of the Kurds in Iraq to seek outside protection. Thus when Saddam Hussein launched an all-out assault on the Kurds in August 1988 after the war with Iran was over, again using poison gas, large numbers of Kurdish civilians and guerrillas were stampeded into flight to Turkey.[16]

International protests against this savagery were ineffective during the period before the invasion of Kuwait in August 1990 set off the Gulf War. In the absence of international sanctions, Saddam Hussein saw no reason to stop attempting to change the demographics of northern Iraq by a second Anfal. Iraqi government documents indicate that 50,000 Kurds were killed in these operations.[17]

The Gulf War of 1990–1991 found Iraq's Kurds still reeling from the brutality of Baghdad's assault the previous year. Thus not until after the Shia of southern Iraq had taken advantage of the disruption of Iraqi security to revolt in March 1991 did Masoud Barzani and supporters of Jalal Talabani began a similar uprising in the north. Yet because this insurrection came after the Shia revolt was mostly crushed, Saddam Hussein was able to shift his troops back to the north, where they rapidly regained control.[18]

A new wave of refugees—perhaps numbering a million and a half—poured out of northern Iraq into adjoining Turkey and Iran. The plight of the Kurds aroused a powerful surge of international sympathy as the media publicized the tragic suffering of women and children displaced in the mountains. This time the international situation was favorable for action. On April 5, 1991, the UN Security Council issued resolution 688 enjoining Saddam Hussein from mistreating his minorities, including specifically the Kurds. To enforce compliance, the international coalition set up a security zone around the towns of Zakho, Dohuk, and Amadiya and their hinterlands in which Iraqi central governmental authority was prohibited. A "no-fly" zone also was imposed from the 36th parallel to the Turkish border, where Iraqi aircraft were forbidden. And a relief operation, Provide Comfort, based in Turkey was begun to alleviate some of the suffering of the Kurdish population.[19]

Taking advantage of this international pressure, by July 1991, Kurdish irregulars gained control of Sulaimaniya in the south. And with the onset of winter 1991 Saddam Hussein's forces pulled back to more defensible positions, leaving almost all the Kurdish-inhabited area outside of Baghdad's control. These lines with minor modifications have marked the extent of Saddam's authority ever since.

After the Kurdish leaders held unsuccessful negotiations with the Iraqi regime in the spring of 1991, Baghdad imposed an economic blockade on the north. That galvanized the KDP and PUK to create a popularly elected governing authority for the area under their control. Accordingly, in May 1992 an election was held in northern Iraq under universal suffrage in the presence of international observers for a parliament to provide an additional measure of self-rule for the Kurdish region of Iraq.[20]

While many observers had expected the Barzanis to win a majority in this election, the delegates ended up evenly divided between the KDP and Talabani's PUK. A government was formed from these two parties under a "prime minister," drawn from the PUK. And to avoid a possibly damaging leadership contest, the two leaders then agreed to share power rather than face a run-off election for president. Even that expedient could not prevent periodic friction from erupting between the two groups.

Formation of this government complicated the regional relations of Iraq's Kurds. Statements in October 1992 advocating a federated Kurdish state within a democratic pluralistic Iraq seemed close to a de facto declaration of independence to Turkish officials. In November, the foreign ministers of Turkey, Iran, and Syria gathered in the first of a series of meetings to condemn this announcement and reiterate their unwavering opposition to Iraq's partition. Nonetheless, Turkey continued regularly to extend permission for the Provide Comfort operation from its territory.[21]

A subsidiary problem for the Kurdish front in Iraq involved relations with the PKK, the organization of Kurds in Turkey which had since the mid-1980s been conducting insurrection. The PKK had periodically used bases in northern Iraq to attack Turkish security forces and village guards in the eastern provinces. That boosted Turkish fears that autonomy for Iraq's Kurds would stimulate separatist tendencies in Turkey. To dampen such concern, the Iraqi Kurdish front opened talks with the Ankara government in 1991, while curtailing PKK freedom of action. In response, the PKK cut relief supplies for a time to northern Iraq.[22]

By the late fall of 1992 relations between the PKK and the Kurdish front in Iraq had deteriorated to the point that the KDP and PUK began military operations against the PKK bases on the Iraqi side of the border with Turkey. Shortly thereafter, the Turkish armed forces moved across the border to hit the PKK bases from the north. That two-pronged attack impelled the PKK forces to surrender to their Kurdish confreres and agree to go to camps near Sulaimaniya, well away from the border with Turkey.[23]

The need not to appear as a separatist movement also pushed the Kurds of Iraq to intensify cooperation in the Iraqi National Congress, an umbrella organization loosely representing Iraqi Arab and Kurdish opposition to Saddam Hussein. To emphasize the pan-Iraqi nature of their activity, the Kurds hosted a meeting of the Iraqi National Congress in September 1992 in northeastern Iraq to concert efforts to change the regime in Baghdad.[24]

This activity helped spur Saddam Hussein to test the resolve of the UN coalition forces by challenging the exclusion zones in January 1993. When these tactics failed, the Iraqis shifted to efforts to scare UN and nongovernmental personnel servicing northern Iraq. Moreover, by tightening the existing economic blockade, the Iraqis caused conditions to deteriorate in the Kurdish enclave in the north. Economic privation was further deepened by Baghdad's sudden demonetization of the widely circulated Iraqi 25-dinar note in May 1993, without allowing those in the north to redeem this currency. And Baghdad permanently cut off electric power to part of the north in the summer of 1993.[25]

Such moves increased Kurdish dependence on outside protectors. At the same time, Iraqi pressure dramatized the dangers to the Kurdish enclave if international support should be withdrawn, and carried the message that Saddam Hussein has by no means given up his intention to bring the Kurds in the north back under direct Iraqi control whenever circumstances permit.

**In Turkey**

Kurds in Turkey faced special problems which assured that, despite their numbers or relative proportion of the population, no movement for autonomy or independence would be easy.

It is well to begin by observing that the Kurds have been primarily on their own in their quest. Suspicion voiced by Turkish authorities of massive Soviet encouragement for Kurdish dissidence in eastern Turkey in the 1970s apparently relied on associating the PKK's Marxist approach with "communist" foreign powers. While there may have been some Soviet involvement, PKK founder Abdullah Ocalan has denied receiving support from Moscow and stressed the hostility of the Turkish Communist party to his movement.[26]

The only significant international support for Kurds in Turkey has come from Syria. The Damascus government's long-term willingness to allow bases for the PKK in territory under Syrian control has been a thorn in Turkey's side; yet as far as one can tell, Ocalan has not been a Syrian puppet, but has maintained a fair degree of independence. The Damascus government has not engaged in training or military supply arrangements of the sort that the Iraqi Kurds received from various Iranian regimes. Unable to procure heavy weapons, Turkey's Kurds have operated as guerrilla bands.

Although the paucity of foreign support played a part, conditions in Turkey were also a major determinant of the inability of Kurds to gain autonomy. In the first place, the Ankara authorities were all along a more powerful foe for Turkey's Kurds than Baghdad was for its Kurdish population. The Turkish government had the resources to control the large expanses of often difficult terrain where Turkey's Kurds lived. Furthermore, the Ankara regime removed tribal leaders for extended periods of internal exile. Well-known and visible rebels were unable to remain on the ground inside Turkey. As a result, those who today are fighting the government lack a fixed address to receive support from abroad and must stay on the move.

Unlike the Iraqi regime, the Ankara authorities did not face direct international intervention to restrict their freedom of action. Amnesty International and other human rights organizations have condemned Turkey's handling of its Kurdish population. But their words have had limited impact. And for decades before such organizations came on the scene, the Turkish government had been free to execute or jail those it suspected of dissidence. As a result, each insurrection of the 1920s and 1930s was led by a different personality. No military leader comparable to Mulla Mustafa Barzani in Iraq emerged inside of Turkey.

After the failure of traditionally based rebellion in the first two decades of the Republic, Kurdish dissidence has been focused, not on the tribe with its strengths as well as weaknesses, but around the loose Marxist ideology of the PKK. Because the PKK was dedicated directly against tribalism, more of its victims were Kurds than Turks. Although that has not stopped it from enjoying prestige and support among the Kurds in Turkey, this opposition to the traditional power structure has complicated the ability of the PKK to gain a political voice in Turkey's democratic system. Up to now it has operated more as a terrorist organization than as a political party.[27]

A major problem for the Kurds in Turkey was the Kemalist policy of assimilation, which worked to deny a separate identity to Kurds. Intermarriage between persons of Kurdish and Turkish background has been common; even some of Turkey's top leaders had Kurdish roots (the late President Turgut Ozal, for example). Moreover, the Turkish political system in practice offered a share in power even to relatively unassimilated Kurds as long as they paid lip service to the principle of a unitary, secular state. Thus over a quarter of the deputies in Parliament and most elected officials in the southeast are now of Kurdish extraction.

Yet the Turkish republic gave no quarter to Kurdish efforts to gain autonomy or independence. Mustafa Kemal Ataturk in 1919 quietly ordered his followers "to proceed in such a manner as to destroy the possibility of a separatist movement by the Kurds." But at the same time, he wooed the powerful Kurdish tribal leaders in order to assure maximum support for the Turkish struggle for independence.[28]

His second-in-command, Ismet Inonu (often thought to have been of Kurdish ancestry because he was born in Malatya), spoke of the Ankara regime as the "government of the Kurds just as much as the government of the Turks" at the 1923 Lausanne Peace Conference that gained international recognition for modern Turkey. This assertion, however, was intended to buttress claims to territory around Mosul inhabited primarily by Kurds and carried no implication that Ankara would countenance autonomy for the Kurds.[29]

Once the Republic was established, the Kemalist regime embarked on secularizing, nationalist reforms that appeared to threaten the interests of major Kurdish leaders. Thus it was not surprising that the Nakshibandi tribal chief, Sheikh Said, revolted in 1925. While Said's insurrection became increasingly tinged with Kurdish nationalism at the end, his movement did not attract the majority of the Kurds in Turkey. Even though it was the most widespread revolt that Ataturk faced, it was put down in short order.[30]

Ataturk moved equally to quash revolts of Kurdish tribal elements near Mt. Ararat in 1930 and in Tunceli (previously known as Dersim) in 1937. These insurrections were limited to only part of the Kurdish population, particularly as the protagonists in Tunceli were the principal Shiite group among the predominantly Sunni Kurds of Turkey. The failure of this latter effort ended the tribal rebellion phase of the Kurdish question in Turkey.

To assure that further Kurdish revolts would not occur, the Ankara authorities imposed stricter administrative controls over eastern Turkey than in the rest of the country. A consistent effort was made to disarm the tribes, and gendarmes were stationed throughout this area. Some Kurdish tribes and especially their leaders were removed from the troubled region. Railway lines were built to facilitate government troop movements on an east-west axis separating the rugged provinces bordering on Iraq from the somewhat more open steppe of the northern tier of the Kurdish region. And the use of Kurdish was prohibited in education or publications.

After multiparty politics began in 1946, the Kurdish issue took a new form. Although barred from separatist agitation, tribal leaders were allowed to enjoy a measure of political power and patronage by running for the national assembly where they could defend their local interests. In fact, the major parties vied for the vote of their constituencies by putting them on their candidate lists for Parliament.[31]

While the system could tolerate exploitation of the Kurdish power structure by the major parties, the efforts by the Turkish Labor party to pander to Kurdish nationalist sentiment was seen as a provocation. For the temerity publicly to return to Inonu's Lausanne formulation that Turkey was a country of Turks and Kurds in its program adopted in November 1970, the Turkish Labor party was summarily closed in mid-1971; its leaders, both Kurds and non-Kurds, were given lengthy jail terms.[32]

This brief attempt at legal activity on behalf of Kurdish interests was succeeded by the terrorist, clandestine operations of the PKK, organized by the Kurdish intellectual, Abdullah Ocalan, in 1977 in Ankara. His feelings of grievance at difficult family experiences in childhood, reinforced by slights as a provincial at the university, radicalized him. Soon recognizing the power of ethnicity, he began building a left-wing organization of Kurds, first with intellectuals, but then with activists of a similar disadvantaged background. Fearing arrest, he left Ankara for southeastern Turkey and by the end of 1979 he fled to Syria. He has not thus far been able to return.[33]

Starting in 1984, Ocalan sent followers back to Turkey to attack the tribal power structure and Kurds cooperating with the Turkish state. Some of these raids were staged from PKK camps on Turkey's border with Syria and Iraq. Over time, this violent defiance of Ankara gained a measure of acceptance among Kurds in Turkey. In part, that may reflect reaction against central government heavy-handedness. Yet his direction of the PKK is autocratic; he has regularly expelled supporters whom he believed had crossed him.[34]

PKK agitation helped provoke the Ankara regime to tighten cultural restrictions, leading to a worsening human rights environment for Kurds in Turkey. Laws were passed further restricting the use of Kurdish in any of its varieties. And in April

1990, a decree gave the regional governor of southeast Turkey extraordinary authority to censor the press, exile those who "act against the state," control unions, and evacuate villages "for security reasons."[35]

These measures aroused deep dissatisfaction among the Kurds in Turkey as well as generating a wave of protest in the burgeoning Kurdish community in Europe. A group of Kurdish deputies from the Social Democratic Populist party publicly took part in a Kurdish émigré gathering in Europe in 1989. When they were expelled from that party for attending, they formed the People's Labor party (HEP), which was tacitly accepted as a purely Kurdish organization. Recognizing that this new body did not meet the criteria to be able to enter national elections in October 1991, HEP's leading members rejoined the Social Democratic Populist party. Once they gained seats in this way, they returned to their breakaway party when the new government launched large-scale military operations against dissidents in eastern Turkey.[36]

Yet the regime's approach toward the Kurds was becoming ambivalent. In 1991, just while violence was rising in the Kurdish areas of the southeast, steps were taken to acknowledge Kurdish identity and to ease restrictions on the use of the Kurdish language in publications. And in June 1992, the government lifted censorship regulations and ended authority to ban "potentially disruptive" elements from the region.[37]

Nonetheless, these steps did not ease the conflict. Although in conjunction with the March 1993 Nowruz holidays Ocalan declared a unilateral ceasefire, it gave only a brief respite. After his followers ambushed Turkish troops at the end of May 1993, Ocalan formally withdrew the "ceasefire"; later that month a rash of Kurdish sit-ins in Turkish installations all across Europe signalled an impressively organized challenge there as well. But this latter activity and sporadic kidnappings of European travelers in Turkey generated ill-feeling against the PKK in Europe rather than a surge of sympathy. Toward the end of 1993, amid renewed PKK-inspired incidents in Europe, France and Germany took action to ban the PKK.[38]

Concomitantly, the Turkish government redoubled its efforts to combat the PKK in eastern Turkey with military force. That was a tacit admission that the system of village guards organized by the government in southeast Turkey in the 1980s to protect villages from PKK raids had not succeeded. Formed from traditional Kurdish opponents of the PKK militants, this force had a vested interest in continuing the battle even if the Ankara government wished to move away from armed conflict.[39]

Resumption of armed conflict did not end efforts at legal activity by Turkish Kurds. The People's Labor party, which appeared likely to pass the elective hurdles erected to keep small parties out of Parliament, was banned by the Turkish Constitutional Court in mid-July 1993 for espousing separatist causes. The successor Democracy party, to which eighteen Kurdish deputies defected from HEP before it was closed, also ran afoul of the law, being succeeded in turn by the People's

Democracy party with a dwindling parliamentary representation. Thus legal activity continued to be compromised, even though newly installed prime minister Tansu Ciller in July 1993 made clear that she favored lifting prohibitions against state radio and television broadcasts in Kurdish. The Turkish Parliament, however, has been unwilling to move in that direction.[40]

## In Iran

Facing an Iranian revolutionary regime that has an extremely restrictive view of human rights and believes that its minorities are an integral part of the Iranian nation, the Kurds of Iran are in many respects further behind their fellows in Turkey and Iraq in terms of political power.

In the first place, geopolitical factors were not favorable to the Kurds of Iran. Their area had few attractive natural resources, seemed of little strategic value to outsiders, and lacked a large or educated population base. Furthermore, the largest Kurdish concentration around Kermanshah was Persianized and less revolutionary than other Kurds in Iran. As a result, only a minority of Iran's Kurds (or less than 5 percent of the total population of the country) actively sympathized with—let alone participated in—efforts to bring Tehran to grant the Kurds autonomy. In Iranian national terms, they could not pose the same kind of challenge that the Kurds in Iraq and Turkey presented.[41]

In addition, the lack of a paramount leader who could operate for long inside of Iran meant that they were, with brief exceptions, unable to gain significant foreign support. Only during the short period when the Soviet Union dominated northern Iran and to a lesser degree when the Iraqis were at war with Iran did foreign connections play a major role. Even then foreign help was neither generous nor reliable.

A serious drawback to pursuing a military strategy for the Kurds of Iran was their lack of experienced military commanders. During the first half of the twentieth century that deficiency was camouflaged by the general weakness of the central government's military apparatus and the wariness of the shahs to confront any of the many tribal groups outside the Kurds as well. But by the 1960s the government felt confident of besting any or all its tribal opponents.

A related problem lay in the exodus of the most talented elements from the Kurdish tribal areas in Iran. Absence of adequate educational facilities and the lack of white collar jobs in the Kurdish area promoted this outflow. That both estranged these Kurds from those they left behind and meant that their skills were not generally available for Kurdish causes at home.

Other more mundane considerations also militated against cohesion. Many observers have pointed to the strong mutual antipathy of Kurds from the north toward those of the south. Also in Iranian culture, there was no tradition of inclusive political parties that would bring together tribal and detribalized elements. And it was the more radical elements within the Kurdish community in Iran that sought to organize; the bodies they formed espoused social doctrines that seemed to violate tribal mores. That served to estrange party and tribe and thus to keep the Kurdish community of Iran divided in purpose.[42]

Taking advantage of the breakdown of central authority in Iran after the First World War, Kurdish tribes led by Ismail Aga Simko managed to set themselves up briefly as independent lords of the Mahabad area near Lake Urumiyah. But after the central government reasserted control over the rest of Persian Azerbaijan in 1922, Simko's move quickly collapsed. By 1930, Reza Shah even was able partially to disarm the tribes.[43]

In the interwar period, Tehran attempted no consistent drive as the Turks did to break up Kurdish tribal organization. Although Reza Shah's regime did not permit Kurdish to be used as the language of education or government, it did allow Kurdish books to be printed and Kurdish programs to be broadcast on the radio. Thus, the Iranian experience formed a middle way between the absolute denial of Kurdishness in Turkey until recent times and the periodic grants of greater autonomy to Kurds in Iraq.

With the occupation of Iran by the Soviet Union during the Second World War, the situation of the Kurds changed significantly. Under Moscow's protection, detribalized Kurds in Mahabad in 1942 took the initiative to organize the Komala, a local organization dedicated to promoting Kurdish separatism. The following year, Qazi Mohammad, the paramount religious figure of the region, began to agitate for formal recognition of Kurdish autonomy. Early in 1946, with Soviet help, Qazi Mohammad proclaimed the Kurdistan Autonomous Republic in Mahabad.[44]

A hastily constructed state, based on an uneasy coalition with the local tribal chiefs and Barzani's Iraqi refugees, this Republic also suffered from a built-in territorial conflict with the Azerbaijan Democratic Republic. The crucial blow to Mahabad, however, was the withdrawal of Soviet forces in 1946. In the absence of a strong foreign protector, traditional interests reasserted their primacy. Kurdish tribal leaders were disturbed by the communist orientation of some of the Komala agitators and a coalition of tribal chiefs offered their submission to Tehran.[45]

With the collapse of the Mahaban republic and the execution of Qazi Moham-mad and his closest collaborators, the Komala party went underground. Mulla Mustafa and five hundred followers fled to the Soviet Union. And hoping to end Kurdish dissidence once and for all, the government stationed the well-armed Third Corps of the Iranian army in the region.

In these circumstances, the wing of the Komala party that became the Kurdish Democratic party of Iran (KDP-I) modified its aims and began to seek merely autonomy for Iran's Kurds within an Iranian democratic state. But conditions in Iran were so difficult that after Qasim took over in Iraq, the KDP-I moved to northern Iraq under Barzani's aegis. That collaboration, though, was disrupted after the shah developed close relations with Mulla Mustafa in the late 1960s. Then except for agitation from sanctuaries in Europe and northern Iraq, the KDP-I became largely dormant.[46]

Conditions of exile fed squabbles within this party. At its second Congress in 1964, under Barzani's protection, the party split. Younger and more radical central committee members tried to set up a liberated area in the Sardasht region of Iran in 1968. They were soon killed or captured. That opened the way for the European-educated Dr. Abdul Rahman Ghassemlou and a group of supporters to take over party leadership in June 1971. But unable to work from Iraq, the party remained in virtual hibernation.[47]

This was a time when the ground for the KDP-I in Iran was progressively deteriorating. The Tehran regime made significant gains in the Kurdish region as elsewhere by expanding the road system and spreading social services into the rural areas. Land reform won peasants to the central government and weakened tribal organization. In this situation, the stringent security measures effectively deprived the Iranian Kurds of potential for causing Tehran serious difficulties as long as the Pahlavis were in power.

The breakdown of authority in the last days of the shah, however, led to renewed agitation in the Kurdish areas. Demands for the formation of an autonomous Kurdish province out of the three existing Kurdish provinces and a freely elected assembly began to be heard. There were also signs that the predominantly Sunni Kurdish population of the north objected to the heavy emphasis on Shiism as the basic rule of law in Tehran.[48]

In this atmosphere, early in 1979 the KDP-I revived. But Abdul Rahman Ghassemlou, whose leadership of this organization was now unchallenged, was unable to project a clear program of action. Moreover, the party lacked military power. Thus the KDP-I proposal of March 28, 1979, for autonomy of the Kurdish region under a federative or autonomous regime was stillborn. And by the spring of 1979, Tehran was able to field newly recruited revolutionary guards to retake the urban areas seized by the Kurds. The Kurdish forces retreated to the hills.[49]

The rebellion sputtered on, with neither side able to prevail, despite the linkup of the KDP-I with a number of small leftist organizations which had passed into bitter opposition to the clerical regime. In an effort to break this stalemate, Ghassemlou declared a unilateral cease-fire in November 1979 and entered into negotiations with the Tehran authorities. But he rejected as too limited the offer of some form of decentralized administration. And KDP-I supporters boycotted the election of the president in the spring of 1980; at the same time, they began to seek contacts across the border with Iraq.[50]

The outbreak of the war with Iraq in September 1980 gave the Kurds of Iran new opportunities. Baghdad offered assistance to the Kurds of Iran as a way to strike a blow at the Tehran regime. But this aid appears to have been pro forma as Saddam Hussein seemed wary of the KDP-I. Nonetheless, until 1983, Ghassemlou and his party were able to hold much of the northwest corner of Iran. They also fought off the small, more radical Komala branch which had resurfaced in 1979 to organize peasants against their landowners around Marivan to the south of the main KDP-I region.[51]

After Iran began to score successes in its war against Iraq in 1983, Ghassemlou fled to Iraq. In 1985 his party split from the leftist Iranian umbrella exile organization, the National Council of Resistance, led by the People's Mojahedin, and set up camps on Iraqi soil quite separate from those of the Mojahedin. Ghassemlou remained in exile, but was assassinated in Vienna by what clearly seems to have been Tehran's agents in July 1989 during further negotiations with representatives of the Iranian regime.[52]

The end of the Iran-Iraq war allowed the Tehran government to regain control of all its territory. But while the KDP-I responded to this setback by insisting that it sought only autonomy for Kurds within the Iranian state, it made clear that it aimed "to topple the clerical regime" as well as to "establish democracy and national rights." Those goals were clearly not acceptable to the Rafsanjani regime. Not surprisingly, therefore, negotiations with Ghassemlou's successor, Sadegh Sharafkandi, also ended in the latter's assassination by agents evidently working for the Iranian state in September 1992.[53]

With its own Kurds thus forcefully repressed, the Tehran regime was able to deal freely with Kurds in neighboring states. The long-term relationship with the Barzanis and Talabanis of Iraq continued its on-again, off-again character, but now with a new wrinkle. Starting in November 1992, Talabani charged the Iranian government with supporting a rebel Kurdish group bent on disrupting the power balance in northern Iraq and sending agents to conduct sabotage. Masoud Barzani, meanwhile, repaired his relations with Tehran, which he visited in October 1994.[54]

At the same time, the question of sanctuary for PKK militants fleeing Turkish and KDP forces operating in northern Iraq began to rile Turkish-Iranian relations. The Turkish press carried stories that these PKK elements were allowed to use Iranian facilities for safehaven to prepare for eventual return to guerrilla warfare in Turkey. Although the Iranians and Turks seem to have reached an understanding on this matter by 1994, it remained on their agenda in the mid-1990s.[55]

## Prospects For Kurdish Separatism

The taste of autonomy that the Kurds in Iraq have had in recent years has encouraged the whole Kurdish people to want permanence in controlling their own affairs. Such permanence can come only with a broadening of democratic procedure in the region that they inhabit. Force of arms cannot be the long-range solution. Neither the Kurds themselves nor outside powers seem likely to be able to compel the collection of central governments with which they must contend to grant self-rule. In the first instance their future is bound up with the future of authoritarian regimes in Iraq and Iran. It is that which provides the essential uncertainty that Kurds face.

Iraq and Iran differ significantly in how they treat Kurds. The Iraqi leaders have always considered frontal assault an option. Yet that is a strategy which is most likely to muster international intervention to keep a protected zone for the Kurds alive. The Iranians, on the other hand, while occasionally raiding across the Iraqi border, depend more centrally on selective assassination to cow Kurdish opposition. Such individual, as opposed to collective, violence is more likely to avoid international intervention of the sort that has protected Kurds in Iraq from Baghdad. And it is likely to keep the Kurds of Iran off balance and in line, though not satisfied.

Yet over the longer run, authoritarianism is probably doomed in both countries. Pressures for increasing democratization are clearly rising in the region. As isolation breaks down and world economic interests entangle even the most recalcitrant state, it is hard to imagine that Iran and Iraq will be removed permanently from international norms. That does not guarantee a smooth course away from the use of force by the regimes in Tehran and Baghdad against their Kurdish populations. But it does suggest that in time Kurds will be able to garner greater political and cultural rights, provided that they stop the internecine fighting that has periodically broken out among the political factions in Iraq.

In Turkey, on the other hand, a democratic structure is in place affording the Kurds the opportunity to share in the direction of the overall state. In fact, if Abdullah Ocalan is to be believed, separation from Turkey is not a feasible option. While Kurds undoubtedly want more freedom of political and cultural expression, there is a solid base on which to build. Legal activity should offer the most promising way ahead.

Unfortunately, however, armed action can only slow the process. It fosters the use of force in return, and dims the prospect that increasing awareness of the different ethnic character of Turkey's Kurds will lead to positive developments. Some Turkish politicians recognize that a measure of political accommodation with their Kurdish population is desirable, not only for domestic considerations but also out of concern to assuage European fears that help keep Turkey out of the European Union. This approach has a long way to go to win the day in Ankara, but may gain momentum as a purely military response to Kurdish dissidence is bound to fail.

In any event, nothing is likely to dampen the underlying demand for greater ethnic recognition and more self-rule. A step forward could be to have provincial governors elected rather than appointed by the central government, an idea once mooted by President Ozal. Such decentralization would represent a major departure from traditional practice and thus may be unlikely—particularly as long as PKK violence persists—though it would probably be a popular move in Turkish majority areas as well.

Fairer distribution of economic resources is a refrain that will be voiced in all parts of the region inhabited by Kurds. More investment, better education, and more good jobs are on the top of the list of demands for the future, as is scrupulous application of world judicial norms. But mere improvement in living conditions and in the economic situation is not likely to still desires for greater political autonomy; it will take considerable political advance to satisfy the general Kurdish desire to go further. And this insistence will undoubtedly be the theme of the 1990s and beyond.

## Notes

1. Mehmet Ali Birand, *APO ve PKK* (Istanbul: Milliyet Yayinlari, 1992), pp. 92–93.

2. Mehrdad R. Izady, *The Kurds: A Concise Handbook* (Washington: Crane Russak, 1992), pp. 131–62.

3. Ibid., pp. 116–20.

4. William Eagleton, *The Kurdish Republic of 1946* (London: Oxford University Press, 1963), pp. 33–40.

5. Edgar O'Ballance, *The Kurdish Revolt: 1961–1970* (Hamden, CT: Archon Books, 1973), p. 87; Edmond Ghareeb, *The Kurdish Question in Iraq* (Syracuse, NY: Syracuse University Press, 1981), pp. 40–41.

6. Sa'ad Jawad, *Iraq and the Kurdish Question* (London: Ithaca Press, 1981) pp. 146–48.

7. Ismet Cheriff Vanly, *Le Kurdistan Irakien Entite Nationale* (Neuchatel: Editions de la Baconniere, 1970), pp. 222–24.

8. Majid Khadduri, *Republican Iraq: A Study in 'Iraqi Politics' since the Revolution of 1958* (London: Oxford University Press, 1969), pp. 274–76.

9. *Keesing's Contemporary Archive, 1970* (Bristol, UK: Keesing's Publications Limited, 1970), p. 23916.

10. Ibid., 1972, p. 25201.

11. "The CIA Report the President Doesn't Want You to Read," *The Village Voice*, February 16, 1976, pp. 70, 85–87; George S. Harris, "Ethnic Conflict and the Kurds," *The Annals of the American Academy of Political and Social Science*, September 1977, pp. 121–24.

12. Geoffrey Godsell, "Shah Tells Why He Made Peace with Iraq," *The Christian Science Monitor*, May 7 1975, p. 3.

13. Izady, op. cit. note 2, p. 69.

14. Ibid.

15. "U.S. Cites Evidence of Attacks," *The New York Times*, April 2, 1988, p. A6; "Crimes against Humanity and the Transition from Dictatorship to Democracy," Report issued by The Executive Council of the Iraqi National Congress, May 25, 1993, Salahuldin, Iraq-London, pp. 19-20.

16. Elaine Sciolino, "Iraqis Reported to Mount Drive Against Kurds," *The New York Times*, September 1, 1989, p. A1.

17. Judith Miller, "Iraq Accused: A Case of Genocide," *The New York Times Magazine*, January 3, 1992, pp. A12–17; *Genocide in Iraq: The Anfal Campaign Against the Kurds*, A Middle East Watch Report (New York: Human Rights Watch, 1993), pp. 17–18.

18. Elaine Sciolino, "Kurds Alone Viewed as Unlikely to Oust Hussein," *The New York Times*, March 20, 1991, p. A12.

19. John Bulloch and Harvey Morris, *No Friends but the Mountains: The Tragic History of the Kurds* (New York: Oxford University Press, 1992), pp. 26–31.

20. Michael M. Gunter, *The Kurds of Iraq: Tragedy and Hope* (New York: St. Martin's Press, 1992), pp. 59-75; "Kurds Convene Parliament," *The New York Times*, June 5, 1992, p. A9.

21. "Iraqi Opposition Picks Leaders," *The Washington Post*, November 1, 1992, p. A35.

22. *Keesing's Record of World Events, 1992* (Harlow, UK: Longman, 1992), p. 39068; Jonathan C. Randal, "Turks Meet With Iraqi Opposition," *The Washington Post*, March 12, 1991, pp. A1, A17.

23. John Murray Brown, "Rival Kurds Embroiled in Battle," *The Washington Post*, October 18, 1992, pp. A29, A34.

24. Caryle Murphy, "Opposition Sets Meeting Inside Iraq," *The Washington Post*, September 20, 1992, p. A29; ibid., May 1, 1993, p. A4.

25. James Dorsey, "Turkey Likely to Let Its Lira Circulate in Iraq's Kurdistan Area," *The Wall Street Journal*, May 25, 1993, p. A10.

26. Turkey, General Secretariat of the National Security Council, *12 September in Turkey: Before and After* (Ankara: Ongun Kardesler, 1982), pp. 176, 247–50; Majeed R. Jafar, *Under-Underdevelopment: A Regional Case Study of the Kurdish Area in Turkey* (Helsinki: Sociaalipolittinen Yhdistyksen tut Kinukia, 1976), p. 144; George S. Harris, *Turkey: Coping With Crisis* (Boulder, CO: Westview Press, 1985), p. 145; Birand, op. cit. note 1, pp. 179–86.

27. Michael M. Gunter, *The Kurds in Turkey: A Political Dilemma* (Boulder, CO: Westview Press, 1991), passim.

28. Mustafa Kemal [Ataturk], *A Speech Delivered by Ghazi Mustapha Kemal* (Leipzig: K. F. Koehler, 1929), p. 109.

29. *Lausanne. Conference on Near Eastern Affairs, 1923* (London: His Majesty's Stationery Office, 1923), pp. 345, 375, 396; [Ismet Inonu], *Ismet Pasa'nin Siyasi ve Ictimai Nutuklari: 1920–1933* (Ankara: Basvekalet Matbaasi, 1933), p. 324.

30. Ugur Mumcu, *Kurt-Islam Ayaklanmasi, 1919-1925* (Istanbul: Tekin Yayinevi, 1991), p. 161; Robert Olson, *The Emergence of Kurdish Nationalism and the Sheikh Said Rebellion 1889–1925* (Austin, TX: University of Texas Press, 1989), pp. 153–56.

31. Harris, loc. cit., p. 116; *Ulus*, December 6, 1960.

32. *Emek*, December 1970, pp. 7-8.

33. Birand, op. cit. note 1, pp. 79-99; Ismet G. Imset, *The PKK: A Report on Separatist Violence in Turkey* (1973–1992) (Ankara: Turkish Daily News Publications, 1992), pp. 19–32.

34. Birand, op. cit. note 1, pp. 134–64; Imset, op. cit. note 33, pp. 83–84.

35. Helsinki Watch, *Destroying Ethnic Identity: The Kurds of Turkey: An Update* (New York: Human Rights Watch, 1990), p. 13.

36. *Keesing's Record of World Events, 1992*, p. 38979; "Turks Meet with Iraqi Opposition," *The Washington Post*, March 12, 1991, p. A1.

37. *Keesing's Record of World Events, 1992*, p. 37969; Helsinki Watch, *The Kurds of Turkey: Killings, Disappearances & Torture* (New York: Human Rights Watch, 1993), p. 42.

38. *Mideast Mirror*, March 13, 1993, pp. 23-25; June 25, 1993, pp. 22–24.

39. *Turkish Probe*, May 11, 1993, pp. 8-11, as quoted in FBIS-WEU-93-097 of May 21, 1993, pp. 72–74.

40. Ibid.; *Ozgur Gundem*, April 27, 1993, p. 6; *Mideast Mirror*, July 15, 1993, pp. 21–22; *Turkish Probe*, September 30, 1994, in FBIS-WEU-94-195, October 7, 1994, pp. 56–58.

41. Izady, op. cit. note 2, pp. 69, 198.

42. Martin van Bruinessen, "The Kurds Between Iran and Iraq," *MERIP Middle East Report*, July–August 1986, p. 16.

43. Hassan Arfa, *The Kurds* (London: Oxford University Press, 1966), pp. 64–67.

44. Eagleton, op. cit. note 4, pp. 33–40.

45. Ibid., pp. 104–16.

46. Abdurahman Kasimlu (Mehmet Acik, translator), *Iran Kurdistani: IKDP 3. Kongere Belgeleri* (Ankara: Pekanin, 1980), p. 92.

47. Ibid., pp. 28–29; Chris Kutschera, *Le Mouvement national Kurde* (Paris: Flammarion, 1979), pp. 344–48.

48. Van Bruinessen, op. cit., note 42, p. 17.

49. Kasimlu, op. cit. note 46, pp. 40–42.

50. Ibid., pp. 37–39.

51. Van Bruinessen, op. cit., note 42, p. 18.

52. Association of Committed Professors of Iranian Universities, *Facts & Myths on the People's Mojahedin of Iran* (no place of publication: no publisher, June 1990), pp. 11–18.

53. "The Baluchi People Fight Against Tyranny and Exploitation," *Voice of Iranian Kordestan* (radio), March 24, 1993, as quoted in FBIS-NES-93-057 of March 26, 1993, p. 25; Stephen Kinzer, "Iran Kurdish Leader Among 4 Killed in Berlin," *The New York Times*, September 19, 1992, p. 4.

54. Caryle Murphy, "Iraqi Kurds Say Iran Is Backing a Rival Faction," *The Washington Post*, November 2, 1992, pp. A18, A20; IRNA, October 9, 1994, in FBIS-NES-94-197, October 12, 1994, p. 88.

55. "Turkey: Iran told to check the PKK," *Mideast Mirror*, July 21, 1993, pp. 17–18; Tolga Sardan, "Iran Supports Turkey's Military Operations," *Milliyet*, May 29, 1994, in FBIS-WEU-94-106, June 2, 1994, pp. 42–43.

# Part III

## Nationalism and the Crisis of the Multiethnic/Multinational State

# 11

# The Relentless Pursuit of the National State

## Reflections on Soviet and Post-Soviet Experiences

### MARK R. BEISSINGER

> The second condition of permanent political society . . . [is] the
> existence in some form or other, of the feeling of allegiance or
> loyalty. This feeling may vary in its objects . . . [but] its essence
> is always the same; viz. that there be in the constitution of the
> state *something* which is settled, something permanent, and not
> to be called in question. . . . But when the questioning of these
> fundamental principles is . . . the habitual condition of the body
> politic; and when all the violent animosities are called forth,
> which spring naturally from such a situation, the state is virtually
> in a position of civil war.
> —John Stuart Mill, *A System of Logic* (1865)

The breakup of the former Soviet Union was more than simply the end of a regime. It was the beginning of an era. When future historians determine the global significance of the chain of events that stretched from 1988 through 1991 in the former USSR, they will be as likely to focus on the death of communism as on the phenomenal growth in nationalist mobilization that accompanied communism's demise and the persisting consequences which that mobilization has had for the rest of the world.

It is the central theme of this chapter that one of the most important developments in Eurasian politics in recent years has been a massive shift, both at the elite and mass levels, towards what I have chosen to call state-seeking attitudes and behaviors. By state-seeking attitudes and behaviors, I have in mind not only the desire on the part of a group for the creation of its own independent state, although obviously that element looms large in any understanding of the breakup of the USSR. But state-seeking attitudes and behaviors also encompass other types of demands as well: for the creation of autonomous state formations within another state; for merging the territory of a group to that of another state; for upgrading the sovereignty and authority of existing territorial units with the purpose of group empowerment; or for changing the rules of the state to gain group control over and access to state resources (for instance, changing the official language or altering group representation in positions of power). The common denominator here is the desire on the part of an ethnic or territorially based group to gain more direct control over or access to a state where such control or access had been denied previously.

State-seeking in this sense may be understood as one of several coexisting, relational dimensions of behavior that fall under the rubric of nationalism. State-expansion (efforts to augment the borders and authority of the state to encompass new territories or groups) and societal engineering (efforts to alter the character of society in order to enhance the position of a particular group) are two other dimensions of behavior that are also characteristic of nationalist politics; others undoubtedly exist as well. Each of these may intersect or overlap with one another.[1] The common element that binds them is that they all deal with the assertion of claims for defining or redefining the physical or human boundaries of the polity, which is the essence of nationalist phenomena. And as they are group-based behaviors, they also have a tendency to evoke their own counter-mobilizations aimed at thwarting them. Conceiving of nationalism in this way—as containing several overlapping and intersecting dimensions of behavior based on how a group seeks to relate to the state, with each of these dimensions itself containing a variety of types of claims and having the ability to provoke its own counter-mobilization—allows us to compare the evolution of nationalist behaviors both between and within these dimensions of nationalism, as well as between them and the counter-mobilizations that they call forth. Of course, none of these forms of behavior is new, either in the world at large or in the post-Soviet world more specifically. Nevertheless, the degree to which mobilization over these issues has exploded in recent years in the former Soviet Union differentiates this period radically from that which preceded it and makes it akin to other periods of world revolutionary change.

The generalization of state-seeking attitudes and behaviors in ethnic politics marks a distinct shift from the period of Soviet power, when these issues were taken as relatively fixed. Indeed, it was the attempt to coopt, institutionalize, and arrest non-Russian state-seeking behavior in the aftermath of the collapse of the Tsarist state that brought about the emergence of the Soviet federal system in the first place. That system was relatively successful at undermining state-seeking; it did so not only through severe repression and limiting group access to and control over state institutions, but also ironically by generalizing state-seeking norms through providing territorial-administrative entities to large numbers of peoples.[2] The unravelling of this formula has caused severe problems for the formation of stable polities throughout the Eurasian region. One of the most profound legacies of Leninism in post-Soviet politics has been a general propensity to seek the resolution of issues of cultural pluralism through the multiplication of territorial autonomies. Ironically, the revolt against communism was supposed to be a revolution against the state, not a struggle for it. The demise of the USSR has often been portrayed in the West as the breakdown of the state and as part of a generalized crisis of government whose implications reach far beyond the USSR's former borders. This crisis did not end with the breakup of the USSR. In the post-Soviet world we have witnessed an extraordinarily large number of conflicts unleashed by the proliferation of state-seeking behavior and the frictions that have ensued between new states attempting to consolidate their sovereignty and groups challenging this sovereignty and demanding greater access to and control over the state.

### State-Seeking and the Generalized Crisis of the State

Figure 11.1, examining mobilization over state-seeking and state-expansionist issues at protest demonstrations in the former Soviet Union from January 1987 through September 1992 ($N = 6,461$),[3] provides us with a general picture of how dimensions of nationalist behavior evolved over time in the former Soviet Union. State-seeking and state-expansion are frequently related activities; as Rogers Brubaker has argued, they have often been two sides of a more general form of triadic politics characteristic of the region that encompasses the actions of national minorities, national homelands, and nationalizing states.[4] Frequently, groups within national homelands seek to expand the boundaries of the state in order to encompass state-seeking diasporic minorities in other states. At the same time, as figure 11.1 indicates, the development of these two dimensions of nationalist politics has been far from identical.

As Figure 11.1 shows, state-seeking was a fixed feature of Soviet politics from approximately June 1988 on, accounting for (on average) about half of the monthly protest mobilization in the country as a whole through May 1991. State-seeking constituted the most important element of the nationalist mobilization that engulfed the former Soviet Union during the years of its demise. While significant mobilization in favor of state expansion (in particular, irredentist mobilization) occurred early in the *glasnost* mobilizational wave, state-seeking soon became a more prevalent form of behavior and arguably the fundamental force behind the country's breakup.

Mobilization over state-seeking issues remained an important element of protest mobilization well beyond the demise of the USSR, lasting at significant levels until July 1992, when demonstration activity in the former Soviet Union began to drop off altogether as a form of political participation. By contrast, state-expansionist mobilization, after declining significantly from mid-1989 through 1991, underwent a revival of sorts after the collapse of the USSR, as groups within new nationalizing states pressed irredentist and expansionist claims against other states.

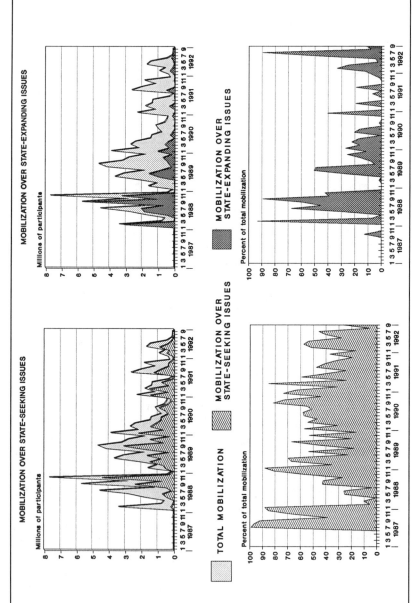

**Figure 11.1.** Mobilization over State-Seeking and State-Expanding Issues at Protest Demonstrations, January 1987 – September 1992.

The decline in mobilization over state-seeking issues at demonstrations in 1992 represented more of a shift in participatory repertoires than an end to state-seeking as such.

In the post-Soviet period, state-seeking both grew more violent and became more institutionalized within official politics than was the case in the late Soviet period. In some parts of the former USSR, democratization and the broadening of the political opportunity structure that it represented allowed elites to pursue state-seeking goals through state institutions themselves. In these cases, state-seeking migrated from the streets to legislatures and local government institutions. In other regions mass violence rather than peaceful protest became the central element in state-seeking behavior in aftermath of the breakup of the USSR.

As figure 11.2 (providing information on the ostensible causes of 1,684 mass violent events from January 1987 through June 1992) indicates, the post-Soviet period was characterized by a growing politicization of conflict over republican borders; efforts to change republican borders have constituted the most frequent cause of mass violence in the post-Soviet period, increasing at an extremely rapid pace with the breakup of the USSR. The vast majority of these conflicts involve minorities seeking to leave the current state in which they are located and to attach their territory to that of a different state. As independent states came to play a more central role in the pressing of state-seeking and state-expansionist claims, violence in some cases became an increasingly prevalent characteristic of disputes over borders. The explanation lies both in the appropriateness of various repertoires of participation to achieving state-seeking goals, as well as the ability of the state itself to act as an organizer of violence. The intrusion of the state into state-seeking activities has meant a significant increase in the level of organization of violence, as well as the destructiveness of the weapons involved. Moreover, for some groups demonstrations and the disruption they seek to cause seemed an appropriate tool of politics when the locus of decisionmaking over border issues rested in Moscow; as Moscow's ability to influence the outcome of these disputes waned, the target of protest shifted more directly onto groups that were less likely to be affected by the politics of disruption.

The development and proliferation of state-seeking behaviors in the former Soviet Union was closely connected with the emergence of a generalized crisis of the state, a crisis questioning what Mill identified as "the fundamental principles" upon which the state is built. I understand these "fundamental principles" as including not only the ideas and practices upon which state legitimacy rests, but also the territorial and human boundaries of the state. Fixed territorial boundaries are one of the central features of the modern state, and all modern states claim to represent a body of citizens constituted as a nation. In the Soviet case, a generalized crisis of the state not only provided the social space necessary for elites to engage in mobilization over state-seeking issues; it also in itself helped to generate the need and desire for a fundamental rethinking of the human and physical boundaries of the polity. Furthermore, this crisis of the state was itself considerably deepened by the proliferation of state-seeking behaviors.

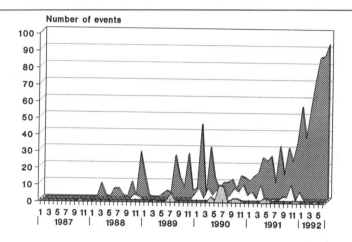

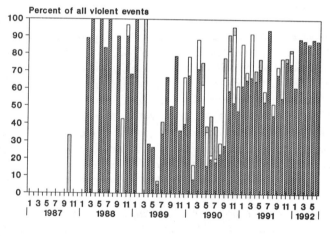

**Figure 11.2.** Violent Mass Events Involving Local, Republican-Level, and Secessionist Territorial Disputes in the Former USSR, January 1987 – June 1992.

A generalized crisis of the state continues into the post-Soviet period, and the enduring ambiguity surrounding the proper boundaries of political communities has formed the main battleground over which post-Soviet national conflicts have been fought. This ambiguity persists in large part because of the historical legacies of empire-building and state-building in Eurasia. As an overland (rather than overseas) empire, Russia could not so easily segment its nation-building and colonial policies, had a difficult time defining who was a citizen and who was a subject, and could not delineate the physical borders of Russia from its occupied territories.[5] Additionally, nationalism came late to the Eurasian land mass; even at the time of the Russian revolution, local, religious, clan, and class identities vied with nationalism for mass loyalties, and in many cases nationalist elites were unsuccessful in mobilizing populations on the basis of ethnicity.[6] The ambiguity of ethnic and territorial boundaries was further accentuated by the Leninist model of state-building and the dual reality of state-building and empire-building that it sustained. If nationalism is essentially about the definition of the physical and human boundaries of the polity, historical experience in this part of the world has led to wholesale confusion and contestation over the definition of those boundaries.[7]

The emergence of a generalized crisis of the state within the former Soviet Union was accompanied by an enormous remaking of national consciousness. No more sharply was this demonstrated than in the proliferation of state-seeking attitudes and behaviors. With the onset of *glasnost*, groups previously denied access to or control over the state quickly began to clamor for change. While a handful of groups had exhibited a mass desire for independent statehood (e.g., the Balts), for gaining autonomous territorial units (e.g., the Crimean Tatars), or for changing the status of their territorial unit (e.g., the Abkhaz) long before arrival of *glasnost*, the same cannot be said for most groups. With some exceptions, most nationalities remained largely demobilized over state-seeking issues throughout most of the Soviet period, and ethnic politics was a game played out by a small coterie of dissidents located on the fringes of the political system. Since the inauguration of *glasnost* almost every group experienced massive attitudinal change and/or mobilization over the issue of the kind of state formation in which they deserved to live.

In reality, the breakup of the USSR was not a single surge of state-seeking, but rather involved successive waves of state-seeking, some of which carried over into the post-Soviet period. Figure 11.3, which examines protest mobilization over state-seeking issues among various categories of ethnic groups,[8] shows a sharp differentiation in the timing and pattern of protest mobilization among ethnic groups and in the emergence of a state-seeking agenda. Not surprisingly, peoples without any representation within the Soviet federal system protested fairly consistently throughout this period over state-seeking issues, although at extremely low levels of mobilization. The absence of access to the state and in some cases geographic dispersal made it difficult for the stateless to engage in effective mobilization of their populations. Levels of protest mobilization over state-seeking issues (as well as protest mobilization overall) were fairly closely tied to the shape of the Soviet federal system itself—further proof of the ways in which Soviet nationalities policies helped to construct the very conditions that eventually undermined the USSR.[9]

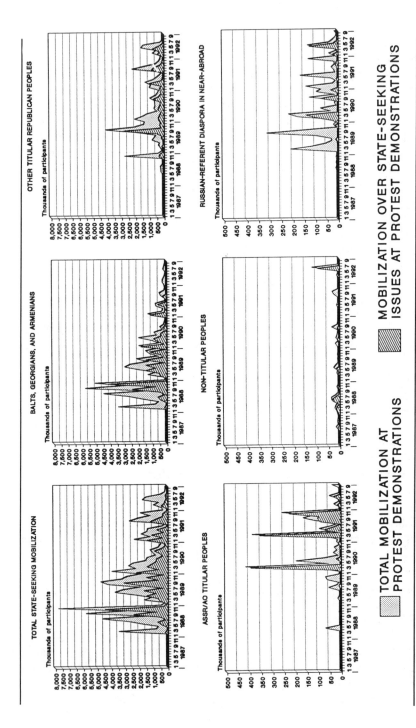

**Figure 11.3.** State-Seeking Mobilization at Protest Demonstrations by Category of Ethnic Group, January 1987 – September 1992.

Balts, Georgians, and Armenians mobilized relatively quickly over state-seeking issues, peaking in late 1989 and early 1990 and declining over the course of 1990, as nationalist governments came to power through the ballot box. By contrast, other titular republican peoples mobilized much later over state-seeking issues (peaking in 1990 and 1991) and only after significant mobilization occurred over other issues. By 1990, most protest in favor of secession was being carried out not by Balts, Georgians, and Armenians, but by Ukrainians, Azerbaidzhanis, Moldavians, and even Russians. Even those who participated in this "revolution of the mind" were surprised by their own behavior. As a liberal Russian Jewish intellectual recounted to journalist John Morrison in May 1990: "If you had told me two years ago I would be out on the street at demonstrations shouting '*Ross-i-ya, Ross-i-ya,*' I would have thought you were crazy."[10]

This second wave of state-seeking mobilization—a time when attitudes toward the state were highly unstable—unleashed the so-called parade of sovereignties, when myriad territories of the former Soviet Union went about formally declaring themselves "sovereign," whatever this most ambiguous of terms actually meant. Indeed, its meaning varied enormously from place to place, in many instances signifying little more than a desire for greater control over local affairs. Not only union republics, but autonomous republics, autonomous districts, urban wards, and even islands participated in this orgy of autonomy-seeking. It was also at this time that most autonomous republics unilaterally declared themselves union republics.

This second stage in the development of state-seeking nationalism was characterized above all by a significant broadening of the peoples involved in state-seeking. As figure 11.3 shows, in early 1991 peoples associated with autonomous republics and provinces began to mobilize over state-seeking issues as well. To some extent, this was a matter of demonstration effects. But other processes were also at work. The growing influence of majority nationalizing movements in the union republics in turn led to efforts by minorities within those republics to separate and gain protection and representation in the context of other state formations. In 1990 and 1991, for instance, both Ossetians and Gagauzy grew active in agitating for separation from their respective union republics in reaction to the rise of nationalism in Georgia and Moldova respectively. New categories and identities, such as Russian-speakers (*russko-govoriashchie*) were called into being as a result of the nationalizing policies of republics; these also became a basis for state-seeking mobilization at this time. Even a year before the State Emergency Committee's aborted attempt to seize power, state-seeking had become so common a form of behavior that it was widely parodied in the Soviet press. In short, the events of 1989–90 provoked a massive pursuit of the state, as groups that were relatively demobilized over state-seeking issues earlier mobilized in search of the national state.

### State-Seeking versus State-Building

A new chapter in attitudes toward the state in this region of the world opened up with the collapse of the USSR in August 1991. At that time, state-seeking attitudes and behaviors became universalized, and a new set of conflicts set in: between the consolidation of new states and the state-seeking behavior of those who remained dissatisfied with the forms of state which they had been designated.

Immediately following the August coup, there was a general consolidation of opinion around the former union republics as new national states. This was particularly so among the titular nationalities of the former union republics, but was not confined to them. It generally affected all populations that had been disaffected from the communist regime, regardless of ethnicity. In the December 1991 referendum on Ukrainian independence, for example, 90.3 percent of the inhabitants of Ukraine voted in favor of secession. Significantly enough, even the heavily Russified Donetsk and Odessa provinces showed 83.9 and 85.3 percent majorities respectively in favor of independence, while 54.1 percent of the voters of Crimea province, populated by a majority Russian population, voted in favor of independence. By contrast, in the post-Soviet era, many of these populations eventually became disaffected from their new homelands and openly began to question the legitimacy of the region's new borders.

Of course, for many peoples independence was unwanted and unexpected, coming without warning and without any effort on their part to achieve it. In a number of these instances populations that had largely been immune to the secessionist disease up to August 1991 (such as the Central Asians) often experienced a radical shift in attitudes in favor of the birth of new states and the collapse of the Soviet center. Whereas before the August coup there was little sentiment in favor of secession in Central Asia, referenda in favor of secession overwhelmingly passed in each of these republics by the fall of 1991.[11] Local communist politicians—often of the most conservative ilk—recycled themselves as national saviors and as founders of national states. In essence, nationalist consciousness and the national state were brought to these peoples from above, through a combination of the actions of elites and the uncontrolled flow of events.

Much of the politics of the past several years in the former Soviet Union can be viewed as an enormous effort at state consolidation, whereby the union republics of the former USSR, having attained international recognition, have sought (often unsuccessfully) to create the basic institutions and practices characteristic of states around the globe: bureaucracies, armies, monetary regulation, police, tax collection, postal service, border control, citizenship control, foreign embassies, and so on. Most important from the point of view of our topic, state-building ran into a third wave of state-seeking unleashed as a direct result of the collapse of the USSR.

There generally have been three sources of state-seeking in the post-Soviet era. First, in the aftermath of the collapse of the USSR, a number of minorities of the former Soviet Union accelerated their agitation for separate statehood and even in some cases declared it unilaterally—this time running directly into the opposition of the former union republics, who only months before were themselves agitating for independence from Moscow. The Soviet federal system, as arbitrary as it was, has served as the basis for legitimation of the post-Soviet state system. The collapse of the Soviet Union led fairly quickly to international recognition of the state independence of the fifteen union republics. But other than Stalin's self-serving decisions about which peoples' deserved their own union republics and which would have units subordinated to union republics, there is no justification for why peoples with union republics deserve independence and those without do not. Kazakhstan and Kyrgyzstan, for instance, were not originally assigned union republican status when the USSR was created, but were instead autonomous republics within the Russian Federation. Had they not been separated by Stalin into union republics in 1936, it is doubtful that they would be independent states today. There is no inherent reason, other than Stalin's manipulations, for why one million Estonians should deserve independent statehood while six million Volga Tartars should not. The post-Soviet configuration of states and the internal structure of the post-Soviet states may in this respect be considered one of the remaining bastions of Stalinism that has yet to be stormed.

Although secessionist sentiment certainly exists among many of Russia's minorities, so far only the Volga Tatars and the Chechens have been bold enough to approach declarations of secession. After the collapse of the USSR Chechnya became de facto an independent state, governed by the corrupt authoritarian regime of Dzhokhar Dudayev, a general in the former Soviet air force who established his control over the region in fall 1991 and imposed a personal dictatorship. For three years Russia hardly exercised any control over the region, and repeated attempts by Yel'tsin to reimpose rule from Moscow failed. Finally, in frustration Yel'tsin ordered an invasion of the region in December 1994, unleashing a bloody war whose consequences are likely to persist for a long time. The international community, of course, did not rush to recognize the Dudayev regime, in large part because of the fear that this would set in motion the further disintegration of Russia. Chechnya's declaration of independence, however, has unleashed other processes of state-seeking throughout the northern Caucasus, weakening further Russia's control over this volatile region.

In the case of Tatarstan, the government of former communist boss Mintimer Shaymiyev for several years defied Moscow's control; rather than complete secession, it preferred to remain associated with Moscow by means of international agreement. In March 1992, Tatarstan held a referendum on whether it was "a sovereign state and a subject of international law," despite the fact that the Russian Constitutional Court had declared the referendum illegal. After 61 percent of the electorate voted to recognize Tatar sovereignty, the republic refused to sign the Russian Federal Treaty. In November 1992, Tatarstan adopted a new constitution that declared it a sovereign state "associated with the Russian Federation" on the basis of an international treaty. During negotiations over the new Russian Constitution in the summer of 1993, the Tatar delegation walked out in protest of what it viewed as backtracking by the Yel'tsin government on the issue of Tatar sovereignty. The Tatars insisted that it was the right of the republics to create a new federation government and not of the center to determine the extent of powers of the republics. Eventually, under heavy pressure from Moscow, the Shaymiyev government signed a bilateral treaty with the Russian Federation in February 1994. However, the agreement itself was ambiguous as to what it actually signified. The Yel'tsin government claimed that it was an internal agreement, whereas Tatarstan described it as a treaty between two sovereign states. Under the agreement, Tatarstan retained the right to conduct its own foreign policy and foreign trade, to decide questions of republican citizenship, and to exempt its youth from service in the Russian army.[12] While the treaty may have put a temporary hold on the quarrel, the issue of defining Tatarstan's relationship with Moscow could easily reemerge in the future.

A second source of the persistence of state-seeking behavior in the post-Soviet period has been the instant Diaspora created by the collapse of the USSR. When the Soviet Union disintegrated in August 1991, 38 million former Soviet citizens who lived outside the union republic of their own nationality (including 25 million Russians) were suddenly thrust into the status of being a minority in another ethnic group's state. While in some cases these minorities have not been excluded from the political process (as in Ukraine), in other cases they have been treated as social or even legal aliens, leading to massive out-migration (as in Central Asia) and, in instances of compact settlement, the growth of regional and separatist movements (as in Estonia and Moldova).

In the case of the Russian minority in northern Estonia, over 90 percent of the participants in a referendum held in the cities of Narva and Sillamae in July 1993 voted in favor of declaring their towns autonomous territories within Estonia. The Estonian government declared the referendum invalid.[13] Within a week of Ukraine's declaration of independence in August 1991, the Supreme Soviet of the majority-Russian Crimea declared its republic's state sovereignty, albeit as a constituent part of Ukraine. In May 1992, the Crimea proclaimed its independence from Ukraine, only to have the declaration immediately annulled by Kiev. There is widespread support in the region for some degree of Russian sovereignty over the area. A 1993 poll conducted by Ian Bremmer in the city of Simferopol found that 75 percent of Russians and 42 percent of Ukrainians in the city preferred that the Soviet Union still existed.[14] In July 1993, the Russian Parliament unilaterally declared Simferopol to be a Russian city. In January 1994, Crimea held a presidential election in which Yuri Meshkov, leader of the Crimean independence movement, won 75 percent of the vote. Subsequent parliamentary elections brought Meshkov's supporters to power with 67 percent of the vote. A simultaneous referendum also showed that 82 percent favored dual Russian/Ukrainian citizenship for inhabitants of Crimea. Meshkov and his group attempted to introduce a separate Crimean citizenship and currency. In response, the Ukrainian Parliament annulled these laws and threatened to dissolve the local government if it did not bring its constitution into line with Ukraine's. By fall 1994, however, a split had developed within Meshkov's own movement, with the Parliament voting to strip him of his powers, while Meshkov called for the Parliament to dissolve itself. This, along with the election of Leonid Kuchma, who is widely seen as favoring the Russian-speaking community in Ukraine, has taken some of the wind out of the Crimean separatist movement.

The self-declared Gagauz republic and Dniestr Moldavian republic remain unrecognized by any government, although four Russian provinces have concluded economic agreements on their own with the Dniestr republic. The Pridniestr republic has at times refused any kind of relationship with Chisinau, while at other times has hinted that it would remain within Moldova if a confederation could be arranged. The Moldavians, by contrast, at first insisted on a unitary state, but have now come to embrace some kind of federal arrangement. In the meantime, the Moldovans have reached a compromise arrangement with the Gagauz, giving them extensive autonomy and reserving for the Gagauz the right to secede if Moldova were to change its international status (i.e., merge with Romania).

While Russian minorities have received the bulk of the attention in the West, it would be wrong to think that the Diaspora issue is confined to Russians alone. The borders of union republics are not ethnic borders, and practically every republic has some minority whose status has been called into question by the transformation of the union republics into national states. In Central Asia, there is a sleeping Diaspora issue which was the cause of considerable communal violence in the *glasnost* period, but in post-Soviet period has not yet grown into an interstate issue. A summit of Central Asian leaders in August 1994 saw the signing of a joint declaration on the inviolability of borders; the signatories committed themselves not to alter former Soviet borders and to prevent activities by groups or individuals on their territory who seek to do so.[15]

A third cause for the growth of state-seeking behaviors in the post-Soviet period has been the crisis of governability that has engulfed the entire former Soviet Union. It has exacerbated severely relations between center and locality and has encouraged locally based groups to vie for control over the state. One sees this not only in the federal crisis that has consumed Russia, but also in the strained relations between Kiev and its Russian minority, and even in the bloody civil war in Tadzhikistan (which is as much a battle among regionally based cliques as an ideological and religious struggle).

The federal crisis that consumed Russia in 1992 and 1993 confirms the critical role played by political opportunity structures in fostering state-seeking behavior. As the Parliament and president became embroiled in a paralyzing power struggle, power drifted to the regions, creating new possibilities for staking claims to state authority. Ironically, it was the 1992 federal treaty and Yel'tsin's state-building strategy which, in a period of confusion at the center, became major threats to the cohesion of Russia. Signed by all the regions and almost all of the republics of the federation (only Tatarstan and Chechnya rejected it), the federal treaty provided, among other things, for extensive local control over natural resources, land, and foreign relations for those territories granted republican status, while territories that were governed as provinces were denied these. This was part of Yel'tsin's state-building strategy: to rely upon the republics in building power and consolidating a new Russia. Indeed, one examination of Russian government spending and revenues showed that republics received more money from the government than they had contributed in taxes, while roughly a dozen provinces have received a fraction of their contribution. Tatarstan, for instance, paid only 93 million rubles in taxes in 1992, at the same time as receiving 38 billion rubles from the government.[16] Policies such as this in turn led to a reaction by the provinces, which are, of course, predominantly Russian. The power of the republics, according to one Russian observer, had "given rise to a situation that can be defined as de jure codification of Russians' statelessness in Russia."[17] This division between republics and provinces became the major issue standing in the way of the acceptance of Yel'tsin's constitution, and it set in motion a rush by provinces to declare themselves sovereign republics. In June 1993, official representatives of forty provinces signed a declaration indicating that they could not initial a new draft constitution for Russia unless their territorial units were given equal status with the republics.[18]

In 1993, center-periphery relations in Russia so deteriorated that six provinces and cities (Amur, Vologda, Sverdlovsk, Kaliningrad, Primorskii krai, and St. Petersburg) unilaterally declared themselves republics, and others promised to follow suit.[19] In the case of Vologda province, a referendum was held in April 1993 in which 80 percent of the electorate voted for turning the province into a "state-territorial entity."[20] The heads of Irkutsk and Krasnoiarsk provinces openly discussed uniting their provinces into a single East Siberian republic. The Cheliabinsk Provincial Soviet voted to transform the province into the Southern Urals republic, and a referendum was scheduled on the issue of the "republicanization" of Chita province. Smelling gold at the end of the republican rainbow, the leaders of six Central Black Earth provinces threatened to declare themselves a republic if they did not receive special credits, price guarantees, and tax dispensations from Moscow.[21] At the same time, the republics were claiming that their rights were inadequate as well. As one regional leader put it, the notion of sovereignty for republics and territorial units of the Russian Federation had become "a bomb under Russia's future," leading to potentially endless conflicts over center-periphery relations.[22] So serious was the challenge to Russia's territorial integrity that Yel'tsin saw fit to warn regional leaders in August 1993 that "the Russian Federation is not a piece of Swiss cheese" and that if Russia could not be kept together peacefully, "it could be done by naked force, by a dictatorship."[23]

The growth of regional separatism and the transformation of provinces into sovereign states were only two manifestations of a broader trend towards state-seeking behavior that encompassed Russia in 1993. On the eastern shores of Sakhalin, the indigenous Nivkhi declared their own autonomous governmental unit, against the desires of the local Russian inhabitants. The Taimyr Regional Soviet declared its secession from Krasnoiarsk krai, and the Khanty-Mansi and Yamal-Nenets Autonomous Regions, both within Tiumen' province, declared themselves sovereign.[24] Chukhotka similarly seceded from Magadan province. The key issue that united all of these cases was natural resources and the question of who would control their exploitation and export from Russia. In some areas of Russia, in particular, in the Kuban' and in Volgograd province, Cossack Hetman rule was introduced. In March 1993 Yel'tsin assigned the functions of military training and policing in the northern Caucasus to Cossack forces. While the Cossack population did not see itself as a separate entity from Russia, there was widespread talk that "an independent Cossack republic will come into being" in the northern Caucasus;[25] in some areas it already existed de facto. The Don Cossacks agitated for the creation of a separate Don Cossack Province that would cut across Russia and Ukraine.

The political crisis between the Parliament and the president was resolved in September and October 1993, when Yel'tsin dissolved Parliament and stormed the Russian White House. The subsequent hardening of the political center led to a sharp drop in the staking of state-seeking claims. And to the disconcertment of many republics, Yel'tsin cut out of the new Constitution any reference to republican sovereignty. He also ordered provincial legislatures to dissolve themselves and to hold new elections by March 1994. This met with considerable opposition, but was carried out. In February 1994 Yel'tsin succeeded in quieting the Tatarstan issue by concluding a bilateral treaty with the Republic. In the views of most analysts, Yel'tsin has successfully reversed the trend towards disintegration of the federation. The real issue, though, is how long this state of affairs will last, given the close connection between disarray in the center and state-seeking in the regions. As patterns of state-seeking in this region of the world demonstrate, should Russian government once again become paralyzed, a proliferation of state-seeking behaviors by Russia's provinces would become likely.

Lest one fall into the trap of believing that the post-Soviet scramble for the state is simply a Russian phenomenon, it is worth reviewing the situation in two republics—Ukraine and Azerbaidzhan—to see how state-seeking remains the product of a generalized crisis of the state throughout the region. Indeed, state-seeking has been an almost knee-jerk reaction to national and regional problems of the most varied sort. In addition to the Republic of Crimea examined earlier, the miners of the Donbass region of Ukraine, who called for the resignation of the Kravchuk government because of excessive taxes and price rises, advocated as well special autonomous status for the Donets region within Ukraine, largely as a means for protecting economic interests and language rights.[26] The Subcarpathian Ruthenians began to agitate for the creation of an Autonomous Republic of Subcarpathian Ruthenia.[27] And Russian communities in four provinces of southern Ukraine have called for combining into a state to be known as *Novorossiia*, or New Russia, in fear of Ukrainian domination.[28] While Ukraine may not yet look like Russia's Swiss cheese (and like Russia, it has experienced some hardening of the state under Leonid Kuchma), no one doubts that under the right circumstances it could still come to resemble Gruyere.

During the June 1993 revolt of Surat Huseinov in Azerbaidzhan, the Talysh, a group of about 22 thousand Iranian-speakers that was once thought to have been completely assimilated by the Azerbaidzhanis, used the confusion to declare into existence a Talysh-Mugan Autonomous Republic on the frontier between Azerbaidzhan and Iran. The local revolt continued for two months before it was put down by the new government of former communist boss Gaidar Aliev.[29] The Lezgins, Sunni Muslims who, since 1922, have been divided by the Azerbaidzhani-Russian border, have also come to challenge Azerbaidzhani territorial integrity with the coming of independence. Depending on who does the counting, there are somewhere between 466 thousand and 1 million Lezgins in the former USSR; while the Azerbaidzhanis claim that only 175 thousand live in Azerbaidzhan, the Lezgins themselves claim that as many as 700 thousand live there and have been subjected over the years to forced cultural and linguistic assimilation. While there had been some agitation among Lezgins in the Soviet period, only with the breakup of the USSR have Lezgins grown politicized over the issue of the unification of all Lezgins within an independent Lezgistan. The Azerbaidzhani government reacted sharply against these developments, causing sharp tensions with Russia.[30] And of course, the Armenian revolt within Azerbaidzhan rages on. Certainly the Russian Federation, with its eighty-nine member units (of which seventeen are national republics) and its huge expanse, represents a degree of complexity not found in the other former republics of the Soviet Union, and for that reason alone is particularly vulnerable to state-seeking behavior. But other republics as well have been experiencing these same forces, perhaps not on the same scale, but certainly in the same spirit and with many of the same consequences.

## Conclusion

It is clear from this presentation that in the case of the former Soviet Union we are dealing with an unusual explosion of state-seeking behavior. And yet, while the former Soviet Union provides us with one example of how state-seeking behavior has proliferated in recent years, it is by no means the only. The late twentieth century has witnessed a more generalized rush to the state not unlike that which was witnessed in East Europe at the end of World War I and throughout most of the Third World in the aftermath of World War II.

How does one explain this new wave of state-seeking conduct, as well as its universalization as a form of behavior within particular contexts? What do the Soviet and post-Soviet experiences tell us about why state-seeking attitudes and behaviors proliferate?

The Soviet and post-Soviet evidence points to the close connection between state disintegration and state-seeking. Indeed, the two appear as opposite sides of the same coin. As we have seen, this is in part because the crisis of the state creates the political opportunities necessary for challenging what Mill calls "the fundamental principles" of the state, making what once seemed impossible fall within the realm of the imaginable. Issues of state formation defy easy settlement, and the mere fact that they are raised itself alters significantly the political opportunities facing those who seek to mobilize populations over these issues. Precisely because state-seeking behavior is dependent upon political opportunities, state-seeking behavior seems to explode at particular points in time, setting off bursts of state-seeking and what appears as a race for the state among numerous groups. Analogous phenomena occurred during earlier eruptions of state-seeking behavior in the twentieth century.

The crisis of the state also provides part of the context that makes state-seeking appear a relevant solution to pursue. It is not simply that state-seeking proliferates because it becomes possible (although in a few cases, such as the Balts, this is a sufficient explanation); state-seeking also proliferates in part because the disintegration of authority defines its own antinomy and itself calls into being efforts to reconstitute political authority on a different basis.

Finally, the crisis of the state in Eurasia, as we have observed, is itself the product of a particular historical legacy of state-building and empire-building that has fostered great ambiguity over the proper definition of the physical and human boundaries of polities. The proliferation of state-seeking is enhanced by this ambiguity and the contestation that it engenders. Moreover, the cultural expectations and norms that have emerged from previous patterns of state-building also have played a large role in fostering state-seeking behavior; the Leninist legacy of state-building helped to generalize norms of state-seeking, making it seem a natural solution to any and all issues of cultural pluralism.

Whatever its causes, the generalization of state-seeking behavior throughout this region of the world makes the long-term creation of stable polities problematic and in many cases elusive. Even if a semblance of stability could be achieved, in some polities cultural conflict is likely to continue to lurk just beneath the surface, waiting for the moment when the state's "fundamental principles" might once again be called into question. It is this inherent "softness" of the Eurasian state which defines the character of cultural politics in this region of the world, and ensures that there will be few easy solutions to the disorder unleashed by the collapse of communism.

## Notes

An earlier version of this chapter was presented at the international conference on "Race, Ethnicity, and Nationalism at the End of the Twentieth Century," sponsored by the Institute on Race and Ethnicity of the University of Wisconsin System, September 1993. Research on state-seeking protest mobilization was carried out under the auspices of grants from the National Science Foundation, the National Council for Soviet and East European Research, the International Research and Exchanges Board, and the Graduate School of the University of Wisconsin-Madison. The author gratefully acknowledges their support.

The source of the epigraph that opens the chapter is John Stuart Mill, *A System of Logic*, vol. 2 (London: Longmans, Green, and Company, 1865), pp. 517–18.

1. Take, for instance, the case of Nagorno-Karabakh. Armenians living in the region who sought to unite the province with Armenia were engaging in state-seeking behavior, while Armenians within Armenia who agitated for incorporating Karabakh into Armenia were engaged in state-expansionist behavior. At the same time, Azerbaidzhanis seeking to expel Armenians from the region were engaged in a form of societal engineering.

2. For an excellent examination of the role of the Leninist federal model in undermining Soviet power, see Ronald Grigor Suny, *The Revenge of the Past: Nationalism, Revolution, and the Collapse of the Soviet Union* (Stanford, CA: Stanford University Press, 1993).

3. For more on the methodology behind this analysis, see Mark R. Beissinger, "Non-Violent Public Protest in the USSR: December 1, 1986 – December 31, 1989," report published by the National Council for Soviet and East European Research, Washington, DC, 1990. *State-seeking issues* were defined as protest mobilization over one of the following issues: against the original annexation of territory to the USSR or Russia; in favor of secession; in support of sovereignty for one's republic or territory; for upgrading the federal status of an administrative unit; for the creation of an autonomous federal unit; for a redefinition of citizenship along national lines; for creation of national military units; for separate representation abroad for a republic; for withdrawal of the Soviet army from the republic; publication or renunciation of the Molotov-Ribbentrop Pact; Siberian regional separatism; for separation of a territory from republic; for foreign recognition of republican independence; for the creation of an independent communist party around a territorial unit; for local control over economic resources; renunciation of Soviet citizenship; for republican control over the KGB; for reunification with Iran; for reunification with Romania; for greater economic autonomy for a republic; for increasing the representation of a nationality within elite posts; in favor of preserving or extending non-Russian linguistic or cultural rights; for making the language of a group the official language; against the Novo-Ogareva agreement; against Russian government interference in local affairs; for creation of a presidency for local government; for creation of Russian presidency; for local control over law enforcement agencies; for restoration of the Soviet Union; for Russian domination in Russia; for secession of a republic; solidarity with Russian separatists in non-Russian republics; against discrimination against population of locality; for full citizenship rights of Russian minority in a

republic; for introduction of dual citizenship; for making Russian a second state language; and for introduction of local citizenship. *State-expansionist issues* were defined as protest mobilization over one of the following issues: irredentist claims against another political unit; for defense of Russians living beyond Russia's borders; for restoration of the Soviet Union; solidarity with Russian separatists in non-Russian republics; for introduction of dual citizenship; for creation of a new Russian Empire; territorial claims against a foreign state; and for Russian intervention in other republican conflict.

4. Rogers Brubaker, "National Minorities, Nationalizing States, and External Homelands in the New Europe: Notes toward a Relational Analysis," paper prepared for the conference on "National Minorities, Nationalizing States, and External National Homelands in the New Europe," August 22–26, 1994, Bellagio, Italy.

5. David D. Laitin, Roger Petersen, and John W. Slocum, "Language and the State: Russia and the Soviet Union in Comparative Perspective," in Alexander J. Motyl, ed., *Thinking Theoretically about Soviet Nationalities: History and Comparison in the Study of the USSR* (New York: Columbia University Press, 1992), p. 130.

6. Suny, op. cit. note 2, pp. 76–77.

7. For a broader explanation for why ambiguity over the physical and human boundaries of polities is widespread throughout Eurasia, see Mark R. Beissinger, "The Persisting Ambiguity of Empire: State and Empire-Building in Post-Soviet Politics," paper prepared for the conference on "National Minorities, Nationalizing States, and External National Homelands in the New Europe," August 22–26, 1994, Bellagio, Italy.

8. Peoples of Dagestan were left out of the analysis because of the ambiguity surrounding whether they had an autonomous republic or were stateless.

9. See Suny, op. cit. note 2; Philip G. Roeder, "Soviet Federalism and Ethnic Mobilization," *World Politics* 43 (January 1991): 196–232.

10. John Morrison, *Boris Yeltsin: From Bolshevik to Democrat* (New York: Dutton, 1991), p. 19.

11. For a review of the results of a number of referenda on independence, see "Presidential Elections and Independence Referendums in the Baltic States, the Soviet Union and Successor States: A Compendium of Reports, 1991–1992," report compiled by the staff of the Commission on Security and Cooperation in Europe, August 1992, Washington, DC.

12. See Elizabeth Teague, "Russia and Tatarstan Sign Power-sharing Treaty," *RFE/RL Research Report* 3.14 (April 8, 1994): 19–27.

13. According to the organizers of the referendum, voter turnout was 54 percent in Narva and 61 percent in Sillamae. The Estonian government claims that voter turnout in the referendum was less than half of the eligible electorate. See *RFE/RL Daily Report*, no. 135, July 19, 1993.

14. Ian Bremmer, "Ethnic Issues in Crimea," *RFE/RL Research Report* 2.18 (April 30, 1993): 27.

15. *RFE/RL Daily Report*, no. 150, August 9, 1993.

16. Leonid Smirnyagin, "The Regions: Political Federalism vs. Economic Federalism," *Sevodnya*, June 25, 1993, p. 2, translated in *The Current Digest of the Post-Soviet Press* [*CDPSP*] 45.25 (July 21, 1993): 7.

17. Ksenia Myalo, in "Debates: The Russian Question in Russia," *Megapolis-Express*, May 5, 1993, p. 29, translated in *CDPSP* 45.17 (May 26, 1993): 11.

18. "Russia's Territories and Provinces Set Conditions," *Rossiiskiye vesti*, June 30, 1993, p. 2, translated in *CDPSP* 45.26 (July 28, 1993): 8.

19. *RFE/RL Daily Report*, no. 138, July 22, 1993. See also Vera Tolz, "Regionalism in Russia: The Case of Siberia," *RFE/RL Research Report* 2.9 (February 26, 1993): 1–9. For a proposal to create a Republic of Moskovia, see Lyudmila Sherova, "Will There Soon Be a Republic of Moskovia?" *Rossiiskiye vesti*, June 2, 1993, p. 1, translated in *CDPSP* 45.22 (June 30, 1993): 16–17.

20. Viktor Filippov, "Vologda Province Is Proclaimed a State Within Russia," *Izvestia*, May 18, 1993, pp. 1–2, translated in *CDPSP* 45.20 (June 16, 1993): 24.

21. Nikolai Yefimovich, "Sovereignty Right Outside Moscow," *Komsomolskaya pravda*, July 13, 1993, p. 1, translated in *CDPSP* 45.28 (August 11, 1993): 6.

22. V. Novikov, Chair of the Krasnoiarsk krai Soviet, quoted in Aleksei Tarasov, "A Bomb Under Russia's Future," *Izvestia*, June 24, 1993, pp. 1-2, translated in *CDPSP* 45.25 (July 21, 1993): 4–5.

23. "Russia Will Allow No Secession, Yeltsin Warns Regional Leaders," *The New York Times*, August 14, 1993, p. A4.

24. Yelena Matveyeva, "Farce of Sovereignties," *Moskovskiye novosti*, May 30, 1993, p. C9, translated in *CDPSP* 45.21 (June 23, 1993): 18.

25. Vladimir Seleznev, "Without Barricades and Whips," *Rossiiskiye vesti*, April 1, 1993, p. 2, translated in *CDPSP* 45.14 (May 5, 1993): 17.

26. Nikolai Lisovenko, "Donets Basin Miners Aren't Asking for Money, They're Demanding Political Changes," *Izvestia*, June 10, 1993, pp. 1–2, translated in *CDPSP* 45.23 (July 7, 1993): 24–25.

27. "Proiavleniia separatizma v Zakarpat'e pod vidom trebovanii avtonomnoi respubliki," *Golos Ukrainy*, August 6, 1993, p. 2.

28. *Nezavisimaia gazeta*, November 16, 1991, p. 2.

29. *RFE/RL Daily Report*, no. 161, August 24, 1993.

30. See Elizabeth Fuller, "Caucasus: The Lezgin Campaign for Autonomy," in *RFE/RL Research Report* 1.41 (October 16, 1992): 30–32.

# 12

# Nationality Questions in the Baltic

## The Lithuanian Example

ALFRED ERICH SENN

In 1988 political developments flipped the question of national minorities in the Baltic republics of the Union of Soviet Socialist Republics (USSR) over on its head. Previously, on the massive Soviet scale, Russians, as the dominant nationality of the USSR, were not considered a minority in the Baltic; Latvians, Lithuanians, and Estonians, the titular nationalities in the Baltic, constituted important minorities, while the Belorussians, Jews, Poles, and Ukrainians in the region constituted minor ones. In the summer and fall of 1988, however, those same Latvians, Lithuanians, and Estonians became majorities on separate smaller stages; the Russians became the largest minority in each republic; and Poles and others became significant minority questions.

Key to the confusion of this turnover was the various groups' attitude toward statehood: Did the new dominant nationalities feel secure? Did the new minorities accept the political changes? What many writers refer to abstractly as "nationalism" can frequently be understood as a question of statehood—the interrelationship of territory, nationality, and political power, as these factors develop over time.

In the post-Soviet states another vital question arises from the inherited tradition of statism. The centralized Soviet structure emphasized the state, whether socialist or nationalist, as the engine of social change, and the new Baltic governments after 1988 accepted the task not just of defending their national cultures but also of helping national cultures recover from the perceived ravages of a half-century of alien rule. In the absence of any laissez-faire traditions, should the new governments encourage the assimilation of their ethnic minorities? encourage diversity? force emigration? employ outright violence? According to Western standards of human rights, the last two alternatives are unacceptable, but they nevertheless have their proponents and practitioners in the post-Soviet arena.

Although some now look at the Soviet system nostalgically for its having avoided open ethnic conflict, there are several considerations that refute such a view:

- Stalin's practice of punishing entire nationalities by deportation and exile intensified national feelings for generations to come; we are just coming to realize the long-lasting consequences of that practice.
- The supposed peace between nationalities was in fact illusory; the Communist party did not resolve the national question but rather suppressed it and left it to ferment.
- National conflicts today are not just an explosion of forces long kept under control by the Soviet system; they also reflect the consequences of Soviet policies. The nationalities themselves changed during fifty to seventy years of Soviet rule, and the Soviet experience in fact contributed greatly to the troubles now plaguing Eastern Europe.

In its program of 1986, the Communist Party of the Soviet Union (CPSU) declared that "the nationalities question inherited from the past has been successfully solved in the Soviet Union."[1] "Nationalism" existed only in capitalist society and therefore, by definition, did not exist in the USSR. Soviet nationalities' policy, though, had within itself severe contradictions, cracks that the regime's repressive forces only papered over without repairing, which the tremors of the late 1980s eventually broke open.

The formal structure of the Soviet system, based on identifying ethnoterritorial units, actually reenforced national consciousness. (Soviet ideologists usually spoke of their policies as "national in form and socialist in content.") When the Soviet Union annexed the three Baltic republics of Latvia, Lithuania, and Estonia in 1940, it accepted their continued existence as politico-geographic units, labelling them constituent republics of the Union of Soviet Socialist Republics. Soviet ideologists then argued that "socialist statehood" was a higher form of social organization than "bourgeois statehood," and they thereby posited what might be better called "national statehood" as the natural antithesis of Soviet rule. So long as Soviet censorship and other repressive forces remained on guard, this presented no problem, but when the central control faltered, this argument released and even buttressed national feelings among those who hated living under Soviet rule.

Few Western observers recognized this problem even in looking at the Baltic republics. In the 1960s, John Armstrong identified the Baltic peoples as "state nations," having a higher self-consciousness than most of the other titular nationalities in the republics of the USSR,[2] but common wisdom among Soviet experts in the United States discounted the national question as a factor in Soviet affairs. In 1984, an official of the American Central Intelligence Agency (CIA) flatly predicted that national minorities in the Soviet Union would play no significant role "in this century."[3]

In the 1980s Soviet nationalities' policy focused on the concept of *sliianie* (merging), an effort to do away with the differences between nationalities by the general acceptance of the Russian language. Soviet educators advocated "bilingualism," providing children with better instruction in Russian than in their mother tongues. Teachers of Russian, moreover, received higher pay than did teachers of the local language. Only after Gorbachev's policy of "openness," *glasnost*, had allowed more free expression, could intellectuals from the minorities complain about these policies.

Those people who specialized in the use of language reacted first to bilingualism. Soviet practice already limited the rights of minority nationalities territorially: Moving out of one's native region could mean giving up one's national culture—except, of course, for Russians—and many persons in fact refused jobs or promotions for just such a reason. One person in a group of thirty people, twenty-nine of whom spoke Estonian, Latvian, or Lithuanian, could force the entire gathering to speak Russian. Within the cultural elites of the various nationalities many saw in bilingualism the decline and even destruction of their basic vehicles of communication. In 1988, the head of the Lithuanian Writers' Union told me of his concern that the Soviet requirement that dissertations be written in Russian would undermine the development of critical thought in the Lithuanian language.[4] In one republic after another, the local writers' union took the lead in demanding stronger efforts to preserve the national language and culture.

Over the course of 1988 and 1989, all three Baltic nations insisted that they had never acquiesced to incorporation into the Soviet Union. The Lithuanians stated this explicitly in their Supreme Council's declaration of March 11, 1990, proclaiming the reestablishment of the Lithuanian state of 1918–40 and dismissing the entire Soviet experience as an occupation by a foreign power. The Lithuanians refused even to consider their right of secession under the Soviet Constitution because, they argued, Lithuania had never been really a part of the Soviet Union—it had been an occupied territory.

Estonians and Latvians expressed similar views, and the tangle of nation, territory, and time implicit in these views had great significance for the evolution of each republic. When asked about treatment of minorities in his republic, an Estonian diplomat objected to calling Russians an "ethnic minority" and argued that the Russians were intruders, introduced by an occupation regime that had deported Estonians. A Latvian politician argued that the Latvians had "reactivated" citizenship for all peoples who inhabited Latvia in 1940 and their descendants; people who had come to Latvia under the aegis of Soviet rule required special legislation. The Russians, he argued, should not be considered a "minority" in the traditional sense; "migrant workers" might be a better category.

It remains here to examine how these thoughts play out in practice, and the remainder of this chapter will concentrate on the Lithuanian example. The three Baltic republics have different histories, different languages and cultures, and different geopolitical situations. As a result they have different national problems.

Of the three republics, Lithuania, which adopted the most liberal citizenship law,[5] has the highest proportion of the eponymous nationality among its population; it has fewer Russians than the other two republics; and it has a second major minority, the Poles. According to the Soviet census of 1989, Lithuania had 3.675 million inhabitants, 79.6 percent of them Lithuanians, 9.4 percent Russians, and 7 percent Poles. Lithuanians constituted a majority in all of the Republic's urban areas except Sniečkus (now named Visaginas, 64 percent Russian) and in all the districts except Ignalina (39.4 percent Lithuanians, 39.4 percent Russians), Šalčininkai (9.4 percent Lithuanians, 79.6 percent Poles), Švenčionys (47.4 percent Lithuanians, 28.8 percent Poles), and the Vilnius district (20.8 percent Lithuanians, 63.5 percent Poles).

The events of 1988 to 1992 changed these census figures in favor of the Lithuanians. For thirty years before 1988, Lithuania had seen a greater immigration than emigration. From 1980 to 1988, the annual net immigration averaged around 5000 persons, with 44 percent of the immigrants being Russians. The net dropped in 1989, and beginning in 1990 emigration exceeded immigration. In 1992, 21,100 more persons emigrated to the former Soviet Union than immigrated. As a result of this change in migration, combined with natural growth, estimates of the population in 1993 reported an increase in the Lithuanian proportion of the population to 80.6 percent, a decline in the Russian population to 8.7 percent, a slight growth in the Polish population to 7.1 percent, and a decline in the Belorussian population to 1.6 percent.[6]

All nationality/population questions are dynamic, changing their features over time, and the Lithuanian capital, Vilnius, offers a remarkable example of this. In 1989 the population of the city of Vilnius was made up of 50.5 percent Lithuanians, 20.2 percent Russians, and 18.8 percent Poles; in 1959 it was made up of only 33.6 percent Lithuanians, 29.4 percent Russians, and 20.0 percent Poles. On my first visit to the city in 1960, I found Russian much more useful than Lithuanian in the streets; in 1970, when Lithuanians constituted 42.8 percent of the population, I found Lithuanian the predominant language in the streets. In the Ignalina district, on the other hand, Lithuanians constituted 77.6 percent of the population in 1959 and 79.9 percent in 1970, but only 39.2 percent in 1989 after the development of the Atomic Energy station in Sniečkus.[7]

Russification policies would seem to have had a greater impact on the Poles and Belorussians in Lithuania than on the Lithuanians themselves. According to the census of 1989, 96.1 percent of the Republic's inhabitants spoke their "native" language, down from 96.9 percent in 1979. Of those who listed themselves as Lithuanian, 99.6 percent spoke Lithuanian (as opposed to 99.7 percent in 1979). Poles and Belorussians showed the greatest decline in speaking their own language, down from 88.5 percent to 85.0 and from 48.6 percent to 40.5 respectively.[8]

When the Lithuanian "rebirth" exploded in 1988, organized by the reform movement "Sajudis," there were, to be sure, Russians who supported the Lithuanians' cause,[9] but the mass meetings, with all their emotional speeches and responses, were conducted entirely in Lithuanian. The process disturbed and frightened people who had calculated that they did not need to know any Lithuanian.

The Lithuanians demanded that their language be the official language of the state. Insofar as would-be reformers in 1988 did not yet dare to challenge the Soviet order directly, the question of state language was the path of least resistance in attacking some fundamental practices of the Soviet state. But for every challenge there naturally arose counterchallenges, both from the sectors favored in the old system and also from other less privileged groups.

Opposition arose primarily among Russians and Poles; in 1988–91 most Russians in Lithuania continued to see themselves as citizens of the Soviet Union rather than as citizens of Lithuania. They shared the values of the metropolis of Moscow, they read the metropolitan press and watched metropolitan television. They had almost no consciousness of being a local community in a smaller, alien territory.

The Poles of Lithuania were a more complicated and diverse group; for one, they formed a more self-conscious community than the Russians did, with their own problems: "The indigenous Poles in Lithuania for the most part constitute a close-knit, impoverished rural community with a low educational level and meager prospects for social and professional advancement. The percentage of Poles who go on to some form of higher education is more than six times lower than the corresponding percentage of Lithuanians; among ethnic groups in the Republic, only Gypsies rank lower."[10] This judgment does not allow for the Poles living in Vilnius, who made up 35–40 percent of the Poles in Lithuania, but it nevertheless carries across the self-image that the Poles of Lithuania had of themselves as being an underprivileged national group.

The Poles were in fact among the more disadvantaged of Soviet nationalities. Not having a territory of their own, like the gypsies and the Jews, they were dependent on local authorities for any recognition of their cultural activities, such as a Polish-language newspaper or the right to hold masses in Polish in local churches. Because of the shifts in political boundaries in this region after World War II, the Poles felt stranded; some declared that they had never emigrated from Poland or immigrated to Lithuania, rather, it was Poland that had moved and had left them behind. (Poles in Belarus and Ukraine have faced analogous problems.) In the late 1940s and early 1950s, about 45 percent of the Poles in Lithuania, 170,000 of 380,000, including most of the intelligentsia, took advantage of the opportunity to emigrate to Poland.[11]

Many of those who remained, faced by a choice of learning Lithuanian or Russian as their official language, chose Russian schools for their children: In the Šalčininkai region, where 79 percent of the population was reportedly Polish, in 1989 only 37.2 percent of the schoolchildren attended Polish schools, while 53.6 percent attended Russian schools. In the Vilnius district where reportedly 63 percent of the population was Polish, there were 2,308 pupils in Lithuanian classes, 3,680 in Polish language classes, and 5,441 (2,745 Poles) in Russian language classes.[12]

In all, as of 1988 and 1989 there were perhaps three major groupings among the Poles on the national question. One, consisting primarily of residents of the city of Vilnius, tended to sympathize with the new currents among the Lithuanians (although the Lithuanians had trouble understanding sympathetic criticism);[13] a second, centered in the southeastern districts of Vilnius and Šalčininkai, preferred to deal with Moscow and the Russians; and the third grouping, spread throughout Lithuania, consisted of Poles who did not particularly want to commit themselves in the choice between Lithuanians and Moscow.

Moscow chose to identify its problems in Lithuania as "interethnic conflict," rather than a challenge to the center, and it claimed to be protecting minority rights. In practice this meant emphasizing the rights of Poles in Lithuania, while at the same time bringing the Poles under a general umbrella of "Russian-speakers" in Lithuania. At Sajudis' founding congress in 1988, for example, Polish and Russian spokespersons used a press conference for what an American journalist called "a joint Polish-Russian offensive"; the first question set the tone: "Poles in Lithuania are uneasy about the growth of Lithuanian nationalism. What is Sajudis' view on this?"[14]

On November 4, 1988, the "Socialist Movement for Perestroika in Lithuania— *Edinstvo*" announced its existence and called for struggle against the Lithuanians. The group demanded that plans to make Lithuanian the official language of the Republic be delayed; it criticized the "indecisiveness" of the Lithuanian Communist party; it called for continued ties with the "union of sovereign republics of the USSR"; and it reaffirmed its faith in "Marxist-Leninist ideology." The group's role as a counter to Sajudis was clear; as the Lithuanian journalist Domas Šniukas wrote, "[i]t is no secret to anyone that you rarely meet a Russian in Sajudis or a Lithuanian in Edinstvo."[15]

The pro-Moscow Poles in Lithuania strongly supported Edinstvo; some observers indeed thought there was stronger Polish than Russian support for the organization. Poles in Warsaw, carrying on their own struggle with Moscow's domination, were sometimes aghast at this spectacle of Polish support for Moscow, but the pro-Soviet Poles in Lithuania simply dismissed the Warsaw Poles as being ignorant of the situation in the Soviet Union.[16]

This pro-Moscow stance compromised the work of other Poles in Lithuania. As Romuald Mieczkowski, editor of the moderate weekly *Znad Wilii*, declared, "If we had been completely correct in our behavior, the Lithuanians would have no pretext to treat us in this way. We have shown a lack of intelligence." Czeslaw Okinczyc, a member of the Lithuanian Parliament, complained, "A pro-Soviet reputation is very difficult to cast off, even if it's unfair. The old system brought so much hardship that once a label has been given, then it sticks."[17]

The Soviet military and the security force, KGB, supported Edinstvo. The military newspaper, *Krasnaia zvezda* (Red Star), enthusiastically endorsed the group, trumpeting reports of discrimination against Russian-speakers. Vadim Bakatin, Gorbachev's last KGB chief, later revealed that the KGB "stood at the sources of the formation of international fronts" and that it pointed to the "activity of these interfronts as an expression of 'the will of the entire people'."[18] As two Radio Free Europe commentators put it, "Now CPSU and KGB representatives encouraged people in these regions to register complaints and make demands of the authorities in Vilnius."[19] Lithuania faced the prospect of a Polish "Karabakh" or a Polish "Trans-Dnistria."

Edinstvo-Jedność-Vienybe, "Unity" as it called itself, held its founding congress in May 1989, amid stormy confusion. Claiming to represent 200,000 sympathizers in 160 primary organizations, the leaders shouted, "The socialist fatherland is in danger," and they physically fought each other for control of the stage. (Organizers criticized Lithuanian television for "tendentiousness" in broadcasting pictures of the combat.) After this meeting it still claimed to represent the Russians and the Poles, but as Jan Sienkiewicz laconically noted, "I would think that the word 'Jedność' is not necessary there."[20]

The pro-Moscow Polish leaders prospered from the confrontation between Vilnius and Moscow in 1989–1991. In the elections of March and April 1989 for the new USSR Congress of People's Deputies, two Poles, Jan Ciechanowicz (in Russian: Tikhonovsky) and Anicet Brodowski, won seats, thereby becoming the first Polish deputies in a USSR Parliament. Both were determinedly pro-Moscow. Ciechanowicz called for the formation of a Polish republic as part of the USSR, and he assured Warsaw journalists that a Pole could indeed be a communist. Brodowski declared Poles must follow Moscow because it offered them more than the Lithuanians did. When Gorbachev blockaded Lithuania in 1990, Moscow made sure that the Polish region of southeastern Lithuania did not suffer.[21]

As the Lithuanians developed their goal of a national state, Polish leaders developed their own national-political program. In April 1989 a Polish "social-cultural association," which had formed a year earlier under the aegis of the Lithuanian Cultural Fund, reorganized itself as the Union of Poles in Lithuania (Związek polaków na Litwie, or ZPL), with 15,000 members, under the slogan, "We have many fatherlands, but only one motherland—Poland" (*Różne mamy ojczyzny, ale Macierz jedną—Polskę*). The ZPL program was at first moderate; they announced that they recognized Lithuania as a "sovereign and independent republic," with its capital in Vilnius.[22] The group's president, Jan Sienkiewicz, indicated that the group would aim to represent the Poles of Lithuania in political, cultural, and civic matters. His first demands focused on educational matters, calling for better Polish language instruction and a Polish institution of higher learning in Lithuania. He also posed the highly symbolic demand of a Polish mass in the Vilnius cathedral.[23]

The pro-Moscow forces among the Poles of Lithuania acted more aggressively. Residents of Šalčininkai and the Vilnius district declared their areas to be autonomous national districts, while Warsaw Poles kept their distance, insisting that this was an internal matter for the people of Lithuania to decide.[24] When the Lithuanian Supreme Council had proclaimed the reestablishment of Lithuanian independence in

March 1990, six Polish deputies abstained on the vote. During Gorbachev's blockade, Moscow encouraged districts of Lithuania to break away, promising to include them in any possible negotiations with the Lithuanian government,[25] and the Šalčininkai and Vilnius districts proclaimed themselves Polish national districts, affirming their loyalty to the Soviet Constitution. In May the Sniečkus municipal council considered joining the Belorussian SSR.[26] The Presidium of the Lithuanian Supreme Council immediately declared the Polish actions unconstitutional.[27]

At the same time, the Lithuanians wanted to avoid pushing all Poles into the arms of the Russians.[28] In the fall of 1989 the government had already created a Nationalities Council, in April 1990 renamed the Nationalities Department, under the direction of a Karaite, Halina Kobeckaitě. When Polish deputies in the Supreme Council complained that no one in the department spoke Polish, Mme. Kobeckaitě appeared in parliament to answer them in Polish, explaining that her office was a state institution, not a "select group of nationalities."

Moscow was now planning to use "interethnic conflict" as a Trojan horse for introducing martial law. In January 1991 Soviet Special Forces entered Lithuania and called out Russian and Polish workers to demonstrate against the Lithuanian government. After the Soviet forces had killed thirteen people in taking the Vilnius television tower on January 13, however, Moscow backed off in the face of world-wide protests.

In many ways the Vilnius action represented both a prelude to the Moscow putsch of August 1991 and also the death warrant of the Soviet regime. The bloodshed encouraged Lithuanian and Polish moderates to join forces, and the ZPL supported the Lithuanian "referendum" of February 1991 on the question of the Republic's separation from the Soviet Union. The Lithuanians, on the other hand, still ignored Polish calls for the inclusion of at least one Pole in the Lithuanian government.[29]

The failed Moscow putsch of August 1991 then changed the game: The Lithuanians took charge and the first conflict came with the Poles. Local leaders in southeastern Lithuania supported the "coup-plotters," and when the Soviet order in Lithuania collapsed in the aftermath of the putsch, the Lithuanian government suspended the local governments, charging that they had been serving as tools of Moscow.[30] In their place the Lithuanian authorities appointed governors, promising that new elections would be held in six months.

The suppression of the councils aroused a storm of protest in Warsaw and elsewhere, where it was seen as oppression of the Polish minority. Eduard Lucas reported in *The Independent* (London) of September 12, "Poles angered by Lithuanian Gauleiters"; Lech Walesa, president of Poland, declared, "There is anxiety over . . . the deteriorating position of people of Polish nationality living in Lithuania"; and Adam Michnik's newspaper *Gazeta wyborcza*, which had in the past been sympathetic, now criticized the Lithuanians (September 16). The agitation calmed down only when Stanislaw Stomma, the president of the Polish Senate who had himself studied in Vilnius in the 1930s, urged calm.[31] The Lithuanians nevertheless stood on notice that henceforth Warsaw would be watching their actions more closely and more critically.

In 1992 the Lithuanian government mended some of its fences with its neighbors. A joint declaration signed in January by Polish foreign minister Krzysztof Skubiszewski and Vytautas Landsbergis eased tensions between the governments, and an agreement signed with Russia in September established a timetable for the evacuation of Russian troops from Lithuania and thereby blunted the threat of Moscow's linking the question of withdrawal with any question of rights of the "Russian-speaking" population of Lithuania. (The category of "Russian-speaking" seemed to include the Poles of Lithuania as wards of the Moscow government.) Both the Polish government and the Russian government henceforth showed little interest in encouraging Polish territorial-administrative ambitions in Lithuania, and the Lithuanian government delayed the reintroduction of local self-government in Šalčininkai and the Vilnius district. In 1994, despite opposition both in Lithuania and Poland, the Polish and Lithuanian governments signed a treaty of friendship.

The position of the Poles nevertheless remained a volatile issue. The ZPL, numbering some 12,000 members, became much more aggressive. (Its former president, Sienkiewicz, apparently retired from public affairs in Lithuania.) Polish grievances and demands include: the Lithuanians are extending the boundaries of the city of Vilnius into "Polish territory"; the Lithuanians have not permitted a regular schedule of Polish masses in the Vilnius cathedral; the Lithuanians should create a Polish university; Lithuanian administrators are unfair to Polish interests; the Lithuanians should dedicate 7 percent of the national budget to the wants and needs of the Polish population; the Lithuanians must recognize the role of Polish military forces, the AK, in Lithuania during World War II. Poles also have demanded that Polish be recognized as an official language in Vilnius and certain other cities of the Republic.[32]

The demands of the Russians of Lithuania contained less drama. Russian spokespersons complained about inadequacies in the school system, problems of border residents in crossing the frontiers, the need for a cultural center, and the spectre of an examination in the knowledge of Lithuanian. Like the Poles, the Russians began to develop their own political spectrum with jockeying for positions of authority; Orthodox Archbishop Khrisostom, who supported the Lithuanians in the crucial days of January 1991, complained that the government no longer wanted to hear him out. Underlying the Russians' grievances was a resentment at having lost their privileged status as the majority.[33]

While history is a major factor in the grievances of Poles and Russians, it is *the* major issue in the Lithuanians' problems of dealing with their Jewish minority. The Jewish population is small, numbering less than 10,000, with a large percentage of it emigrating each year; there are annually more than twice as many deaths as births. According to the Jewish writer Grigorii Kanovičius, there is no official anti-

Semitism,[34] but the Lithuanian government has found itself the target of international scrutiny concerning the memory of the Holocaust during World War II.

The problem of Lithuanian-Jewish historical relations eloquently illustrates the dangers of building historical interpretations on stereotypes. Many Jewish writers, noting that Lithuanians participated in pogroms during the Second World War, condemn the Lithuanian nation as a whole; many Lithuanians, on the other hand, noting the support and service that Jews provided to the Soviet authorities in 1940 and 1941 condemn the Jews as a whole. When Lithuanian Prime Minister Adolfas Šleževičius, in September 1994, expressed regrets for the participation of Lithuanians in anti-Jewish actions during the war, *The New York Times* reported Jewish complaints that his statement was inadequate, and Lithuanian nationalists at home demanded prosecution of the individuals who had participated in the persecution and deportation of Lithuanians in the aftermath of the Soviet occupation of the country.[35] Until both sides can move beyond negative stereotypes of the other, there will be little progress in resolving this sort of dispute.

In creating their *national* state, the Lithuanians proclaimed broad civic rights for the minority nationalities, but however justifiable the Lithuanians may consider their own cultural goals, emphasizing a program of national statehood stimulates thoughts of territorial identity on the part of the other nationalities of the Republic. Nationalists think in terms of a state serving the interests of the Lithuanian "nation," and one can find groups and publications suspicious and even intolerant of other nationalities. The fact that the minorities of Lithuania supported Algirdas Brazauskas and the Lithuanian Democratic Labor party (LDLP) in the elections of 1992 and 1993 evoked comparisons with the situation in 1926, when a coup overthrew a coalition government supported by the minorities and installed a nationalist government. The discussion quickly passed away, but commentators have continued to express concern about the attitudes and intentions of the Poles.

A number of journalists criticized the socialist government as being too soft toward the Poles. On April 24, 1993, *Lietuvos aidas*, which calls itself the "state newspaper," carried a headline, "The Union of Poles Plays the Tune, the LDLP and the VRK [i.e., the elections commission] Dances." Writing in *Atgimimas* of August 18, 1993, Audrius Bačiulis declared: "Having made a preelection bargain with the Union of Poles, the LDLP is now paying its debts."[36] When the treaty of friendship between Warsaw and Vilnius came before the Parliament for ratification in 1994, nationalists complained that the Polish government had not apologized for General Lucjan Żeligowski's seizure of the city of Vilnius in October 1920.

In all, the policies of the Lithuanian government have reinforced the corporate identity of the two major minority national communities, Russians and Poles; the Poles even have guaranteed representation in the Lithuanian Parliament. Spokespersons of the regime hope in this way to guarantee their loyalty: In the fall of 1993, Romualdas Ozolas argued that Pope John Paul II, in calling "Lithuania's Poles Lithuanians of Polish Ancestry," had emphasized "not only the civil integrity of peoples living in Lithuania but also the significance of the state orientation of culture."[37]

The Lithuanian government's Department of Nationality Affairs, run by the Karaite Halina Kobeckaitě from 1989–94, nonetheless took a different approach. Kobeckaitě emphasized civil rights for the Republic's 109 nationalities and 13 operating religions. It is the obligation of the state, she argued, "to make laws and create legal, juridically based opportunities for realizing the basic needs connected with national self-consciousness." She called for separating citizenship from nationality and criticized the provision of the Lithuanian Constitution that declares, "Ethnic communities of citizens shall independently administer the affairs of their ethnic culture, education, organizations, charity and mutual assistance" (article 45). "In my opinion," she explained, "this concept should be changed since it raises juridical problems," and she objected to the thought that an individual must belong to an association in order to enjoy national rights.[38] In 1994 the department was absorbed into another government agency, and Kobeckaite became the Lithuanian ambassador to Estonia.

In sum, the relations between the nationalities of Lithuania are still developing. So far the Lithuanians have avoided major ethnic conflict—this despite the determined efforts of its eastern neighbors to arouse such conflict. The decisions of individuals, continuing economic crisis, and possible intervention by neighbors may, of course, all yet play significant roles in its evolution. Negative images from the past still linger to cause problems; but the general trend has been positive.

**Notes**

1. Martha Brill Olcott et al., eds., *The Soviet Multinational State: Readings and Documents* (Armonk, NY: M.E. Sharpe, 1990), p.27.

2. See John Armstrong, "The Ethnic Scene in the Soviet Union: The View of the Dictatorship," reprinted in *Journal of Soviet Nationalities* 1 (1990): 37-38.

3. Robert Blackwell, as cited in *Congressional Roundtable on U.S.-Soviet Relations: 1984 Report* (Washington, D.C.: Peace Through Law Education Fund, 1984), p. 22. A conference on Soviet affairs in December 1986, sponsored by the Harriman Institute at Columbia and the Rand/UCLA Center, completely ignored the nationalities question. See *The 27th Congress of the Communist Party of the Soviet Union: A Report from the Airlie House Conference*, December 1986.

4. See Alfred Erich Senn, *Lithuania Awakening* (Berkeley: University of California Press, 1990), p. 8.

5. See *Lietuva, Litva, Lithuania. Sbornik materialov* (Vilnius, 1989), pp. 35–46; *Lietuvos Tarybų Socialistines Respublikos pilietybes istatymas* (Vilnius: LTSR AT, 1990).

6. See *Lietuvos rytas*, April 2, 1993. Lithuanians explain the declining Russian population as follows: The Russians received citizenship and with it vouchers for

buying property; they used the vouchers to buy their apartments. Those who wanted to move to Russia could sell their apartments, and in Russia they could buy new apartments for less money and have cash left over.

7. When the atomic energy plant was being built, managers were under orders to hire Russians in preference to Lithuanians. In 1960, on the other hand, I discovered that many people whom I heard speaking Russian in public were, in fact, Poles.

8. *Sovetskaia Litva*, March 3, 1990.

9. Cf. the memoir by Georgii Efremov, *My liudi drug drugu* (Moscow: Progress, 1990).

10. Saulius Girnius and Anna Sabbat-Swidlicka, "Current Issues in Polish-Lithuanian Relations," in Radio Free Europe, *Report on Eastern Europe*, January 1, 1990, p. 42.

11. In his account of "the view of the dictatorship," Armstong had written, ". . . in view of their low degree of social mobilization . . . the Poles scarcely pose a significant problem for the regime." Armstrong, op. cit. note 2, p. 39.

12. Girnius and Sabbat-Swidlicka, op. cit. note 10, p. 41; *Sovetskaia Litva*, March 3, 1990.

13. For an example of Lithuanian expectations of reporting, see Inija Trinkuniene, "Respublikos persitvarkymo procesų atspindys Lietuvos laikraščiuose rusų ir lenkų kalbomis (kontentanalize)," in A. Matulionis et al., eds., *Lietuva ir Sajudis* (Vilnius: LMA Filosofijos, sociologijos ir teises institutas, 1990), pp. 25–28.

14. *Czerwony sztandar*, October 28, 1988.

15. Senn, op. cit. note 4, pp. 240–41.

16. Girnius and Sabbat-Swidlicka, op. cit. note 10, pp. 43–44.

17. See *Index on Censorship* 10 (October 1992): 26.

18. Vadim Bakatin, *Izbavlenie ot KGB* (Moscow: Novosti, 1992), p. 49. For an admission of the military's role, see *Izvestiia TsK KPSS* 3 (1991): 100.

19. Girnius and Sabbat-Swidlicka, op. cit. note 10, pp. 39–50.

20. *Komjaunimo tiesa*, May 6, 1989.

21. See interviews with Ciechanowicz in *Lithuania* (Warsaw, in Polish) 1 (1990): 56–58, and in *LAD*, October 15, 1989; and interview with Brodowski in *Vil'nius* (Vilnius, in Russian) 2 (1990): 84–93.

22. *Lithuania* 1 (1990): 147-51; Grinius and Sabbat-Swidlicka, op. cit. note 10, p. 44.

23. *Komjaunimo tiesa*, May 6, 1989. Vilnius was still officially part of the Polish church province. When I asked Vincentas Cardinal Sladkevičius about this in 1988, he smiled and confirmed this, but he then added, "In practice we treat it as our own." Interview, October 6, 1988.

24. Steve Burant, "Polish Lithuanian Relations: Past, Present, and Future," *Problems of Communism*, May–June 1991, pp. 67–84. Cf. the interview with the Polish ambassador in Lithuania, "Istorija-istorikams, gyvenkime del ateities," *Respublika*, April 6, 1993.

25. Cf. the reaction by Romualdas Ozolas, as recorded in his *Pirmieji atkurtosios nepriklausomybes metai* (Vilnius: Valstybinis leidybos centras, 1992), pp. 47, 63.

26. *Lietuvos Respublikos Aukščiausios Tarybos [LRAT] Stenogramos*, vol. 1 (Vilnius: Lietuvos Respublikos Aukščiausioji Taryba, 1990), pp. 114–15; see also 7: 164–70; 8: 355–88. For a more recent view of attitudes in Sniečkus, now renamed Visaginas, see the interview with V. N. Shevaldin, general director of the Ignaline power plant, in *Vil'nius* 4 (1993): 10–15.

27. *LRAT Stenogramos*, 6: 168.

28. Author's interviews in Lithuania, August 1990.

29. Czeslaw Okinczyc interview, *Pasaulis* 8 (1991): 34–38.

30. See Juozas Matakas, "The Problems of Ethnic Minorities in Lithuania: The Polish Ethnic Minority," *Lithuania Today: Politics and Economics* (Vilnius) 6 (1992): 14.

31. See his "Rozmyślając nad etapami," *Lithuania* 1 (1990): 4–10.

32. Although a Lithuanian government official told me that the Polish ambassador intervenes far more on behalf of his compatriots than does the Russian ambassador, Polish nationalists in Lithuania have expressed considerable discontent with what they see as a lack of support from Warsaw. An American official characterized the job of the Polish ambassador as the toughest diplomatic position in Vilnius.

33. The best-known Russian of Lithuania, Nikolai Medvedev, argues that the Lithuanians have handled the national question better than the Latvians and Estonians, that Russian youth are more comfortable in Lithuania than the older generation, and that Russians are doing best where they form a community and feel needed, as in Sniečkus/Visaganas. Interview, Vilnius, June 22, 1993.

34. Interview, Vilnius, June 17, 1993. See also his farewell interview before emigrating, *Lietuvos rytas*, July 27, 1993, reprinted in *Golos Litvy* 30 (1993).

35. On sympathies within the Jewish community for Soviet rule in 1939–40, see Ben-Cion Pinchuk, *Shtetl Jews under Soviet Rule* (Oxford: Basil Blackwell, 1990). In 1941 the Soviet authorities also deported Jews from Lithuania.

36. Bačiulis also complained that other Lithuanian parties had made little effort to find support among the Polish population. See also the complaint that the ZPL filed with the Lithuanian government, reprinted as "Lenkų Sajunga puola," *Atgimimas* 28 (1993): 5.

37. See Romualdas Ozolas, "Popiežiaus dovanos kiekvienam musų" *Lietuvos rytas*, September 14, 1993.

38. On Kobeckaite's views, see her interviews and articles, including: *Lithuania* 1 (1991): 22–27; *Vechernye novosti*, April 2, 1991; *Vil'nius* 6 (1991): 117–19, 10 (1991): 3–18 (especially on Russians), 6 (1992): 150–56; *Atgimimas* 9 (1993): 9; "My grazhdane gosudarstva," *Vil'nius* 5 (1993): 108–16. Among the publications of the Department of Nationalities are: *National Minorities in Lithuania*

(Vilnius: Centre of National Researches of Lithuania, 1992), and *Tautines mažumos Lietuvos Respublikoje* (Vilnius: Valstybinis nacionalinių tyrimų centras, 1992). The Russian community in Lithuania has published *Russkie v Litve—problemy i perspektivy* (Vilnius: Prezidium Soveta Russkoi obshchiny Litvy, 1992).

# 13

# Ethnonationalism and the Disintegration of Yugoslavia

## ROBIN ALISON REMINGTON

Nationalism, like fire, can build or destroy. For politicians and societies blessed with stable political institutions and viable economies, nationalism is an element of power signifying commitment to a nation-state. In this sense nationalism functions as an instrument for mobilizing support for national interests, national goals. Such nationalism contributes to political cohesion. Yet under conditions of political/economic instability nationalism fuels aggression, ignites wars, and like a forest fire devastates everything in its path.

This analysis starts from the assumption that "nationalism is a state of mind"[1] and that a nation is a collection of individuals who by self-definition have become a nation. Nations may be, but in the Balkans usually are not, coterminous with states. Ethnonationalism is a conscious bond between members of a nation whether or not they are living in the same state, the conceptualization of "us" defined by the presence of "them."[2]

This chapter investigates the role of ethnonationalism in the disintegration of Yugoslavia. It explores the tentative hypothesis that the popular stereotype of historically determined Balkan tribalism as the primary culprit in reducing this once peaceful, multiethnic society to savagery is an oversimplification of a complex interaction of variables: including flawed Yugoslav and international institutions, criminally irresponsible political leaders manipulating national/ethnic tension for personal gain, and an unstable international security environment. The focus is on what defines the nature of relations between "us" and "them" among the southern Slav nations battling for new borders. Since the disintegration of Yugoslavia is unlikely to stop—the four-month cease-fire did not hold long enough to stop the fighting in Bosnia and Herzegovina on the "basis of" the international contact group's (Great

Britain, France, Germany, Russia, and the United States) 1994 effort at map-making—acceptance of Slovenia, Croatia, and Bosnia and Herzegovina as members of the United Nations in May 1992, provides a manageable cutoff point for this analysis.

### The Nationalism of Nonstate Nations

It is important to understand the origin of ethnonationalism in the former Yugoslavia. For centuries this part of the Balkans has been a crossroads of competing empires. The second Yugoslavia (1945–91) was a young state trying to meld together first five then—with the addition of the Bosnian Muslims—six nations with very different historical experiences and political cultures, along with literally dozens of nationalities. Ethnonationalism as it influenced the dynamics that led to the collapse of Yugoslavia involves the primary Serb-Croat relationship, the Serb-Albanian clash over whether history or demography should control the balance of power in Kosovo, backlash Slovene and Bosnian Muslim nationalism, and the Macedonian question that never dies.

The overarching problem is that both Croats and Serbs developed their national identities as nonstate nations in the womb of competing empires. During centuries of separation, these identities survived on myths of past glories and independence. Such ethnonationalism was essential to preserve and save the nation. It is not unique. Rather, much like the postcolonial nations of Asia and Africa, the first and second Yugoslav states emerged from imperial domination divided by history, religion, arbitrary boundaries, conflicting political cultures, and incompatible expectations in relation to their shared futures.

Although the international community and media have focused on the evil of Serbian aggression in the name of "greater Serbia," memories of past glories mingle with present aspirations in Croatia as well. In his interview with Croatian president Franjo Tudjman, Steve Coll describes the picture of King Tomislav in battle armor above Tudjman's desk and the picture in the lobby of decapitated Turkish Muslims, as Croatian knights ride through a conquered village beneath angels carrying a banner that reads "Glory and Victory"[3]; both conjure up images of past glories.

In addition to the dysfunctional role of nonstate nation ethnonationalism for state-building, there are three subthemes from Serbian history that haunt those who struggle to restore or keep the peace within or among the successor states of post-Communist Yugoslavia. First, the territory being fought over in the newly independent state of Croatia, largely—though not totally—corresponds to the military frontier where Serbs have lived for generations. Second, the Bosnian Serbs have a long history of rebelling against international decisions forcing them to live under what they consider unacceptable foreign administration. The 1878 Congress of Berlin that led to Austrian annexation of the region in 1908, must share the blame for the 1914 assassination of the Austrian Archduke Franz Ferdinand in Sarajevo and the start of World War I. Finally, Kosovo, now populated by an estimated 85 percent ethnic majority of Albanians is the beating heart of Serbian history: the sacred birthplace of the Serbian church in 1346.

Unfortunately, Kosovo is also the cradle of modern Albanian nationalism and the home of 1.6 million of the 2.05 million ethnic Albanians recorded in the 1991 census. Of 3.5 million Albanians in the world, more than one-third live in Yugoslav successor states, and by far the majority of these reside in Kosovo. Just as Serbian politicians play upon fears for the safety of Serbs living in Croatia, as well as in Bosnia and Herzegovina, Albanian politicians demand protection for their "martyred brothers" in Kosovo. In short, notwithstanding some media exaggeration, there is good reason to worry that Kosovo is the weakest link for those whose nightmare is a widening war in the Balkans.[4]

Bosnian Muslims are perhaps the hardest nation to categorize. These are Slav Muslims, not ethnically distinct from Serbs and Croats. Indeed, among Bosnian Muslims themselves, as well as among both Serbs and Croats, there are those who would argue that all Bosnian Muslims are Croats or Serbs respectively.[5] In this view, Bosnian Muslims are an artificially created nation, the product of President Josip Broz Tito's attempts to contain Serb-Croat conflict in Bosnia and Herzegovina, and also designed to advance the cause of nonalignment in the Middle East. The category "ethnic Muslim" was used by the regime as of 1968. By the 1981 census, some two million respondents (8.9 percent of the total population of Yugoslavia) identified themselves in this category.[6] By the 1991 census, that number had gone up by roughly 65,000, with 1.9 million of the total making up 43 percent of the population of Bosnia and Herzegovina—that is, before policies of "ethnic cleansing" changed the population ratios in ways yet to be recorded.

To return to the larger picture, having established that Serbian and Croatian ethnonationalism alike were largely dysfunctional during the attempted transition to a shared southern Slav state, it is important to look at the political/institutional context through which these nations expressed their hopes and fears. Indeed, in 1918 neither Croats nor Serbs were engaged in nation-building in the Western sense of that concept. Rather, both wanted to imprint their own preferred organizational model. These conflicting state-building agenda continued throughout the second Yugoslavia, and are central to the 1991 collapse into civil war.

### Continuity with Interwar Yugoslavia

Given their experience with Hungarian promises made and promises unkept, Croats brought a deep suspicion of unequal relationships to the 1917 negotiating table in Corfu. Not surprisingly, the Council of Croats and Slovenes wanted a confederal Yugoslavia, a partnership of equals. Equally predictable, Serbs saw the proposed southern Slav state as the road to a restoration of Tsar Dusan's medieval Serbian Empire. In the 1990s, Slovenia and Croatia again turned to a confederal community of nations (EC, consociational model) as the appropriate constitutional framework for post-Communist Yugoslavia. Serbs again looked to an integrated federation in which the Serbian population (roughly 9 million of the 23 million total) would translate into political advantage.

Here the failure of interwar Yugoslavia underlines the conflicting political cultures that divided the Kingdom of Serbs, Croats, and Slovenes. When King Aleksander disbanded Parliament and established a Serbian dictatorship in 1929, Serbs accepted this as an appropriate law and order measure and blamed Croats for the parliamentary gridlock. Conversely, Croatians perceived these measures as de facto martial law, what many saw as Serbian colonization of Croatia.

Croatian militants responded by organizing a violent resistance movement, the Ustashe, that retaliated by participating in the assassination of the Serbian king during his trip to France in 1934. When the Nazi war machine carved up the first Yugoslav state in 1941, Hitler sent back the leader of the Ustashe, Dr. Ante Pavelic, as head of the putatively Independent Kingdom of Croatia. This was the first independent Croatian state in eight hundred years, and it included Bosnia and Herzegovina.

## Fascist Croatia and WWII

Having a clear idea of "what's in a name," the Croats invited an Italian duke, who never left Italy, to rule under the title of King Tomislav II. Pavelic's SS set out on a campaign of "ethnic cleansing," killing hundreds of thousands of Serbs, Jews, and Gypsies. Croatians who resisted the slaughter died with them in death camps run by indigenous Croatian fascists.[7] Men, women, and children were herded into Orthodox churches and burned alive. Jasenovac became the symbol of a Serbian holocaust. Serbs blamed Bosnian Muslims for allying with or at least not resisting Croatian brutalities, and committed atrocities in retaliation against both Croats and Muslims.

## Ethnonationalism and Communist Yugoslavia

Given the legacy of the failed interwar experiment with national integration and mutual wartime atrocities, it is not surprising that Communist Yugoslavia attempted to blacklist ethnic politics from the political stage.[8] The goal was to replace the first Yugoslavia, seen by non-Serbian nations as a de facto greater Serbia, with a southern Slav federation pledged to the brotherhood, unity, and equality of all participating nations.[9] The myth of wartime partisan solidarity became the cornerstone of a "revitalized belief system"[10] that was institutionalized in the form of a multinational federalism, which was designed to buy time while the revolution redirected nationalist passions into class identity.[11] Thus, from the start, the legitimacy of Communist

Yugoslavia rested on the Communist party's performance in meeting not only socialist but also ethnonationalist expectations.

The implicit social contract committed the party's leaders to a socialist revolution in which some nations were *not* more equal than others. On the one hand, class identity would provide the needed national cohesion for state-building and national integration. On the other, as Serbs were quick to point out in the 1990s, this amounted to reinstating the Slovene and Croatian community of nations model of how to live together, thereby punishing the Serbs.

### *Socialist Self-Management: the Yugoslav Alternative*

In 1948, the break with the Soviet Union forced Yugoslavia to detour off the Soviet road to socialism.[12] Notwithstanding the intentions of those who proclaimed the brave new world of self-management at home and nonalignment abroad, the Yugoslav challenge to Moscow inadvertently opened the back door to ethnic politics in the guise of in-system territorial/ bureaucratic bargaining. Perhaps inevitably, insistence on Yugoslav's national road to socialism within the international communist movement legitimized demands for increased autonomy by the constituent nations of the Yugoslav Federation. This had repercussions for center-republic power sharing, reducing the Yugoslav Communist party to a League of Communists—the League of Communists of Yugoslavia, (LCY)—more vulnerable to challenges from strengthened regional party organizations. Since these republics and autonomous provinces were largely synonymous with national identities, this essentially rehabilitated the nation.

Over time these problems were further compounded by a lack of political development that, according to Samuel Huntington's criteria, amounted to a low-level of political institutionalization[13]—that is, the failure of Communist Yugoslavia to create a viable, autonomous political machinery for resolving ethnonational conflict. And so, contrary to the intent, by the 1960s the ideological propositions of nonaligned, self-managing socialism combined with targets of opportunity created by a booming Yugoslav economy to form a volatile mix.

The campaign for market socialism divided republic/provincial party organizations along territorial and bureaucratic lines. This created regional political actors motivated by acceptable, in-system economic nationalism. Less acceptable national spokesmen reemerged in the wake of foreign policy strategies that saw Yugoslavia's multinational society as a bridge to other key parts of the Balkans and the Middle East. As part of the same package, support for Macedonian nationalism became an instrument in Yugoslav-Bulgarian relations.[14] In those days, the Bosnian Muslim campaign for national status appeared to have been an acceptable price to pay for Yugoslav influence-building among Muslim countries in the Middle East and North Africa.[15]

In short, Yugoslav domestic and foreign policy imperatives alike worked to erode the distinction between good and bad nationalism, setting off cycles of centralization-decentralization that weakened the federal center. Despite President Tito's crackdown of 1970–71 on Croatian ethnonationalism in the form of a mass national movement, the balance of power between republic party organizations and the LCY shifted steadily towards the regional parties.

In this context, four repercussions of Yugoslavia's self-managing alternative to "real socialism," Soviet style, belong on the list of long-term causes of the 1991 collapse of post-Communist Yugoslavia into civil war:

1. Much like the West during the Cold War, Yugoslav policymakers became used to a security situation in which external threat papered over ethnonational differences rather than resolving the them.
2. As a result, the Yugoslav armed forces became politicized and accustomed to a privileged economic and political position within Yugoslav society.
3. The permanent identity crisis of the LCY over its relationship to proliferating self-managing institutions limited party adaptability, undermined coherence, and essentially substituted Tito's charismatic authority for political institutionalization.
4. An unintended de facto association of territorial/bureaucratic politics with ethnonational political agenda reopened the back door to national/ethnic politics.

### From Charismatic Authority to Collective Leadership

President Tito was the George Washington of Communist Yugoslavia, and an architect of the Nonaligned Movement. He walked on the world stage. Tito was the Godfather who called the shots, and banged heads where necessary to broker ethnonational conflict. When he died in 1980, Tito left his people a complex, cumbersome political machinery that was fundamentally grounded in his own charismatic authority, for which there was no substitute. Known as the Titoist solution,[16] and enshrined in the Constitution of 1974, this was a deliberate diffusion of power designed to contain debilitating power struggles among would-be successors.

Party-state collective leadership based on four key elements assured that all the republic/provincial party organizations would have their turn in the room at the top of the pyramid of power:

1. federalization of the party into nine parts (the regional parties plus the JNA party organization);
2. interrepublic and provincial consensus as a decisionmaking procedure;
3. territorial/ethnic keys for political jobs at all levels; and

4. rotation schedules designed to de-professionalize politics in theory, and prevent any vestige of cadre job security in practice.

This quota-system expanded the number of unofficial political actors in what inevitably became an interrepublic/provincial and center-regional political tug-of-war. Notwithstanding its continued responsibility for foreign policy, defense, and an amorphous "united market," the federal government did not stand a chance. With all undesignated powers devolving to the republic/provincial level, the immediate result was a hemorrhaging of power from the federal center to regional party organization. The federal party was rapidly reduced to mediating between powerful republic/provincial fiefdoms for declining resources.

Contradiction number one: *While it may have been the best that could be done at the time, nothing in the political apprenticeship during Tito's lifetime prepared his successors to operate the complex, post-Tito, political machinery he left behind.*

Tito's economic legacy was still more of a liability. Tito had ignored economic advisers who, as early as 1978, were pressing the president to do something about the growing hard-currency debt.[17] His luckless successors did not have that choice. The roughly $20 billion hard currency debt became subject to continual IMF demands for an austerity budget that required steadily declining standards of living. For Yugoslav workers, housewives, and pensioners facing the post-Tito economic facts of life was a painful shock. Thus, "the sacrificed generation" paid for Tito's economic mistakes. Given the fact that the Tito myth was essential to political stability, those stuck with cleaning up his economic act could not even say don't blame us.

### Rise of the National Gladiators

Clearly, legitimacy via economic performance was not in the cards, yet all politicians crave and need legitimacy to govern. The political merry-go-round of collective leadership denied name recognition and institutionalized legitimacy to those who jumped in and out of the room at the top with dizzying speed. The lack of slots reserved for those who thought of themselves as Yugoslavs on the collective presidencies or in the foreign service was a serious flaw in relation to ethnonationalism. It was well to speak in the name of Yugoslavia, but one's political career depended on appealing to voters closer to one's home base. Step-by-step, ethnonationalist politics became the only truly political game in town.

Contradictions two and three: *The imperatives of economic reform and political consolidation of a viable, integrated Yugoslavia were fundamentally at odds, while the Titoist solution simultaneously weakened the federal government and removed incentives for post-Tito politicians to think of themselves as Yugoslavs.*

**Ethnonationalist Precipitants**

*Kosovo: Albanian, Serb, and Slovene Perspectives*

By giving the Serbian Autonomous Province of Kosovo direct, if not exactly equal, access to the ruling party/state bodies, the Constitution of 1974 escalated ethno-nationalist ambitions of the Albanian majority of the province. The issue centered on demands for republic status. After all, if 1.7 million Slovenes, 1.3 million Mace-donians, and 577,000 Montenegrins could have their own republic, why not 1.6 million Albanians—the majority of the population in Kosovo? The irredentist struggle between Serbian historical claims and Albanian demographic demands entered a new stage in which, for the first time, federal institutions worked to the favor of the Albanians who held de facto control, but denied them real juridical control.

Militants, ranging from those most intent on republic status to out-and-out separatists, became an open part of the Kosovar Albanian political spectrum. Nation-alists riots in March and April of 1981 led to a state of siege, with federal troops acting as what the Albanian population viewed as an occupation force. In these con-ditions, many Kosovar Serbs and Montenegrins began to leave the province, further weakening Serbia's demographic case.

In turn, the resulting Serb, Montenegrin, and Macedonian backlash proliferated "nationalist excesses" throughout other federal units.[18] That process culminated in 1986 with a controversial draft of a memorandum by the Serbian Academy of Sciences which attacked the Constitution of 1974, warned of Albanian sponsored genocide against Kosovar Serbs, accused Croatia and Slovenia of obstructing Yugo-slav unity, and insisted that Serbs were deprived of their national identity and deliberately divided in Tito's Yugoslavia.[19]

This memorandum provided the platform for Slobodan Milosevic's transforma-tion from a relatively unknown party boss into a virtually iconic defender of the Serbian nation, which came in April 1987 with his pledge to protect Kosovar Serbs. Pandering to Serbian backlash ethnonationalism, Milosevic vowed to derail eco-nomic reform until the issue of counter-revolutionary activity in Kosovo was solved; Kosovo reintegrated into Serbia proper.

The Serbian godfather's populist, street politics were particularly threatening to the Slovenes, who feared that if Serbian hegemonic demands could eliminate the constitutional rights of the 1.6 million Albanians in Kosovo, the rights of 1.7 million Slovenes were also at risk. In this sense, the crisis in Kosovo intensified what was gingerly called the "Slovene Syndrome." Undeniably, Slovene internal politics and Ljubljana's positions on all-Yugoslav political/economic issues were discernibly different from those of the other republics.

Whether or not such differences added up to a syndrome, three of them came to play a crucial role in the collapse of Yugoslav. First, the Slovene liberal media policy horrified hardline Serbian politicians, who were furious that Slovene journalists would suggest that Serbia's historically heavy-handed policies in Kosovo, indeed

Serbian historical nationalism, had contributed to the ongoing difficulties Serbia faced in the province. Second, the very economic prosperity of Slovenia, where there was virtually no unemployment and per capita income was roughly twice the national average, led to resentment at the flow of Slovene foreign currency to the federal government or in the form of subsidies to their southern neighbors.[20] In this regard, Slovenes began to talk about "defensive nationalism."[21] Finally, long-standing tensions between Slovenia and the Yugoslav military escalated over the arrest and trial of three Slovene journalists accused of leaking military secrets. Thus began the events that led Janez Jansa, to his fateful position as Slovene defense minister in June 1991.

### The Romanian Revolution

Mikhail Gorbachev's "new political thinking" for his country and the world reposi-tioned Yugoslavia from the engine of East European systemic change to the caboose. With the end of the Soviet military veto over East Central European reform, com-munist governments crumbled with the Berlin Wall. Previously hegemonic commu-nist parties became stragglers on the road to multiparty democracies and market economies. In Yugoslavia, politicians, workers, students, and housewives all knew that the system was in crisis, but there was no agreement on what was to be done.

The violent overthrow of the Romanian president and dictator, Nicolae Ceausescu, in December of 1989, lacerated the concept of "socialism in one family," and shook the party and society alike. Amid a growing sense of frustration and anger at political gridlock, the LCY accepted the principle of opposition parties and gave up its formal monopoly of power at the January 1990 14th Extraordinary Party Congress.

Still, the League of Communists of Yugoslavia stood deadlocked over the long-standing conflict among the nations of Yugoslavia concerning political organization and the rules of state-building, that is, over incompatible visions of Yugoslavia as a community of equal nations (the European Community [EC] model) or Yugoslavia as an integrated federal system (a "greater Serbia" model)—the very issue upon which the first Yugoslavia had floundered. The 14th LCY Congress could not resolve the differences between those who thought that the Titoist solution had gone much too far and those who felt it had not gone far enough. Although officially the Congress was only postponed, committees charged with working out a compromise platform never had a chance. By July 1990, even Milosevic had abandoned the LCY and established his own Socialist party of Serbia (SPS).

### Multiparty Regional Elections

With the failure of the federal party to survive in the new political environment of multiparty politics, all eyes now turned to the new cast of political actors emerging from regional multiparty elections.[22] Center-right parties dominated the elections in Croatia and Slovenia, while nationalist coalitions shared power in Bosnia and Herzegovina, and Macedonia. Milosevic stayed on as president of Serbia. The SPS won control of the Serbian Parliament and found a willing ally in the winning Communist party of Montenegro, headed by Momir Bulatovic. The interests and constituents of these winners had little in common beyond their strategy of appealing to ethnonational fears vis-à-vis their ethnonational agenda.

Yugoslav Prime Minister Ante Markovic's favorable rating in the polls[23] did not translate into any significant victory for his hastily constructed Alliance for Reform Forces in any of the six republics. Markovic had organized too late. The defeat of his party further weakened the authority of the already staggering federal government. Worse still, the prime minister came to lose credibility as a neutral broker as he engaged contending forces in the electoral arena.

There can be no doubt that the victory of Franjo Tudjman's Croatian Democratic Union (CDU) in the spring of 1990 reflected an intensified ethnonationalism among Croats. Like the nationalist fever that swept Serbia in 1987–88, Croatia was gripped by political euphoria. The Croatian voters saw Tudjman's victory as the chance to make Croatia the republic of Croatians.

Monuments against fascism disappeared, along with reference to the political rights of the 600,000 Serbian minority in the Republic's new Constitution.[24] Croatian history was rehabilitated. That history, along with the flag of the ancient Kingdom of Croatia, aroused very different emotions in Croats and the Serbian minority that had survived the massacres of Serbs living in the fascist Independent Kingdom of Croatia.[25]

Serbs in Knin, the heart of the Krajina region, immediately warned that if Croatia could leave Yugoslavia, they would leave Croatia. Serbian militants responded to Croatian "sovereignty" and attempted to implement their own self-proclaimed sovereignty by harassing tourists and blocking the main road from Zagreb to the Adriatic coast. This cut the artery of Croatian tourism. Tudjman retaliated with an "ethnically pure" Croatian paramilitary police. Croats agreed with the measure as an appropriate response to a law and order problem. Krajina Serbs saw it as a return to policies of Croatian fascism.

Thus, Serbian memories of what happened to the Serbian minority in the last independent Croatia combined with Croatian fears of Milosevic's hegemonic ambitions to destroy the fabric of Yugoslav national/ethic coexistence. As these ethnonational passions flared, Croats and Serbs still committed to the founding principle of brotherhood, unity, and equality for all Yugoslav nations were pushed aside. In Serbia and Croatia alike, fear was manipulated by the would-be defenders of the nation for political advantage. Just as Milosevic's god/savior image was enshrined by his skillful playing on fears for the safety of the shrinking Serbian minority in Kosovo, Tudjman cast his Serbian counterpart as a villain, while ever the more glorifying Croatian historic symbols, thereby expanding Serbian fears pertaining to the safety of Serbs in Croatia.

Serbs considered Croatian declarations of sovereignty short of independence as a threat to the integrity of the Yugoslav state. Conversely, Croats interpreted Milosevic's warning that if Croatia became independent, he would reopen the question of borders as a blatant Serbian landgrab. The operatic, increasingly sectarian nature of political rhetoric on all sides magnified the politics of distrust and suspicion.

Milosevic attempted to bring the army into this political fray—in order to strengthen his hand vis-à-vis Croatia, and to deal with the growing Serbian internal opposition that brought Belgrade to a halt following the March 9, 1991, student and opposition party mass demonstrations—to no avail. When the March 15 Serbian resolution to give the army emergency power was voted down by one vote in the collective presidency, Borisav Jovic, Serbia's representative resigned. Milosevic's own refusal to recognize the authority of the presidency[26] left little doubt that he also was unwilling to play by the extant rules.

The subsequent role reversal in which the "sovereign" republics of Slovenia and Croatia came to the defense of the federation, allows one to assume that as late as March 1991 all parties still engaged in a choreography of struggle over a shared Yugoslavia. That brief opportunity for reconciliation did not survive the Serbian/ Montenegrin attempt to abort the normal rotation schedule of the state presidency, and prevent the Croatian representative, Stjepan Mesic, from taking over as president in mid-May 1991 as mandated.

## Slovenia and the Army

Given the erosion of normally understood meanings attached to the term "sovereignty," and interviews in Ljubljana the week before Slovenia declared its "independence" at the end of June 1991,[27] there is reason to believe that this step was yet another stage in the jockeying to control what kind of post-Communist Yugoslavia would emerge. By itself, the Slovene declaration might or might not have led to actual separation and civil war. However, what was seen in Ljubljana as the less than friendly decision of the Croats to piggy-back on the Slovene initiative complicated matters. More seriously, the attempt by Slovene policymakers to renege on their agreement to allow joint customs presence on the borders during ongoing negotiations with the federal government[28] resulted in a bungled show of federal military force. Once the shooting started, it threw control of the Slovene political spectrum into the hands of those who equated "independence" with immediate separation.

Slovene defense minister Janez Jansa—the former journalist tried by the military for intending to print military secrets, and who had reason to dislike the JNA—escalated the conflict by proclaiming that the army had "declared war" against Slovenia.[29] It was an overstatement, yet use of the army to demonstrate federal authority[30] was a milestone on the road to civil war.

The European Community brokered a cease-fire, a three months cooling-off period. But the damage to the corporate identity of the JNA as having been defeated on the ground by the Slovene Territorial Defense Forces, and the effect of television pictures showing army recruits in pajamas being sent back to Belgrade with the Red Cross, had fateful repercussions. A most dangerous casualty of the Slovenia prelude to civil war was that of moderates within the JNA leadership. As a consequence, when local Serbian authorities in the self-proclaimed autonomous region of Krajina went on the offensive and declared that they were uniting with Bosanka Krajina in Bosnia and Herzegovina to form "a greater Serbian community," a very different army responded.

### Germany and the Internationalization of Civil War in Croatia

Unfortunately for all concerned, the civil war in Croatia broke out just as a united Germany was trying out its foreign policy wings, and still smarting from the criticism that Bonn had shirked its responsibility by sending money instead of men to the Desert Storm operation. Croatian guestworkers in Germany and Germans who saw the small Dalmatian towns where they vacationed and made friends attacked, and the wondrous walled city of Dubrovnik shelled on their nightly television screens, demanded action.

Whether or not German foreign minister Hans-Dietrich Genscher genuinely believed recognition would teach Milosevic a lesson and end his campaign to recreate a "greater Serbia,"[31] Serbs had a more sinister interpretation. In Belgrade, German warnings that Bonn would recognize Croatia if the federal army did not exercise restraint were attacked as policies of a "Fourth Reich." Tudjman was cast as a 1990s Ustashe pawn in a revanchist German game to gain control over the Adriatic. Regardless of whether such accusations were largely paranoia, the empirical effect of the German attempt at deterrence was an escalation of the very violence that it sought to contain.

Moreover, the warning to Belgrade was heard as a call to fight harder in Zagreb. Croatian forces blockaded JNA garrisons in Croatia and then attacked them. This strategy changed the character of the war in Croatia. With 25,000 soldiers and their families hostage, JNA imperatives were no longer those of the federal government or even Serbian political goals. This was a corporate military establishment whose primary mission had become to protect its own. Army leaders warned that for each army installation that was destroyed something of value to Croatia would pay a price.[32] Objections from the federal government, as well as demands by the prime minister for the resignation of then Defense Minister Kadijevic and other high-ranking military leaders were swept aside. In December 1991, Prime Minister Markovic resigned to protest the army's share of the proposed federal budget.

**War in Bosnia and Herzegovina**

For months the European Community and United Nations brokered cease-fires were a revolving door to the next round of violence, as Serbs fought to expand territory under their control before the fighting stopped, while Croats fought to hold on to what they had and search for weapons. Then, on the fifteenth try, the U.N. special envoy, former American Secretary of State Cyrus Vance, negotiated a ceasefire that held together long enough to bring in 14,000 U.N. peacekeepers. Thus began the saga of the United Nations Protection Forces (UNPROFOR) in Croatia.

However, reducing the Croatian front to low-level intermittent conflict could not prevent the looming destruction in Bosnia and Herzegovina. Vance and the president of the Bosnian collective presidency, Alija Izetbegovic, both warned the EC that yielding to German pressure for recognition of Croatia and Slovenia by an arbitrary January 15, 1992, deadline would push the war into this vulnerable multiethnic heartland of Yugoslavia. The Bosnian president appealed to the U.N. for assistance to prevent rising violence in response to the republic's declaration of sovereignty, and the subsequent demand for constitutional independence by the Parliament of Bosnian Serbs.[33] He was denied, but as a gesture the U.N. made Sarajevo the headquarters for U.N. forces in Croatia. It was not enough to stem the tide. As predicted, the EC-mandated referendum[34] was accompanied by a spread of the war to Bosnia and Herzegovina. U.N. membership for Slovenia, Croatia, and Bosnia and Herzegovina followed on May 22, 1992.

**An Obituary for Yugoslavia: Some Concluding Thoughts**

In analyzing the role of ethnonationalism in the disintegration of the second Yugoslav state, it is helpful to one to focus on the categories of long-term causes, precipitants, and accelerators of war within and among the successor states of post-Communist Yugoslavia. In relation to long-term causes, the findings of this analysis point to ethnonationalism and a failure of political institutionalization as inseparable culprits in the collapse of both interwar and post–World War II southern Slav efforts at state-building. And in both cases international events derailed what might have been successful attempts to overcome conflicting nationalist agenda, that is, the rise of Hitler's Germany in the 1930s and the collapse of communist regimes and parties in East Central Europe in the 1990s.

As for precipitants, undoubtedly both Milosevic and Tudjman rode the tiger of ethnonationalism to power. Yet it was the flawed "Titoist solution" that left his successors with a political machinery with no incentives or rewards for politicians who thought of themselves as Yugoslavs. It was the power-brokers of the international financial community, for example, the IMF and the World Bank, that created conditions that deprived post-Tito politicians of economic performance. When the chips were down, Milosevic's maneuvering in the spring of 1991 was not as the savior of the Serbs but to save his own skin from growing Serbian opposition. The 1991 declaration of independence by Slovenia was as much to be free of the economic burden of its southern neighbors, in response to the vision of a New Europe, as it was to assert an ethnonational identity. In this sense, ethnonationalism must be seen as one of a package of precipitants, and not as *the* precipitant in Yugoslavia's fragmentation.

With respect to accelerators of civil war that led to disintegration of the juridical Yugoslavia that existed in 1991, it appears that Serbian and Croatian ethnonationalism was less important than the JNA's behavior as a corporate military establishment run amok, and much less important than the fact that the EC caved in to German pressure on the timetable for recognition of Croatia before Zagreb had met the conditions of the EC's own commission with regard to protection of the rights of the Serbian minority.

With the end of the 1994 cease-fire between the Bosnian Serbs and the Bosnian Muslim–led government, intense fighting resumed in the spring of 1995.[35] In the flux that has accompanied the disintegration of Yugoslavia, the dead must be counted among the ongoing repercussions of the EC's arbitrary decision that any former Yugoslav republic seeking recognition had to request it by December 23, 1991 (the only criterion for according such recognition to Bosnia and Herzegovina was a referendum boycotted by the Bosnian Serbs), that continue to unfold in rising body counts, untold numbers of wounded, and the 2–3 million refugees created by war and deliberate policies of "ethnic cleansing."

The destructive potential of ethnonationalism must be reckoned with as the international system seeks for a new world order to replace the power vacuum left by the collapse of communism in East Central Europe and the Soviet Union, especially in the light of the shared search for democracy, which raises the persistent question: democracy for whom?—the citizen, the nation? In the changed political environment, those who seek democracy as a nation have more opportunities for political organization and access. This can be most threatening, particularly to those with competing historical or demographic claims and agenda. Expanded opportunities to participate in multiparty systems and procedural democracy often foster increased expressions of ethnonationalism. However, in the successor states of Yugoslavia and their Balkan neighbors—as in Canada, Spain, and Great Britain— such ethnonationalism is the political condition within which democracy must be built and/or nurtured if it is to exist at all.

**Appendix A:**
**Ethnic Composition of Yugoslav Successor States**

| | | | |
|---|---|---|---|
| **Slovenia** | | **The Federal Republic of Yugoslavia** | |
| (UN May 22,1992) | | (not recognized by US/EU 1/19/95) | |
| Slovene | 91% | **Montenegro** | |
| Croats | 3 | Montenegrins | 61.8% |
| Serbs | 2 | Muslims | 14.6 |
| Other | 4 | Serbs | 9.3 |
| **Croatia** | | Albanians | 6.6 |
| (UN May 22, 1992) | | Yugoslavs | 4.0 |
| Croats | 77.9% | Other | 2.7 |
| Serbs | 12.2 | **Serbia*** | |
| Yugoslavs | 2.2 | Serbs | 85% |
| Muslims | 1.0 | Yugoslavs | 5 |
| Other | 6.7 | Muslims | 3 |
| **Bosnia and Herzegovina** | | Montenegrins | 2 |
| (UN May 22,1992) | | Romanies | 2 |
| Muslim | 43.7% | Other | 3 |
| Serbs | 31.4 | | |
| Croats | 17.3 | **Vojvodina** | |
| Yugoslavs | 5.5 | Serbs | 65% |
| Other | 2.1 | Hungarians | 20 |
| | | Croats | 5 |
| **TFYR Macedonia** | | Romanian | 2 |
| (UN April 7, 1993) | | Other | 4 |
| Macedonians | 64.6% | | |
| Albanians | 21.0 | **Kosovo** | |
| Turks | 4.8 | Albanians | 82%** |
| Romanies | 2.7 | Serbs | 10 |
| (Gypsies) | | Muslims | 3 |
| Serbs | 2.2 | Romanies | 2 |
| Others | 4.7 | Other | 3 |

*Sources*: Ruza Petrovic, "The National Composition of Yugoslavia's Population, 1991," *Yugoslav Survey*. 33.1 (1992) based on 1991 census data.

*Notes*:

\* The Petrovic article does not give a breakdown of Serbia proper, Vojvodina, and Kosovo; these figures are taken from the CIA, *The Former Yugoslavia: A Map Folio* (Washington, DC, 1992).

\*\* Official Yugoslav figures. Kosovar Albanians boycotted the 1991 census.

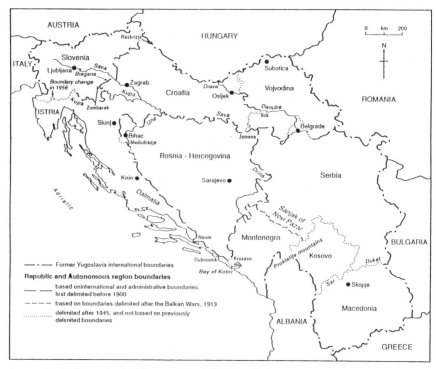

**Appendix B.** Yugoslavia: Former Republic Boundaries

## Notes

1. Hans Kohn, *The Idea of Nationalism: A Study of Its Origins and Background*, 2nd. ed. (New York: Macmillan, 1961), p. 16.

2. Peter Zwick, *National Communism* (Boulder, CO: Westview Press, 1983), p. 4.

3. *The Washington Post National Weekly Edition* (March 8–14, 1993), p. 8.

4. Brian Hall, "A Holy War in Waiting," *The New York Times Magazine*, May 9, 1993. See also, Dusan Janaic, "National Identity: Movements and Nationalism of Serbs and Albanians," *Balkan Forum* 3.1(10 )(March 1995): 19–84.

5. Pedro Ramet, "Primordial Ethnicity or Modern Nationalism: The Case of Yugoslavia's Muslims," *Nationalities Papers* 13.2 (Fall 1985): 170.

6. *Statisticki kalendar Jugolavije 1982* (Belgrade, 1982), p. 37.

7. Serbian author Dr. Lazo M. Kostich, cites German sources to substantiate his estimate of 750,000, *Holocaust in the Independent State of Croatia* (Chicago:

Liberty Press, 1981), p. 4; British historian Fred Singleton puts the figure at 350,000, *Twentieth-Century Yugoslavia* (New York: Columbia University Press, 1976), p. 88.

8. See Paul Shoup's pioneering study, *Communism and the Yugoslav National Question* (New York: Columbia University Press, 1968).

9. Phyllis Auty, *Tito* (New York: Ballantine, 1972), p. 81.

10. M. George Zaninovich, *The Development of Socialist Yugoslavia* (Baltimore: The John Hopkins University Press, 1968), p. 44ff.

11. See Shoup, op. cit. note 8. Also see Walker Connor, *The National Question in Marxist-Leninist Theory and Strategy* (Princeton, NJ: Princeton University Press, 1984), p. 222ff.

12. This section draws upon my earlier chapters "Self-Management and Development Strategies in Socialist Yugoslavia," in Gerasimos Augustinos, ed., *Diverse Paths to Modernity in Southeastern Europe: Essays in Development* (Westport, CT: Greenwood Press, 1991), pp. 57–87; and "The Collapse of the Yugoslav Alternative," in Zoltan Barany and Ivan Volgyes, eds., *The Legacies of Communism in Eastern Europe* (Baltimore: The Johns Hopkins University Press, 1995), pp. 267–88.

13. Samuel P. Huntington, *Political Order in Changing Societies* (New Haven and London: Yale University Press, 1968), pp. 12–24.

14. Stephen E. Palmer and Robert R. King, *Yugoslav Communism and the Macedonian Question* (Hamden, CT: Shoe String Press, 1971).

15. Dennison I. Rusinow, "Yugoslavia's Muslim Nation," *Universities Field Staff International (UFSI) Report*, no. 8 Europe, 1982.

16. See Robin Alison Remington, "Nation versus Class in Yugoslavia," *Current History* 86.523 (November 1987).

17. Interviews with economists in Belgrade May–December 1981. Indeed, reportedly until a team of outside experts came to assess the damage, post–Tito policymakers did not know the actual amount of that debt.

18. Sabrina P. Ramet, *Nationalism and Federalism in Yugoslavia, 1962–1991* (Bloomington, IN: Indiana University Press, 1992), p. 198.

19. This memorandum was illegally distributed by the Belgrade daily *Borba*, then officially banned. Excepts in *Vecernije novosti* (Belgrade) September 24, 1986; *RFE Research Report* (October 16, 1986).

20. According to one member of the Slovene LCY presidency, Slovenia accounted for 25 percent of Yugoslavia's hard currency exports while 20–30 percent of the Slovene national product went to less-developed regions. *The New York Times*, July 13, 1986.

21. *Frankfurter Allegemeine*, August 21, 1986, cited by Sabrina Ramet, op. cit. note 18, p. 209.

22. For a detailed analysis see, Lenard J. Cohen, "Yugoslavia's Pluralist Revolution: The Democratic Prelude to Civil War," *In Depth: A Journal for Values and Public Policy* 3.1 (Winter 1993): 115–50.

23. *Borba* (Belgrade), May 21, 1990. Markovic was seen as the politician "pulling Yugoslavia forward" by ratings that ranged from 60 percent to 92 percent in Bosnia and Herzegovina; above those of Milosevic, Tudjman and Kucan.

24. Robert M. Hayden, "Constitutional Nationalism in the Formerly Yugoslav Republics," *Slavic Review* 51.4 (1993).

25. For a powerful description of the Serbian minority reaction, see Misha Glenny, *The Fall of Yugoslavia: The Third Balkan War* (London: Penguin Books, 1992), pp. 82–84.

26. For an English language text of Milosevic's speech, see *Politika: The International Weekly* (Belgrade), March 23–29, 1991.

27. Based on meetings with a member of the Slovene foreign ministry and academic colleagues in Ljubljana, June 20–21, 1991.

28. Based on conversations with Yugoslav colleagues and Warren Zimmerman, American Ambassador, Belgrade, June 30 – July 9, 1991.

29. BBC, Belgrade, June 28, 1991.

30. Who gave orders to whom and who was responsible for what remains in doubt. Prime Minister Markovic said on Belgrade television that his order had been exceeded. The army insisted that it was acting in accordance with decisions of the government and the presidency, *Narodna Armija* (Belgrade), July 6, 1991. Whereupon Markovic went on to accuse the army of acting on its own in Slovenia, *Vreme* (Belgrade), September 23, 1991, pp. 5–12.

31. John Newhouse, "The Diplomatic Round—Yugoslavia," *The New Yorker*, August 24, 1992.

32. *Politika: The International Weekly* (Belgrade), October 5–11, 1991.

33. National Public Radio, March 28, 1992. For an analysis see Milan Andrejevich, "More Guns, Less Butter in Bosnia and Herzegovina," *RFE/RL Research Report* (March 13, 1992).

34. Text of EC "Declaration on Yugoslavia," (Brussels, December 17, 1991), *Review of International Affairs* (Belgrade) 42.998–1000 (December 1, 1991): 28; Also see Predrag Simic, "Europe and the Yugoslav Issue," *Review of International Affairs* (Belgrade) 43.1001 (February 5, 1992): 1–5.

35. Editor's note: Indeed, so severe did the fighting become that the U.N. reinforced its peace-keeping contingent with "rapid reaction" forces. As the hostilities continued, the Bosnian government deployed an estimated 30,000 troops in June in an attempt to lift the Serbian three-year siege of Sarajevo. However, the Serbs captured Srebrenica and Zepa, two of the six U.N. "safe areas" (Gorazde, Sarajevo, Tuzla, and Bihac being the others), in July of 1995. Shortly thereafter the United States Congress passed a bill to lift the arms embargo on Bosnia and Herzegovina, which was vetoed by President Bill Clinton on August 10, 1995. Three days earlier, Croatian soldiers marched into Kinin, the capital of the Krajina region, which the Croatians captured in culminating a three-day campaign. This occasioned the exodus

of more than 160,000 Serbs into Bosnia and Serbia, thereby reducing Croatia's Serbian minority from 12 percent to 3 percent of the population.

The Croatian capture of the Krajina region, a ferocious NATO air campaign against the Bosnian Serbs (after two Serbian shells killed forty-three persons in central Sarajevo on August 28, 1995), and intense diplomatic pressure eventually led to face to face peace nogotiations by President Franjo Tudjman of Croatia, President Alija Izetbegovic of Bosnia, and President Slobodan Milosevic of Serbia in Dayton, Ohio. The negotiations, begun on November 1, 1995, and brokered by the United States, with Assistant Secretary of State Richard Holbrooke and Secretary of State Warren Christopher playing the leading roles, resulted in the initialing by the three presidents of what was termed "The Dayton Accord: A Peace Agreement for the Balkans" on November 21, 1995. The Bosnian peace agreement was signed by them on December 14, 1995, at the Elysée Palace in Paris, France—in the presence of President Bill Clinton of the United States, Prime Minister John Major of the United Kingdom, Prime Minister Viktor Chernomyrdin of Russia, President Jacques Chirac of France, and Chancellor Helmut Kohl of Germany. The signing of the agreement cleared the way for 60,000 NATO troops, including 20,000 Americans to be installed in Bosnia and Herzegovina to oversee the disengagement of the warring factions, effect the unification of Sarajevo, and foster an atmosphere of security whereby the reconstruction of Bosnia and Herzegovina, as well as other war-torn areas of the former Yugoslavia, could begin in earnest.

# 14

# China and the Containment of Ethnonationalism

## DAVID D. BUCK

China has tens of millions of minority peoples. The 1990 census listed the number of non-Han peoples as 91.2 million, or 8 percent, of China's total population of 1.13 billion.[1] More than three-quarters of China's minorities belong to the nine largest groups: the Zhuang (15.5 million), Manchu (9.8 million), Hui (8.6 million), Miao (7.4 million), Uygur (7.2 million), Yi (6.6 million), Tujia (5.7 million), Mongols (4.8 million), and Tibetans (4.6 million). Most of these peoples still live in their traditional homelands at the periphery of the Chinese state, although they often share those lands with Han Chinese settlers. Others, like the Hui and many of the Miao, are scattered among central regions long dominated by the Hans.

Since 1949, the People's Republic of China has classified most non-Han peoples as national minorities, granting many of them a measure of autonomy within specified administrative boundaries. Autonomy does not mean that they are free to secede from the People's Republic of China, but that they enjoy certain special rights as part of the "Chinese family of nations."[2] The new Communist government adopted an approach giving all minorities legal equality, and promising economic improvement, and better transportation and communication linkages. The new order banned derogatory terminology about minorities in published pronouncements, improved minority peoples' schools and education in their respective languages, and tolerated the practice of many of minority customs and life styles that differed from the Han majority. China's minorities, however, have had to meet certain standards established by the modernizing Marxist state. When religious institutions and practices are involved, the minority peoples have faced the same general denigration of religion that has marked the communist approach since coming to power.

Overall the Chinese government's policies are a modification of the Soviet nationality policy. As in the case of the former Soviet Union, the reality of central control through a disciplined Leninist party structure greatly reduces the real independence of supposedly autonomous minority peoples. In particular in China, the adoption of increasingly radical forms of social revolution after 1956 in what culminated as the Great Leap Forward, the minority peoples found themselves caught up in the same great tide as did the Han Chinese majority.[3]

In addition, minority peoples and the territory they inhabit have experienced increasing cultural and economic pressures from the growing numbers of the Han nationality who have emigrated or been resettled into their regions. This wave of outward movement by the Han Chinese began over two hundred years ago, but has accelerated in the last half of the twentieth century. China's population has doubled over the past forty years. That factor alone created an ineluctable force pushing tens of millions of Han Chinese into the less densely populated territories occupied by these minorities. Also, national security considerations and penal policies caused the resettlement of millions of Han Chinese to the border regions. In some locations, these Han settlers have completely displaced the original inhabitants, in others, their presence challenges the ways of ethnic groups who consider these lands or urban settlements their home territory.[4] Probably the most obvious case is the Xinjiang Autonomous Region, where the proportion of Han Chinese inhabitants rose from 8.1 percent (300,000) in 1949, to 38 percent (3,800,000) in 1975.[5] Many minority nationalities live in contiguous areas and operate as special autonomous units. For example, China's Moslems—who themselves include many different nationalities such as the Uygur, Kazak, Kirgiz, in addition to the Hui—can be found in two autonomous provinces (the Xinjiang Uygur and the Ningxia Hui Autonomous Regions), four autonomous prefectures, and thirteen autonomous counties, as well as in regular administrative units throughout China.[6]

Throughout the Maoist era, government policies produced a system in which minority peoples received relatively few special considerations. However, since 1978 during the Reform era in the People's Republic of China, minority peoples in China have enjoyed three marked advantages: they generally have not been subject to the harshest strictures of family planning policies; they find it easier to change their residence within China than most Han Chinese; and they have been permitted to revive religious practices previously suppressed. Freedom of religious practice is a key variable particularly among 30 million peoples who practice Islam and it has given increased dynamism to their ethnonationalism.[7]

J. Richard Walsh argues that since the disintegration of the Soviet Union, the principal goal of China in Central Asia is to maintain the status quo by offering political and economic support to the emerging republics of Central Asia in hopes that this can check the forces of Islamic resurgence or pan-Turkic nationalism in the region.[8] Among China's many minorities there is reason to be concerned that certain groups—particularly the Tibetans, the Moslem peoples of Central Asia, and possibly the Mongols or Koreans—may try to break the existing political order to establish their own states or associate with preexisting nation-states. Typically, there are external forces such as Saudi-financed Sunni Muslim movements or the autonomous state-in-exile of the Dalai Lama which can provide both leadership and material support for such changes.[9] In the case of the Mongols, the economic difficulties facing the independent state of Mongolia, now free from both the political control and economic subsidization of the former Soviet Union, do not make it an active center capable of attracting support from the Mongol population of China. Other minority peoples such as the Yao (2.1 million), the Dong (2.5 million), or the Dai (1 million), all of whom live in the southwestern Yunnan-Guizhou plateau region, will inevitably remain minority populations within some larger polity. Nevertheless, the People's Republic of China is going to have to make adjustments in its nationalities in order to respond to the greater role that ethnic and religious identity have in today's world.

This chapter offers a general appraisal of ethnonationalistic movements in China and their prospects. Another way of approaching the question would be to examine several specific situations in detail such as the Tibetans, Uygurs of Central Asia, the Koreans of Northeast China, or the Yao of the Southwest. Several recent monographic studies have utilized that approach;[10] so within the limited confines of this chapter, I stress general characteristics of ethnonationalism in China and the world today.

My approach is based on three crucial factors: First, the general dynamics of ethnonationalism in our times have wide applicability throughout the world, including the People's Republic of China. Second, at the same time, however, ethnonationalism in China has developed in a particular set of circumstances over the past two hundred years, and those historical experiences strongly shape the present and future there. Finally, some characteristics of ethnonationalism and Leninism at work in China clearly parallel the experience of the former Soviet Union and other European communist states. When these three factors are combined, the potential for ethnonational division within China seems strong. But a fourth and probably decisive factor, namely, the strong economic growth which China has experienced over the past decade, undercuts forces that might produce division.[11] Fifth, and finally, there is the character of Han or Chinese nationalism itself, now undergoing a major redefinition, which will have a great influence on the future of the minority peoples in China. I should like to discuss briefly each of these five.

**General Character of Contemporary Ethnonationalism**

Ethnonationalism is built around appeals to a combination of characteristics including a language, a home territory, a religion, a historical experience, even a sense of special economic roles and a heritage of social practices. Such shared characteristics exist in many times and places. Often, these remain as secondary qualities within the identities of individuals and communities. The nature and intensity of ethnic identity vary tremendously according to time, location, and even among individuals within a given community. For some Italian-Americans, for example, ethnicity may be no more than acknowledgment of an Italian heritage, where for others, it becomes a source of livelihood, a career, or a central defining characteristic that shapes and colors their entire lives.

Yet in none of these manifestations is ethnonationalism a political force. Only when these familiar components of ethnic identity become the basis for a political program—almost always a separatist political agenda—can ethnonationalism become a significant force in political history. The potential for ethnonationalism to become a basis for political movements has been limited historically, because creating and maintaining a state has had only a limited connection with the consent of the governed. More typically, a ruler and his state's authority rested on some combination of military might and an appeal to a universalistic political system or religious authority.

Since the eighteenth century, the spread of Western-derived political concepts about the state have radically altered the potential for ethnonationalist movements. First, there is a right of the governed to determine under what system they shall be governed, and second, there is a belief that governments are operated best by people of the same heritage as the governed. Either or both of these tenets give a measure of instant political and moral authority to those who make use of these concepts to ground their political projects.

Political leaders find it convenient to invoke common characteristics of ethnicity as a source of political identity. Large numbers of individuals and groups find response to these invocations both comprehensible and emotionally satisfying because the sense of identity is bound up with language use, religious practice or some sense of territory, all of which are strongly compelling. Following the interpretations of the British scholar, John Breuilly, I stress how ethnonationalism is best understood as the transformation into an oppositional political movement of what are really mundane characteristics of regional, religious, economic, and social identity.[12]

Political authority in modern secular nation-states must rest on some appeal to the consent and participation of the governed. In practice, that political authority can operate with little reference either to the governed or their elected representatives. Still, the consent of the governed stands both as a check on autocracy and as a principle around which opposition can easily take form. When political movements are based on appeals to ethnonationalism, it often proves possible to reorder existing political alignments. Politicians throughout the world are finding that themes of religious, linguistic, or other attributes of ethnic identity can quickly cut across the prevailing notions of class, ideology, and political parties to provide the kind of mass support on which contemporary political power rests.

A common consequence of these appeals are movements to create new, independent nation-states. This process itself is highly disruptive to the economic life of both the new state and its predecessors, as one can readily see throughout the former Soviet Union and Eastern Europe.[13] Moreover, ethnonationalism may bring in its wake the kind of brutal, senseless murdering of former neighbors that has scarred Bosnia and Herzegovina, and Chechnya, for example.

Ethnonationalism need not be a divisive force leading to bloodshed. Some observers see the reassertion of religious authority as working against the largely unchecked power of the nation-state.[14] Still, present evidence of ethnic conflict in Bosnia and Herzegovina, Rwanda, Kashmir, and Sri Lanka, to mention only the most obvious, is not promising. A possible historical parallel for the breakdown of the large nation-state exists in the Protestant Reformation in Europe, where the challenge to the older, central authority of the universal church in Rome did not result in a revival of paganism, but rather an intensification of Christianity in new forms. From that example, it would seem likely that ethnonationalism will produce only new forms of the nation-state, rather than anticipate its demise and death.

This means that the nation-state, either in its older familiar forms that have shaped world history for the past two hundred years, or in its newer, more fissile forms that have come to increasing attention since the 1980s, will continue to predominate in the political life of the world's people. Specifically, in China, we should expect both the oppositional politics of ethnonationalism and a strong, dominating nation-state to continue to be primary elements in any future events.

### Ethnonationalist Policies in Chinese History

Stevan Harrell argues that over the past 350 years China has seen three separate "civilizing projects" in which the center has tried to win over peripheral peoples to its claim of a superior civilization. He calls these projects the Confucian, the Christian, and the Communist. Harrell finds that the response of the peripheral peoples is to develop a sense of ethnicity.[15]

The present territorial dimensions of the People's Republic of China were inherited largely from the Qing dynasty which ruled China from 1644 to 1911. The Qing rulers were not Chinese themselves, but Manchus who consciously attempted to maintain their identity as separate from the Han Chinese. The Qing Empire operated on principles of suzerainty and territoriality which had no easy equivalency with those of the Western system of nation-states or the Western conception of international relations. They also lacked the conception that state authority was strictly confined within boundaries fixed by law or custom. In terms of its relations with the Han Chinese majority, the Manchus followed the accepted neo-Confucian approach of having a class of men specially trained in ethics govern the empire as a whole and its individual territorial subdivisions on the basis of a universal set of principles. This Chinese approach stressed largely indirect control of communities as long as they paid taxes, avoided quarrels, armed clashes or potential subversion. Thus, in theory, the Qing state did not favor the Han nationality against others, but it found it difficult to establish administrative practices that helped protect minorities—including, even, themselves—from increasing pressures of sinification.[16]

An example of Qing policy can be drawn from the late eighteenth and early nineteenth centuries, when under both the Qianlong and Jiaqing emperors efforts were made to stop Han Chinese settlers from occupying Mongol grazing lands in what is now called Northeastern China (Manchuria). The Qing dynasty policy was to protect the lands, livelihood and culture of its non-Han subjects against Han emigration. The Qing was most adamant about such protection in those sections of the Northeast where enormous forested regions supported varieties of hunting and gathering economies similar to that of the Manchus themselves before they conquered China.[17] Among their Mongol allies, and among the Tibetans or the Moslem peoples of the Central Asian oasis, the Qing attempted to maintain firm control over their rulers and religious leaders without permitting the Han Chinese to settle in any significant numbers in their land.

In practice though, the Qing were not able to stop the Chinese emigration into Mongolia, primarily because the Mongol princes residing in Beijing, wishing to maintain elaborate lifestyles, became so dependent upon the income from the sale and rental of their lands that they would not follow imperial directives. Wherever the call of potential farming land beckoned, the Han Chinese moved rapidly to occupy and displace its former inhabitants, especially in the western reaches of Sichuan, the southwestern plateau region bordering on Southeast Asia, on Taiwan, and north of the Great Wall in Manchuria.

By 1860 and afterwards, the Qing found that the pressures of other expanding states were such that they had to give up control of territory inhabited by minority peoples to Russia and Japan. Faced with a wide set of challenges from the Western powers and Japan, the Qing moved away from their traditional role of protecting themselves and other minorities from the Han, to opening Manchuria to Han residence and generally favoring Han expansion in ways they had previously not accepted.

The Qing Empire faced challenges both on its periphery and at the very center of its political and economic strength. As Czarist Russia took over Siberia, Japan became the recognized dominant power in the Ryukyus and Korea, while making Taiwan a colony. The French took Vietnam completely out of the Chinese orbit, and the British penetrated Tibet. Even more threatening, were the steady increases in foreign privileges in the home provinces of China where extraterritoriality gave foreign residents special legal, tax, commercial and residence privileges that all compromised the authority and independence of the Qing state.

The Chinese response to foreign encroachment was a borrowing of the Western concept of nationalism to defend themselves against what appeared to be an inevitable tide of foreign conquest and domination. The Qing rulers generally managed to keep pace with the growing demands for reform and self-assertion of the Chinese majority against the foreigners. But by 1911, with the Qing state led by an child-emperor and the spirit of nationalist revolution thoroughly permeating the educated urban populace as well as the military service, the dynasty fell—to be succeeded by a series of weak and inept governments whose leaders lacked the vision, power, and the will to make the sacrifices necessary to truly meld China into a modern nation.[18]

In the years after 1911, Chinese nationalism picked up more adherents who came to envision a new China controlling the full territory of the former Qing dynasty, even to recover the break-away state of the Mongolian People's Republic, which, with Soviet backing, became fully independent in 1924.[19] In the minds of Chinese political leaders of the early twentieth century, race and nation were closely linked. The place and function of the minority peoples in the Chinese nation were always somewhat unclear. They were to be part of China, but the terms of their membership were vague and ill-defined.

The American scholar Owen Lattimore, who had been raised and worked as a young man in China, came, in the 1920s, to be fascinated by the peoples of Inner Asia, especially the Mongols. Much of Lattimore's writing and politics flowed from his sympathy and understanding of the Mongol situation in the nationalistic China of the 1920s and 1930s.[20] In Lattimore's work, he advanced a deep concern for the fate of China's minority peoples. As he saw the problem, there were three possibilities. First, the Central Asian minorities faced a fate of steady encroachment from the Han Chinese, who, like locusts, would move inexorably to occupy the land and destroy the minorities' way of living. This had been a recurring possibility throughout history, as a strong China expanded towards its Asian frontiers. In the twentieth century, the Chinese were even more irresistible. Lattimore, noting the effects of technology, wrote, "[y]et, the effective range of these inevitable forces had been expanded by something new . . . [by] the use of railways, modern arms, and new financial, commerical and industrial enterprises.[21]

Second, the minority peoples faced conquest by Japan. Once part of a Japanese Empire, pockets of their culture would survive while most of their land and resources were put to use to benefit the home empire and its rulers.

Finally, there was the potential for some autonomous control of their own territory, with a preservation of language, social practices, and indigenous political leadership through the Soviet Union's nationality policy. To Lattimore in the 1930s, the Russian nationality program, as embodied in the Soviet Union and in the state of Mongolia, was a better bet for minority peoples than either the Chinese or the Japanese approach. In Lattimore's appraisal, the Chinese communists led by Mao Zedong, were not significantly different from other Chinese in terms of their attitudes toward minority peoples. Present-day scholars echo his appraisal. Frank Dikotter, for example, has concluded that

[a]lthough there is nothing in Mao's writings which deals directly with the idea of race, it is clear that his sense of nationalism was based on a strong racial consciousness and a sense of biological continuity. Like most politicians who grew to maturity in Republican China, he perceived the Chinese "nation" (minzu) as a biologically distinct group: being Chinese was a mater of "culture" as well as "race."[22]

Thus, the new order in China continued to share many of the established Chinese attitudes toward minorities. In the 1930s, Lattimore had concluded that no Chinese leader could hold in check the expansionistic and absorptive nature of Chinese society. The Chinese would continue to expand into contiguous land as long as it could sustain the Chinese style of life. In Lattimore's judgment, China, under any conditions, could be expected to keep expanding, and the best hope of minority peoples lay with the Soviet-style of semi-autonomous administration. What happened in China after World War II comes close to fulfilling Lattimore's vision. The Han Chinese have kept expanding into minority lands, while a Soviet-style nationalities policy has helped the non-Han peoples retain a modicum of leverage within the political system.

After the Chinese Communist movement won full control over China, driving out the Chinese Nationalists under Chiang Kai-shek, they adopted a general policy of imitating Soviet examples. In this new People's Republic of China, the Constitution enshrined the general principles of the Soviet approach to autonomous government for minority peoples. Consequently, special regions, districts, and other territorial units were established, in which the principles of self-rule combined with efforts at sustaining cultural autonomy of the minority peoples.

The structure of minority nationalities' autonomy was undercut, however, by five factors. First, following the general principle of all communist rule, those in power were under the full discipline of the Party. Second, military occupation by the People's Liberation Army—inevitably largely Han Chinese in terms of composition and leadership—was necessary in order to preserve the new Chinese state from its foreign enemies. Third, in line with the increasingly universalistic application of state policy in the People's Republic, the minority regions were drawn into the same general political and economic campaigns. Fourth, in the style of complete general adherence to the directives of Beijing, there was almost no room for minorities to sustain a significant give-and-take relationship with the center and thereby preserve some measure of autonomy. Finally, the state sponsored settlement of Han Chinese in large numbers in frontier regions.

In sum, the Chinese political system had some potential for minority autonomy, but in practice it highly circumscribed minority identity while minority lands were being occupied by new Han Chinese settlers sponsored by the state. As the anthropologist Dru Gladney argues, the minority peoples of China came to be exoticized as a kind of primitive "other" who shared China with the Han, but whose quaint costumes, easy sexuality, and male bravado were all to be avoided by the sober, disciplined, and hard-working Han.[23]

### The Leninist State and Ethnonationalism

Owen Lattimore's optimistic hopes about Soviet nationality policy were never realized. As has been exposed in the collapse of the Soviet Union, ethnonationalism became not a bulwark of the socialist order, but one its first and strongest sources of opposition. Although during the Cold War, states such as the Soviet Union and Yugoslavia presented themselves and were regarded by most authorities, both domestically and from outsiders' perspectives, as nation-states, they have since quickly disintegrated. Some claim now that the Soviet Union was never a nation, only a modern state wedded to an older concept of empire, which inevitably broke apart.[24]

From some perspectives, the Leninist state is not a protector of cultural differences, but a dedicated enemy of ethnic difference, and regards ethnic communities as "outmoded, mere living fossils." Mindful of this, Edward Friedman argues forcefully that

> the politics of anthropology in Leninist-Stalinist societies finds little progressive value in the cultures of minority peoples. They are mere economic moments whose time has passed. To be rid of them is like removing the dead but unburied. . . . Combining [Lewis Henry] Morgan's anthropology with Marx's telos, the Leninist state acts on the colonialist categories of orientalism.
>
> The rulers define the people of other regions by an anthropology of advanced or backward, with the most industrialized areas tied to the capital treated as the most advanced. In other regions, people have to make themselves over in the image of an artificial "socialist" culture or be treated as primitive and reactionary. What is demanded is deculturation.[25]

From Friedman's perspective, the present Chinese state combines the terrible failings of Soviet nationality policy intensified by the combination a blind faith in their own vision of Marxist truth, the age-old Chinese assumption of cultural superiority, plus a passion for modernization that calls on everyone, including Han Chinese, to give up most of their traditional cultural practices.

From this approach, the dissolution of present People's Republic of China might seem almost inevitable, for if the Soviet Union fell apart in the moment of a failed coup in August 1991, how can the People's Republic of China avoid some crisis that will shatter it in the same fashion? In the case of Tibet, for example, where the Han Chinese find control necessary, but little to praise in either past or present Tibetan culture, it is easy to imagine the breaking away of the region as a parallel to

Mongolia's independence in the 1920s. If Tibet can go its own way, why would not large sections of Inner Mongolia become part of an enlarged Mongolian republic, or the Korean minority in Northeast China be joined in some way to the burgeoning state of South Korea with all its wealth and dynamism? Clearly, these most populous minority groups, with strong linguistic, cultural, and religious identities who occupy an identifiable territory, have all the standard markers of ethnonationalism. If political leadership emerges, and the increasingly familiar politics of ethnonationalistic fragmentation appear, they could break away.

Once underway, could not the People's Republic of China's Kazaks be joined to Kazakhstan, the Uzbeks become part of Uzbekistan? Such cross-boundary national couplings seem to come easily to mind, but as Gerald Segal points out, the Kazaks in the People's Republic of China number 1.1 million, but the Uzbeks are only 14,500, the Kirgiz 142,000, and the Tajiks 33,500.[26] Numbers like these hardly seem capable of participating in the ending of the most populous nation-state in the world.

This reveals another question about the future, for whatever kind of a state did emerge from a dismembered China, it would, like the successor states to the Soviet Union, still have to deal with questions of minority peoples and their rights. For example, where would the nearly ten million Manchu's go? Their traditional homeland has been completely transformed by more than a century of Han Chinese settlement and modernization, while most Manchus themselves lived in China as privileged conquerors for more than 300 years. These Manchus no longer have a traditional homeland; nor do many of them know how to live any kind of a rural life. Simply put, the collapse of the existing nation-state does not solve the problems of minority peoples; it only casts those problems in a new form.

One consequence of ethnonationalistic fragmentation seems inevitable: it generates streams of refugees. In China, we must imagine that Han Chinese settled in some of the most remote and least desirable locations along the state's frontiers would rush to return to the Han heartland, while pockets of Mongols and Tibetans living now in "Han Chinese" provinces such as Sichuan or Jilin, would move into Mongolia or Tibet. In fact, these minority peoples have lived in their present locations long before the Han Chinese arrived, but would be forced to abandon their real homes for a national homeland. Consequently, even the most ardent supporters of ethnonationalism in China might well pause before the prospect of such dislocations and disruption.

Finally, one cannot escape the fact that Leninism also has served, in a fashion, as a refuge protecting ethnonationalism by providing an identity, however weak it might have proven to be in practice, that might possibly buffer individuals and families from the worst excesses of the Leninist state. Even during the height of Maoist centralization when everyone throughout China was supposed to be caught up in the same current campaign of anti-imperialistic nationalism, national minorities had some slight shielding from the full impact of change provided by a combination of distance and their autonomous administrative arrangements. After 1978, as China's leadership has realized that state required compliance does not successfully unleash the creative powers of labor, various kinds of economic, religious, and cultural activity, independent of the Communist party and the nation-state, have been tolerated, and sometimes even encouraged.

In religious terms, in regard to population policy, and on questions of residence and freedom of economic activity, several non-Han Chinese minorities have benefited directly and indirectly from this pattern of liberalism. To many Han Chinese, those benefits look like special privileges which the Chinese envy and may even rush to embrace, if they can claim that they themselves should be reclassified as members of a particular minority people. Liberalization in the People's Republic has developed a new generation of minority leaders, who, much like their older predecessors from the Maoist era, cannot escape the thought that their own leadership positions probably are tied to the survival of the existing order.

### Economic Growth and Ethnonationalism

Whatever advantages the existing political order affords minorities and their current leaders, alone it cannot provide enough incentives to insure that they will remain tied to Beijing. However, for some large minorities in China, the results of recent economic growth, combined with the promise of the future, will serve as a major break on the genesis of new ethnonationalist states. In markets and streets in China's largest cities, Central Asian minorities prosper through trade and commerce. If they lost their ability to travel and do business in China through national separation, they would lose access to the source of their prosperity. For millions of other minorities, such as the Manchus or most Hui who live in the inner provinces of China, there is no place they really want to live on the periphery. They have no "homeland" to which to return.

China has had a remarkable period of economic growth and development since the early 1980s. Foreigners who do not like the present regime in Beijing still flock to China to invest and do business, simply because it is a dynamic center of economic growth in today's world.[27] Why should China's ethnic minorities deny themselves of access to this opportunity any more than Japanese or American capitalist businesses? Whatever their philosophic objections to the Chinese Communist party or their own experience of discrimination, expropriation, or exploitation by the Beijing government in the past, there is a strong rationale for swallowing one's memories in favor of present and future profits.

Still, the leadership of ethnonationalist movements rarely derive from the commercial strata among an ethnic group. It often comes from religious and cultural leadership that casts a wary eye on their own people who are involved in commercial dealings. Among Moslem peoples, religion clearly has displaced short-term economic advantage as a rationale for political action. In China, Central Asian Moslem groups may repeat this pattern, while small minority groups such as the Naxi (278,000) or the Ewenki (26,000), who still live in close-knit villages, may find little desirable in the commercialization of life by anyone.

Yet, economic advantage will no doubt operate as a brake against ethno-nationalist fissures. The situation is thus the opposite of what obtained in Eastern Europe and the Soviet Union, where freedom from Moscow's grasp seemed to contain a promise of more economic opportunity. The attraction of the Chinese economy for some of its own minorities probably will continue in the future, as long as economic benefits of belonging to the Chinese nation-state remain so tangible and enticing.

### The Changing Nature of Han Chinese Nationalism

When one looks at what is called the ethnic make-up of the People's Republic of China, what is most amazing is that over one billion people are all classified as "Han Chinese." This uniform identity covers over enormous linguistic and cultural differences within the Han Chinese themselves.[28] Like most Western interpreters, I see Chinese nationalism as a modern phenomenon of the late nineteenth and twentieth centuries spreading outward from a Western influenced elite to widening circles of ordinary people who saw their culture, their way of life, and their very identity threatened by foreign imperialism after 1840. National consciousness led to a fear of being overwhelmed and produced a unifying, defensive reaction. Nationalism in China has constructed a style of fearless resistance to foreign intervention, which is supposed to motivate all true Chinese.

When the Communist party in China captured the flag of nationalist resistance, it borrowed economic policies from the Soviet Union that stressed how all surpluses that could be wrung from the agricultural sector must be devoted to industrial and urban development in a largely autarkic economy. Policy implementation resulted in an increasingly stagnant and retrograde economy after an initial period of success. In contrast, economic policies which linked strong states to market mechanisms and world trade in three Chinese communities—Singapore, Hong Kong, and Taiwan—generated enormous economic growth. There is strong evidence of a whole new national project emerging in China, built around the dynamic, commercialized, and adaptive South, which contrasts itself with a narrow, conservative, and bureaucratic North.[29]

We know that the supposedly united Han peoples of China are shot through with linguistic, regional, and even ethnic differences (for example, the Hakka) that make the future of the present Han unity seem questionable. Political leaders calling on identities such as Cantonese, or Fujianese, organized political movements of some strength in the early twentieth century and could do so again. Political movements based on such identities could potentially enlist many tens of millions in their ranks, far more than any of the individual officially recognized minorities in China. In Taiwan, exactly such a movement, long feared by the ruling Nationalist party, emerged into the open in the 1980s.

In the summer of 1995, a private visit to the United States by the president of the Republic of China on Taiwan, Lee Tung-hui, plus a bid by that government for a seat in the United Nations, touched on a diplomatic squabble in which the government in Beijing revealed how deeply it was concerned over the possibility of fissiparous tendencies among the Han majority. In the official Beijing version of these events, the United States was behind the scenes manipulating Lee Tung-hui into an effort at pulling China apart.[30]

Post-1978 policies in China have lessened central control, increased regional autonomy, provided small but nonetheless greater degrees of independent authority for political leaders outside Beijing. Leaders in Canton, Shanghai, Chengdu, and Wuhan, as well as the people in their surrounding regions, seem to have as much to gain from increased autonomy from the center as would the Tibetans, the Mongols, and the Uygurs. Thus, I have concluded that the future of the People's Republic of China is more likely to be determined by the changing nature of Han Chinese nationalism than by problems deriving from the non-Han minorities, who numerically are so much smaller a factor in Chinese politics.

**Conclusion**

Ben Kerkvliet, writing about reform in Vietnam, suggests that the Vietnamese Communist party since 1986 may have recaptured some of the qualities that brought it to power in the North, and eventually enabled it to unify Vietnam. Among those qualities is what Kerkvliet calls "mass regard," that is, a kind of shorthand for the leadership's concern with policies that meet the aspirations and needs of the vast majority of the people. These included national self-determination and autonomy in the face of foreign colonialism. Once the foreigner had been expelled, the Vietnamese felt they had a pattern—agricultural collectivization and economic autarky in the Chinese Communist model—for economic and social organization of the new order, but, in fact, this approach proved to be as unsatisfactory in Vietnam as it had proven to be in China. Then, says Kerkvliet, the Vietnamese Communist party returned to the secret of its former successes and became "mass-regarding," again by adopting policies of household farming and other forms of economic liberalization acceptable to the people.[31]

What Kerkvliet argues about the Vietnamese Communist party may also be true of the Chinese Communist party. Many specialists think that the Chinese have little potential to develop in the near future anything like a democratic or representative government and, in fact, China will produce some form of "neo-authoritarianism."[32] Should a neo-authoritarian leadership develop and prove itself to be "mass-regarding," it could well continue to exercise leadership. Certainly, the reform programs instituted by the Chinese Communist party under Deng Xiaoping's leadership have been generally well received. These policies have occasioned greater regional autonomy, as well as increased personal freedom and economic opportunities for both urban and rural residents. At the same time, the reforms have not seriously threatened the position of the military, nor the livelihoods of the tens of millions of workers for state enterprises and the state bureaucracies. Everyone has had to make adjustments and certainly many are not in full support of the changes. Yet none of the challenges to its authority, not even the Tiananmen Incident of 1989, has proven effective enough to topple the existing order.

In its policies toward minorities, as in other areas, the People's Republic can be said to have found ways to keep significant support, if not majority support, within most minority nationalities. So, there is a case to be made for seeing the Chinese Communist party not as an ossified and outmoded group, but one still capable of maintaining the existence of the People's Republic of China.

The process of liberalization and devolution of authority from Beijing is not over. For China to continue as a single nation in its present form, some liberalization must continue. To reiterate what I said at the outset, it is primarily those minority peoples with real or potential strong outside support—the Tibetans, the Muslims of Central Asia, and possibly the Koreans of the Northeast—who seem to present the greatest threat to the present boundaries of the Chinese state. China, however, is much more threatened by changes in the character of Han Chinese nationalism. New visions of the meaning and goals of Han Chinese nationalism will constitute a much greater problem than any of those that may emerge among the ethnonational minorities in China.

## Notes

1. *Beijing Review*, December 24–30, 1990, p. 34.

2. Thomas Heberer, *China and Its National Minorities: Autonomy or Assimilation* (Armonk, NY: M. E. Sharpe, 1989), pp. 20, 40.

3. June Teufel Dreyer, *China's Forty Millions* (Cambridge, MA: Harvard University Press, 1976), pp. 159–71.

4. For the situation on Mongolian grasslands see, Burton Pasternak and Janet W. Salaff, *Cowboys and Cultivators: The Chinese of Inner Mongolia* (Boulder, CO: Westview Press, 1993).

5. Heberer, op. cit. note 2, p. 94.

6. "China's Moslems," *Beijing Review*, June 12–18, 1995, p. 10.

7. Dru Gladney, *Muslim Chinese: Ethnic Nationalism in the People's Republic* (Cambridge, MA: Harvard University Press, 1991).

8. J. Richard Walsh, "China and the New Geopolitics of Central Asia," *Asian Survey* 33.3 (March 1993): 848–68.

9. Émigré politics among Tibetans is focused on this question. See Pierre-Antonie Donnet, *Tibet: Survival in Doubt* (New Delhi: Oxford University Press, 1994). For reports of similar movements in Xinjiang, see Nicholas Kristoff, "A Muslim Region is Tugging at the Ties that Bind," *The New York Times*, August 14, 1993, pp. A1, A3.

10. See Melvyn C. Goldstein, *A History of Modern Tibet: The Demise of the Lamaist State* (Berkeley: University of California Press, 1989); Chae-jin Lee, *China's Korean Minority* (Boulder, CO: Westview Press, 1986); Jacques Lemoine and Chiao Chien, eds., *The Yao of South China: Recent International Studies* (Paris: Panggu, 1993). Stevan Harrell is editing a new series, "Studies on Ethnic Groups in China," for the University of Washington Press and has produced the first volume, *Cultural Encounters on China's Ethnic Frontiers* (Seattle: University of Washington Press, 1995), in which elements of identity among many different ethnic groups in China are discussed by ten contributors.

11. Thomas Heberer, writing in 1989, before the full impact of China's growth became apparent, reached an opposite conclusion. He believes that economic growth will be a force leading to the fragmentation of ethnic groups in China, op. cit. note 2, p. 130.

12. John Breuilly, *Nationalism and the State* (Chicago: University of Chicago Press, 1986), 2nd ed.

13. The experience of division within Yugoslavia and Czechoslovakia may not be directly applicable to China, but the forces that led to the particular congeries of new states that have succeeded the Soviet Union may be more relevant. See Abbas Hamdani, "An Overview of the Current Status of Muslim Countries of the Former Soviet Union," a paper presented to the Parliament of World Religions, Chicago, September 3, 1993.

14. See Mark Jurgensmeyer, *The New Cold War: Religious Nationalism Confronts the Secular State* (Berkeley: University of California Press, 1993).

15. Harrell, op. cit. note 10, pp. 3–36.

16. On the question of racism in China, see Frank Dikotter, *The Discourse of Race in Modern China* (London: Hurst & Co., 1992) pp. 31–38. Dikotter argues that the concept of racialism existed in eighteenth-century Chinese life, long before such ideas were introduced in the West, pp. 31–38.

17. Robert H. G. Lee, *The Manchurian Frontier in Ch'ing* (Cambridge, MA: Harvard University Press, 1970), pp. 116–37.

18. See Germaine Hoston, *The State, Identity and the National Question in China and Japan* (Princeton, NJ: Princeton University Press, 1994), for a detailed consideration of how Japanese and Chinese thinkers, particularly the Marxists, have struggled with the national question.

19. Charles R. Bawden, *The Modern History of Mongolia* (New York: Praeger, 1968).

20. James Cotton, *Asian Frontier Nationalism: Owen Lattimore and the American Policy* (Manchester: Manchester University Press, 1989).

21. Owen Lattimore, *The Inner Asian Frontiers of China* (New York: American Geographical Society, 1940), pp. 17–18.

22. Dikotter, op. cit. note 16, p. 192.

23. "Representing Nationality in China: Refiguring Majority/Minority Identities," *Journal of Asian Studies*, 53.1 (February 1994): 92–113. See Harrell, op. cit. note 10, pp. 8–17, where he argues that civilizing societies regularly classify the peripheral peoples as women (a sexual metaphor), children (an educational metaphor), or ancient (a historical metaphor).

24. Mark Beissinger, "Demise of an Empire-State: Identity, Legitimacy and the Deconstruction of Soviet Politics," in Crawford Young, ed., *The Rising Tide of Cultural Pluralism: The Nation-State at Bay* (Madison: University of Wisconsin Press, 1993), pp. 93–115.

25. Edward Friedman, "Ethnic Identity and the De-Nationalization and Democraticization of Leninist States," in Young, op. cit. note 24, pp. 232–33.

26. Gerald Segal, "China and the Disintegration of the Soviet Union," *Asian Survey* 32.9 (September 1992): 272–84.

27. For one of the most forceful analyses of China's current economic growth, see William H. Overholt, *The Rise of China: How Economic Reform is Creating a New China* (New York: W. W. Norton, 1993). Overholt argues that China was the world's fastest-growing economy during the 1980s and will continue in that fashion in the 1990s. He sees a complete reshaping of the Pacific region economy and China's emergence as a world superpower.

28. There are only a few recent studies that try to treat this diversity among the Han Chinese in a systematic fashion. See Leo J. Moser, *The Chinese Mosaic: Peoples and Provinces of China* (Boulder, CO: Westview Press, 1985).

29. Edward Friedman, "Reconstructing China's National Identity: A Southern Alternative to Mao Era Anti-Imperialist Nationalisms," *Journal of Asian Studies* 53.1 (February 1994): 67–91.

30. Li Jiaquan, "Lee's Visit Defies Agreements," *Beijing Review*, June 26 – July 2, 1995, pp. 19–20. The Chinese Foreign Ministry's official spokesmen repeated these sentiments on numerous occasions in the summer of 1995.

31. Ben Kerkvliet, "De-collectivizing the Land: Everyday Politics, Policy Changes and Village-State Relations in Vietnam," *Journal of Asian Studies* 54.2 (May 1995): 290–316.

32. Richard Baum, "Political Stability in Post-Mao China: Problems and Prospects," *Asian Survey* 38.6 (June 1992): 491–505. Baum correctly associates Zhao Ziyang and his circle with the theory of neo-authoritarianism in Beijing politics. See Baum's, *Burying Mao: Chinese Politics in the Age of Deng Xiaoping* (Princeton, NJ:

Princeton University Press, 1994), pp. 220–22, 238–39. The appeal of this approach to governing China reaches far beyond Zhao Ziyang, who was the chief loser in the political shake-up following the Tiananmen Incident of June 1989. It continues to be a favored approach among the top leadership in Beijing.

# 15

# Political Ethnicity and State-Building in Nigeria

## CLAUDE AKE

Ethnicity is a complicated social fact. It is not clear whether ethnic groups actually exist or whether they are merely ideological constructs. What is clear enough is that there is ethnic consciousness, which is a living presence produced and driven by material and historical forces. Ethnicity has to be understood in the complex dialectics of imagination and reality, of construction, dissolution, and reconstitution.

For the purpose of understanding ethnic politics and their implications for the integrity of the state, it does not matter very much whether ethnicity is real or imagined. Even if it is real, there is not, as is often assumed, a necessary connection between ethnicity and political conflict. All too often, ethnic conflict is perceived too ubiquitously in ethnic misrepresentations of strategies of survival, strategies of power, and in emancipatory struggles against oppression sustained with ethnic ideologies. What we need to explore is how ethnicity becomes politicized and associated with exclusivism and conflict, a phenomenon that may be called political ethnicity. Political ethnicity is an elemental force which will, for better or for worse, be decisive for the peace and well-being of humankind. The planet has had a taste of its enormous power and its daunting possibilities in the decomposition of the Soviet Union, Yugoslavia, Somalia, Liberia, and Czechoslovakia. In the North, it threatens the world economy; it has turned Europe into a fortress against the South, and it has demonstrated its capacity to engender xenophobia, racism, and many other forms of regressive consciousness.

The purpose of this chapter is not to theorize about the global resurgence of political ethnicity. It is, rather, to show how it was engendered in Nigeria, and what its implications have been especially for the viability of Nigeria as a nation-state.

## Political Ethnicity in Nigeria

An account of political ethnicity in Nigeria must begin with the character of the colonial state. Mechanically held together by force, this state was an incoherent assortment of peoples. It was not so much a state as a state project, an implausible state project ultimately defeated by its own contradictions. One source of these contradictions was that the colonial state in Nigeria inevitably relied heavily on force to subjugate the indigenous peoples and to carry out its mission. That made it threatening, and induced some of its subjects to regard it as a hostile force. Many of them were driven to traditional solidarity groups such as ethnic or national groups, or even some hastily contrived ones such as literacy clubs or community development associations. These solidarity groups became centers of resistance, means of self-affirmation against the colonizers' aggressive de-culturing of the indigenous people, as well as networks for survival. Somewhat paradoxically, the colonial state was strengthening the traditional solidarity groups and social formations on whose ruins it was supposed to stand.

Even in the urban areas which were considered the melting point of parochial identities, colonial rule was recreating them. Colonial rule was cheap rule. It had no social welfare system. This was particularly difficult for the new city-dwellers, lonely first-generation urbanites who had to battle the notorious problems of colonial cities. In the pressure of the cities they sought the companionship of people akin to themselves, usually from the same rural community or those who spoke the same language. Every colonial town in West Africa quickly spawned a rich harvest of "improvement" or urban associations of people from the same community, ethnic, or national group. With varying emphasis, these associations, which sponsored development in their indigenous rural communities, became interest groups for their members and their groups of origin. They became vehicles of political participation as well as group solidarity against the impositions of an arbitrary and coercive state.

Most important, many of them, notably the Ibo State Union, the Egbe Omo Oduduwa, the Ibibio Welfare Union, and the Edo National Union became social welfare systems providing scholarships for education, assistance for people in difficulty with the law, helping members to set up small businesses or to find employment, as well as giving material and moral support to the sick, the bereaved, and the needy. The educational schemes of these associations played a major role in producing the elite which led the nationalist movement. The majority of the first generation nationalist leaders such as Nnamdi Azikiwe were beneficiaries of these education programs. Thus, instead of being a melting point, the new West African cities tended to recreate old solidarities and loyalties and gave them greater significance. Because these ethnic formations were such a highly functional safety net in the face of a predatory state and a total absence of a social welfare system, they effectively displaced the state as the primary focus of political loyalty.

**The Nationalist Movement and Political Ethnicity**

Since Nigeria was already "ethnicized" in this sense, the nationalist movement, following the line of least resistance, initially evolved as a network of ethnic associations and mass organizations. When the Nigeria National Council, which heralded the coming of age of the nationalist movement in Nigeria, was launched on August 28, 1944, it was a coalition of 8 professional bodies, 11 social clubs, 2 trade unions, 2 fledgling political parties, 4 literary societies, and 101 urban ethnic associations which constituted the bulk of its membership.

The strategy of de-colonization adopted by the colonial government gave impetus to political ethnicity. In the spirit of indirect rule, the major administrative and political units of the country were made to coincide with the spatial locations of the three major ethnic groups, Hausa-Fulani, Yoruba, and Ibo. Then under pressure from nationalist forces, the British devolved power to these regions. The Constitution of 1954, sometimes described as the "regionalist constitution," gave residual powers to the regional governments and also granted them self-government under regional premiers, who would be the leaders of majority parties in the regional legislatures. The three major nationalist leaders, Alhaji Ahmadu Bello, in the North, Dr. Nnamdi Azikiwe in the East, and Chief Obafemi Awolowo in the West opted for power in the region instead of remaining in the central government which was still controlled by the British. Each of them won his regional premiership and consolidated his power base in his region with the result that Nigeria came to be dominated by three regional, ethnic parties. The National Council of Nigeria and the Cameroon's (NCNC), which initially had a strong national orientation, settled down to being the party of the Ibos in the East; the Action Group (AG) became the party of the Yoruba in the West; and the Northern Peoples Congress (NPC) became the party of the Hausa-Fulani in the North.

As political independence approached, the leaders of the ethnic groups who had cooperated in the nationalist coalition began to maneuver for power. In the course of these rivalries those ethnic groups which did not feel that they were strong competitors for power in the postcolonial era began to worry about marginalization and domination. Thus ensued a rash of minorities movements making a wide variety of demands—separatism, federalism, confederationism, the guarantee of human rights, minority rights, affirmative action for minorities, strong local autonomy within the regional framework, and so on. In 1957, the Secretary of State for the Colonies appointed a Commission of Inquiry to ascertain the facts concerning the fears of the minorities throughout the country and to propose means of allaying those fears.

The tour of the commission through the country between 1957 and 1958, the open hearings, the campaign of the affected groups, as well as the lively debates heightened political consciousness pertaining to the issues of human rights, minority rights, and political participation. Many small groups which had been politically apathetic came alive and became organized and assertive. The episode increased political pluralism as some of these groups formed political parties. A famous example is the Benin-Delta People's party formed in 1953 under the presidency of the Oba of Benin; another was the Niger Delta Congress formed in 1959 from the Rivers Chiefs and People Conference. In the end, the commission found against the demand for the creation of states and constitutional provisions which might encourage ethnic separatism. Instead, it came out strongly for guaranteed rights and for political arrangements which favored incorporation and equity rather than exclusion and discrimination.

Still, politics remained ethnicized as the major political parties—NCNC, NPC, and the AG—remained essentially confined to their respective regional base. At the same time, some minority parties came into being in the struggle of given minority groups to resist marginalization by the dominant national group in their region. The notable examples are: the Northern Elements Progressive Union (NEPU) led by Mallam Aminu Kano; a party of the Hausa Talakawa, formed to resist Fulani domination in the North; and the United Middle Belt Congress led by Joseph Tarka, formed to resist Fulani domination in North Central Nigeria. The United National Independence party was formed to counter the NCNC, which Eastern minorities considered to be a vehicle of Ibo domination. Another notable minority political formation was the West State movement, formed to challenge the domination of the Yorubas through the Action Group in the West.

### Constitutional Development and Political Ethnicity

Political ethnicity reinforced the tensions and centrifugal tendencies of the Nigerian polity which were inherent in the mechanical unity of the colonial state, and eventually pulled Nigeria away from the unitary state that the colonial power had envisaged in relation to federalism. When the British administration took the first serious step towards independence for Nigeria with the Richard's Constitution of 1945, it was clearly thinking in terms of a unitary government. The Constitution had the following structure: At the base, was the Native Authority system, whose representatives were to constitute a regional council in each of the three regions into which Nigeria had been divided North, East, and West. Each region in turn had representation in a central legislature based in Lagos. The essentially unitary character of the Constitution could be seen in the fact that legislative power was concentrated in the central legislature in Lagos, leaving the regional councils little more than the power to advise on local problems.

This Constitution was short-lived because it lagged far behind the development of nationalist consciousness. Nationalist leaders found it unacceptably authoritarian. It was replaced by the MacPherson Constitution of 1951. By now the Nigerian bourgeoisie knew that the British administration would soon hand over political power; the bitter war of succession had already begun. The MacPherson Constitution not only advanced Nigerian independence, it also reflected the deep divisions within the Nigerian political class and began the movement of the Nigerian political system towards federalism. The three-region structure was retained. The regional legislatures were empowered to legislate on all matters of internal policy, although their legislation could be reviewed and rejected by the central legislature. This Constitution was a considerable advance towards self-determination for Nigerians. By the time it was enacted, it was clear that power would be transferred to the regional level first before being transferred, if it at all, to the center. This realization induced a scramble for a regional base of power among the Nigerian political class and contributed immensely to its regionalization. With the increasing regionalization of the political class, ethnicity moved into the center of Nigerian politics. This was inevitable, since the three administrative regions also coincided with the locations of the three major tribal groups in Nigeria—northern region (Hausa-Fulani), eastern region (Ibo), and western region (Yoruba).

It is not surprising that when in 1953, a legislature from the Western Region moved a motion to the effect that the British grant Nigeria independence by 1956 the Northerners opposed it, apparently because they felt they were unprepared (by education, etc.,) and so could be dominated. They proposed an Eight-Point Programme, which was essentially a bid for making Nigeria a confederation—the central government would have only a few areas of jurisdiction, mainly foreign policy, defense, and customs. The Northerners only agreed to put aside this program after the Eastern and Western leaders accepted a federal arrangement which granted specific powers to the federal government, and left all other powers in a residual category under the jurisdiction of the regional governments. Along with this, the civil service and the judiciary were regionalized. Even so, the fears of ethnic domination continued to mount as regional elites fought out the battle for succession and mobilized ethnic consciousness to secure a political following. On account of these fears, Nigeria came to independence in 1960 with a federal constitution which was so complex that it never really had a chance of working. It soon collapsed, giving way in turn to anarchy, civil war, and military rule.

**Political Ethnicity and Political Conflict in Postcolonial Nigeria**

As expected, in the pre-independence election of 1959, each of the three major parties won decisively in its regional base, with the final standing in the House of Representative at 148 seats for the NPC, 89 seats for the NCNC, and 75 for the Action Group. But no party was strong enough to rule alone. The NPC and NCNC duly went into a coalition and formed the government. However, the premium on power was so high that both the government and the opposition were narrowly fixed on gaining as much power as possible by whatever means. Eventually, the government used all its powers to harass the Action Group, which in turn remained confrontational as Nigerian quickly headed towards deep political crisis. The government capitalized on factional strife in the AG-controlled Western House of Assembly to go for the liquidation of the Action Group. A state of emergency was declared, and an administrator whose powers were virtually limitless was appointed. The administrator came down heavily on the Action Group. Its leader, Obafemi Awolowo, was tried for treason and imprisoned. The machinery for the creation of another state from the region was set in motion. Members of the embattled party defected *en masse*, and its strength in the House of Representatives fell from 75 to 13.

The political crisis deepened following the announcement of the census result of 1962–63, which bore heavily on how power would be distributed. This time the battle between the Action Group opposition and the government was compounded by a bitter conflict between the coalition partners, the NCNC and the NPC, a conflict associated with an explosion of ethnic animosity. The crisis came to a head in 1965 when the highly controversial and violent elections for the House of Representatives and the Western House of Assembly were held. The political system had broken down, but without degenerating to a general state of anarchy. Nonetheless, on January 15, 1966, the army seized power. Soon afterwards, a long bloody civil war ensued. It was not until 1979 that Nigeria returned to civilian rule, in what proved to be only a brief interlude, for in 1983 the military took power again, and has ruled Nigeria ever since.

It is important to underline the continuity between military and civilian rule in the Nigerian context; they are points on the same continuum. To begin with, in Nigeria politics is equated to warfare. The Nigerian state, reflecting its colonial origins, lacks autonomy. It is not an objective force standing above and mediating the contradictions of social life but largely an instrument which those who control it use openly to promote their own interests, often to the disadvantage of others. To all but the few who control state power, the state tends to be seen as a hostile, predatory force with enormous power. Because everyone places the highest priority on controlling this force, political competition becomes immensely intense and unrestrained, indeed, Hobbesian. This has been compounded by the use of state power for accumulation and aggrandizement, a tendency which renders state power all the more attractive. To all this must be added the effect of political ethnicity. The resort to ethnic ideology as a means to power has unleashed strong antipathies, and engendered fears about being under the power of other ethnic groups—fears verging on paranoia. All this has made the competition for power a war of all against all.

Because politics has become warfare, it was inevitable that the specialists of war would become the major players in politics. The descent to military rule was entirely logical and inevitable. However tempting it may be, it is not very useful to dichotomize between military rule and civilian rule in the context of Nigeria; it is far more useful to regard them as moments of the same political dynamics. This is related to the failure of both civilian and military rule.

Military rule, which was justified as a redemption from political collapse and the efficient facilitator of the state-building process, appears to have failed by its own standard, for behind the outward conformism and apparent stability, divisive tendencies were growing and the state was loosing its bid for loyalty. These particular problems of military rule in Nigeria appear to have been widely recognized, for in the run-up to civilian rule there was great concern about disintegrative tendencies arising especially from ethnicity, but also from minority status and class. These concerns were amply reflected in the Constitution with which Nigeria returned to civilian rule in 1979.

The Constitution introduced a presidential system with a singular concentration of power in an executive president. At the same time, it attempted to restrict political competition through the powers of the National Electoral Commission (NEC)—the government-appointed body designed to oversee the forming and functioning of political parties, as well as the conduct and adjudication of elections. These measures only reinforced the problems they were supposed to solve. They placed a very high premium on the capture of the presidency, and so intensified the competition for power. The four years from 1979 when the military handed over power to civilians were notable for a single-minded and lawless struggle for the presidency. The election of 1983 was contested with such intensity and lawlessness, and amidst such paranoid fears of ethnic domination, that the political system broke down again, paving the way for the return of the military on December 31, 1983. More than a decade has passed since the coup and the military is still in power.

**Political Ethnicity and the Nigerian State**

Nigeria is no closer to being a viable state in the 1990s than it was in 1960 when the country gained its independence. Indeed, the state-building project must now be pronounced a failure, inasmuch as the state has lost the bid to be the repository of the primary loyalty of Nigerians to ethnic and national groups as well as local communities. The official Nigerian state—for all its apparatuses, its enormous power, and all of the resources that it controls—is only nominally a state. It is no *res publica*. Its citizens do not constitute a "public." They share no strong sense of corporate identity, and do not see the state as a collective enterprise of overriding importance deserving commitment.

Rather, the Nigerian state is perceived as an exploitable resource, a contested terrain where all struggle to appropriate and privatize some or all of the enormous powers and resources of the state. Those who wage these struggles are interest groups, but more significantly ethnic groups and communities. The importance of this struggle is that the state disappears in a process of parceling and privatization, its place taken by communities and ethnic groups, nationalities and subnationalities. These are invariably the social formations to which loyalties are given, they are the *res publica*. It is in this context that the notorious problem of public morality in Nigeria is to be understood. The monumental scale of corruption, for which Nigeria is rightly notorious, is associated with the fact that the citizenry is not a public with a "public" morality; it is an arena where groups who define themselves as strangers and contestants are fighting for a precious prize. By all indications, many Nigerians think that it is quite proper to appropriate and privatize the resources of the state. Indeed, this belief is the one thing that comes close to a public morality; in Nigeria it is a morality which negates the state.

Military rule was supposed to neutralize political ethnicity and get the state-building project back on course. The rationalization for military rule offered by its supporters was always that it was more conducive to political stability, rational and efficient management, the crystallization of collective purpose and to the building of the state, which like the army is a rational/bureaucratic organization. This rationalization carries the implication that the military would have a better sense of the requirements of state-building.

But, far from enhancing state-building, military rule has undermined it. To begin, it is well to observe that once the army entered politics it became not only politicized but ethnicized, and could not rise above developing contradictions. The military has ruled Nigerian like a unitary state, and in doing so has exacerbated fears of domination, since the military is popularly perceived to be ethnicized. Political anxiety arising from this has been compounded by the concentration of power and its arbitrary exercise. While exacerbating tensions and nurturing destabilizing tendencies, military rule in Nigeria was able to maintain a surface stability by its repressive capability. But beneath the surface of stability the state project regressed.

The military has learned that force alone will not do, and has made some concessions to the social plurality of Nigeria as well as to federalism, particularly by making much of its commitment to the "federal character" principle. The federal character principle enjoins equitable distribution of offices, opportunities and rewards among the different peoples of Nigeria. And so, Nigeria's military regimes have created more states and local governments to give more groups a sense of autonomy. In 1967 the number of states of the federation was increased from three to twelve, then to nineteen in 1975, and to thirty in 1993. Yet the pressure for more states continues.

In a limited way, the process of redivision reflected the existing structure of power and helped to crystallize it. The major ethnic groups subdivided themselves more than others and they have collectively increased their dominance. Some of the minority groups got a measure of political space without diminishing their marginalization. They may have been more inclined to reconcile themselves to their continuing marginalization if they had some real autonomy in their state or local government. However, there was not much prospect of local autonomy under a military dictatorship. In any case, the economics of federalism in Nigeria was not conducive to autonomy. The states and local government areas were created without any regard to their economic viability. Indeed, none of the thirty states is viable, only Lagos state is potentially so. They are too revenue-dependent to have autonomy. And now, their multiplication has worsened their prospects for autonomy. The more they grow in number, the weaker they are in relation to the federal government. There are now thirty starving states and 596 local government areas struggling over diminishing resources.

### Political Ethnicity and the Antipathy to Military Rule

It appears that the unpopularity of military rule in Nigeria may be its lasting contribution to the state-building project. The military has been blamed for presiding over the squandering of the oil boom, as well as for corruption so brazen and pervasive as to obliterate all faith in the rule of law and the possibility of getting justice. The military is blamed for the gross mismanagement of the economy; for wasting Nigeria's oil wealth; for saddling Nigeria with an impossible debt burden; and for causing the steady decline of real income since its return to power. The military suffers from its association with the Structural Adjustment Program of the World Bank and the IMF; it is held responsible for creating the conditions that forced Nigeria to adopt the program in 1986, and also for the miseries it has brought by way of high inflation, unemployment, high interest rates, a virtual abolition of the social service sector, and apparent collapse of social consensus concerning the Nigerian state.

With few exceptions such as Abuja and Kaduna, Nigerian cities are littered with mounds of garbage, which in some cases have rendered roads unusable. Hospitals have no drugs, large parts of Nigerian cities go without light or running water for weeks or months. Armed robbers operate at will, sometimes brazenly holding up traffic at midtown in broad daylight while they rob one car after another. This has caused a rush to self-sufficiency. Nigerians who can afford it, now provide their own garbage disposal system, their electric and water supply through generators and bore-holes, and their own security through private guards or hired policemen. The urban poor and rural dwellers have developed a wide variety of survival strategies, often reinforced by sophisticated networks. In the course of all this, associational life is thriving. The Nigerian state, already displaced by ethnic and national groups as well as local communities, is becoming increasingly irrelevant except as a nuisance.

This is the background of the opposition of Nigerians to military rule. The objective of ending military rule has become a uniting force to them. It has diverted some attention from the ethnic, religious, nationalist, and regional particularisms which have dominated Nigerian politics for four decades. The presidential election of 1993 was a stunning expression of this new political reality. Quite unexpectedly, the country turned against the National Republic Convention (NRC), the more conservative party reputedly preferred by the military government as well as the dominant faction of the political class. The presidential candidate of the party, Alhaji Bashir Tofa, was soundly beaten by Chief M. K. O. Abiola, the candidate of the Social Democratic Party (SDP). The SDP was identified with changing the status quo, including a better deal for the poor. The manifesto of Chief Abiola and the SDP was entitled *Farewell to Poverty*.

It was the manner of the SDP victory that was significant. To understand this, it should be noted that the basic political dichotomy in Nigeria is between the North and the South of the country. The North—which is predominantly Moslem and is more populous but more backward economically and educationally—has had a virtual monopoly of political power. It was always expected that the North would use its numerical strength to ensure the election of a Northerner and a Moslem as president, in order not to compound its economic disadvantages with the loss of political power. Yet in 1993 the North voted for Chief Abiola, the Southern candidate, who took more states there than the NRC candidate who came from Kano. It was just as significant that Abiola won so decisively in the South. It was assumed that he would perform disastrously in the Eastern States—Abia, Imo, Enugu, and Anambra—ones peopled by the Ibos who are supposedly the "traditional enemies" of the Yoruba, Chief Abiola's ethnic group. Yet he made an unexpectedly strong showing in this region.

Moreover, Chief Abiola, who is a Moslem, ran with a Moslem running mate. According to conventional wisdom, it should have been suicidal for Abiola not to have a Christian on the ticket in order to attract Southern voters. But conventional wisdom was confounded starkly when the South voted overwhelmingly for the Moslem-Moslem ticket (see appendix).

The military government rejected the result and resumed its rule, promising another democratic transition. This decision has plunged the country into a deep crisis, which some fear may yet lead to another civil war and disintegration. The polity has been polarized into those who believe that the democratic verdict of June 12, 1993, must be upheld, and those who believe in letting the government have its way in canceling an election which was certified to be free and fair by the government's own National Electoral Commission, the Center for Democratic Studies (CDS), as well as by all independent Nigerian monitoring groups and all foreign monitoring groups. The crisis of the presidential election has immensely increased the opposition to military rule, amidst widespread belief that the cancellation was made to extend the transition to civilian rule. Now the country is polarized politically between those who insist on democracy and those who are still attached to the old politics in which power is brokered by military and political chieftains of the political class, a politics in which power is based on ethnicity, religion, and region. It would appear that Nigeria's chances of making a success of the state-building project, and liberating her politics from political ethnicity, depend on the success of this fragile democratic constituency. If the election of June 12 is any guide, we may expect that this democratic constituency will win in the long run. The election indicates that a new political reality is emerging and will not be denied. But it promises to be a very long run which will, in all probability, be traumatic.

### Conclusion: A Democratic Solution?

A great deal will depend on the form and content of Nigeria's evolving democracy. The commitment to democracy, especially on the part of the elite leading the democracy movement is, with minor exceptions, shallow. For most of them, democratization is essentially a strategy of power. They concede the need for elections, but, only the election of themselves, by the free choice of the people if possible, by fraud and coercion if necessary.

Democracy is not yet being customized to the historical realities of Nigeria. The elite which leads the democracy movement is quite content with a simplified version of liberal democracy as electoral competition. Theirs is a democracy which presupposes social atomization and individualism, and a commitment to formal equality and abstract rights. But most Nigerians are very poor and struggling to survive; many are illiterate and in poor health. They are not served by abstract rights but by concrete rights that will allow them to improve their material well-being, to conquer ignorance and participate meaningfully in democratic politics. They are attached to their communal identities, which importantly form their sense of freedom and well-being, and which are not easily reconciled to the rugged individualism of liberal democracy.

In so far as democracy in Nigeria is situated in the social location and consciousness of ordinary people, as it must eventually in order to mean anything and to survive, it becomes clearer that far from fueling ethnic conflict as is so often assumed, the process of democratization will likely reduced it. A democratic Nigeria will minimize those tendencies which underlie the robustness of ethnicity: the divorce of public policy from social need, the image of the state as a hostile force, the marginalization of all but the few who control state power, and the overvaluing of state power as a means of security.

The initial shaky steps which Nigeria has taken towards democratization are encouraging greater political expression of social pluralism. Economically and politically marginalized groups are more articulate. There is a resurgence of minority rights movements and calls for a sovereign national conference to reexamine, if possible renegotiate, the basis of political association. These are not really signs of stress and instability but assets to democratization and state-building. The Nigerian state cannot attain viability until it begins to negotiate the consensus and accommodation which will give it legitimacy before its heterogeneous peoples. And it cannot find this accommodation unless it comes to terms with Nigeria's social pluralism through the negotiated consensus of democratic practice.

**Table 15.1. The June 12, 1993 Nigerian Presidential Election**

| S/No | State | S.D.P | S.D.P Score % | N.R.C | N.R.C Score % | Total Score | |
|---|---|---|---|---|---|---|---|
| 1 | Abia | 105,273 | 41.04 | 151,227 | 58.96 | 265,500 | (bc) |
| 2 | Adamawa | 140,875 | 45.72 | 167,239 | 54.28 | 308,114 | (a) |
| 3 | A/Ibom | 214,787 | 51.86 | 199,324 | 48.14 | 414,129 | (be) |
| 4 | Anambra | 212,024 | 57.11 | 159,258 | 42.89 | 371,282 | (bc) |
| 5 | Bauchi | 339,339 | 39.27 | 524,836 | 60.73 | 867,175 | (a) |
| 6 | Benue | 246,830 | 56.94 | 186,302 | 43.60 | 433,132 | (ae) |
| 7 | Borno | 153,496 | 54.40 | 128,684 | 45.60 | 282,180 | (ae) |
| 8 | C/River | 189,303 | 52.23 | 153,452 | 44.77 | 342,755 | (bc) |
| 9 | Delta | 327,277 | 69.30 | 145,001 | 30.70 | 427,278 | (be) |
| 10 | Edo | 205,407 | 66.48 | 103,572 | 33.54 | 308,979 | (be) |
| 11 | Enugu | 263,101 | 48.09 | 284,050 | 51.91 | 547,151 | (bc) |
| 12 | Imo | 159,350 | 44.86 | 195,836 | 55.14 | 355,186 | (bc) |
| 13 | Jigawa | 138,552 | 60.67 | 89,836 | 39.33 | 222,388 | (a) |
| 14 | Kaduna | 389,713 | 52.20 | 356,860 | 47.80 | 746,573 | (a) |
| 15 | Kano | 169,619 | 52.28 | 154,809 | 47.72 | 324,428 | (a) |
| 16 | Katsina | 171,162 | 38.70 | 271,077 | 61.30 | 22,329 | (a) |
| 17 | Kebbi | 70,219 | 32.66 | 144,808 | 67.34 | 215,027 | (a) |
| 18 | Kogi | 222,760 | 45.60 | 265,732 | 54.40 | 488,492 | (ae) |
| 19 | Kwara | 272,270 | 77.24 | 80,209 | 22.78 | 52,479 | (a) |
| 20 | Lagos | 883,965 | 85.54 | 149,432 | 14.46 | 1,033,397 | (db) |
| 21 | Niger | 136,350 | 38.10 | 221,437 | 61.90 | 357,787 | (ae) |
| 22 | Ogun | 425,725 | 87.78 | 59,246 | 12.22 | 484,971 | (bd) |
| 23 | Ondo | 883,024 | 84.42 | 162,994 | 15.58 | 1,046,018 | (bd) |
| 24 | Osun | 325,266 | 83.52 | 72,068 | 16.48 | 437,344 | (bd) |
| 25 | Oyo | 536,011 | 83.52 | 105,788 | 16.48 | 641,799 | (bd) |
| 26 | Plateau | 417,565 | 61.68 | 259,394 | 38.32 | 676,959 | (ae) |
| 27 | Rivers | 370,578 | 36.63 | 640,973 | 63.37 | 1,011,551 | (ca) |
| 28 | Sokoto | 97,726 | 20.79 | 327,250 | 79.21 | 469,976 | (a) |
| 29 | Taraba | 101,887 | 61.42 | 64,001 | 38.58 | 165,888 | (ae) |
| 30 | Yobe | 111,887 | 63.59 | 64,061 | 38.41 | 175,948 | (a) |
| 31 | Abuja | 19,968 | 52.16 | 18,313 | 47.84 | 38,281 | (FCT) |
| Total | | 8,341,309 | 58.36 | 5,952,087 | 41.64 | 14,293,396 | |

*Key*

| | | | |
|---|---|---|---|
| Northern States | (a) | Western States | (d) |
| Southern States | (b) | Minority States | (e) |
| Eastern States | (c) | Federal Capital Territory | (FCT) |

## References

Ake, C. 1985. "The Nigerian State: Antimonies of a Periphery Formation." In C. Ake, ed., *Political Economy of Nigeria*. London: Longman.

———. 1993. "What is the Problem of Ethnicity in Africa?" *Transformations* 22.

———. 1994. "A World of Political Ethnicity." In R. van den Berg and U. Bosma, eds., *Historical Dimensions of Development Change and Conflict in the South*. Hague: Ministry of Foreign Affairs.

Anderson, Benedict. 1983. *Imagined Communities: Reflections on the Origin and Spread of Nationalism*. London: Verso Editions and New Left Books.

Arrighi, G., T. K. Hopkins, and I. Wallerstein. 1989. *Antisystemic Movements*. London and New York: Verso.

Awolowo, Obafemi. 1974. *Path to Nigerian Freedom*. London: Faber and Faber.

Azikiwe, Nnamdi. 1961. *Zik: A Selection from the Speeches of Nnamdi Azikiwe*. Cambridge: Cambridge University Press.

Bamissaiye, A. 1971. "Ethnic Politics as an Instrument of Unequal Socio-economic Development in Nigeria's First Republic, African Notes." *Bulletin of the Institute of African Studies*. University of Ibadan.

Banton, M. 1983. *Ethnic and Racial Competition*. Cambridge and New York: Cambridge University Press.

———. 1960. *West African City: A Study of Tribal Life in Freetown*. London: Oxford University Press.

Brass, Paul. 1976. "Ethnicity and National Formation." *Ethnicity* 3.3.

Buell, R. L. 1928. *The Native Problem in Africa*. New York: Macmillan.

Cohen, A. P. 1978. "Ethnicity: Problems and Focus in Anthropology." *Annual Review of Anthropology* 7: 379–403.

———. 1985. *The Symbolic Construction of Community*. Chichester: Horwood.

———. 1981. "Variables in Ethnicity." C. Keyes, ed., *Ethnic Change*. Seattle: University of Washington Press, 307–31.

Conner, W. 1973. "The Politics of Ethnonationalism." *Journal of International Affairs* 27: 1–21.

———. 1973. "Ethnonationalism in the First World: The Present in Historical Perspective." In M. J. Esman, ed., *Ethnic Conflict in the Western World*. Ithaca: Cornell University Press, 19–45.

Chazan, Naomi, et al. 1992. *Politics and Society in Contemporary Africa.* Boulder, CO: Lynne Riener Publishers.

Chretian, J. P. 1985. "Hutu et Tutsi au Rwanda et au Burundi." In Jean Loup Amselle and Elikia Mbokolo, eds., *Au Coeur de L'Ethnie.* Paris: Editions la Decouverte.

Coleman, James. 1958. *Nigeria: Background to Nationalism.* Berkeley: University of California Press.

Crowley, Daniel J. 1963. "Politics and Tribalism in the Katanga." *The Western Political Quarterly* 16.1 (March).

Dashefsky, Arnold. 1975. "Theoretical Framework in the Study of Ethnic Identity: Toward a Social Psychology of Ethnicity." *Ethnicity* 2.

Devereux, G. 1975. "Ethnic Identity: Its Logical Foundations and its Dysfunctions." In G. de Vos and L. Romannuci-Ross, eds., *Ethnic Identity.* Palo Alto: Mayfield Publishing Company.

Ekeh, P. 1975. "Colonialism and Two Publics in Africa: A Theoretical Statement." *Comparative Studies in Society and History* 17: 19–112.

Enloc, C. 1973. *Ethnic Development and Political Conflict.* Boston: Little Brown and Company.

Fish, S. 1980. *Is there a Text in this Class? Theory of Interpretive Communities.* Cambridge, MA: Harvard University Press.

Giddens, A. 1980. *Modernity and Self-Identity: Self and Society in the Late Modern Age.* Stanford, CA: Stanford University Press.

Hechter, M. 1976. "Ethnicity and Industrialization: On the Cultural Division of Labour." *Ethnicity* 3: 214–24.

Horowitz, Donald L. 1985. *Ethnic Groups in Conflict.* Berkeley: University of California Press.

Jakubowics, A. 1984. "State and Ethnicity: Multiculturalism as Ideology." J. Jupp, ed., *Ethnic Politics in Australia.* London: G. Allen & Unwin.

Keyes, C. 1981. "The Dialectic of Ethnic Change." In C. Keyes, ed., *Ethnic Change.* Seattle: University of Washington Press.

Kirk-Greene, A. H. M. 1971. *Crisis and Conflict in Nigeria.* 2 vols. London: Oxford University Press.

Lema, Antoine. 1993. *Africa Divided: The Creation of "Ethnic Groups."* Lund: Lund University Press.

Mare, G. 1992. *Brothers Born of Warrior Blood: Politics and Ethnicity in South Africa.* Johannesburg: Ravan Press.

NcNeil, W. 1985. *Polyethnicity and National Unity in World History.* Toronto and Buffalo: University of Toronto Press.

Montville, J., ed. 1990. *Conflict and Peacemaking in Multi-Ethnic Societies.* Lexington, MA: Lexington Books.

Okamura, J. Y. 1981. "Situational Ethnicity." *Ethnic and Racial Studies* 4.4: 452–65.

Olzak, S. and J. Nagel. 1986. "Introduction. Competitive Ethnic Relations: An Overview." In S. Olzak and J. Nagel, eds., *Competitive Ethnic Relations.* Orlando: Academic Press.

Patterson, O. 1983. "The Nature, Causes, and Implications of Ethnic Identification." C. Fried, ed. *Minorities: Community and Identity.* Berlin and New York: Springer-Verlag.

Peil, Margaret. 1975. "Interethnic Contacts in Nigerian Cities." *Journal of International African Institute* 45.2.

Ringer, B. B. and E. R. Lawless. 1989. *Race-Ethnicity and Society.* New York: Routledge.

Rothchild, Donald and Victor A. Olorunsola, eds. 1983. *State Versus Ethnic Claims: African Policy Dilemmas.* Boulder, CO: Westview Press.

Sanda, Olu Akin. 1974. "A Comparative Analysis of Political Leadership and Ethnicity in Nigeria and Zaire." *Journal of East African Research and Development* 4.1.

St. Jorre, John de. 1972. *The Nigerian Civil War.* London: Hodder and Stoughton.

Smock, Audrey. 1971. *Ibo Politics: The Role of Ethnic Unions in Eastern Nigeria.* Cambridge, MA: Harvard University Press.

Smith, A. D. 1986. *The Ethnic Origins of Nations.* Oxford and New York: Basil Blackwell.

Smith, S. J. 1984. "Negotiating Ethnicity in an Uncertain Environment." *Ethnic and Racial Studies* 7.3: 360–73.

Stack, J. F. Jr., ed. 1986. *The Primordial Challenge: Ethnicity in the Contemporary World.* Westport, CT: Greenwood Press.

Stein, H. 1980. "Culture and Ethnicity as Group-fantasies: Psycho-historic Paradigm of Group Identity." *Journal of Psychology* 8.1: 21–51.

Volkan, V. 1990. "Psychoanalytic Aspects of Ethnic Conflict." In J. Montville, ed., *Conflict and Peacemaking in Multi-Ethnic Societies*. Lexington, MA: Lexington Books.

Wallerstein, I. 1991. "The Construction of Peoplehood: Racism, Nationalism, Ethnicity." In E. Balibar and I. Wallerstein, eds., *Race, Nation, Class: Ambiguous Identities*. London: Verso.

Wright, J. 1991. "Ethnicity and History: Towards Discussion of the Zulu Case." Unpublished seminar paper, Critical Studies Group, University of Natal, Pietermaritzburg.

# 16

## Canada and the Challenge of the Quebec Independence Movement

MARC V. LEVINE

After nearly two decades of challenge to Canada's political order, most observers agreed that by the mid-1980s Quebec nationalism had entered a period of quiescence. The stunning election in 1976 of the separatist Parti Québécois (PQ) to control of Quebec's provincial government had inaugurated a bona-fide national unity crisis in Canada. However, the PQ was thwarted in its 1980 referendum seeking a mandate from Quebec voters to negotiate "sovereignty-association," its version of independence. By 1985, fragmented and dispirited, the "separatists" were voted from power, replaced by the resolutely federalist Quebec Liberal party. The "national question," as it is called in Quebec, seemed settled for a generation.

In this context, it seemed perfectly reasonable to conclude that "Canada's most serious political crisis . . . appear[ed] to have run its course."[1] Some analysts even argued that Quebec had entered a post-nationalist era. Dominique Clift, perceiving an epochal shift in Francophone Québécois values from the collective (nationalist and social-democratic) to the individualistic (anti-nationalist and resolutely capitalist), insisted that Quebec nationalism "is destined to decline as a political movement. It can no longer be expected to dominate public debates as it has done now for more than twenty years. Timelier and more concrete concerns will be taking its place."[2] William Coleman went even further, arguing that "as Quebec's Francophone community has come to participate more fully in the continental economy, its culture has become more similar to others active in that economy. In the view of many, this has led to a situation where that inner quality burning in the hearts of Québécois will soon be extinguished. If this does happen, then the nationalist movement in Quebec will have failed and may itself die."[3]

But the burial of Quebec nationalism was premature. By the early 1990s, in the wake of two disastrously botched federal-provincial government efforts to restructure the Canadian Constitution in ways that would recognize Quebec's distinctiveness, Canada once again faced the possibility of national disintegration. Politicized Francophone nationalism re-emerged with renewed force in Quebec, with support for Quebec independence reaching unprecedented levels. In 1985, polls showed a mere 15 percent of Quebecers supporting independence; by late 1990, in the bitter aftermath of the failure of the Meech Lake constitutional agreement, support for independence reached 70 percent in one poll.[4] The Parti Québécois returned to power in the 1994 Quebec provincial elections, and in October 1995 held another referendum on Quebec sovereignty. In a result that sent shock waves throughout the rest of Canada, the sovereignists came within 50,000 votes of winning and beginning the process of secession. The inevitable next referendum may be held as early as 1997 or 1998, and although a victory for separation is hardly assured, the odds have swung sharply in favor of the breakup of Canada by the year 2000.

What happened? How did the "Quebec question" return with such force, after appearing settled following the devastating defeat of the *indépendantiste* forces in the 1980 referendum and the mid-1980s decline of the Parti Québécois? What is the likelihood that predominantly French-speaking Quebec will become an independent country by the end of the twentieth century?

I argue in this chapter that, although Quebec nationalism was dormant through most of the 1980s, a powerful combination of large-scale social, economic, and political changes in Canada and Quebec was setting the stage for a nationalist revival. In addition, the repoliticization of Quebec nationalism provides almost a textbook case-study of the mismanagement of social conflict in culturally divided societies. The misguided strategy deployed by Canadian Prime Minister Brian Mulroney and Quebec Premier Robert Bourassa to secure passage of the Meech Lake Accord was perhaps the single most important factor in rekindling independence sentiment in Quebec when the agreement was not ratified in 1990. Political leadership makes a difference, particularly in societies such as Canada that are seriously divided by ethnonationalist cleavages. Structural factors may have set the stage for an inevitable revival of Quebec nationalism sometime in the future, but it was the miscalculations of Canada's two most important political leaders in the late 1980s that brought the country to the brink of political disintegration.

This chapter is divided into four main sections. First, it provides a brief overview of the rise and fall of the modern Quebec independence movement, seeking mainly to explain the nationalist quiescence that seemed to take hold by the mid-1980s. Second, it offers a short narrative of the political events that helped rekindle separatist fervor in Quebec, including an assessment of the constitutional strategies of Mulroney and Bourassa. Third, it examines the large-scale social and economic factors that I believe provided a structural basis for the Quebec nationalist renaissance of the 1990s. Finally, it presents some informed speculation on "whither Quebec" in the 1990s.

**The Rise and Fall of the Quebec Independence Movement, 1968–1985**

Although French Canadian nationalism has always existed in Quebec, during the 1960s a more assertive Francophone "neo-nationalism" emerged to dominate the political landscape and challenge Canada's federal order. Spearheaded by a "new middle class" of Francophone teachers, journalists, and policy professionals, a great cultural and political awakening known as the "Quiet Revolution" swept through French Quebec during the 1960s.[5] At the heart of the Quiet Revolution was the assertion that the cultural survival and *épanouissement* (blossoming) of Francophone Quebec depended upon Francophones becoming "maîtres chez nous" (masters in our own house). This was no longer the traditional French Canadian nationalism of *la survivance* in which French cultural survival was predicated on ruralism, avoidance of modern (read: English) influences, and total fealty to the Catholic Church. Historically underdeveloped and economically dominated by a Montreal-based English-speaking minority, French Quebec would begin during the Quiet Revolution a full-scale *projet de société* of modernization and *rattrapage* (catching up) aimed at building a society in which the French language and culture could flourish in a dynamic, modern North American context. Put simply, the Quiet Revolution aimed to permit Francophones "de vivre à la fois en français et à la moderne."[6]

The central tenet of Quiet Revolution nationalism was that the Quebec provincial government, the chief governmental unit in Canada controlled by Francophones, would be the primary instrument responsible for safeguarding and developing the "French fact" in Quebec. Since 1960, when the ideology of the Quiet Revolution took hold, every Quebec provincial government has sought additional powers from the federal government in Ottawa for the purposes of building an autonomous, fully developed French-speaking state. The result, of course, has been thirty years of on-and-off confrontation between power-seeking Quebec governments and the Canadian federal government. Moreover, this combination of *étatisme* and neo-nationalism has produced in Quebec what Stéphane Dion calls "the most powerful subnational government in all of the OECD countries in terms of its share of resources and its scope of intervention."[7] By itself, this legacy of the Quiet Revolution, a well-developed subnational government controlled by a culturally anxious and nationalistic Francophone community, institutionalized an inherent source of challenge to the Canadian federal system.

Thus, after 1960, a clear majority of Francophone Québécois were nationalists in the Quiet Revolution sense of the term: strongly identifying with Quebec territory as "*la mère-patrie*" of Francophones in North America, and believing in the need for a strong, autonomous Quebec state to oversee societal development in a manner consistent with Francophone cultural security.[8] However, a logical step beyond the Quiet Revolution ideology was the emergence, in the late 1960s, of a modern Quebec independence movement. If, as the architects of the Quiet Revolution argued, an autonomous Quebec state were to be the *moteur principal* of Francophone security and development, would it not best serve that function as a *sovereign* state, unimpeded by a Canadian federal government in which Quebec Francophones would always represent a minority interest?

Several fringe political parties in Quebec began advocating independence in the early 1960s, and a small but noisy terrorist group, le Front de Libération du Québec, brought national-liberation type tactics to Montreal in support of the cause before flaming out in the "October crisis" of 1970. But the modern Quebec independence movement really began in 1968 with the formation of the Parti Québécois, a mass political party whose goal was to achieve Quebec independence through democratic (i.e. electoral) means. Led by the charismatic René Lévesque, a high-profile nationalist minister in the provincial Liberal governments of 1960-66, the PQ immediately mobilized the growing hard-core separatist constituency. In addition, as a party with a moderately social-democratic *projet de société*, it also attracted the support of labor, civil servants, teachers, and other classes of Québécois nationalists with a progressive social bent.[9]

The growth of the PQ during the 1970s was meteoric. In its first run in Quebec provincial elections in 1970 it received 23 percent of the popular vote; in the 1973 elections PQ support rose to 30 percent (including 44.5 percent of the vote in predominantly Francophone ridings on Montreal Island).[10] An *indépendantiste* party was now Quebec's main political alternative to the ruling Liberal party.

Through the mid-1970s, though, surveys still showed support for Quebec independence never exceeding 18 percent of the electorate.[11] Nonetheless, by the mid-1970s, the PQ was able to augment its core separatist support by appealing to a significant number of moderate nationalists concerned about the most burning policy question in Quebec: the issue of language policy. The continuing strength of English in Montreal through the early 1970s, as the city's language of work and of upward mobility, was an ongoing grievance for Francophone nationalists feeling the cultural pride and new economic possibilities of the Quiet Revolution. In addition, by the early 1970s, linguistic trends in Montreal seemed to threaten the *cultural survival* of Francophones. In overwhelming numbers, immigrants to Montreal were sending their children to the city's English-language schools. Francophone nationalists feared that, as these immigrants integrated into the Anglophone community, the demographic position of Francophones would erode and the future of French would be threatened. Indeed, one highly publicized demographic study suggested that Francophones could become close to a minority on Montreal Island by the year 2000.[12] In this context, by advocating restrictive language laws to protect the French language in Quebec, the PQ became the electoral vehicle for Francophone nationalists concerned about *la question linguistique*, thus expanding the party's political base. In fact, the PQ's support has always swelled when the language issue is at the top of the Quebec political agenda.[13]

The PQ was also able to attract electoral support from nonseparatist nationalists by adopting in 1974 a strategy of *étapisme*, or independence in stages. The *étapiste* strategy decoupled provincial elections from a declaration of independence by promising that the PQ would hold a referendum on sovereignty *after* coming to power. Thus, Quebec Francophone voters could feel free to express their nationalistic concerns by voting PQ—or, for that matter, voting against the ruling Liberal party for any number of reasons—without necessarily opting immediately for the uncharted waters of Quebec independence.[14]

This strategy paid off in 1976 when, a mere eight years after its founding, the Parti Québécois ousted an unpopular Liberal government in the Quebec provincial elections. For the first time in an advanced Western democracy, an ethnonationalist separatist party was elected to control a subnational government (even if, given the workings of *étapisme*, the PQ's mandate in 1976 was merely to provide "good government" rather than build an independent Quebec).

The four years of PQ government leading to the 1980 sovereignty referendum represented a high-tide of Quebec separatism. Within a year of its election victory, the PQ passed a far-reaching language law, Bill 101, which radically reshaped Quebec's linguistic landscape: It required all new immigrants to send their children to French-language schools, mandated French as the primary language of the workplace, and proscribed, with only minor exceptions, languages other than French in commercial signs in the province. As the PQ declared in its language policy White Paper:

> There will no longer be any question of a bilingual Quebec. . . . The Quebec we wish to build will be essentially French. The fact that the majority of its population is French will be clearly visible—at work, in communications, and in the countryside. It will also be a country in which the traditional balance of power will be altered, especially in regard to the economy; the use of French will not merely be universalized to hide the predominance of foreign powers from the French-speaking population.[15]

In a very real sense, then, Bill 101 was viewed by Quebec separatists as the legislative prelude to Quebec independence: the linguistic character of an "embryonic nation-state" was being defined, in fundamental challenge to the policies of national bilingualism pursued by Canada's federal government.[16]

After four years of sparring with the Canadian federal government, led by federalist Quebecer Pierre Elliot Trudeau, the PQ finally held its referendum in May 1980. Sixty percent of Quebec voters, including a slight majority of Francophones, rejected the PQ effort to secure a mandate to negotiate its option of "sovereignty-association": political sovereignty with economic association with the rest of Canada. The referendum results revealed clearly that, although nationalism was a dominant ideology in French Quebec, there were profound divisions among Francophones over how their national interests should best be pursued. Moreover, the economic development of Francophone Quebec was still such that fears over the economic costs of sovereignty were a major issue in voter decisionmaking; questions about the economic viability of an independent Quebec colored much of the referendum debate, and clearly discouraged a significant percentage of voters from supporting sovereignty. Finally, some analysts have suggested that the "PQ-as-government" may have unwittingly undermined the "PQ-as-independence-movement" by such policies as Bill 101, which may have helped reduce by 1980 the cultural anxieties that had fueled the growth of Quebec separatism throughout the 1970s. Bill 101 seemed to buttress the status of French in Quebec *before* the advent of independence, channeling immigrant children into French schools, reducing the status of English in the economy, and engendering a French face in the province. If these cultural and economic advances were possible under federalism, voters may have wondered how compelling was the need for independence, especially in view of the economic uncertainties attending such a shift.

The referendum clearly revealed what political scientist Louis Balthazar has called Francophone Quebec's three "publics,"[17] a cleavage that has persisted since the referendum. Quebec Francophones are generally divided into three main camps on the "national question": federalist, confederalist, and separatist. About 15–20 percent of the Francophone electorate is solidly federalist, with a firm attachment to Canada, and about 15–20 percent is hard-core separatist, supporting Quebec independence *pur et dur*. The remaining 60 percent or so of Francophones, called confederalists by Balthazar, are moderate-to-strong nationalists who, while finding the federalist status quo unacceptable are normally, for a variety of reasons, leery of independence. Their preferred constitutional options range from "renewed federalism," with greater autonomy for Quebec, to perhaps some milder forms of sovereignty, such as the "sovereignty-association" espoused by the PQ (although polls have consistently revealed an astonishing confusion among Québécois over precisely what sovereignty-association would entail).[18] During the 1980 referendum, the majority of confederalists—perhaps for economic reasons, maybe for reasons of wanting to give Canada "one last chance"—were unable to support the PQ option. But, despite general quiescence on the national question in the 1980s, these confederalists did not become ardent supporters of Canadian federalism and, as we shall see, when political conditions changed dramatically by the early 1990s, many were ready to declare themselves in favor of an independent Quebec.

In the aftermath of the bitter referendum defeat, the PQ nevertheless regained its footing to score a mildly surprising reelection victory in the 1981 provincial elections. However, things unraveled quickly thereafter for the party, and for Quebec nationalism in general. Pierre Trudeau's successful "repatriation" of the Canadian Constitution, without the assent of the Lévesque government, further weakened the PQ. A bitter strike pitted the PQ against Quebec public employees in 1982–83: in the midst of the deep recession, the PQ rolled back wage increases for teachers and civil servants. This action placed the party in opposition to some of its historically core constituencies, and further fragmented the PQ coalition. As Graham Fraser has written, a general post-referendum fatigue, moroseness, and disorientation overtook party militants, its leadership, and indeed the separatist movement.[19] Bill 101 had taken the edge of off the language question, historically the prime stimulant of nationalist mobilization. Furthermore, at least in the short-term, the rise of a Francophone business culture—ironically, in part a product of the successes of PQ language and economic policies aimed at nurturing a Francophone capitalist class— also helped undermine the nationalist project. As Kenneth McRoberts points out, this new business culture "through its attack on the desirability or efficacy of state intervention . . . served to undermine a central premise of the neo-nationalist argument for Quebec sovereignty."[20] By the mid-1980s, Francophone "entrepreneurialism" was all the vogue in Quebec, *étatisme* in general was discredited in an increasingly conservative political climate, and state-oriented nationalism was presumed *passé*.

Its sovereignty rejected by Quebec voters, its social-democratic *projet de société* and progressive coalition in tatters, and its leadership undermined by defections and political fatigue, the PQ's "*indépendantiste* moment" appeared to have passed. In 1984, the federal Conservative party under bilingual Anglo-Quebecer Brian Mulroney swept to office, winning a landslide in Quebec with promises to undo the "wrongs" visited on Quebec by the 1982 Trudeau Constitution (and with a substantial number of highly nationalistic MPs elected to the Mulroney government from Quebec). In this climate, PQ leader René Lévesque officially declared the sovereignty option in "mothballs" as he endorsed the "*beau risque*" of Mulroney federalism. In 1985, "normalcy" returned in the Quebec provincial elections as the exhausted Parti Québécois was routed by the Liberals, led by Robert Bourassa. Quebec seemed to have entered a post-nationalist era.

### Meech Lake, Charlottetown, and the Repoliticization of Quebec Nationalism

To institutionalize this nationalist quiescence and pursue their business-oriented, neo-conservative policy agenda without the distraction of the "national unity question," the Mulroney and Bourassa governments quickly began actions to gain Quebec's approval of the Canadian Constitution (which had been lacking since Trudeau's 1982 repatriation). The timing seemed propitious: with Quebec nationalism quiescent, it was hoped that a modest set of constitutional reforms could bury for the foreseeable future the spectre of Quebec independence.

The Bourassa government offered five conditions necessary for Quebec to accept a new constitutional accord:

1. Formal recognition of Quebec as a "distinct society" in the Canadian Confederation;
2. Constitutional formalization of a 1978 federal-provincial agreement (the Cullen-Couture agreement) giving Quebec primary control of immigration to the province;
3. A Quebec veto over future constitutional amendments changing federal institutions;

4. Restrictions on federal spending in areas of provincial jurisdiction, and guarantees of Quebec's right to "opt out" with compensation from any programs that were transferred by other provinces to the federal government; and

5. Quebec participation in the appointment of judges to the Canadian Supreme Court.[21]

These "five minimum conditions," as the Bourassa government called them, became the basis for a constitutional accord hammered out by Prime Minister Mulroney and the ten provincial premiers at Meech Lake in April 1987, and signed in June of that year. As specified in the Canadian Constitution, provincial legislatures would then be required to ratify the Meech Lake Accord within three years for its provisions to become part of the Constitution.

Expected to be a pro-forma ratification, the process unraveled over the next three years. In three provinces (New Brunswick, Newfoundland, and Manitoba), premiers who had signed the accord were voted out of office during the ratification period, and replaced by premiers who were critical of significant elements of the accord. In particular, the "distinct society" clause became a lightening rod for concern in English Canada, critics suggesting that the clause might confer a "special status" on Quebec, placing it above other provinces.[22] In Quebec, as English Canadian politicians attacked the distinct society clause, it quickly assumed importance as a symbolic constitutionalization of Quebec's sociocultural uniqueness and special place in confederation as the *foyer* of French Canada. Even if most legal experts argued that the distinct society clause would have little real impact on the distribution of powers in confederation, the symbolic importance of the provision was enormous. In culturally divided societies, these symbols take on a political life of their own. Each time criticism was levied against the distinct society clause, Francophone anxiety grew in Quebec. As Charles Taylor points out: "The Meech Lake Accord was important because it was the first time that recognition of Canadian duality and the special role of Quebec was being written into a statement of what Canada was about. . . . Anyone who can use the expression 'just symbolic' has missed something essential about the nature of modern society."[23]

Several other events during the 1987–90 ratification period also divided Quebec and the rest of Canada, placing the accord in jeopardy and paving the way for a resurgence in Quebec nationalism. The 1988 federal elections, in which the Canada-U.S. Free Trade Agreement was the most prominent political issue, found Quebec and large portions of English Canada on opposite sides (with Quebec, led by its burgeoning Francophone *entrepreneuriat*, strongly supporting the agreement). As Philip Resnick has written, many anti-free trade voters in English Canada felt strong resentment at the Quebec position. Resnick's own writing, in his "letters" to an imaginary Québécois friend, conveys these feelings: "You voted in this election with supreme indifference to the issues of both Canadian identity and appropriate models of society so clearly posed in the rest of Canada. What mattered to your political elites (and their big business backers) were the gains (real or hypothetical) that Quebec stood to make from the deal. . . . Your attitude bespoke a sacred egoism bordering on contempt."[24]

The anti-Meech and anti-Quebec backlash in English Canada intensified in late 1988 and early 1989 with another language dispute in Quebec. In December 1988, the Canadian Supreme Court struck down portions of Bill 101 mandating unilingual French commercial signs. However, a firestorm of Francophone reaction, including some of the largest street demonstrations in Quebec history, persuaded Quebec Premier Bourassa to invoke a provision in the 1982 Constitution, the so-called "notwithstanding clause," which permitted him to nullify the Court's decision. In addition, in a disastrous effort at linguistic compromise, the Bourassa government passed Bill 178, a new language law that still limited outdoors commercial signs to French-only, but permitted, under certain conditions, other languages along with French (i.e., English) on signs *inside* some stores. This so-called "inside-outside" compromise satisfied no one. In Quebec, Bill 178 provided an impetus for Francophone nationalist mobilization, while anti-Meech forces in English Canada portrayed Bill 178 as a disturbing indication of what policies Quebec might pursue under Meech's distinct society clause.[25]

Thus, in the wake of the election of recalcitrant premiers, divisions over free trade, and the controversy surrounding Bill 178, it became apparent by mid-1989 that the Meech Lake accord was in serious trouble. It was at this point that Bourassa and Mulroney, facing the constitutionally determined June 23, 1990, deadline for ratification of Meech, undertook a fateful, high-risk gamble that ultimately opened the way for a full-scale repoliticization of Quebec nationalism and an unprecedented surge in support for Quebec independence. In an effort to persuade the balking premiers in English Canada to support Meech, both Bourassa and Mulroney deliberately fostered a crisis atmosphere, explicitly raising the threat of renewed separatism in Quebec if Meech were rejected.

In Quebec, this rhetoric transformed Meech Lake from a relatively innocuous constitutional agreement—up to this point the PQ and most nationalists had scoffed at its importance—to a potent symbol of whether Quebec's distinctiveness as a Francophone society would be recognized by the rest of Canada. Moreover, by raising apocalyptic scenarios of what could happen if Meech were rejected, Bourassa and Mulroney seemed to legitimize sovereignty as a rational response to English Canada's failure to ratify the accord. In culturally divided societies, leaders interested in conflict management normally try to defuse explosive cultural issues by attempting to focus debate on technical, nonloaded issues.[26] Bourassa and Mulroney literally rolled the dice by politicizing the most sensitive of issues: Quebec's sense of cultural self-esteem. Meech was no longer a technical discussion of Canada's division of powers, left chiefly to constitutional law specialists; it was now about whether English Canada would "accept" Quebec's distinctiveness, an explosive debate, as Charles Taylor points out, over "recognition."[27]

Moreover, by playing the separatist "card" and invoking the threat of a revived Quebec independence to pressure the other provincial premiers, Bourassa unwittingly created a self-fulfilling prophecy. There were, for example, less extreme alternatives to Bourassa's "it's either Meech or the separatists" strategy for securing passage of the accord. Bourassa could simply have said that if the rest of Canada did not accept his constitutional proposals, Quebec would continue to boycott constitutional reform until it did. Instead, the "sleeping dog" of independence was awakened, and events soon surged well beyond Bourassa's control.

The Bourassa-Mulroney strategy backfired monumentally when Meech failed, and an unprecedented surge of Quebec nationalism and sentiment for independence swept across the province. As table 16.1 shows, the period after Meech witnessed the highest support for Quebec independence among all Quebec voters since pollsters began asking the question in the early 1960s.[28]

Clearly, in the aftermath of Meech, with leaders articulating sentiments of cultural "humiliation" and "rejection," Quebec Francophone public opinion was mobilized for something radical.[29] As Jean-François Lisée has argued in his exhaustive two-volume study of the post-Meech period, there was a "window" of public opinion consensus: virtually 80 percent of Quebec Francophones were in favor of sovereignty. There is little doubt that had Bourassa been so inclined, he could have called a snap referendum on Quebec sovereignty, linked arms with the PQ, and launched an independent Quebec.[30]

Instead, in the period after Meech, although Bourassa refused to meet in any further constitutional discussions until the provisions of Meech Lake were accepted in English Canada, his pro-Canada confederalist proclivities became more and more evident. Two working groups convened by Bourassa, the Allaire group within his Liberal party and the "blue-ribbon" Commission on the Political and Constitutional Future of Québec (the Bélanger-Campeau Commission), issued radical reports calling for a massive transfer of powers to Quebec, far beyond those contained in Meech and bordering on de facto sovereignty. Bélanger-Campeau also pushed for a 1991 referendum on sovereignty. Bourassa essentially ignored the substantive demands of the two groups—he labeled them bases for negotiation, not Quebec's definitive position—and modified the referendum deadline and its subject. "The master of time," Bourassa delayed holding a referendum until 1992 (to let Quebec public opinion demobilize from the sting of Meech) and changed the content of a potential referendum to either sovereignty or credible constitutional offers from the rest of Canada.[31]

Although his approach was clearly running against Quebec public opinion at the time, Bourassa's stature as the most admired leader in Quebec (derived largely from his dignified public interventions in the immediate post-Meech period and from his courageous battle with cancer beginning in mid-1990) enabled him to stall successfully on the sovereignty referendum. By mid-1992, with his own deadlines approaching, Bourassa returned to the federal-provincial conference table and a new

**Table 16.1. Quebec Public Opinion on Independence, 1965–1993 (all adult Quebec citizens)**

| Year of Survey | In Favor | Opposed | Undecided |
|---|---|---|---|
| 1965 | 7 | 79 | 14 |
| 1968 | 10 | 72 | 18 |
| 1970 | 11 | 74 | 16 |
| 1973 | 17 | 64 | 19 |
| 1976 | 18 | 58 | 24 |
| 1979 (March) | 16 | 72 | 12 |
| 1979 (November) | 19 | 72 | 9 |
| 1980 (March) | 28 | 64 | 8 |
| 1981 | 22 | 62 | 16 |
| 1985 | 15 | 74 | 11 |
| 1989 | 29 | 56 | 15 |
| 1990 (February) | 47 | 52 | 1 |
| 1990 (May) | 53 | 44 | 3 |
| 1990 (June) | 70 | 23 | 7 |
| 1990 (November) | 53 | 33 | 14 |
| 1991 (May) | 43 | 47 | 10 |
| 1992 (July) | 34 | 54 | 12 |
| 1993 (April) | 40 | 47 | 13 |
| 1994 (September) | 35 | 51 | 14 |
| 1995 (February) | 38 | 57 | 3 |

*Sources*: Edouard Cloutier et al., *Le virage* (Montreal: Quebec/Amerique); Philip Authier, "No 60%, Yes 40%: Poll," *The Gazette* (Montreal), February 17, 1995, p. A1; Sarah Scott, "Divide and Conquer," *The Gazette* (Montreal), September 10, 1994, p. B1.

set of Meech look-alike proposals were hammered out, the so-called Charlottetown accord. In October 1992 the accord was presented to Canadians in a nationwide referendum. Seven of Canada's ten provinces, including Quebec, voted down the accord, and it entered the growing historical dustbin of failed constitutional proposals.

But Bourassa's tactics succeeded, at least in the short-term. By avoiding an early referendum, the "Meech moment," a period of astonishing consensus within Quebec for radical constitutional action, passed. By 1992, Quebec was suffering from palpable constitutional fatigue; the supercharged atmosphere of *après Meech* seemed ended. The Quebec sovereignty movement hardly faded away, though. Indeed, with the election of the PQ in 1994 and the promise of a referendum in 1995, Canada seemed poised for yet another national unity crises. The 1990–92 crisis, which witnessed unprecedented levels of support for independence in Quebec, saw radical action stifled by an age old political strategy: "muddling through". What remains to be seen is if muddling through will suffice for the next round.

### The New Quebec Nationalism: Structural Determinants of the Post-Meech Surge

As I have argued, the political fiasco surrounding the Meech Lake Accord and, in particular, the questionable tactics deployed by Bourassa and Mulroney in pushing the accord, played a major role in rekindling Quebec nationalism. Leaders who deliberately politicize cultural issues, and heighten ethnonational feelings of rejection and humiliation, unleash powerful forces that are difficult to control.

But Meech was just a catalyst for the reemergence of nationalism. After all, as Maurice Pinard has pointed out, the past thirty years of Canadian history is littered with failed constitutional agreements, and while these failures all helped stoke the fires of the Quebec independence movement, none engendered quite the explosive reaction as did the failure of the Meech Lake Accord.[32] Even the image of nine English Canadian provinces "ganging up" with Pierre Trudeau to repatriate the 1982 Constitution over the objections of the Quebec government did not generate the kind of response that followed in the wake of Meech. In my view, several changes occurring in Quebec's social composition and economy during the 1980s rendered Francophones more susceptible to a nationalist resurgence than they appeared during the post-1980 referendum period.

First, although Bill 101 significantly improved the status of French in Quebec in the 1980s, an evolving set of cultural anxieties continued to preoccupy Francophones. As has been well-documented,[33] Bill 101 altered Quebec's linguistic dynamics in several areas seen as vital by nationalist Francophones: channeling immigrant children into French-language schools, and establishing French as Quebec's language of work, business transactions, and commercial signs.

However, during the 1980s new concerns arose over the linguistic and cultural security of French Québécois. Studies showed that English still remained a powerful force attracting immigrants in Quebec, even as massive numbers of Allophones—non-English, non-French residents—were compelled by Bill 101 to send their children to French schools.[34] Moreover, the influx of Allophone children into Montreal's historically ethnically homogeneous French schools resulted in something of a "culture shock" in Francophone quarters: by the late 1980s, over one-fifth of Montreal's French-language schools contained a *majority* of students whose native tongue was not French. In 1990, a nasty conflict erupted in Montreal's largest French school system over efforts by the school board to prohibit Allophone children from using English as a language of communication outside the classroom (i.e., in the cafeteria or schoolyard) in these multiethnic French schools. Although the policy was opposed by numerous Francophone groups and was never implemented, the

"English in the schoolyards" controversy nevertheless revealed growing tensions over French Montreal's cultural transformation, as did several highly publicized clashes at a number of Montreal-area schools between Allophones and Franco-phones *de souche* (native-born Francophones). These episodes left little doubt that there was considerable anxiety in the Francophone community over the new cultural and linguistic dynamics in Montreal's French schools, and, by extension, in Quebec society as a whole.

Since Bill 101 was enacted, French-language schools and other Francophone social institutions have had to make major adjustments, in a relatively short period of time, to integrate diverse cultural communities into a heretofore homogeneous Francophone society that has little experience with intracommunity ethnic diversity. Fundamental questions of cultural redefinition—to what degree should multicul-turalism recast French-Québécois culture and what will be the place of diverse ethnic and racial communities within a French-speaking society—became almost overnight central preoccupations for intellectuals and policymakers.[35]

In Montreal, the persistent strength of English in the officially French-speaking *métropole* means that immigrant integration occurs in an ambiguous, dualistic linguistic context, "where," as political scientist Daniel Latouche puts it, "the French language and Québécois culture have only a *relative* predominance."[36] The integration of immigrants into new societies is a difficult and often conflictual process under any circumstances, but Montreal's unique linguistic heritage makes this process especially problematic. Thus, notwithstanding the impact of Bill 101, the growing proportion of non-Francophones in Montreal's population (see table 16.2) became a source of cultural unease in the Francophone community during the 1980s.

This anxiety became all the more palpable in the 1980s with a series of well-publicized studies on the continuing demographic lag among Quebec Francophones *de souche*. Once "the breeders of North America" as René Lévesque colorfully observed, the Quebec Francophone birthrate is now 1.2 children per childbearing woman, among the lowest rates in the West. As one demographer's analysis puts it: *Naître ou ne pas être* (Give birth—or cease to exist).[37] A polemical television docu-mentary in 1989, entitled *Disparaître* (To Disappear), caused quite a stir in Quebec by raising the specter of a disappearing native Francophone population, displaced by growing numbers of immigrants, especially those who in Canadian parlance are called "visible minorities": nonwhite immigrants from places such as Haiti, Jamaica, Vietnam, Pakistan, and North Africa. This was an especially controversial issue as the Quebec government had just embarked on a program that significantly increased the number of immigrants admitted to Quebec, in part to counteract the province's low birthrate, and numerous analysts questioned the ability of Francophone society to successfully absorb and integrate a radical increase in immigrants.[38] (The govern-ment also initiated a series of "natalist" policies, such as offering a "baby bonus" that reaches $6,000 for a third child.)

**Table 16.2. The Linguistic Composition of Montreal, 1971–1991**
(% of persons of French mother tongue in total population and in the schools
on the Island of Montreal)

| Population | 1971 | 1976 | 1981 | 1986 | 1991 |
|---|---|---|---|---|---|
| Total Population | 61.2 | 60.1 | 59.7 | 60.1 | 56.8 |
| Schoolchildren | 63.8 | 58.9 | 56.4 | 54.2 | 51.2 |

*Sources*: Statistics Canada; Conseil scolaire de l'Île de Montréal; Conseil de la langue française.

In short, demolinguistic data offered a mixed reading on the future of French in Montreal—significant progress combined with formidable obstacles and persistent risks. These ambiguities were compounded by the lack of a clear consensus within the Francophone community regarding the relationship of multiethnicity and immigration to an evolving redefinition of Québécois culture. As François Rocher and Guy Rocher aptly observe, "these circumstances occur at a moment when Quebec Francophones do not know exactly who they are."[39] Thus, the Meech debacle came at a time of gnawing unease in the Francophone community over cultural change and linguistic security, a time when Francophone Québécois were likely to be highly sensitive to perceived cultural slights such as those discerned in the anti-Meech backlash in English Canada.

A second structural factor paving the way for a rapid recrudescence of Quebec nationalism was the declining demographic and economic weight of the Anglophone community in the province. English-speakers were historically a *minorité majoritaire* in Quebec. They were a demographic minority in the province, but part of the Canadian English-speaking majority and unquestionably the group controlling economic power in the province. Indeed, well into the mid-twentieth century, most major Canadian corporations were headquartered in Montreal, controlled by Anglophones and operating in English. The Quiet Revolution, the rise of the Parti Québécois, and Bill 101 helped change all that, with the result that over 250,000 Anglophones had left Quebec since the 1970s, chiefly for Ontario and the booming Toronto region.[40] Moreover, Toronto's displacement of Montreal as the preferred location for corporate headquarters further diminished the weight of Anglophone economic power in Quebec. To be sure, English Canadian businessmen remain firm opponents of Quebec separatism. But, with Montreal increasingly functioning as a French-speaking regional economic center, instead of its historical status as Canada's national economic center, these Anglophone capitalists are less likely to view a sovereign Quebec in the same apocalyptic manner that they did in the 1960s or 1970s. Furthermore, with fewer powerful Anglophone interests located in Quebec, and with the demographic strength of Anglophones reduced after two decades of outmigration, the ability of Quebec Anglophones to function as a counterweight to separatism is much more limited today than even at the time of the 1980 referendum.

This development is closely related to a third structural factor underpinning the new Quebec nationalism, namely, the rise of a Francophone capitalist class in Quebec. The 1980s witnessed the full flowering of Quiet Revolution and PQ initiatives aimed at creating a Francophone corporate establishment in Quebec. As Anglophone capital continued its withdrawal from the province, Francophone enterprises assumed a more prominent role in the economy. As current PQ Premier Jacques Parizeau notes: "When all those English Canadian companies were pulling out during the PQ's first few years in power, I maintained my equanimity. I realized it would simply open the way for French Canadians to step in and take control over those fields."[41] Across Quebec, the percentage of workers employed by establishments under Francophone control increased from 47.1 percent in 1961 to 54.8 percent in 1978 and 61.6 percent in 1987.[42]

By the mid-1980s, under the popular label "Quebec, Inc.," a formidable network was in place of Francophone-controlled state corporations, private financial institutions, and large as well as medium-sized, export-oriented businesses. Large public corporations such as Hydro-Québec and the Caisse de Dépôt et Placement provide natural resource and financial underpinnings to Quebec enterprise. The Caisse de Dépôt was particularly important in reducing Quebec's dependence on non-Quebec capital, clearly a concern in earlier years when the threat of "capital strikes" against an independent Quebec where routinely invoked to dampen Francophone nationalism. The Caisse de Dépôt manages funds collected by the Quebec Pension Plan (Quebec opted out of Canada's plan in 1965), now has assets approaching $50 billion, and has since the late 1970s often used "nationalistic" criteria in its investment decisions, often supporting Francophone entrepreneurs in corporate merger and acquisition battles.[43] Other Francophone-controlled financial giants, such as the Banque nationale du Canada and the Mouvement Desjardins, are major forces in the Quebec economy, and corporations such as Bombardier, SNC-Lavalin, and Canam-Manac have carved out international market niches as Quebec private enterprise "success stories."[44]

The rising profile of a Francophone business class has been an important element in the new wave of Quebec nationalism. Unlike the 1980 referendum, when questions concerning the economic viability of an independent Quebec seriously undermined support for the PQ option, there is little doubt today in the minds of virtually all serious analysts that an independent Quebec, with or without economic association with the rest of Canada, would be economically viable. There are serious disagreements over the economic costs of separation, ranging from projections of minor "transition costs" to major long-term increases in unemployment and a precipitous drop in Quebecers' standard of living.[45] But there is no longer any suggestion, as there was in 1980, that the withdrawal of Anglophone capital in the event of sovereignty would leave the Quebec economy totally crippled. The rise of prominent Francophone enterprises, particularly its strong, autonomous financial network, puts Quebec a long way from infamous episodes such as the so-called "Brinks Show" during the 1970 provincial elections when, to discourage support for the PQ, the Royal Trust Company assembled a convoy of nine Brinks trucks, allegedly carrying securities from its Montreal headquarters to Toronto, to visibly frighten Quebec voters about the consequences of a PQ victory. The rise of Francophone capitalism has undercut what was the Anglophone establishment's staple argument against Quebec independence: that Anglophones were the effective managers of the Quebec economy and, therefore, to avoid a massive flight of capital from Quebec, Francophones should resist the false allure of nationalism and separatism.

Another important nationalist consequence of the rise of Francophone capitalism is that unlike 1980, when Francophone and Anglophone businessmen were virtually united in their opposition to the PQ project, there are now at least some influential Francophone business elites who view sovereignty as desirable for Quebec's economic development. Symbolically, Jean Campeau and Michel Bélanger, two powerful Francophone businessmen, were the co-chairs of the Quebec's sovereignty-oriented blue ribbon commission. Although Bélanger subsequently returned unequivocally to the federalist fold—in 1995 he accepted co-chairmanship of the "Non" committee in the referendum on Quebec sovereignty—Campeau became a member of the PQ government, along with former head of the Canadian Manufacturer's Association, Richard Le Hir. Claude Béland, president of the powerful financial institution Mouvement Desjardins, has been an outspoken advocate of Quebec sovereignty since Meech. While some observers became carried away during the post-Meech period and argued that Francophone businessmen would "lead" the *démarche* to sovereignty, the majority of the Quebec business elite still favor some form of federal relationship; indeed, the Quebec Conseil du Patronat remains one of the strongest opponents of sovereignty. However, with business no longer monolithically opposed to sovereignty, and with some powerful corporate interests now squarely on the pro-sovereignty side, a major obstacle to an independent Quebec has been lessened. Certainly, during the post-Meech period, Francophone businesses were active participants in the nationalist mobilization, a marked shift from Quebec's past, and the "market nationalist" orientation of the new Quebec sovereignty movement bespeaks this business influence.

Two additional structural factors that made the Quebec environment in the late 1980s conducive to nationalist resurgence need to be mentioned briefly. First, as symbolized by the strong support of Quebec elites for the Canada-U.S. Free Trade Agreement and NAFTA, the globalization of economic life has attenuated economic links between Quebec and the rest of Canada. To be sure, Canadian markets still represent the vast majority of Quebec's exports and imports, and a sovereign Quebec would undoubtedly need to maintain friendly access to these markets. But data on interprovincial trade flows show that between 1974 and 1989 the proportion of Quebec's manufacturing shipments destined for the rest of Canada declined from

37.3 percent to 24.8 percent; a similar decline occurred in trade flows between other Canadian provinces and Quebec. Between 1989 and 1994, in the aftermath of the two trade agreements, aggregate interprovincial trade in Canada declined by over 15 percent, while trade between the United States and Canada rose by over 70 percent.[46] It is difficult to avoid the conclusion that, as the Quebec economy is more integrated into global markets and, in particular, the U.S. market, that Quebec's economic commitment to Canadian federalism will diminish. As Quebec becomes less dependent on Canadian markets, the historical argument that sovereignty entails too many economic risks—the most powerful anti-independence weapon in the 1980 referendum—loses much of its potency. As Richard Simeon observes, "global and North American integration promotes Canadian disintegration."[47] If, as Simeon, Thomas Courchene, and others argue, globalization shifts economic power from central-states to smaller units of government, then clearly the rapid globalization of economic life in the 1980s helped resuscitate Quebec nationalism at the end of the decade.

Finally, the Mulroney Conservatives' attack on the Canadian state after 1984 also unwittingly helped unleash centrifugal tendencies in the country. Put simply, cutbacks in social programs and, in particular, slashes in transfer payments to provinces helped lessen the importance of the central government in the daily lives of Quebecers (and other Canadians) and refocused citizens' attention on provincial governments as their primary states. "Fiscal decentralization" from Ottawa during the Mulroney years resulted in important expenditure shifts that de-emphasized the centrality of the federal government in Canadian life: federal spending on social programs and transfers to the provinces, as a percentage of GDP, declined from 15.0 percent in 1984 to 13.5 percent in 1991.[48] According to Pierre Fournier, 30 percent of Quebec government revenue in 1980 derived from federal funds; by 1992, the figure had declined to 18 percent. This trend was bound to reduce not only Quebec's reliance on the federal government but also its allegiance.[49]

Despite significant cuts, the federal budget fell deeply out of balance by the early 1990s, with Canada running a deficit, relative to GDP, higher than any country in the G7. This "crisis of public finance" in Canada undermines what had historically been one of the strongest arguments in Quebec against independence. As Jeffrey Simpson notes, "federalists who fought the 1980 referendum on sovereignty-association warned Quebecers about separating from a fiscal powerhouse. A decade later, federalists were reduced to warning that secession would require Quebec to absorb roughly a quarter of Canada's staggering national debt."[50]

Furthermore, the anti-state rhetoric of the Mulroney government depreciated the value of the central government, an approach to political economy that could only enhance nationalists' argument that Ottawa offered little of importance to Quebecers. Each time the Mulroney government reduced the scope of national institutions—the CBC or Via Rail, for example—it eliminated some of the glue binding together Canada's regions. The Quebec nationalist rhetoric that "Canada doesn't work anymore," received ample support in the devaluing of the Canadian state that occurred during the Mulroney years. Thus, by attacking the state as well as "unloading" social programs on the provinces, Mulroney unwittingly undercut his government's ability to bridge Canada's regional/linguistic cleavages.

In sum, the reemergence of independence sentiment in Quebec was much more than a post-Meech reaction, although the aberrantly high levels of support for sovereignty immediately after Meech did reflect the feelings of cultural rejection and humiliation articulated by many Francophone leaders. As we have seen, structural changes in Quebec and Canadian society, economy, and political institutions paved the way for a renewed nationalism whose full dimensions were undoubtedly obscured by the post-referendum fatigue and depression that gripped nationalist forces after 1980. Meech Lake and its 1990-92 aftermath were to lay bare new fissures that had been germinating during the eighties; the 1995 Quebec sovereignty referendum confirmed their intensity. The question now is: whither Quebec and Canada in the 1990s?

### The Future of Quebec Nationalism

The past five years have witnessed extraordinary swings in Quebec public opinion on "the national question." In the eyes of most observers, the independence issue was thought to have been settled for a generation after the 1980 referendum; however, by 1990 and 1991, at the apex of the "Meech moment," there was virtual unanimity among Quebec Francophones in favor of political sovereignty. Most analysts thought the separatists would be dealt a decisive defeat in the October 1995 referendum; yet the secessionists fell short by a scant 50,000 votes of launching Quebec on the road to independence. Thus, any crystal-ball gazing must be done with appropriate caution and humility.

The October 30, 1995, referendum profoundly and perhaps, irrevocably, reshaped Canada and Quebec's political landscape. In 1980, just over 40 percent of Quebec's voters and just under 50 percent of the province's Francophones voted "Oui" to a "mandate to negotiate" sovereignty-association with the rest of Canada. In 1995, provincial voting on a stronger referendum question, which though somewhat contorted, pointed inexorably to an independent Quebec, 49.4 percent of the province, including almost 60 percent of Quebec Francophones, voted "Oui." The separatists swept voting districts throughout the province, losing only on the Island of Montreal, where Quebec's Anglophone and immigrant population is concentrated, in federalist pockets near the Canadian capital of Ottawa, and in scattered districts elsewhere in the province. By any reckoning, it was a stunning result.

The referendum result provided vivid evidence, notwithstanding the ebb and flow of support for independence during the 1990's, that something fundamentally "snapped" for Quebec Francophones in their allegiance to Canadian federalism after the Meech Lake debacle. The separatist campaign trailed badly in the polls through early October. Oriented mainly around the rather technocratic vision of independence articulated by then-PQ leader, Jacques Parizeau, there seemed to be little passion behind the "Oui" forces or little belief that they could triumph. However, when Lucien Bouchard—Quebec's "hero" of Meech, who resigned from the Mulroney government in protest over the "humiliation" of Quebec during the final stages of Meech's collapse—effectively took over leadership of the "Oui" forces, there was an immediate surge in support for the "Oui," almost carrying them to victory on October 30. Having served since 1993 in Ottawa as the head of the Bloc Québécois, a Quebec separatist party sitting in the federal Parliament, Bouchard took over as head of the PQ and Quebec premier in January, 1996, when Jaques Parizeau resigned following the referendum's defeat. As the living incarnation of the Meech "humiliation," the extraordinarily popular Bouchard is the kind of charismatic leader able to articulate cultural themes that resonate with Quebec Francophones. In the aftermath of the 1995 referendum, few are betting against Bouchard's ability to inspire Quebec Francophones to take the final step out of Canada into a sovereign Quebec.

The referendum also provided evidence that the structural changes in Canada's and Quebec's political economy, noted earlier in this chapter, have altered the arithmetic of independence in the eyes of Quebec Francophones. To be sure, the vast majority of Quebec's business elite, both Francophone and Anglophone, sided with the "Non" during the campaign. "Non" leaders relentlessly argued that voting "Oui" in the referendum would promote economic catastrophe: Federal Finance Minister Paul Martin even hyperbolically maintained separation would cost Quebec a million jobs, around a third of its employment base. Francophone voters, nonetheless, appeared to shrug off these economic arguments, convinced of the economic viability of an independent Quebec and apparently willing, in the name of cultural affirmation, to absorb some "transition costs." Moreover, the cutbacks in social programs and federal institutions, continued under the federal Liberal government which replaced the discredited Conservatives in 1993, further enhanced the sovereignists' argument that Ottawa increasingly offered little of importance to Quebecers. Paul Martin's austerity budget, which entailed major cuts in national institutions such as the CBC, and Lloyd Axworthy's social policy and unemployment insurance reform program, all reduced the scope of the national government, and, it would appear, also helped reduce Quebecers' fears that they would be losing substantial benefits from Ottawa by separating from Canada.

In the aftermath of the referendum, linguistic tensions rose perceptibly in Quebec and the rest of Canada. In Quebec, relations between the Francophone majority and English-speaking and immigrant minorities were severely strained by an ugly referendum night speech by then-PQ leader Jacques Parizeau, in which he attributed the separatists' defeat to "money and the ethnic vote." Parizeau's words dealt a serious blow to the ongoing efforts of the PQ to build a "civic nationalism" in

Quebec, more inclusive than simply French Québécois "ethnic nationalism." In addition, for the first time, a serious movement emerged within the Anglophone community in support of the "partition" of Quebec in the eventuality of secession, carving out areas of Montreal, the Ottawa Valley, and perhaps the Eastern Townships as territory staying within Canada. "If Canada is divisible, so is Quebec," became the partitionists' rallying cry."[51] PQ leaders rejected the notion out of hand: "[Anglophones] are a little panic stricken and are looking in all directions, including the creation of an Ulster on the West Island [of Montreal]," said PQ minister Jacques Brassard.[52] Many Anglophone opinion leaders cautioned against this serious and potentially dangerous escalation in rhetoric. "Partition Montreal?," wrote former editor Norman Webster in the Montreal *Gazette*. "Remember Belfast, and then let the idea go."[53]

However, the partition idea continues to gain steam, particularly as federal Prime Minister Jean Chrétien and several of his ministers warn Quebec's separatist leaders that they regard it as a realistic possibility. Moreover, the Chrétien government added to the partition scenario by raising the possibility that lands belonging to the Crees, Mohawks and other native peoples in Quebec could also be declared Canadian territory in the event of Quebec secession. In short, as the explosive questions of borders and territorial rights entered into political discourse, the spectre of Northern Ireland or Yugoslavia-type violence in Quebec—once viewed as far-fetched—became scenarios about which serious analysts began to worry. Whatever the divisions among Anglophones about the wisdom of partition, there was no gainsaying the malaise and anxiety that swept over the community in the aftermath of the October 1995 "close call" referendum.

By early 1996, it was abundantly clear that Canada had reached a crossroads. The irreconcilable visions of Canadian nationhood held by Quebec nationalists and the rest of Canada, brought to a head during the Meech Lake crisis and unresolved during the 1990s, left Quebec within an eyelash of having voted to secede from Canada in 1995. There will be a short period of breathing space for Canada on "the Quebec question." Newly installed Quebec Premier Lucien Bouchard has promised to take care of "the nightmare of our public finances," before even considering when to hold the next referendum on sovereignty (Quebec's huge budget deficit and fragile economy will occupy his energies in the near term).[54] At the federal level, there is the Chrétien government accommodationist "Plan A," to offer constitutional reforms to satisfy Quebec's traditional demands for autonomy and recognition; and its hard-ball "Plan B," to challenge the legality of secession and to raise the spectre of partition as a realistic scenario if Quebec were to opt out of the confederation. It remains to be seen whether either strategy can halt the impetus toward independence that accelerated in Quebec in 1995.

Although the movement for Quebec independence has an undeniable momentum—a certain aura of inevitability—following the 1995 referendum, the list of uncertainties surrounding Quebec sovereignty remains imposing. Would a sovereign

Quebec be able to negotiate a satisfactory economic "association" with Canada, especially in view of the hardening attitudes toward Quebec in English-speaking Canada? Could Quebec gain easy access to NAFTA, a centerpiece in the separatists' arguments about the economic viability of an independent Quebec? Would the rest of Canada, as well as minorities within Quebec, accept the borders of the *province* of Quebec as legitimate for an *independent* Quebec? How would the current federal debt be divided between a sovereign Quebec and Canada? What would be the impact were various minorities in Quebec to insist that they wish to remain a part of Canada? Would there be a massive exodus of English-speakers and head-officers of Canadian corporations from Montreal, wreaking serious havoc with the city's already damaged economy? The reality, of course, is that it is impossible to predict the precise aftermath of a Quebec vote in favor of sovereignty.

In the past, these uncertainties seemed to place a ceiling on the support for independence in Quebec. As noted earlier, the "soft nationalist" component of Francophone public opinion historically appeared unwilling to take the radical leap to separatism, in light of the difficult questions that have just been posed. However, the 1995 referendum changed everything: almost 60 percent of Francophones decided to take the leap into the unknown and support separation. Much can happen between now and the next referendum. Political leaders may come up with a constitutional formula that satisfies Quebec nationalists and is acceptable to the rest of Canada, an unlikely possibility. Soft nationalists in Quebec may shy away from separation, fearing economic catastrophe or violence. Indeed, by early 1996, some surveys showed support for Quebec independence dropping precipitously among Francophone voters who thought violence was a realistic outcome of sovereignty.[55] Dissatisfaction may grow with the PQ government as it attempts to restore Quebec's public finances, and in so doing undercut support for the PQ sovereignty option. The odds have now shifted in favor of separatism, but there are still likely to be many twists and turns until "the Quebec question" is resolved.

## Notes

1. Kenneth McRoberts, *Quebec: Social Change and Political Crisis* (Toronto: McClelland and Stewart, 1993), p. 440.

2. Dominique Clift, *Quebec Nationalism in Crisis* (Montreal: McGill-Queen's University Press, 1982), p. 126.

3. William Coleman, *The Independence Movement in Quebec, 1945–1980* (Toronto: University of Toronto Press, 1984).

4. Maurice Pinard, "The Dramatic Reemergence of the Quebec Independence Movement," *Journal of International Affairs* 45.2 (Winter 1992): 480, 483. As Pinard and others have pointed out, how one poses this basic question affects the answer. For example, polls consistently show higher support for "sovereignty," or "sovereignty-

association," than for "independence" or, lowest of all, "separation." These variations make the potential wording of a referendum question all the more crucial.

5. See, for example, McRoberts, op. cit. note 1, pp. 128–208; and Réjean Pelletier, "La Révolution tranquille," in Gérard Daigle and Guy Rocher, eds., *Le Québec En Jeu: Comprendre les grands défis* (Montréal: Les Presses de l'Université de Montréal, 1992), pp. 609–24.

6. Louis Balthazar, "L'évolution du nationalisme québécois," in Daigle and Rocher, op. cit. note 5,

p. 648.

7. Stéphane Dion, "Explaining Quebec Nationalism," in R. Kent Weaver, ed., *The Collapse of Canada?* (Washington, DC: The Brookings Institution, 1992), p. 78.

8. See Balthazar, op. cit. note 6, p. 651.

9. Vera Murray, *Le Parti québécois: de la fondation à la prise du pouvoir* (Montreal: Hurtubise HMH, 1976).

10. See Marc V. Levine, *The Reconquest of Montreal: Language Policy and Social Change in a Bilingual City* (Philadelphia: Temple University Press, 1990), p. 98.

11. Pinard, op. cit. note 4, p. 480.

12. Reprinted in Jacques Henripin, "Quebec and the Demographic Dilemma of French Canadian Society," in Dale C. Thomson, ed., *Quebec Society and Politics: Views from the Inside* (Toronto: McClelland and Stewart, 1973), p. 162.

13. For a history of these various episodes, including detailed analyses of Quebec's language legislation since the 1960s, see Levine, op. cit. note 10.

14. On the strategy of *étapisme*, see Murray, op. cit. note 9, pp. 177–200; and the brief discussion by the *père* of *étapisme*, Claude Morin, in his book *Les choses comme elles étaient: Une autobiographie politique* (Montréal: Editions Boréal, 1994), pp. 311–24.

15. Gouvernement du Québec, *La politique québécoise de la langue française* (Quebec: Editeur officiel, 1977), p. 34 (author's translation).

16. See William Coleman, "From Bill 22 to Bill 101: The Politics of Language Under the Parti Québécois," *Canadian Journal of Political Science* 14.3 (September 1981): 463.

17. Balthazar, op. cit. note 6, pp. 653–56.

18. Polls have shown for example, that almost one-quarter of Quebecers believe that a sovereign Quebec would still send representatives to the Canadian House of Commons.

19. Graham Fraser, *PQ: René Lévesque and the Parti Québécois in Power* (Toronto: Macmillan of Canada, 1985), pp. 242–372.

20. McRoberts, op. cit. note 1, p. 341.

21. For an analysis of the content of the Meech Lake Accord, see Jeremy Webber, *Reimagining Canada: Language, Culture, Community, and the Canadian Constitution* (Montreal: McGill–Queen's University Press, 1994), pp. 125–56.

22. See Patrick J. Monahan, *Meech Lake: The Inside Story* (Toronto: University of Toronto Press, 1991).

23. Charles Taylor, *Reconciling the Solitudes* (Montreal: McGill–Queen's University Press, 1993), pp. 170, 195. The quotations are spliced together but in context.

24. Philip Resnick, *Letters to a Québécois Friend* (Montreal: McGill–Queen's University Press, 1990), p. 57.

25. Levine, op. cit. note 10, pp. 131–38.

26. See, for example, the entire literature on consociational democracy, as in Arend Lijphart, *Democracy in Plural Societies* (New Haven: Yale University Press, 1977).

27. Taylor, op. cit. note 23, p. 195.

28. Typically, support for "sovereignty-association," the PQ option, has been approximately 10 points greater than for "independence" in surveys.

29. Taylor, op. cit. note 23, p. 170.

30. Indeed, one writer entitled his short book on Meech, "The Accord—How Robert Bourassa Will Make Independence." See Georges Mathews, *L'accord—Comment Robert Bourassa fera l'indépendance* (Montreal: Le Jour, 1990). The most detailed account of the post-Meech period, with particularly critical treatment of Bourassa, is Lisée, *Le Tricheur: Robert Bourassa et les Québécois, 1990–1991* (Montréal: Editions Boreal, 1994), and Lisée, *Le Naufrageur: Robert Bourassa et les Québécois, 1991–1992* (Montreal: Boréal, 1994).

31. See Guy Laforest, *De la prudence: Textes politiques* (Montreal: Editions Boréal, 1994), pp. 119–56.

32. Pinard, op. cit. note 4, p. 489.

33. Levine, op. cit. note 10, pp. 138–227; and Marc V. Levine, "Au délà des lois linguistiques: la politique gouvernementale et le caractère linguistique de Montréal dans les années 1990," in Levine et al., *Contextes de la politique linguistique québécoise* (Quebec: Editeur officiel, 1993), pp. 3–40.

34. See, for example, Mireille Baillargeon and Claire Benjamin, *Caractéristiques linguistiques de la population immigrée recensée au Québec en 1986* (Quebec: Ministère des Communautés culturelles et de l'Immigration, 1990).

35. See, among others, François Rocher and Guy Rocher, "La culture québécoise en devenir: les défis du pluralisme," in Fernand Ouellet and Michel Pagé, eds., *Construire un espaces commun: pluriethnicité, éducation et société* (Quebec: Institut québécois de recherche sur la culture, 1991), pp. 43–77.

36. Daniel Latouche, *Le bazar: des anciens Canadiens aux nouveaux Québécois* (Montreal: Editions Boréal, 1990), p. 123.

37. Jacques Henripin, *Naître ou ne pas être* (Quebec: Institut québécois de recherche sur la culture, 1989).

38. See, among others, Marc Termotte, "Ce qui pourrait être une politique de migration," *L'Action nationale* 78.2 (February 1988): 308–22.

39. Rocher and Rocher, op. cit. note 35, p. 52.

40. Levine, op. cit. note 10, pp. 120–24.

41. Ibid., p. 174.

42. François Vaillancourt and Josée Carpentier, *Le contrôle de l'économie du Québec: la place des francophones en 1987 et son évolution depuis 1961* (Montreal: Office de la langue française, 1989).

43. On the history of the Caisse de Dépôt, see Mario Pelletier, *La Machine à milliards* (Montreal: Québec/Amérique, 1989).

44. See Yves Bélanger and Pierre Fournier, *L'entreprise québécoise: développement historique et dynamique contemporaine* (Montreal: Hurtubise HMH, 1987).

45. See, for example, Patrick Grady, *The Economic Consequences of Quebec Sovereignty* (Vancouver: The Fraser Institute, 1991); and John McCallum and Chris Green, *Parting as Friends: The Economic Consequences for Quebec* (Toronto: C. D. Howe Institute, 1991).

46. Thomas Courchene, *In Praise of Renewed Federalism* (Toronto: C. D. Howe Institute, 1991), pp. 20–21.

47. Richard Simeon, "Globalization and the Canadian Nation-State," in G. Bruce Doern and Bryne B. Purchase, eds., *Canada at Risk? Canadian Public Policy in the 1990s* (Toronto: C. D. Howe Institute, 1991), p. 51.

48. See Courchene, op. cit. note 46 (all), and Mel Hurtig, *The Betrayal of Canada* (Toronto: Stoddart Publishing, 1991), pp. 330–31.

49. Pierre Fournier, *A Meech Lake Post-Mortem: Is Quebec Sovereignty Inevitable* (Montreal: McGill–Queen's University Press, 1991), p. 115.

50. Jeffrey Simpson, *Faultlines: Struggling for a Canadian Vision* (Toronto: Harper Collins, 1993), p. 295.

51. Paul Wells, "Chrétien, Ministers see Logic of Partitioning," Montreal *Gazette*, January 30, 1996, p. A1.

52. Presse canadienne, "L'integrité du territiore fait consensus à Québec," *Le Devoir* (Montreal), January 23, 1996, p. A-2.

53. Norman Webster, "Partition Montreal? Remember Belfast, and then let the idea go," Montreal *Gazette*, December 16, 1995.

54. Philip Authier, "Quebec Finances a Nightmare," Montreal *Gazette*, February 26, 1996.

55. Paul Wells, "Potential for Violence Making Yes Votes Think Again: Survey," Montreal *Gazette*, February 25, 1996.

# Epilogue

## WINSTON A. VAN HORNE

The text of this book was submitted to the publisher in August of 1995. Since then, there have been many events around the globe that are most germane to this volume. In the fall of 1995 the IRA resumed its armed struggle against Britain, though early in 1996 there were signs that the peace process was not dead; the integrity of the Canadian state was preserved by a scant 50,000 votes after the referendum in Quebec; Ken Saro-Wiwa—poet, playwright, and a leader of the Ogoni people in their struggle for greater autonomy—and eight others were executed by the Nigerian military regime, despite international censure and pleas for clemency by world leaders including the pope; and a peace agreement was signed in Paris by the presidents of Bosnia and Herzegovina, Croatia, and Serbia. In early 1996, China mounted considerable pressure on Taiwan in the run-up to the Taiwanese presidential election on March 30, by holding high-powered war games close to Taiwan; the Russians succeeded in killing Dzhokhar M. Dudayev, the leader of the Chechen separatists, but the war in Chechnya showed no signs of abating; there was talk of civil war in Russia should Gennadi A. Zyuganov, the Communist party's candidate, win the presidency in the election scheduled for June 16; Aum Shinrikyo religious leader Shoko Asahara went on trial for his role in the sarin gas attack on the Tokyo subway system; and former football star O. J. Simpson was acquitted for the murders of his ex-wife Nicole Simpson and her friend Ronald Lyle Goldman, a decision which spotlighted ever so intensely the jagged edges of the deep racial fault lines in the United States. Each and all of the developments just mentioned should be elaborated in some detail, but in a short epilogue such as the present one, I have elected to focus on a set of events that was not called out but is most relevant to the chapters by Galia Golan and Muhammad Hallaj.

On November 4, 1995, Prime Minister Yitzak Rabin was assassinated by Yigal Amir, an Israeli, less than two months after Shimon Peres and Yasir Arafat initialed the accord of September 24, 1995, which, returned significant portions of the West Bank to the Palestinians. At the time of the initialing, Peres said: "[W]hat we are doing today is not a normal political or economic enterprise; it is history in the real meaning of the word. . . . I really feel the Lord has offered us a real opportunity to change the course of hopelessness and desperation and bloodshed into something more promising, more noble, more humane."[1] The nobility of purpose and humaneness of deed that Peres expressed were obviously not shared by Amir, who was outraged by what he perceived to be the Rabin's government betrayal of Israeli interests in the peace process with the Palestinians. (I find it distressingly ironic that Rabin's military genius paved the way for him to be murdered by a man who was not even born at the time when Rabin enjoyed his greatest triumph on the battlefield, to wit, the victory in the Six-Day War of 1967.)

Amir's disaffection with the peace process was mirrored on the opposite end of the divide in culture and political economy by Hamas, which underwrote in blood a series of suicide bombings in Israel from July 24, 1995, through March 4, 1996, that killed dozens of persons and injured scores more. These bombings occasioned both fear and rage among the Israeli populace, and impelled Prime Minister Shimon Peres, Rabin's successor, after the suicide bombing in Jerusalem on March 3, 1996, to declare "'a war in every sense of the word' against Hamas."[2] And when, on the very next day, a suicide bomber "struck just before 4 p.m. outside the Dizengoff Center, the biggest shopping mall in Tel Aviv,"[3] Peres said: "I have been asked where we will act[?] . . . My answer is everywhere. . . . I have been asked if we will break the law[?] . . . There is one law we will not break. That is the law of national and personal security of the state of Israel. It is legal for a nation to defend its existence."[4] It is interesting to note here that Peres cast the series of suicide bombings not just in terms of personal security and national security, but also in terms of the very existence of the state of Israel itself. It is doubtful that the bombs which shattered and scattered the bodies of so many endangered the existence of Israel, but in portraying them as threats to the integrity and very existence of the state Peres gave himself much room to maneuver in striking out against the enemies of the state. And strike he did, not only against Hamas, but also against Hezbollah and other enemies of Israel.

He destroyed homes of relatives of the bombers, restricted the movement of Palestinians, and closed off access to jobs in Israel for them. He also fought a two-week low intensity war against Hezbollah guerrillas operating out of bases in southern Lebanon, from where they launched Katyusha rockets and mortar rounds on northern Israel. This fighting was marked by an Israeli artillery barrage that hit a United Nations peace-keeping camp, resulting in the deaths of seventy-five Lebanese civilians and the wounding of more than one hundred. "Israel said the attack on the base was a grave error. It [nonetheless] prompted worldwide outrage and a rapid intensification of diplomatic efforts to bring a halt to the conflict."[5] A formula was found, brokered by U.S. Secretary of State Warren Christopher, to bring an end to the killing of civilians on both sides of the Israeli-Lebanese border, even though it did not proscribe continued fighting between the combatants.

Given the bullets of Amir, the suicide bombings of Hamas, the Katyusha rockets and mortar rounds of Hezbollah, and Peres' low intensity warfare, many expected the peace process to stop dead in its tracks; perhaps undermined irretrievably. But this did not happen. On April 24, 1996, in Gaza, the Palestine National Council (PNC) by 504 to 54, with 14 abstentions and 97 absent, "voted . . . to revoke those clauses in its 32-year-old charter that called for an armed struggle to destroy the Jewish state [Israel]. . . . Formally, the resolution adopted by the council consisted of two simple clauses. The first declared that the council 'decides to amend the Palestine National Covenant by canceling clauses which contradict the letters exchanged between the PLO and the Israeli Government.' The second ordered a new charter to be drafted within six months."[6]

In an age conspicuous for all sorts of drivel concerning the putative end of history and a vapidity in the use of the term historic, the action of the Palestine National Council was truly historic. *The New York Times* observed that "[t]hough time and the Israeli-Palestinian agreements have rendered the charter largely obsolete, the formal revocation of the hostile clauses carried great symbolic importance for Israelis."[7] In symbol there is substance, and the substance of symbol is no less important than the symbol of substance. Peres was acutely attuned to the relation of symbol and substance when he observed that "[i]deologically, it [the action of the PNC] may be the most important change in the last hundred years [of Jewish-Palestinian relations]."[8]

The vote by the PNC, which was well in excess of the two-thirds needed to amend the charter, could, symbolically and substantively, turn a page in history insofar as it opened a path to the construction of strong institutional bridges between Israelis and Palestinians. For the more the two peoples act to confute rather than corroborate the dire warnings of Neguib Azoury and Arthur Ruppin that opened Golan's chapter, the more compromises they find it possible to make without abridging cultural norms upon which their respective national identities rest. Thus, for example, " [i]n response [to the PNC's action] Mr. Peres was expected to go ahead with the withdrawal from Hebron, the last West Bank city from which Israel agreed . . . to [withdraw in the accord of September 1995]. The withdrawal was suspended after the suicide bombing attacks [that were renewed in February of 1996. Moreover,] Mr. Peres' Labor party [was] expected to revoke from its platform its formal opposition to the formation of a Palestinian state."[9] Indeed, "[t]he actions of both sides clear[ed] the way for the start of the . . . final phase of negotiations, the 'final settlement' talks [in which] the most difficult issues, such as the status of Jerusalem, the future of Israeli settlements in Palestinian lands, and water resources [would be addressed]."[10] And so, in spite of the severe hits that it took, the peace process was not destroyed. Though Rabin had been murdered most foul by being shot in the back, the integrity of the 1993 handshake between himself and Arafat still beamed above the blood-drenched handiwork of those for whom *compromise* is a dirty word, and the work of traitors to *the cause*.

In 1993, on the occasion of the signing of the Israeli-Palestinian accord, Rabin said: "We have come to try and put an end to the hostilities so that our children, [and] our children's children, will no longer experience the painful cost of war: violence and terror. We have come to secure their lives and to ease the soul and the painful memories of the past—to hope and pray for peace. Let me say to you, the Palestinians, we are destined to live together on the same soil in the same land. We, the soldiers who have returned from battles stained with blood; we who have seen our relatives and friends killed before our eyes; . . . we say to you today, in a loud and clear voice: enough blood and tears. Enough. . . . We are today giving peace a chance—and saying to you and saying again to you: enough."[11] How well were Rabin's sentiments echoed by "Mufid Abu Rabbo, 39, a member of the new Palestinian legislature [and a member of the PNC, who observed after the vote to amend the charter:] 'It's a dream for us to be here and say 'enough is enough of the old style, it's time to face a new era.'"[12]

The potency of Golan's concept of fed-up-ness is ever so evident in the observations of Rabin and Rabbo, anecdotal though they be. It is a commonplace for one to hear that the power of emotion should never be underestimated. As ever the more Palestinians and Israelis say "enough is enough," increasingly the unthinkable becomes thinkable, and the impossible does become possible, to borrow Hallaj's language. Put differently, the emotive force of fed-up-ness conjoined with the rational force of carefully drawn legal and technical compromises do hold out the prospect of Israel living in peace and security alongside a Palestinian state. Fed-up-ness, then, the carnage of suicide bombers and costly reprisals notwithstanding, could well be a crucial contributory factor to the creation of a Palestinian state, and the consummation of the two-state solution envisaged by Hallaj and the PNC.

Could a true peace between the Israelis and the Palestinians, that is, a peace reinforced by sound institutional arrangements and nurtured by good trans-generational memories, pave the way for the emergence of that "larger vision" which bridges the "us/them" "we/they" divide, for which Muhammad Hallaj, Martin Marty, and Claude Ake call? Many years ago when I taught graduate students, I once gave a doctoral examination in which I asked why was the twentieth century noted for so many century-dominant physicists, mathematicians, philosophers, and economists but no political philosophers—such as a Thomas Hobbes, John Locke, Jean Jacques Rousseau, G. W. F. Hegel, John Stuart Mill, Friedrich Engels or Karl Marx? Each of these political philosophers was animated by a larger vision, one that spanned his century and transcended it. Regarding race, ethnicity, and nationalism, the globe is sorely in need of an individual, or perhaps more than one individual, who matches the stature of the ones just mentioned, and who is able to design concepts, ideas, hypotheses, and theories which have the sort of normative and empirical grounding that impel people, regardless of their particular cultural mooring, to behave in ways that are consistent with given prescriptions and pro-scriptions. What I said in the Introduction concerning cultural relativism would, at first blush, appear to be inconsistent with what has just been said. Yet I do not believe that there is an inconsistency insofar as cultural relativism is amenable to transcultural constructs and norms pertaining to honor, fairness, decency, integrity, and well-being. Cultural distinctiveness is not incompatible with transcultural beliefs, attitudes, and behaviors.

However, the sorts of beliefs, attitudes, and behaviors fostered by rapacious capitalist production and its corollary inequities; bankrupt socialist/communist statism and its attendant miseries; stultifying theocratic dogmas and their accom-panying conformities; and vulgar racial/ethnic indoctrination and its concomitant arrogance, hardly afford the sorts of constructs and norms whereby a larger trans-cultural vision that does not dissolve "us" into "them" nor "them" into "us," but recognizes and values equally the integrity of "them" and "us" separately, within a shared framework of "we together," could guide human conduct. Should Palestine and Israel realize the hope of Rabin, Arafat, and Peres, perhaps, just perhaps, such a larger vision may come to pass, with benefits that redound globally. Of course, the very obverse could happen, and then the warning of Brian Porter concerning nationalism and the *ethnie* looms ever so large.

In bringing this epilogue to a close, it may be well to observe that the enduring value of this volume lies in its global reach and the patterns that it calls out. It has made plain that the state is no salvation in relation to national chauvinism, ethnic exclusivism, and/or racial paranoia. Indeed the state—or the desire for it—is often a consummative force, if not the efficient cause, of these phenomena. Still, the state has much potential to transcend hard divisions wrought by race, ethnicity, and nationalism. And so, in the chapters of this book one discerns both the destructive force of "us/them," as well as the boundless possibilities of "we together." May that larger vision for which Ake et al., hope become a reality in the twenty-first century.

## Postscript

*Israeli Elections*

The assassination of Yitzhak Rabin on the evening of November 4, 1995, after a peace rally attended by over one hundred thousand persons in Tel Aviv, exposed starkly the crosscurrents of hope and fear in Israeli society over the peace process. Rabin—a sabra (native-born Israeli), a classic warrior, a war hero, an archetypal Israeli in flesh and spirit—"was frequently denounced by ardent foes [of the peace process] as a 'traitor,' or pictured with an Arab head scarf or a Nazi swastika" (*The New York Times*, November 6, 1995, p. A6). How this must have pained him, perhaps more than the three bullets lodged in his body which, as he lay dying, he said, "hurts, but its not so bad" (*The New York Times*, November 7, 1995, p. A. 9).

In the aftermath of the assassination, the new prime minister, Shimon Peres, and the Labor party, were to enjoy a 16-point lead over Benjamin Netanyahu and the Likud, which many, including Leah Rabin, the wife of the slain prime minister, accused of fomenting the social vitriol from which Rabin fell. National elections were scheduled for May 29, 1996, and, prior to the first of four suicide bombings between February 25 and March 4, the conventional wisdom was that Peres and the Labor party would be victorious over Netanyahu and the Likud. But after each suicide bombing Peres' lead shrank in the polls, and his low intensity war with Hezbollah did little to help him. Eventually the contest became a dead heat, and after all the ballots had been counted two days following the election Netanyahu had defeated Peres. *The New York Times* of June 1, 1996, reported the following: "After counting absentee ballots through much of the day, the Israeli Election Commission finally declared [Benjamin] Netanyahu the winner over Prime Minister Shimon Peres by 29,457 votes, 1,501,023 to 1,471,566" (p. A1). Interestingly, though the Labor party won two more seats than the Likud (34 to 32) in the 120 seat Knesset, Israel's Parliament, both lost seats to religious and other special-interest parties. The Labor party lost ten seats and the Likud eight seats. In the new Parliament, nine parties with from two to ten seats would constitute a near majority, though they split from left to center to right along the political spectrum. This outcome led one television commentator in the United States to observe that "Israel is returning to her tribes," a comment that made Martin Marty's chapter flood my mind.

Just as Yitzhak Rabin had become the first Israeli prime minister to be born in Palestine, so too Netanyahu, a sabra, became the first Israeli prime minister to be born after the state of Israel was created. And just as Rabin the warrior had become an architect for peace, many of those in favor of the peace process began to wonder aloud whether Netanyahu would also become a consummator of peace—given the hard line against concessions to the Arabs that he had taken during the campaign, and for which he was well-known. Recognizing the sharp and bitter divisions in the Israeli populace, and mindful of the United States' and international interest in the peace process, Netanyahu said the following in his first major public address after the election: "In the last few years, the division of Israeli society has widened, and the tensions have increased between various parts of society. . . . I see my first mission as Prime Minister to reunite the people, to reduce the tensions and to strengthen the unity of the people. And I want to say to you . . . that the peace must start at home. . . . I call on the citizens of Israel, the non-Jewish citizens of the state of Israel . . . I see you as part and equal in everything that goes on in the state of Israel. . . . I plan to be the Prime Minister of everyone without any exception.

"I [have] said that peace begins at home, but we must continue it outside of Israel. And *we plan to advance the peace and the negotiating process* with all of our neighbors in order to get a stable peace, a real peace, peace with security. . . . I stretch out my hand in peace to all the Arab leaders and all of our neighbors, our Palestinian neighbors. I call on you to join us on the road to real peace with security.

Let us go in a way of security for everyone, for all the nations of the region. The government we will form . . . with God's help, will strengthen the peaceful relations that have already been established with the Jordanian kingdom and with Egypt, and will continue negotiations with the Palestinians, and we also [will] try to advance the negotiations with other Arab states. I call on those states to join the peace process.

"I see our friend, the United States, as part of the peace process. The relations between the United States and Israel are strong as a rock, and I am sure that they will continue in the coming four years . . ." (*The New York Times*, June 3, 1996, p. A6. Author's italics). Clearly, Netanyahu set a conciliatory tone. He saw all around him and knew well the costs of what a political analyst for the newspaper *Maariv*, Chemi Shalev, captured ever so poignantly and ominously: "Half of the public in Israel is now going around with a feeling that redemption is at hand, and the other [half] believes that it is trapped in a hell on earth. . . . Some rejoice; others weep" (*The New York Times*, June 1, 1996, p. A4). Moreover, he was cognizant that lacerations of the nation's soul had to be healed. The role of the peace process in the healing of the nation's soul will thus test the mettle of Prime Minister Benjamin Netanyahu and the Israeli government. For there are those like Yossi Leibowitz who believe that Netanyahu's victory "was all God's plan," and there are other's such as Nabil Osman who believe that "[w]hoever won, the next Prime Minister would have little choice but to continue the Middle East peace process, because any deviation from the peace process would create a big reaction against Israel in [the Middle East]" (ibid., p. A5).

*Russian Elections*

In a field of ten candidates, Russian president Boris N. Yel'tsin defeated Gennadi A. Zyuganov (35.28 percent to 32.03 percent) in the first round of elections on June 16; in the runoff of July 3, Zyuganov lost to Yel'tsin 40.31 percent to 53.82 percent.

**Notes**

    1. "Israel and P.L.O. Reach Accord to Transfer West Bank Areas," *The New York Times*, September 25, 1995, p. A1.

    2. "Israeli Rage Rises as Bomb Kills 19, Imperiling Peace," *The New York Times*, March 4, 1996, p. A1.

    3. "4th Terror Blast in Israel Kills 12 at Mall in Tel Aviv; Nine-Day Toll Grows to 59," *The New York Times*, March 5, 1996, p. A1. From the time that I prepared the Introduction to this volume (July 1995) to the present (May 1996), my clip file from *The New York Times* shows the following headlines regarding suicide bombings in Israel—in addition to the two that have been mentioned already: "2 Suicide Bombings in Israel Kill 25 and Hurt 77, Highest Such Toll," February 26, 1996; "22 Killed in Terrorist Bombing of Bus in Tel Aviv; 46 Wounded," October

20, 1995; "In a Shaken Tel Aviv, Fear Now Rides the Buses," October 21, 1995; "Bus Bombing Kills Five in Jerusalem; 100 are Wounded," August 22, 1995; "Suicide Bomber Kills 5 in a Bus Attack Near Tel Aviv," July 25, 1995.

4. *The New York Times*, March 5, 1996, op. cit. note 3, p. Al.

5. "Israeli Barrage Hits U.N. Camp in Lebanon, Killing at Least 75," *The New York Times*, April 19, 1996, p. Al.

6. "P.L.O. Ends Call for Destruction of Jewish State," *The New York Times*, April 25 1996, pp. Al, A6. It also was noted that "[t]he formula was designed to satisfy the Israeli-Palestinian agreement signed in Washington on Sept[ember] 28, [1995], which declared that within two months of the inauguration of an elected legislative council, the P.L.O. would change its charter to comply with letters in which Mr. Arafat recognized the right of the state of Israel 'to exist in peace and security,' and renounced 'the use of terrorism and other acts of violence.' In exchange, the [p]rime [m]inister at the time, the late Yitzhak Rabin, recognized the P.L.O. [which former Prime Minister Menachem Begin and former Defense Minister Ariel Sharon had tried to destroy in the 1982 war in Lebanon,] and agreed to open formal negotiations with it." p. A6.

7. Ibid.

8. Ibid.

9. Ibid.

10. Ibid.

11. "Rabin and Arafat Seal Their Accord as Clinton Applauds 'Brave Gamble," *The New York Times*, September 14, 1993, p. A6. Author's italics.

12. *The New York Times*, op. cit. note 6, p. Al.

# Index of Persons, Places, and Organizations

# Subject Index

357